Etymologies and Genealogies

The University of Chicago Press
Chicago and London

Etymologies and Genealogies
A Literary Anthropology
of the French Middle Ages

R. HOWARD BLOCH

R. Howard Bloch, professor of French at the University
of California, Berkeley, is the author of *Medieval French
Literature and Law*.

The University of Chicago Press, Chicago 60637
The University of Chicago Press, Ltd., London

© 1983 by The University of Chicago
All rights reserved. Published 1983
Printed in the United States of America
90 89 88 87 86 85 84 83   5 4 3 2 1

Library of Congress Cataloging in Publication Data

Bloch, R. Howard.
   Etymologies and genealogies.

   Includes index.
   1. French literature—To 1500—History and criticism.
2. Philosophy, Medieval—History.   3. Literature—
Philosophy.   I. Title.
PQ151.B64   1983   840'.9'001   82-20036
ISBN 0-226-05981-2

This book is dedicated to
Bert, Virginia, Ellen, Ben, and Becca Bloch.

Contents

Acknowledgments

The excruciating final stages in the preparation of a book—proofreading, checking of sources, indexing—are compensated only by the pleasure of thanking those who have participated in its genesis all along the way. First among these are two close friends and intellectual companions, Alexandre Leupin and Eugene Vance, who will recognize in the present work glimpses of an often heated, sometimes maddening, always challenging dialogue of the last few years. I am also indebted to Daniel Poirion, who permitted me to present my ideas in their early stages to his seminar at the Ecole Normale Supérieure, and to Charles Méla and Michel Zink, whose comments partially reshaped my thinking at that time. It is, of course, impossible to acknowledge all the colleagues whose erudition and generosity lie hidden beneath the surface of the essay which follows; I mention only in passing Leo Bersani, Alan Bernstein, Tom Bisson, Joe Duggan, Sepp Gumbrecht, Denis Hollier, Marie-Hélène Huet, Leo Löwenthal, and the group around *Representations*. A special note of thanks is due Peter Haidu and Bernard and Jacqueline Cerquiglini who read the manuscript in its entirety, as well as Charles Bernheimer, Geoff Nunberg, and Paul Rabinow who, from the viewpoints of the critic, the linguist, and the anthropologist, offered a wide range of perspectives upon the Introduction. Finally, I would like to express my gratitude to Jann Matlock, whose assistance with everything from the sleuthing of sources to typing facilitated my task at every stage, to the Humanities Research Council of the University of California, and to the John Simon Guggenheim Foundation, which afforded me a delicious sabbatical year.

Abbreviations

In order to reduce the number of footnotes, I have adopted the following abbreviations for frequently cited texts:

Aucassin *Aucassin et Nicolette*, ed. M. Roques (Paris: Champion, 1967).

De Planctu Alain de Lille, *De Planctu Naturae*, in *Satirical Poets of the Twelfth Century*, ed. T. Wright (London: Longman, 1872).

Etym. Isidore of Seville, *Etymologiarum sive originum libri XX*, ed. W. M. Lindsay (Oxford: Oxford University Press, 1911).

Historia Abelard, *Historia Calamitatum*, ed. J. Monfrin (Paris: J. Vrin, 1959).

Huth *Huth Merlin*, ed. G. Paris and J. Ulrich (Paris: Firmin-Didot, 1886).

Marcabru *Les Poésies de Marcabru*, ed. J. Dejeanne (Paris: Champion, 1909).

Metalogicon John of Salisbury, *Metalogicon*, ed. C. I. Webb (Oxford: Clarendon Press, 1929).

Notices C. Thurot, *Notices et extraits de divers manuscrits latins pour servir à l'histoire des doctrines grammaticales du moyen âge* (Paris: Imprimerie Royale, 1868).

Perceval Chrétien de Troyes, *Le Roman de Perceval*, ed. W. Roach (Geneva: Droz, 1959).

PL *Patrologia Latina*, ed. J.-P. Migne (Paris: Garnier, 1879).

Priscian Priscian, *Institutionum Grammaticarum libri XVIII*, ed. H. Keil (Hildesheim: Georg Olms, 1961), vol. 2.

Roland *La Chanson de Roland*, ed. J. Bédier (Paris: H. Piazza, 1964).

Rose *Le Roman de la rose*, ed. D. Poirion (Paris: Flammarion, 1974).

Varro Varro, *De Lingua Latina*, ed. R. G. Kent (Cambridge: Harvard University Press, 1951).

William IX *Les Chansons de William IX*, ed. A. Jeanroy (Paris: Champion, 1913).

Introduction: Toward a Literary Anthropology of the Middle Ages

In Classical mythology the invention of writing is alternately ascribed to the Phoenician Cadmus, the Greek Hermes, and the Egyptian Thoth.[1] The medieval figures most associated with writing are Odin, the inventor of runes, and Merlin—magician, enchanter, and prophet. Merlin is said to have written two books. The first, dictated to his mother's confessor and protector Blaise, contains Merlin's account of events prior to and during the Arthurian reign as well as the story of his own birth and precocious rhetorical gifts. Through it we are privy to the legends of the Round Table: "Et Merlins s'en ala a Blaise en Norhomberlande, si li raconte tot et dist, et Blaise le mist en escrit et par son livre le resavons nous encore."[2] The second book, divinely inspired and transcribed by the counselors at the court of Uter and Pendragon, is prophetically disposed: "Et nostre sires qui est poissans sour tout m'a donné sens de savoir toutes choses qui sont a avenir en partie."[3] Merlin is the patron saint of letters within the Arthurian world. In Geoffrey of Monmouth's *Vita Merlini* he supervises the construction of a *scriptorium* for the recording of his predictions; in the *Didot-Perceval* he retires from the world to a "writing house" or *esplumoir*.[4] The numerous dispatches which circulate between lovers, between enemies, between Arthur and his barons are the product of Merlin's prolific pen, as are the inscriptions on tombstones, swords, boats, and hermes scattered throughout the realm. Merlin is as powerful an image of the writer as the Middle Ages produced and, indeed, an embodiment of the principle of writing itself.

The pluralistic possibilities of writing are subsumed in the magician's many shapes. At times a young child, adolescent, old crone, woodsman, shepherd, monk, and *preudom*, Merlin moves about under continually shifting guises. His interlocutor in the Welsh *Dialogue of Merddin and His Sister Gwendydd* addresses him successively as the "Judge of the North," the "Prophet," the "Master of Song," the "Melancholic," the "Warrior of Arderydd," the "Wise," and the "One Who Has Completely Read the Distichs of Cato."[5] The author of the Huth text confides that the other characters "do not know that Merlin can take other forms and other appearances (*samblance*) than his own"; and the polymorphous *enchanteor* himself boasts that "those who believe they know me know nothing of my being."[6] Merlin is the representation of that which cannot be said and of everything that can be said—a shifter, trickster, joker, arbiter of value and of meaning. Also omniscient, his special knowledge of the past, of men's thoughts and intentions, of paternity, of the future, places him in relation to the other figures of the text as the author stands in relation to his work: a privileged observer of its every aspect.

Merlin personifies the figure of the paradox—the prophet who is everywhere, yet nowhere. Representative of Satan, recuperated by God, he retains the knowledge imparted by both. A fatherless being without discernible origin, his conception having occurred without his mother's awareness, he is at the same time the protector of paternity. A latter-day Hermes, he is the inhabitant of the forest—the Wild Man—who is simultaneously the bringer of culture, the master of arts and of science, the practitioner of music, medicine, astronomy, mathematics, and calculation.[7]

Merlin is no less adept at human relations. Also like Hermes—the god of clever speech, the wise child, flatterer, and liar—he represents the skilled rhetorician, master of juridical discourse, guardian of technology, and engineer of the physically impossible.[8] We are told that Hermes took a special delight in the affairs of men, particularly in commerce, deals, in barter as well as in buying and selling; he was the herald and messenger of the Gods. Merlin, like his Classical counterpart, acts as messenger, go-between, matchmaker, mediator, peacemaker; and, these failing, as military strategist—master of ruse, maneuver, and surprise. His military triumphs are supplemented by political savvy during peacetime. The foundation of the Round Table is the product of Merlin's ingenuity as is Arthur's elaborate succession to Uter's kingdom.[9]

Merlin's polysemous nature, invisible omnipresence, and superhuman perception of the past and future incorporates a savoir that permits the governance of men and that poses generally the question of the relation between knowledge and power. More precisely, his special knowledge—inherent in writing—implies the existence of a power distinct from immediately physical, military domination; the kind of power afforded by know-how, technical competence, mastery of the signs of a culture, including its music.[10] Here the confrontation between Merlin and the counselors at Vertigier's court is highly instructive.

In what constitutes the first political episode of the thirteenth-century prose romance, King Vertigier concludes a pact with the Saxons. He then seeks repeatedly to build an impregnable tower which crumbles mysteriously after each attempt at construction. Vertigier summons his counselors whose wisdom consists of their skill in the practice of astronomy.[11] What these official arbiters of truth read in the stars is, in fact, a premonition of their own death at the hands of "a child of seven years conceived without earthly father" ("un enfant de set ans qui estoit nés sans pere d'oume terriien [et conceus] en une feme" [*Huth*, 1:41]).

The Oedipal overtones of the astronomical prediction are obvious: like Laius, the counselors seek to destroy that which the oracle reveals; and like Oedipus himself, they pursue the knowledge which destroys. For the struggle between the sanctioned discipline of astronomy and Merlin's art is sealed in the lie, presented to Vertigier's court, that only the blood of the fatherless child will make the tower stand (". . . et qui porroit cel sanc avoir et metre ou mortier, si tenra la tours et sera tous jors mais bonne" ibid., 1:42]). Thus the *sages hommes*, in their search for the object of the menacing omen, come upon a group of children playing:

> Et en cel camp avoit une compaignie d'enfans qui choulloient. Et Merlins, qui toutes les choses savoit, i estoit et vit les messages le roi Vertigier qui le queroient. Si se(s) traist Merlins lés un des plus riches enfans, pour chou que il savoit bien que il le mesaesmeroit, si haucha la croche, si en feri l'enfant en la gambe; et li enfes commencha a plourer et Merlin a laidengier et apieler fius sans pere. Quant li message qui le queroient oirent l'enfant ensi parler, si alerent tout quatre viers l'enfant qui ploroit, si le demanderent: "Qui est cil qui t'a feru?" Et il dist: "C'est (li) fieus d'une feme que onques ne seult qui l'engendra, ne onques n'ot pere." Quant Merlins l'oi, si vint viers les messages tout en riant et lour dist: "Signour, je sui chieus que vous querés et que vous avés juré(s) que vous ochirrés et devés porter mon sanc le roi Vertigier." [Ibid., 1:43]

In this field there was a group of children playing with ball and club [Fr. *chouler*]. And Merlin, who knew everything, was there and saw King Vertigier's messengers who were looking for him. Merlin drew alongside one of the richest children because he knew he would dislike him; he raised the club and struck the child in the leg, and the boy started to cry and to curse Merlin and call him "fatherless son." When the messengers who were looking for him heard the child speak thus they approached the crying child and asked him: "Who is the one who struck you?" And he said: "He is the son of a woman who never knew who engendered him, nor did he ever have a father." When Merlin heard this he approached the messengers and said, laughing: "Lords, I am the one you are seeking and that you have sworn to kill in order to take my blood to King Vertigier."

Merlin's triumph over the astronomers is by no means unique. He systematically usurps the officially sanctioned discourses—scientific, juridical, political, technological, even theological—of a culture that is transformed by his pervasive presence. The entrapment of Vertigier's counselors is merely the first of a number of founding episodes which serve to establish the authority of a point of view indistinguishable from the authorial voice—ubiquitous, omniscient, present in all its ruses. More

Boys playing from Bede, *Life of Saint Cuthbert,* Ms. University College 165, Bodleian Library, Oxford University, England. (Printed with the permission of the Masters and Fellows of University College, Oxford.)

generally, it poses the possibility of a vision that presents itself as comprehensive and of a system of meaning adequate to such an all-encompassing horizon. Nothing escapes the watchful eye of the "wise child." The "wise men" can neither plot against him nor approach him without being seen; the rich boy cannot retaliate without his foreknowledge. As Merlin admits in the type of explanation that often concludes an episode like the above, "because I knew they were against me, I identified myself to them by means of a child whom I struck in order that he name me." Even after the astronomers have promised not to kill him, Merlin retains a perfect perception of their innermost intention. And in bringing them before Blaise for the purpose of written confession, the magician-inquisitor reminds those who until then held sway at court that "he wants them to know that he will know if they tell a lie."[12]

Merlin's totalizing regard places him at once outside and at the center of the tale which he narrates and in which he participates. It incorporates the vision of the scientist, the supposedly neutral observer, and that of the actor within a drama of cultural mutation in which superstition is vanquished by a higher law, a more efficient discourse—in this instance, that of poetry and prophecy combined. Merlin's dominating presence is the necessary condition of complicity with the reader; and his victory creates the illusion of a reliable point of view from which to further dominate the text until he delegates that power—the secret of writing's power—and is himself trapped by it (*Huth*, 2:196–198).

The impossibility of locating Merlin within this enormous prose work, which like its protagonist defies generic classification, creates a rich confusion with far-reaching implications for our understanding of Old French literature and its historical background. His role as observer and participant, his status as poet and actor, suggest the subtle beginnings of what might be termed a literary anthropology of the Middle Ages. I say "anthropology" because Merlin's central (inclusive, neutral, and fundamentally ethnocentric) vision of a society which, as his lack of paternity infers, is radically *other* takes as its own point of departure the comprehensive index of cultural elements and the deduction of its innermost laws. I say "literary" because the vehicle of such a supposedly scientific undertaking is itself poetic and indissociable from the polyvalent capacity of language both to inform—to maintain its "transparence"—and to delude. The man possessed of superior insight, both outside and above the official discourse of the court astronomers, embodies the principle of writing in all its reliable and illusory dimensions. And his rearrangement within a work of romance of the prevailing "orders of discourse" merely affirms the centrality of poetry within a process of broad social transformation.

The situation of the poetic text can be considered to be anthropological in the strictest sense: like Merlin, it offers unique insight into the workings of a society which it also conditions. And just as the magician-inquisitor is both the bringer of writing and its corruptor—faithful witness and perfidious abuser—medieval poetry is both the reflection and the agent of permutation of the object it reflects. We will have occasion shortly to return to each of these points, which are by no means evident given the fact that Old French literature is sufficiently alien to our own sensibilities to require something on the order of an "anthropological" explanation. But first a glance at the archetypal anthropological moment in the history and practice of that discipline as we know it.

In a central chapter of *Tristes Tropiques*, C. Lévi-Strauss offers a "lesson in speaking" as important in its ramifications as the famous "leçon d'écriture." The anthropologist, having spent some time among the Nambikwara of Brazil, remains unable to penetrate that culture until, in his own phrase:

> Un jour que je jouais avec un groupe d'enfants, une des fillettes fut frappée par une camarade; elle vint se réfugier auprès de moi, et se mit, en grand mystère, à me murmurer quelque chose à l'oreille, que je ne compris pas, et que je fus obligé de lui faire répéter à plusieurs reprises, si bien que l'adversaire découvrit le manège, et, manifestement furieuse, arriva à son tour pour livrer ce qui parut être un secret solennel: après quelques hésitations et questions, l'interprétation de l'incident ne laissa pas de doute. La première fillette était venue, par vengeance, me donner le nom de son ennemie, et quand celle-ci s'en aperçut, elle communiqua le nom de l'autre, en guise de représaille. A partir de ce moment, il fut très facile, bien que peu scrupuleux, d'exciter les enfants les uns contre les autres, et d'obtenir tous leurs noms. Après quoi, une petite complicité ainsi créée, ils me donnèrent sans trop de difficulté, les noms des adultes.[13]

In order to understand the full significance of Lévi-Strauss's "discovery," it is important to know that proper names are a subject of taboo among the Nambikwara: "l'emploi des noms propres est chez eux interdit" (p. 254). The anthropologist had, until then, relied upon a language as artificial in its attributions as the Morse code which resonates even in the chapter heading ("Sur la ligne"): "pour identifier les personnes il fallait suivre l'usage des gens de la ligne, c'est-à-dire convenir avec les indigènes des noms d'emprunt par lesquels on les désignerait. Soit des noms portugais, comme Julio, José-Marie, Luiza; soit des sobriquets: *Lebre* (lièvre), *Assucar* (sucre)" (p. 294). An accurate perception of the true proper name—and not just of one but of the multiple names (both of children and of adults) that constitute a differential system—is the necessary prelude to a "cracking" of the cultural code. With the deliverance from unmotivated signs, the relations between those designated henceforth by supposedly determined "proper" names are assumed to fall into place. And if the anthropologist's revelation occurs by chance, it is no accident, as J. Derrida notes, that the episode of discovery directly precedes the chapter on family life ("En famille").

Lévi-Strauss's uneasy interaction with the children of the Nambikwara marks the liminal anthropological moment—the instant at which the outsider as observer penetrates the object of observation and play is converted into "science." Here, in fact, is where the *Huth Merlin* and *Tristes Tropiques* seem to join. The children's game, hidden identity, give and take of tort and retaliation signal a certain episodic similarity. Beyond that, the drama of demystification by nomination, which serves to establish meaning, is in both cases symptomatic of the beginning of a complicity between author and reader (or listener) which radicalizes the literary and scientific enterprise. Merlin names *himself* and is thus implicated in the exposure of his own intention. It is, in fact, this dissolution of the distinction between author and invention that renders the literary narrative problematic. A crippling openness characterizes Merlin's stature as universal signifier; and so comprehensive and contradictory is the novel which exposes even the mechanism of its own production that it never generates the kind of dramatic interest dependent upon "narrow mimesis" in the Aristotelian sense. Lévi-Strauss, on the other hand, learns only the names of *others* and thus remains firmly outside of the problematics of nomination that he thematizes. This is not to suggest that such a savvy observer of the savage mind allows the dialectical possibilities of such an encounter to pass unnoticed. On the contrary, he is keenly aware of the fact that intellectual penetration cannot be dissociated from cultural transformation. What escapes the scientist's gaze is the extent to which any objectively conceived regard upon the other throws into question the very premises of the scientific undertaking and the extent to which it is itself productive of literary form.

Lévi-Strauss's appearance upon the primal anthropological scene contains the seeds of his own loss of innocence alongside that of the Nambikwara. His access to the secret of social organization is, moreover, associated with a loss of transparency. Like Merlin, he passes from invisibility ("the Nambikwara were easy-going and unperturbed by the presence of the anthropologist") to a visibility which destroys. Here, however, the resemblance ends, since the question of the effects of self-exposure, of what is destroyed, is not susceptible to evenhanded response. In naming himself, Merlin also names the enterprise of fiction synonymous with his being. For Lévi-Strauss, by comparison, the consequences of naming the other are merely incidental. The encounter with the children of the Nambikwara implies the dissipation of his sources. His appearance to the adults, and own investment with meaning, render further understanding more difficult: "Lorsque ceux-ci comprirent nos conciliabules, les

enfants furent réprimandés, et les sources de mes informations taries"
(p. 294). Later, an even more dramatic encounter with the chief of the
Nambikwara results in the anthropologist's momentary disorientation,
loss of photographic equipment and weapons, and eventual recovery, as
if he had just participated sympathetically in a ritual isolation, initiatory
testing, and return (pp. 315–316).

If the effects upon the anthropologist of the anthropological moment
par excellence are temporary and anecdotal, its aftermath for the Nambikwara is catastrophic and determining. The dissipation of one source
does not prevent Lévi-Strauss from pursuing another; and this at the
center of the culture whose integrity, by his own account, is annihilated
by his presence armed with the tools of the anthropologist's trade. Here I
refer to the famous "writing lesson" in which the tribal chief, attracted by
the scientist's note-taking, inexplicably grasps the "purpose of writing,"
which the ethnologist equates with social domination:

> L'écriture avait donc fait son apparition chez les Nambikwara; mais non
> point, comme on aurait pu l'imaginer, au terme d'un apprentissage labo-
> rieux. Son symbole avait été emprunté tandis que sa réalité demeurait
> étrangère. Et cela, en vue d'une fin sociologique plutôt qu'intellectuelle. Il
> ne s'agissait pas de connaître, de retenir ou de comprendre, mais d'ac-
> croître le prestige et l'autorité d'un individu—ou d'une fonction—aux dé-
> pens d'autrui. [P. 316]

Lévi-Strauss, again like Merlin, is the bringer of civilization through
writing, which in turn disrupts the very cultural fabric that he originally
sought to describe: "Ceux qui se désolidarisèrent de leur chef après qu'il
eût essayé de jouer la carte de la civilisation (à la suite de ma visite il fut
abandonné de la plupart des siens) comprenaient confusément que l'écriture et la perfidie pénétraient chez eux de concert" (p. 319).

For Lévi-Strauss, writing is synonymous with the exertion of power,
exploitation, "the strengthening of dominion"; but a power whose effects
are uneven. On the one hand, penetration of the Nambikwara incurs a
temporary setback for the scientist; on the other, it portends a momen-
tous cultural breakdown mythologized in terms of a primal expulsion—
the fall from stone-age innocence into the corruption and strife that
Lévi-Strauss, in the tradition of Rousseau, associates with the passage
from culture to society. In the question of this imbalance lies the difference between the archetypal anthropologist and the medieval Merlin.
More precisely, Lévi-Strauss depicts the unilateral effects of writing upon
the other whose names permit not only anthropology but an exertion of
the power that the unaffected scientist exposes. In this respect the ethnologist reserves for himself a position of innocence inspired by an unperturbed belief in the transparency of his own discourse about the other,
while he shows that he has not learned an even more fundamental

"lesson" about writing that J. Derrida undertakes to teach him in his own founding meditation on language, *De la Grammatologie*.

Derrida accuses Lévi-Strauss of what he terms "phonologism," a privileging of the voice over writing which falsifies the scientific project from the beginning. According to the philosopher of language, the "writing lesson" that the anthropologist localizes historically at a precise moment in the evolution of culture is already contained in the speaking lesson. Rather, the distinction which Lévi-Strauss draws between speech, associated with innocence, and writing, identified with difference, hierarchy, and corruption, is already operative in the "espacement" of speech subsumed in the category of "archi-écriture." Thus the violence inherent in language has occurred even before the anthropologist arrives upon the scene with his writing pad; it exists in the suppression of proper names and, beyond that, in their original instigation: "Il y a écriture dès que le nom propre est raturé dans un système, il a 'sujet' dès que cette oblitération du propre se produit, c'est-à-dire dès l'apparaître du propre et dès le premier matin du langage."[14] The violence of the chief's appropriation of writing, which Derrida classifies as a "tertiary empirical" act, simply mirrors a primal expropriation of "le vocatif absolu" endemic to any use of language whatsoever—"la violence de l'archi-écriture, la violence de la différence, de la classification et du système des appellations" (p. 162).

For the philosopher, the fragility of the anthropological project lies in the confusion of a supposedly neutral scientific discourse with an essentially colonial endeavor. He faults Lévi-Strauss for what he terms an "epigenetic" concept of writing whose ultimate consequences are more ethnocentric than the ethnocentrism that the structuralist seeks to avoid. Because of his ready acceptance of the distinction between voiced utterance and writing, Lévi-Strauss falls into the trap of what for Derrida is an illusory and even dangerous distinction between idealized cultures without orthography and cultures possessed of writing along with the repressive technologies that it implies. Ample evidence both of innocence and exploitation is, he maintains, to be found on either side of the barrier of writing; and any attempt to assign priority to one side or the other excessively dramatizes the role of the Western observer in a mythopoetic reenactment of the Fall. According to Derrida, Lévi-Strauss is guilty finally of bad faith, of a Rousseauistic wallowing in ethnological confession that blinds him to the liberating as well as the enslaving effects that writing, psychologically as well as historically, has always enjoyed.

I am aware that the above opposition is itself somewhat dramatized, that its overly simple terms do justice to the more subtle strategies of neither the anthropologist nor the philosopher. It is nonetheless germane to the medieval example which, I think it also can be shown, even points toward one possibility of a historically situated reconciliation of the two.

Stated simply, Lévi-Strauss's romanticized encounter with the Nambikwara offers: the psychic satisfaction of a well-centered perspective upon the other, a pleasure perhaps not divorced from that of "dominion"; the esthetic satisfaction of a narrative in the broadest sense, that is to say, a meditation upon origins or beginnings verging on the pleasure of the literary text;[15] and a certain intellectual satisfaction implicit in the possibility of cognitive certainty which, in its power to reassure, reinforces the seduction of central vision. On the other hand, Lévi-Strauss's unwillingness to identify, much less to come to grips with, the speaking and writing subject leads at best to self-delusion and at worst to a complicity in the anthropological project transformed, by a decisive intrusion upon its object, into a neocolonial one. Ultimately, it elicits the kinds of questions that Derrida poses and which threaten the very foundations of anthropology as a scientific discourse. "Can there be an anthropology in which the contradiction of a continuous description of difference does not inhere?" "Can anthropology exist without the exertion of power?" Put another way, "Is it possible to imagine a non-Western ethnology?" and "What would such a regard of the other upon *its* other look like?"

Derrida's critique of the anthropologist offers, in turn, the philosophical satisfaction of a rigorous reexamination of the assumptions underlying all scientific discourse, including the assumed "transparency" of its written form; it offers the pleasure attached to thoroughness of argument and to the carrying of initial premises to their logical conclusion, even when these menace the continuity of overall presentation. Yet it leads to the reestablishment of a new principle of certainty according to which, wherever language is involved, there can be no certainty of the type that Lévi-Strauss takes for granted; and this paradox is not without difficulties of its own. For if the ethnologist unconsciously dramatizes, that is to say, overparticularizes, an "empirical violence" by making it appear accidental, if he maintains an illusory and potentially dangerous distinction between the empirical and the essential, between the self and the other, the philosopher in turn generalizes to such an extent as to obliterate the particular altogether. By reducing the violence of representation to such a basic level—pushing it from writing, to speech, and back to thought—Derrida himself inflicts a violence equal to that of which he accuses Lévi-Strauss: he refuses the specificity of the object of representation, denies its materiality, to such an extent as to pose the question of whether one can, finally, distinguish between the annihilating effects of the anthropologist's ethnocentric vision and those of the philosopher's homogenizing regard.[16]

The gulf between the ethnology of Lévi-Strauss and the philosophy of language of Derrida seems absolute and overdetermined from the beginning. Lévi-Strauss's vision of the other and of the other's relation to writing is, in some fundamental sense, overdetermined by the choice, in responding to the question "What is man?" of men without writing. Derrida's response to the same question is similarly decided by the impossibility of separating speech from a universal writing operative even at the level of thought, and hence a universalizing of the human condition. Nevertheless, it can be shown that in this radical disjunction resides the interesting possibility of an anthropology of the West. A certain turning of the Lévi-Straussian project upon the Derridean problematics of the sign constitutes a powerful tool for the analysis of a culture like that of the Christian Middle Ages, one whose specificity consists precisely in a meditation upon language unrivaled in any era except perhaps our own.

The idea of a "Western anthropology" is hardly original. The monumental work of M. Foucault, to take the most prominent example, can be situated in the disjunctive space between Lévi-Strauss and Derrida. Foucault traces the various exclusionary provinces of our own others—the madman, criminal, sexual deviant; and he places the various practices of exclusion, and thus the problem of identity, within the general context of what he terms an "archeology" of the discourses of man.[17] The situation of the Middle Ages is, however, different, and not just in the sense that M. de Certeau intends when he defines all history as anthropological because it deals, alongside the madman of the psychoanalyst and the wildman of the anthropologist, with the *dead man* as the other.[18] The distinguishing trait of the medieval example has to do with the fact that we are so massively cut off from the signs of an age which we even now continue to define as a lacuna between two more familiar cultural moments. This is more than a question of linguistic competence, learning another language; it involves the philological endeavor in the highest sense of the term—the attempt to understand the presuppositions, semantic range and context, material conditions, the social, theological, psychological points of reference of the signs of a culture alien enough from our own to allow very little to be taken for granted.[19]

Some of the most powerful readings of the medieval period to appear in recent years are, in fact, those which capitalize upon the obligation to view its strangeness with unfamiliar eyes, with the eyes of the anthropologist before he has "cracked the code," learned the proper names, of a culture riddled with centuries of ready-made interpretations. In particular, P. Zumthor's *Langue et technique poétiques à l'époque romane* and his *Essai de poétique médiévale* encourage the reclassification of vernacular literary modes according not to the romantically inspired notion of genre but rather to the enunciative distance ("écart linguistique") which each establishes with respect to Latin and with respect to each other.[20] H.-R.

Jauss, more in the German hermeneutic tradition than in that of the linguistic schools of Copenhagen, Paris, and Prague, associates the otherness of the Middle Ages—what he calls its "alterity"—with the principle of esthetic identification.[21] In what remains a fundamentally anthropological gesture, he seeks to transform strangeness into a virtue by which a necessary reflection upon the other becomes the pleasurable basis for knowledge of the self.

Given that what we call the Middle Ages is sufficiently inaccessible to habitual modes of perception and understanding to solicit anthropological inquiry, "What," it may be asked, "would such an anthropology look like?" Here is where Derrida challenges Lévi-Strauss on his own terms. For any satisfactory answer to this question itself entails exactly the kinds of issues that the grammatologist prescribes. An anthropology of the Middle Ages must, first of all, take as its point of departure the appropriateness, even the primacy, of the consideration of language. This was a period marked by intense debate about the nature and function of verbal signs. Linguistics, within the medieval order of human (conventional or socially determined) discourse, constituted a proper field of legitimation capable of producing in the first instance knowledge of the perceptible world. Moreover, the millennium between the fifth and the fifteenth centuries was an age in which speculation about linguistic signs was fundamental to speculation about the larger universe.[22] Not only was medieval culture a culture of the Book, its epistemology an epistemology of the Word and of words, but disciplines that today are considered primary were, until the Renaissance, subordinate to the "artes sermocinales." Economics, for example, was a subset of general sign theory (see below, pp. 164–170); history was often considered under the heading of grammar; philosophy dealt extensively with questions like the status of general verbal terms; and theology was haunted by such issues as the search for an adequate name for God, the efficacy of divine grace in human speech, and the symbolic nature of the sacraments.

Second, any anthropology of the Middle Ages must take into account, along with the centrality of linguistics, a certain *practice* of texts, which is where Lévi-Strauss's "epigenetic" concentration upon difference turns upon Derrida. The philosopher's reduction of all meanings to one essential meaning, whence derives the power of his analysis, also marks the parameters of a blind spot that falls within the anthropologist's domain. Bearing only tangentially either upon the general phenomenology of language or upon the ontological conditions of its production (or metaphysical implications), this field has to do with the question of reception, what H.-R. Jauss (after Gadamer) refers to as a text's "horizon of expectation," as well as with the global issue of use and social function.[23] It involves the ways in which a culture ritualizes—ignores, appropriates, suppresses, disseminates, banalizes, fetishizes—the corpus of symbolic possibilities available to it at a given moment. And, finally, it entails the modes by which various means of textual production mediate and are mediated by other cultural discourses (e.g., familial, scientific, economic, legal).

We begin from the premise that the twelfth and thirteenth centuries offer a unique opportunity for an anthropology based upon the practice of the text. Unique because, as C. S. Lewis claimed, this period represented one of the few moments of true historical mutation the West has ever known. But unique also because the nature of the transformation which affected virtually every area of social and cultural life was so intimately connected to a profound shift in the status and uses of writing. Its situation at the *terminus ad quem* of the so-called Dark Ages can, in fact, mean only this: that the period between the collapse of the Carolingian Empire and what G. Duby designates as the "watershed years" of the last quarter of the eleventh century left relatively few written traces. This is not to infer that writing was not practiced regularly by a small group of assiduous annalists and scribes but rather that, during this "ebbtide of history," the locus of writing was severely restricted. Literally displaced from the center to the margins of society, to the monasteries and high princely circles scattered throughout Europe of the invasions, both the place of writing in the polis and its function were marginalized. The Renaissance of the High Middle Ages, in contrast, was practically synonymous with a collective "writing lesson"—the irruption of a basically illiterate secular culture into writing, and the break, within writing, of a universal Latin culture into the disparate vernacular tongues. For the first time since the fall of the Roman Empire, the lay aristocracy of Western Europe possessed a cultural vehicle adequate to express its innermost tensions and ideals.[24] And for the first time since the triumph of Christianity, the techniques of writing heretofore reserved for a caste (clerical and male) were massively disseminated among those exercising an ecclesiastical function as well as not.

What is to be learned from this collective "writing lesson," this intrusion of writing into many activities conducted until then without it (e.g., government, secular law, business, poetic performance)? First, that the unidirectional catalyzing effect which Lévi-Strauss assigns to history because of writing does not hold for the medieval example. Cultures possessed of writing lose it, repress it, displace it, only to rediscover and reappropriate it even centuries later. Second, that the idyllic, tension-free state that the anthropologist associates with an ignorance of writing cannot be said to be universal and certainly does not pertain to the period in question: the "Dark Ages" were characterized by the most extreme conflict and chaos; the "age of writing," in comparison, offers the first peaceful fruits of civil administration—the discipline of the state—along with the displacement of the anarchy of internecine conflict toward foreign crusade. Finally, the absolute association of writing with a hierarchization of social relations is much more problematic than the ethnologist would allow. Lévi-Strauss posits as a necessary corollary of writing the reinforcement of the ability of some individuals to dominate others.[25] And while it is true that the twelfth and the thirteenth centuries witness a gradual centralization of political power—the consolidation of a monarchic presence within an expanding royal domain along with the revival of towns—the role of writing per se in such an evolution is highly ambiguous. Its dissemination produced almost limitless possibilities for the dispersion of power alongside of its concentration. If anything, this "second feudal age" (M. Bloch) testifies to a persistent tension between those ready to capitalize upon the institutional forms of power that writing permits—administrative, legal, economic—and those for whom it represents (consciously or not) the possibility of their subversion. Writing is not, as the ethnologist asserts, the *cause* of social conflict; it is, in the absence of Derrida's "tertiary empirical violence," at once the vehicle of such conflict and the terrain upon which it occurs.

This brings us to our second premise, which is that the literary text represents a privileged forum for the realization of such tensions and, in fact, a key to the anthropology of the age. In an era in which historical documents are still relatively rare and culturally biased (in favor of aristocracy and clergy), in which the intellectual output of "high culture" is ideologically oriented and detached from everyday life, literature opens a *via regia* to the only kind of anthropology that can have any meaning within the context of the "writing culture" of the High Middle Ages. This will change, of course, with the fundamental reorganization of the orders of knowledge and of discursive practice at the time of the Renaissance (in particular, with the intrusion of the vernacular upon areas of historical and scientific inquiry formerly reserved for Latin, and with printing). Until then, however, poetry remains crucial to the anthropological endeavor. And if we have begun with what at first appears like a fantasy-filled work of fiction, it is because a literary text like the *Huth Merlin*, situated at the confluence of documentary evidence and ideological prescription, furnishes the richest answers to the questions that ethnology poses (more later); it yields the most dynamic indication of what A. Borst calls "life forms." Merlin embodies the possibility of an anthropology of difference, as outlined by Lévi-Strauss, combined with a grammatological reflection upon the role of language (and of the subject) within such an undertaking, as articulated by Derrida. The magician-politician stands on neither side of writing. At once within and outside of the tale, he both names himself and is associated with writing in all its potential to exert and to subvert the power it names. Simultaneously scientist and poet, Merlin's status as witness and participant in this drama of social transformation above all marks the literary work as a privileged locus—a point of departure—for the anthropology of the later medieval period.

Merlin's stature as author also indicates the degree to which the literary object is itself implicated in the process it exposes. Here lies a centering paradox of the project at hand: namely, the vernacular poetry of the High Middle Ages both reflects its cultural moment, thus enabling anthropological description, and is a prime vehicle for the change of that which it reflects. Such a dialectical relation is, of course, characteristic of the bivalent role of literature in every age. Yet the medieval situation is particular, and the nature of this particularity bears special meaning for the anthropologist of the Christian West.

In the era before the book, before all that the book implies by way of an autonomous article consumed by a public of solitary readers, the literary object constituted an anthropological space in the strictest sense. Here is where the dichotomy that Lévi-Strauss (in the mainstream of Western linguistics) draws between voice and writing takes on significance in spite of Derrida's critique. For the defining mode of literature was, until the fourteenth century, that of the oral recitation. Even those texts of which we possess the (often fragmentary) written traces were themselves intended to be either read aloud or sung. What this means is that poetry enjoyed a public, collective status denied to it in the age of printing. And its practice remained indissociable from the kinds of symbolic activity that the anthropologist normally studies. The "performed text" represented a periodic ritual enactment of the most basic values and innermost code of the lay culture of the High Middle Ages—the affirmation with only limited variation of that which is ideologically manifest elsewhere. But with this crucial distinction: where the ritual of the anthropologists is an essentially conservative force of social cohesion, literature stands at the crossroads of medieval social practice and ideology. It is at once the representation of that which occurs outside of the realm of textual production and, as A. Adler and E. Köhler have shown, an inverted mirror of the possible.[26] The poetic performance stands as a ratification of the ideals of the community and as a forum for the articulation of responses to shared dilemmas, and thus as an instrument of change. This is another way of saying that the relation between the medieval poet and his audience is more dynamic than that of the shaman and his clan. And while the literary ritual always commemorates the common past of the group, it also attests to a deep complicity between what Zumthor calls the "vouloir-entendre" and the "vouloir-dire."

The Old French text is a "generator of public consciousness," which can be said to exist *through* it just as society can be said to exist through language.[27] The most compelling proof of this is, of course, a negative one—the fact that so few texts are ascribable to an author invested with more personality than a mere name. Medieval literature before the age of Dante constituted a kind of common property belonging to no individual poetic voice but to the voice of the community as a whole, and occupying a liminal space between that which it reflects and affects. Written vestige of an oral performance, it is the relic of a society which once relied only tangentially upon writing. Symptom of an immense process of textualization operative throughout the culture, it is at the same time the catalyst of change. A literary anthropology of the Middle Ages is situated, then, in the interstices between Lévi-Strauss's "epigenetic" privileging and Derrida's radical denial of the difference between oral and written expression—in the zone where "archi-écriture" lends itself to discussion in terms of social practice.

One final premise governs the present study: that we are currently in a unique position for such an undertaking. Recent advances by historians make it possible to begin to answer for the Middle Ages the kinds of questions that concern the anthropologist (e.g., kinship, economic exchange, symbolic practice). The study of medieval literature has, moreover, begun to emerge from the exhaustion of idealist and positivist criticism which has for some time now adequately answered the questions of nineteenth-century philology (e.g., chronological and regional situation, sources, manuscript affiliation, genre). More important, the reassessment of the relation between the social sciences and the humanities, as it has occurred over the last twenty years, renders the narrow distinctions between academic disciplines inappropriate to the intellectual project atuned to the exigencies of its own age. This implies the necessity of interdisciplinary study, but only as a prelude to study of the relation between the various orders of knowledge pertaining elsewhere and at other times, only as a first step in the global attempt to assimilate the contemporary discourses of man—their underlying determinations, practical consequences, methods—to any consideration of the other.

This blurring of the borders between traditional domains is especially appropriate to the universalizing culture of the Middle Ages. It points in the direction of a dialogue between the past and the present of which the exchange between Lévi-Strauss and Derrida, mediated by Merlin, is merely emblematic. More precisely, the issues that define our own intellectual temper were sufficiently crucial to the period we designate as our "historical other" as to render such a dialogue compelling. Merlin, faithful witness and unwitting anthropologist, enlightens us about his own time. But beyond that, his curiously ambiguous status encourages speculation about the structuralist ethnologist, the writer on writing unconscious of his own poetic gesture, as well as about the poststructuralist philosopher whose analysis denies, to cite T. Adorno, that "everything is not possible at all times." What I am suggesting is that the choice of the Middle Ages is really a choice motivated by, and in favor of, the present—and not just in the sense of Jauss's "otherness" provoking identification. On the contrary, this temporally distant and logically inaccessible era speaks directly to our time as a kind of challenge to many of the burning issues of the day. Its pertinence is writ large, there to be read in:

1. *The centrality of semiotics.* As we have already affirmed above (p. 12), the place of the language arts is fundamental within the medieval orders of knowledge. Linguistics will lose its centrality at the time of the Renaissance and only since F. de Saussure has it begun to recapture its pride of place. This is one of the defining themes of the essay which follows, and we will have occasion to return to it over and over again.

2. *The status of the subject.* For the structuralist, the existence of a community without writing serves as a testing ground for what E. Said terms "life at the zero point," that is to say, the possibility of a culture without the relations of power that the idea of social life has, since the eighteenth century, implied. Similarly, the High Middle Ages represent an ideal test case for the radical questioning of the subject characteristic of many of the most powerful minds from Hegel, Nietzsche, and Freud to Barthes, Derrida, Lacan, and Foucault. Here the problem of whether the discourse of the individual is, to invoke the medieval expression, "founded," or whether a transpersonal discourse speaks through the individual, is crucial and cannot be separated from broader linguistic concerns. The Dark Ages represent a kind of "zero point" of the subject. Whether for theological reasons, for reasons connected to the underlying structure of a warrior society, or because of the reduced role of writing, the status of the individual was, from the time of the Carolingian Renaissance to that of the twelfth century, reduced to a minimum. This "middle age" of the Middle Ages signals an absolute rupture between Classical notions of the self and those of our own age. Conversely, the reign of Louis VII onward marks a founding moment in the history of the self as we know it (and as it will be modified during the Renaissance and the Enlightenment).

One of the guiding tenets of the present study as well as of my previous book on medieval literature and law is that Old French poetry played a crucial role in this evolution.[28] Both symptom and vehicle, vernacular literature was the privileged locus for the articulation of a notion of the self as a distinct inner space with a law of its own. This will culminate in the thirteenth century with the appearance of long allegorical poems offering a full-blown dynamic model of the mind. But it is obvious more generally in the constant ideological tension between collective (epic) and individualizing (courtly) forms as well as in the relative lack of specificity of the individual work within its generic mode, its status, in Zumthor's phrase, as a "nuance within a register." Again, these are issues fundamental to the discussion which follows, and they will recur repeatedly.

3. *The coincidence of the linguistic and the social.* The orders of language and of society were, in the period under scrutiny, considered to be connatural. In the first place, language was held to be proper only to man and the necessary condition of human society. "Deprived of speech," as John of Salisbury asserts in what remains the keynote of the age, "men would degenerate to the condition of brute animals, and cities would seem like corrals for livestock, rather than communities composed of human beings united by a common bond for the purpose of living in society, serving one another, and cooperating as friends."[29] The language arts stood as the sine qua non of social order; and in the tradition passed to the Middle Ages by Cicero, the foundation of the city and of rhetoric are conceived as simultaneous gestures implicated in each other:

> Nam fuit quoddam tempus cum in agris homines passim bestiarum modo vagabantur et sibi victu fero vitam propagabant, nec ratione animi quicquam, sed pleraque viribus corporis administrabant; nondum divinae religionis, non humani offici ratio colebatur, nemo nuptias viderat legitimas, non certos quisquam aspexerat liberos, non, ius aequabile quid utilitatis haberet, acceperat. . . .
>
> Quo tempore quidam magnus videlicet vir et sapiens cognovit quae materia esset et quanta ad maximas res opportunitas in animis inesset hominum, si quis eam posset elicere et praecipiendo meliorem reddere; qui dispersos homines in agros et in tectis silvestribus abditos ratione quadam compulit unum in locum et congregavit et eos in unam quamque rem inducens utilem atque honestam . . . , deinde propter rationem atque orationem studiosius audientes ex feris et immanibus mites reddidit et mansuetos.[30]

> There was a time when men wandered at large in the fields like animals and lived on wild fare; they did nothing by the guidance of reason, but relied chiefly on physical strength; there was as yet no ordered system of religious worship nor of social duties; no one had seen legitimate marriage nor had anyone looked upon children whom he knew to be his own; nor had they learned the advantages of an equitable code of law. . . .
>
> At this juncture a man—great and wise I am sure—became aware of the power latent in man and the wide field offered by his mind to great achievement if one could develop this power and improve it by instruction. Men were scattered in the fields and hidden in sylvan retreats when he assembled and gathered them in accordance with a plan; he introduced them to every useful and honorable occupation . . . , and then when through reason and eloquence they had listened with greater attention, he transformed them from wild savages into a kind and gentle folk.

Thus the Classical anthropological moment represents a curious blend of elements familiar both to the ethnologist and the philosopher of language. "Epigenetic" in its dramatic unraveling, Cicero's concern with origins assumes the possibility of a primordial state before the existence of the city, religion, reason, justice, and the family—the law of exogamy which Lévi-Strauss equates with culture itself. Yet the Latin rhetorician remains closer to Derrida in his situation of the primal social law somewhere between Aristotle's "inarticulate noises made by brute beasts" and Lévi-Strauss's graphic writing—that is, in a refinement of speech synonymous with rhetorical eloquence and reason itself. The "time before the law" is, moreover, not that of the structuralist's sentimental rendering of the Golden Age; on the contrary, that which precedes eloquent speech and social order is defined by "blind and unreasoning passion satisfied by misuse of bodily strength."[31]

Augustine in many ways comes closest to the Derridian imbrication of socialization and signification. For the Bishop of Hippo, appellation does not coincide with thought but is coterminous with a primary instance of the social: "Since," he maintains, "man remains incapable of forming solid social bonds without words, through which he communicates in some way his soul and his thoughts to another, reason understood that it was necessary to give names to things. . . ."[32] Similarly, Aquinas acknowledges in the advent of meaningful language the expression of man's nature, which "because he is a social and political animal, made it necessary for his ideas to be transmitted to others. . . ."[33] The law of language, whether located in appellation, speech, or eloquent expression, is synonymous with the law. Their common origin is not merely chronological, as, for instance, in the patristic association of Hebrew letters and the reception of the law through Moses, but logical as well. In the tradition stretching as far back as the Latin grammarian Varro, speech and justice are allied: "Dico 'I say' has a Greek origin, that which the Greeks call δεικνύω 'I show.' . . . From this moreover comes *dicare* 'to show, to judge,' because the *ius* 'right' is spoken; from this *iudex* 'judge,' because he *ius dicat* 'speaks the decision.' . . ."[34]

Historically and logically related, the orders of language and of society are also ontologically intertwined. Here we touch upon the Platonic theme of man the microcosm of the greater universe and, in particular, upon the conceptualization of the latter in terms of a written text. The twelfth century was one of the great ages of Platonism in the West, and the analogy between man and the elements of the cosmos received both doctrinal and literary elaboration in the Chartrian commentaries upon the *Timaeus* (William of Conches, Gilbert of Porreta), Bernard Silvestris's *De Mundi universitate*, Godfrey of Saint-Victor's *Microcosmos*, and later in the physics and "naturalist anthropology" of Albert the Great, Bonaventure, Aquinas, and Jean de Meun.[35] For the theologians, philosophers, and speculative poets of the High Middle Ages, the world is, on the one hand, the ambiguous mirror of God, at once the source of illusion for man's fallible senses and a source of knowledge about its Creator. Man, on the other hand, is the reflected image of the natural universe whose laws he embodies, a "workshop," in the phrase of John Scotus, in which the principles of nature are constantly renewed. Under such an analogical articulation of subsistent categories, the distinction between the natural order of the universe and social order is minimized. To know nature is to know an ideal order of relation between men since natural law is the equivalent of psychic law. And the bond between human psychology and cosmic order, one of the major themes of Boethius's *De Consolatione*, becomes in the twelfth century the basis of moral science. As Hugh of Saint-Victor observes, "nature and justice are allied."[36] Finally, to complete the syllogism, if man and nature, nature and society, are analogous, so too is man analogous to the human community. This idea is developed most fully in the topos of the Body Politic. Urania's speech of the *De Mundi universitate* equates natural law with a harmonious balance of bodily parts. John of Salisbury gives elaborate expression in the *Policraticus* to the organic metaphor of bodily health and social equilibrium.[37]

If I have introduced the theme of man the microcosm (a dangerous gesture for the scholar who risks being caught in the analogical movement he describes), it is because the natural order equated with social order itself rests upon an essentially linguistic model. The *speculum Dei* is conceived as a function of writing. For Hugh of Saint-Victor, for example, "the entire sense-perceptible world is like a sort of book written by the finger of God." According to Alain de Lille, "every creature in the world is, for us, like a book and a picture and a mirror as well." "There marked down by the finger of the Supreme Scribe can be read the text of time, the fated march of events, the disposition made of the ages"—so affirms Bernard Silvestris.[38] Even more important, the moral order that mediates the relation between individual and community was, throughout the period in question, subject to analysis in specifically linguistic terms. The medieval language arts provided the framework for discussion of the mental images which, because they are held to be universal, define the parameters of a universal psychology. This is true, for instance, of Augustine whose economy of conversion is, as M. Colish has shown, overdetermined by the model of rhetoric.[39] It is equally applicable to the case of Abelard who equates mental images with general verbal terms and for whom the logic of ideal linguistic relations is equivalent to the subsistent order of the world. Then, too, the assimilation of linguistics and psychology among the speculative grammarians of the thirteenth and fourteenth centuries yields the global project of reconciling through universal grammar the mind's modes of signifying the ontological categories of the real with the voice's modes of material expression.

The coincidence of the orders of language and society, mediated by a linguistically defined psychology, obviously cannot be separated from the centrality of semiotics and the question of the subject; and, as with these first two points, it informs our inquiry into the relation between language theory, family structure, and poetic form. I am aware, of course, that not all literary critics, much less those whose specialty is the Middle Ages, acknowledge such a problematics and that those who do disagree radically as to how to define it. I am conscious also that this particular combination of elements risks appearing somewhat arbitrary to the anthropologist, who habitually deals with the correlation of linguistics and kinship; to the historian, who uses literary material to document the history of the family; to the critic, for whom the connection between grammar and poetry is crucial; and to the philosopher, who may be used to the mutual consideration of all three but not to their historical situation. The project proposed does, in fact, cross the customary boundaries between ethnology, linguistics, philology, philosophy, and intellectual, social, institutional, and literary history; and it is perhaps worthwhile to situate it within the often overlapping histories of these domains.

If asked to identify the beginning of modern formulations of the relation between the structure of a given society and its language, one would have to point to eighteenth-century "philosophical anthropology," which is itself rooted in the much older search for an original language and in a growing consciousness of the political consequences of such a determination.[40] Rousseau, for example, equates three basic types of writing—allegorical figures, conventional characters, and alphabetic signs—with three corresponding types of social order: "Ces trois manières d'écrire correspondent assez exactement aux trois divers états sous lesquels on peut considérer les hommes rassemblés en nation. La peinture des objets convient aux peuples sauvages; les signes des mots et des propositions, aux peuples barbares, et l'alphabet aux peuples policés."[41] Giambattista Vico posits a similar linguistic trio corresponding to three stages of evolution and of political organization. The Age of Families at the dawn of humanity is characterized by "a silent language using signs or objects having a natural relation with ideas"; the Age of Heroes, by "heroic emblems founded on resemblances, comparisons, images, metaphors, natural descriptions"; and the Age of Men, by "conventional signs appropriate to popular republics and monarchic states."[42]

Though the first edition of La Scienza Nuova appeared almost a century before the constitution in the Romantic period of the discipline of comparative philology, Vico laid the foundation of historical linguistics and of history based upon the study of language. Thus, he attempts to prove, for example, that nouns existed before verbs since "in order to have a meaning . . . a sentence must start with a noun, either explicitly or understood, which governs it." And, in a gesture which anticipates by some two hundred years R. Jakobson's famous studies of aphasia and language acquisition, Vico cites the example of a man who, "struck dumb with apoplexy, retained his mastery of nouns even though he lost control completely of verbs."[43] The Neapolitan philosopher's deduction of the development of language and of the individual from the logic of grammatical construction is crucial to the thought of the early comparative philologists, who seized upon the evolutionary significance of typological difference.[44] But where Vico saw in the principles of internal structure an indication of the accretional ontogenesis of human language in general, F. Bopp, F. Schlegel, J. Grimm, and R. Rask, following the lead of comparative anatomy, found a key to the history of particular language and to their genetic relation. Their attempt to establish a historical linguistics coterminous with the natural history of mankind obscured, in fact, the analogy between grammatical and political order.

The publication of W. von Humboldt's *Über die Verschiedenheit des menschlichen Sprachbaues* (1836) marks a turning point in the history of our topic. The aristocratic diplomat and amateur linguist, armed with the wealth of empirical data amassed ever since Sir W. Jones's positing of a common origin of Sanskrit, Greek, Latin, Gothic, and Celtic (1786), returned to the question which obsessed Vico, namely, the equation of the formal structure of a particular language and the spirit of the people who speak it: "Ihre Sprache ist ihr Geist und ihr Geist ist ihre Sprache."[45]

Von Humboldt's assimilation of grammar and national identity itself enjoyed a rich heritage, leading, on the one hand, to linguistic and comparative psychology and, on the other, to ethnolinguistics. Yet it was his reformulation (from the paradigms of A. G. Schlegel and F. Bopp) of a tripartite system for the classification of languages according to morphology that spawned what remains the most outlandish articulation of the relation between linguistic and social order of a most extravagant age. I am referring to M. Müller's assimilation of isolating, agglutinating, and inflecting languages to societies built respectively around the institutions of family, tribe, and state. Family tongues, of which Chinese is the prototype, are ideally suited for conversation within the consanguineal group: "It is a style of thought and speech, not unusual between mother and daughter. The one generally knows what the other is going to say, and words are used more to indicate than to describe thought. Long sentences are hardly thought of . . . and particular intonations, familiar accents, are sufficient to prepare the mind of the hearer. . . ."[46] Müller thus posits a perfect adequation between a language composed of numerous unchangeable independent units and a culture consisting of numerous autonomous living groups with little global integration.

Similarly, the Turanian or Nomadic languages, "which express in words not only ideas, but the relation of ideas," are suited to tribal organization: "The Turanian life is no longer a family life, or the life of a troglodyte Muni. It is the life of tribes, where the individual and the family are separated only by the floating walls of tents, and in daily contact with their clansmen. It is an indispensable requirement in every nomadic language, that it should be intelligible to many, though their intercourse may be but scanty. The introduction, therefore, of elements expressing as clearly as possible the grammatical relation of words, the invention of signs, whether natural or conventional, for distinguishing between nominal and verbal roots, the avoidance of everything that might obscure the meaning of words or the intention of their grammatical exponents, distinguishes the Turanian from the Chinese."[47] And, finally, only the so-called State languages are appropriate to life within the political community: "In the Arian and Semitic languages we find institutions, laws, and agreements, which, like the law of inheritance and succession at Rome or in India, show the stamp of an individual will impressed on the previous traditions of scattered tribes."[48]

From the field of comparative philology the problem of relation between language and culture passed to that of anthropology and ethnolinguistics; these, less heavily imbued with nineteenth-century naturalism and Darwinian evolutionism, could ignore neither the question of universals nor the trend toward cultural relativism. Early anthropologists like Frazer, Morgan, McLennan, Kroeber, and Rivers turned to semantics over grammar; and where family structure is concerned, they were obsessed by the attempt to reconcile the conflict between the so-called descriptive and classifying systems of kinship terminology.[49] At the same time, linguistically inclined ethnographers and linguists either denied altogether the importance of physical determinism or fell into a kind of relativism that endows every language with the power to produce independently an adequate system of cultural reference. F. Boas, for instance, contends that "it does not seem likely that there is any direct relation between the culture of a tribe and the language they speak."[50] E. Sapir rejects "all attempts to correlate particular types of linguistic morphology with certain stages of cultural development," though he does accept that "the vocabulary of a language more or less reflects the culture whose purpose it serves."[51] Sapir's student B. L. Whorf posits thought as a cultural problem solvable by linguistics; and this through the distinction between vocabulary, which is taken to be the "natural product of motor reactions," and syntax, or the culturally determined "factors of linkage between words and morphemes which make the categories and patterns in which meaning dwells."[52] Whorf thus reintroduces the core of Müller's evolutionism through the back door of cognition.

It is among the componential analysts that ethnolinguistics appears to break definitively with nineteenth-century naturalism and to abandon grammar in favor of descriptive semantics. More precisely, in an age dominated by behaviorism in psychology, functionalism in anthropology, and structuralism in linguistics, they seek to discard the question of meaning altogether, or, in the words of F. G. Lounsbury, "to do for meaning what 'structural phonetics' (phonemics) was intended to do for the structure of sounds in language, namely, to isolate its distinctive features and build descriptions on these."[53] Indeed, the parallel between Kroeber's proposals for the study of kinship as a differential system (1909) and Saussure's definition of language as a distributional field (1916) is striking.[54] But it was not until the post–World War II era that such ethnologists and linguists as Goodenough, Lounsbury, Wallace, Atkins, Conklin, and Greenberg found, in the phonemics of the Prague School, an apparatus capable of bridging the gap between the two. Thus, as Lounsbury maintains, the phone, a unique linguistic event, is held to be equivalent to the unique individual or kinsman; the phonotype, a class of phones heard and transcribed as the same by the phonetician, corresponds to the kintype, a class of kinsmen given the same designation by the ethnologist; and, finally, the phoneme, a class of noncontrastive phonotypes sharing distinctive phonetic features, parallels the kinclass, or kintypes which "are not contrasted terminologically and which share the same distinctive bundle of semantic features."[55] A. F. C. Wallace and J. Atkins outline the steps of a componential analysis as follows: (1) recording of a complete set of terms of reference or address; (2) definition of these terms according to traditional kintypes (Fd, FaBr, DrHuBr); (3) identification of two or more conceptual dimensions, each of whose values ("components") is signified by one or more of the terms; (4) definition of each term by means of a symbolic notation, as a specific combination or set of combinations of the components; (5) statement of the semantic relationship among the terms.[56]

Componential analysis was born out of the tremendous anxiety of the ethnologist vis-à-vis the linguist who, it was feared, had found either in the language of generative grammar or in that of Boolean logic the means of rivaling the "hard" sciences. The results often look like some Brave New Anthropological World. J. H. Greenberg, for example, proposes to represent the prohibition of marriage between parents and children by the equation $xMy \supset \sim (xPy \ v \ yPx)$, and cross-cousin marriage as follows: $xMy \supset: (\exists u) \ (\exists w) \ (\exists z): \ wPx \cdot z \ Py \cdot u \ Pw \cdot u \ Pz : w\epsilon\mu \cdot z\epsilon\varphi \cdot v \ w\epsilon\varphi \cdot z\epsilon\mu.$[57] Lounsbury captures the essence of Pawnee kinship in the formula $A^{n+1}UA^{-n}/A^nUA^{-n}/A^nUA^{-n-1}.$[58]

The immediate aim of the componential analysis is the definition of a "cultural grammar," what Greenberg outlines as the creation of "a meta-language describing the syntax of the formulas for the relationship terms of a particular system."[59] Its eventual goal is, however, the comparison, through such a metalanguage, of various kinship systems whose material means of expression varies, and, ultimately, the articulation of general rules of relation between functional social roles and the terms of their classification. Thus G. Murdock proposes a universal grammar of kinship based upon a worldwide ethnographic sampling of over two hundred and fifty cultures; and he establishes the thirty postulates and axioms by which "the elements of social organization, in their permutations and combinations, conform to natural laws of their own with an exactitude scarcely less striking than that which characterizes the permutations and combinations of atoms in chemistry or of genes in biology."[60]

Lévi-Strauss offers in three articles reprinted in *L'Anthropologie structurale* at once the most interesting and frustrating reflection upon the relation of anthropology and linguistics. It is here, in fact, that the centuries-old dream of discovering the "general but implicit" rules of culture reaches an apogee, and, to be more specific, that the dream of wedding the laws of kinship to those of language is consummated. Marriage and language are, for the structural anthropologist, analogous systems of communication designed to insure, respectively, the circulation of women and of messages.[61] They participate coequally in the "identical unconscious structures" which furnish such a fertile meeting ground for social and psychological order and which, in the absence of any more teleological definition of culture, provide an interpretative goal. Thus the ultimate anthropological project, outlined in the essay entitled "Language and the Analysis of Social Laws"—the establishment of a congruence between the languages of the world and the systems of kinship that language simultaneously reflects and encodes. According to Lévi-Strauss:

1. The Indo-European system of kinship assures "the density and fluidity of the population" through a minimum of negative prescriptions just as the Indo-European languages "have simple structures utilizing numerous elements 'competing' to occupy the same positions in the structure."[62]

2. The Sino-Tibetan kinship systems are derived from the simplest forms of Indo-European "general reciprocity"; and where language is concerned, they function in accordance with complex structures containing few elements, "a feature that may be related to the tonal structure of these tongues."

3. African kinship represents an "extension of the bridewealth system, coupled with a rather frequent prohibition on marriage with the wife's brother's wife." This leads to a system of general reciprocity more complex than in the Sino-Tibetan example, "while the types of unions resulting from the circulation of the marriage-price approaches . . . the statistical mechanism operating in our own society." African languages, in turn,

have "several modalities corresponding in general to a position intermediate between 1) and 2)."

4. Oceanic kinship and linguistic patterns demonstrate simple structures and few elements.

5. And, finally, American Indian paternity of the Crow-Omaha type combines elements of special and general exchange, whereas the appropriate linguistic patterns demonstrate "a relatively high number of elements which succeed in becoming organized into relatively simple structures by the structures assuming asymmetrical forms."[63]

Lévi-Strauss thus brings us full circle. We recognize in his comprehensive conceptualization of the relation between the world's languages and systems of kinship none other than the global project of comparative philology. The ethnologist's discovery of the physical and mechanical laws of paternity and syntax—whether of many elements and few rules or of complex structure and few elements—differs little from von Humboldt's discovery of inflecting and isolating languages; the identification with cultures practicing general and restricted exchange is close indeed to Müller's application of von Humboldt's categories to state versus family societies. Like the historical linguistics of the nineteenth century, the universal classification that Lévi-Strauss proposes rests upon the assumption that language and kinship are subject to the methods of the natural sciences, to the "exactitude" of atoms in chemistry or genes in biology, according to the latter-day naturalism of Murdock. More serious, Lévi-Strauss falls into the same trap as the componential analysts who confuse the operative concept of a metalanguage with the untenable notion of a metasociety. By universalizing "mental structures," he affirms the essential unity of mankind, which, despite the synchronic cast, merely reintroduces a certain outworn physiological ethnology dressed in the clothes of the unconscious processes. Which poses an important question: Can we think the problem of unity as the anthropologist proffers it without at the same time postulating a unified origin? Can one imagine the Family of Man without a common ancestor? Or different linguistic families without the *Ursprache* of the comparative philologist?

Lévi-Strauss's global strategy for the perfect adequation of linguistics and kinship is Darwinism in disguise. Just as A. Schleicher sought "to do for the organism of language what Darwin did for animals and plants," the ethnologist seeks to do for the species of family relations what the philologist did for language.[64] And if his totalistic undertaking, unlike the fastidious descriptions of the componential analysts, remains purposefully vague, it is because there has never been a successful correlation of language type—monosyllabic, polysyllabic, tonal, or morphological—with the structure of a particular society.[65] On the contrary, societies with vastly different infrastructures speak the same tongue; and societies with a similar institutional base speak languages of the most diverse types (e.g., Eastern Europe where we find Slavic, Finno-Ugric, Germanic, and Romance patterns). Instances abound of societies that have undergone sudden transformation with only superficial (lexical) effect upon current usage (e.g., France and Russia at the time of their popular revolutions). Conversely, examples of relatively rapid linguistic change, as in periods of intense immigration, are to be found in the absence of a corresponding social shift.

The anthropological dream of union between language and culture, the occulted naturalism of the structuralist, is rich in lessons for the literary anthropology of the Middle Ages. It points to the incapacity of ethnology to transcend certain philological issues like the reciprocity of unity and origin as well as to the broader issue of what Derrida terms "epigeneticism." It calls into question any formulation of the problem that is rooted in the essentially philological project of adequation between kinship and spoken grammar. Furthermore, it serves as a reminder of the extent to which the linguistics of the past century, which subtends both the universal anthropological project and standard medieval studies, is itself defined by a particular family model. This is as true of the initial undertaking of comparative philology, the reconstitution of a lost original Indo-European ancestor, as for the abiding interest in etymological roots. Historical linguistics, infused with the terminology of the family (e.g., mother and sister languages, families and subfamilies of tongues), depends upon the *Stammbaumtheorie* of Linnean biology for the classification of speech according to genera and species.[66] That branch of philology concerned with the establishment of texts takes as its point of departure the organization of manuscripts into a pedigree (*stemma*) descended often from a lost original prototype, as a genealogical model of poetic production mirrors that of historical linguistics.[67] When added to the family oriented theories of genre which have dominated literary studies until recently, the task seems hopelessly complex.

Here is where the medieval problematics of language theory, family structure, and poetics steps into the breach opened by anthropology when it moves beyond the immediate ethnological analysis, and where it also renders traditional medievalism conscious of its own anthropological underpinnings. For in the following pages the degree to which the foundations of romance philology are shaped by its object of study—which is anthropological in the strictest sense—will become increasingly clear. Not only do the genetic roots of historical linguistics stretch back to the period under scrutiny (and beyond that to Biblical notions of an original language), but the literary text, as we have affirmed and shall now proceed to demonstrate, occupies a singularly ritualized anthropological space between ideology—what Lévi-Strauss might call a "mental structure"—and institutions. The choice of the medieval period presents, finally, a way out of the impasse encountered by the heretofore unsuccessful attempt to link a particular language as it is spoken with social structure. This possibility of resolution lies not in language but in the sustained reflection upon language unique to the West.[68] Philosophical anthropology, comparative philology, and ethnolinguistics have failed until now because of the arbitrariness of all "cultural" definitions of linguistic structure. The syntactic independence of the word within the inflecting sentence can, for example, be used to emphasize the freedom of choice of the individual within a system of "general exchange," while its morphological intricacy stands, at the same time, as proof of the integrative complexity of the political state. What a closer look at the medieval language arts offers, in contrast, is a definition of linguistic structure abstracted from any particular idiom, a key not to the rules governing concrete instances of writing or speech but to the rules governing all such rules. It is, to invoke the Foucaultian terminology, not merely one representation among others but the representation of the laws of representation.

The literary anthropology which follows takes shape, then, around the attempt to trace the relation between such a privileged map of the conditions of representation and the symbolic activities which are both determined and mediated by it. If it is organized somewhat in the manner of what the classicists call a "ring structure," that is, according to an initial progression reversed by that of the end, its symmetry should not be confused with the substantive disposition of the matter at hand. Thus, we shall begin with what John of Salisbury terms "the cradle of philosophy," early medieval grammar, which was heavily oriented around the concepts of signification and definition as well as around the practice of etymology. The thesis of the first chapter, simply put, is that a genealogically defined linguistic model informs not only the discipline of grammar (both internal grammar and historical linguistics), but remains fundamental to an entire epistemological mode manifest in the discourse of history, theology, and Biblical exegesis.

Chapter 2 traces the relationship between the "etymological" grammar of this formative period and the radical reorganization of the aristocratic family of the twelfth century around the notion of genealogy and, in particular, around certain lineal institutions (e.g., strict exogamy, restriction of marriage, primogeniture). We shall see how the patterns of noble kinship prevalent until the time of the French Revolution are themselves rooted in a particular linguistic model, and, further, how such a system of paternity is sustained by certain aristocratic practices of the sign (e.g., heraldry, patronymics). More important, we shall see how they are mediated by a range of representational fields encompassing the visual arts (stained glass and manuscript illustration), genealogical narrative, "literary" genealogies, and epic poetry. The first part of Chapter 3 is, in fact, devoted to the homological identity between the Old French *chanson de geste* and grammatical and familial models based, respectively, upon etymology and genealogy. In the remainder of this section, pivotal point of the "ring," we explore the various modes of radical disruption of the epic; in particular, we see how the Old French and Provençal love lyric served to interrupt a poetic code supporting both an implicit model of representation and the biopolitics of lineage. The bulk of Chapter 4 situates the "disruptive" *chanson d'amour* in relation to the "disruptive" linguistic movements of the latter Middle Ages (nominalism and modal grammar) and in relation to the advent, alongside of lineage, of a system of kinship closer to the early modern conjugal unit or household. I argue in Chapter 5 that the courtly romance constituted a privileged forum for the mediation of conflicting grammatical, familial, and literary modes. In the novel more than anywhere else the issues that concern the literary anthropologist—marriage, succession, narrative continuity, representational integrity, the connection between economic and linguistic property, sexual desire—are both thematized and productive of form. Finally, our conclusion focuses upon the role of such mediatory literary models in the massive reorganization of the relation between power and writing that accompanied the reconstitution of the Capetian state.

ONE

Early Medieval Grammar

As the three knights who are to complete the Arthurian quest approach the locus of transcendence—the Grail—they come upon three objects identified as Solomon's boat, David's sword, and three pieces of wood.[1] Each has its own history, meaning, and relation to the others. The boat is connected to Solomon's prophetic vision of his own descent and to the desire to indicate to "the last of his lineage" his foreknowledge of Galahad's coming: "Si pensa coment il poïst fere savoir a celui home derreain de son lignage que Salemons, qui si lonc tens avoit devant lui esté, seust la verité de sa venue."[2] The Old Testament king is thus projected apocryphally into what was, from the perspective of the High Middle Ages, the equivalent of early modern history. More important, his perception of a future conception focuses upon what is taken to be a natural relation between genealogy and signification. Solomon's certainty about "the truth of the ending of his line" elicits almost automatically the urge to leave a readable trace of his own existence, as the issue of *generation—*

what constitutes a natural link between members of the same family—entails that of *representation*—how signs signify and, more precisely, how they signify through time.

The second object encountered by the Grail Knights is David's sword passed down through his son Solomon and signaling, according to the anonymous author(s) of *La Queste del Saint Graal*, an adventure waiting for Galahad. It too has a medieval and Biblical past. This is the weapon with which the Fisher-King of Arthurian legend was wounded—an act, we are told, that repeats the original crime of the Old Testament as well as its redemption in the New:

> Et la mort que Abel reçut par traïson a cel tens qu'il n'estoient encore que troi home en terre senefia la mort au verai Crucefié, car par Abel fu il senefiez et par Caym fu senefiez Judas par qui il reçut mort. Et tout einsi come Caïns salua Abel son frere et puis l'ocist, tout ausi salua Judas son seignor, et si avoit sa mort porchaciee. Einsi s'acorderent bien les deus morz ensemble, non pas de hautece, mes de senefiance. [P. 217]

> And the death of Abel by treachery in the days when there were only three men on earth signified the death of the true Crucified, for Abel signified Our Lord, and Cain prefigured Judas, who brought about his death. And just as Cain greeted his brother Abel and then slew him, even so did Judas greet his Lord, although he had been compassing his death. There are then many points where these deaths correspond, not in degree, but in their outward signs.

In the similarity of outward signs coupled with deeper differences of degree and meaning, the question of signification is linked to that of history, and to a particular vision of history as repetition. In fact, this passage shows, as well as any in Old French literature, how, according to the medieval sense of typology or figura, one event prefigures another as the signs of divine Providence become manifest through time.[3] History, whose original Old Testament version is interpreted by a second rendering in the New Testament, represents a text whose unfolding meaning will become fully evident only at the end of human duration. Here the central issue is triple. For the question of *signification*—how signs signify—informs that of *prefiguration*—how history works. Both coincide, moreover, in a reversible cycle of fall and redemption. Just as Christ's sacrifice redeems Cain's founding infraction, Galahad's coming will redeem—cure—the wounded Fisher-King. Signification and prefiguration are thus subtended by the issue of transgression, as sign theory and history meet in the question of the origin of the law.

The third object, or set of objects, encountered by the Grail Knights consists of three sticks of wood which, we learn, are vestiges of three Biblical trees. The first, a white twig, is part of the original Tree of Knowledge situated at the site of the birth of sexual desire. Like Solomon's boat, it too signifies foreknowledge of future generations, in this case those of Eve, "just as if she were speaking to her heirs who would come after her"; and, like David's sword, it is bound up in a cycle of decline and recovery: "Et ce fu senefiance que par la Virge Marie seroit li heritages recovrez qui perduz estoit au tens de lors."[4] The second twig, which is green, belonged originally to the Tree of Life located outside of Eden at the place of copulation. It seems, in fact, to embody the principle of procreation: "Car si tost com il en ostoient un raim, il le fichoient en terre, si reprenoit tantost et enracinoit de son gré. . . ."[5] Finally, the third stick, which is red, represents a piece of the Tree of Death, which stood at the locus of the original crime and which was used, the author(s) indicates, in the construction of Solomon's boat. The red stick is also set in opposition to its green counterpart in that it is associated with a failure of reproduction and an economics of dearth: "Ne de celui ne pooit nus autres aengier, ainz moroient toutes les plantes que len en fesoit. . . ."[6] This last series of relics seems to embrace the earlier two, as the issues of generation, signification, prefiguration, and transgression are structured by that which, for lack of a better term, I shall call *insertion*—how a part relates to a whole, and, by extension, how the model of such a relation affects the representation of the family as a system for the insertion of individuals within a group.

The medieval text thus makes a surprising connection between the seemingly distinct fields of sign theory (how signs represent), family structure (how the parts of a lineage are, through signs, related), history (which is precoded according to a system of Christological salvation), and the origin of the law. What is more, not only do the elements of this equation define a nexus of key symbolic activities within any culture (the family, history, the law), but they serve, for the period in question, to define one of the basic models of representation itself. These specific figurations of family, history, and signification articulate a common principle in that each contains parts bound by relations of contiguity, mutual participation, imbrication, and temporal—diachronic—sequence. First, a sequence of objects (Cain's weapon transformed into David's sword passed to Solomon, and eventually to Galahad)—and a series of trees and graftings (white, green, and red, used for Solomon's and then for the Questors' boat). Second, a series of events linked to the trees—disobedience leading to conception, conception to death, death to sacrifice and resurrection. And, finally, a genealogical series: Adam is the ancestor of David, Solomon, and Christ as well as of the three Grail Knights.[7]

The image of the tree is a powerful symbol of the problematics which the text seems so naturally to expose. Like the technique of the "mise-en-abyme" of medieval blazonry, it both captures the movement of that which it structures and constitutes a designation—a kind of map—of representation itself. Or of what we might, with consciousness of the complexity of any such rhetoricizing of history, think of as a metonymic representation—one that involves a contiguous link of part to whole, container to contained, penetration of subsequent by prior events, a linear unfolding of history across time. The tree, in this instance, is doubly significant, since the thirteenth-century audience was probably aware that, according to legend, the Tree of Paradise was linked vestigially to the Cross. The Tree of Knowledge of Good and Evil proved to be an instrument of sin and death before becoming the vehicle of redemption; the *lignum vitae* of paradise prefigures the new dispensation.[8] Thus the metonymically linked trees imply a system of relations in which every part is, through the seamless web of a lost beginning (an original wholeness at the outset of time), embedded in a hierarchical and chronological series. Where kinship is concerned, the Questors (Bohort, Perceval, and Galahad) are the descendants of Joseph of Arimathea, who, since Christ could not reproduce, nonetheless preserved his lineage by gathering his blood in the Grail. Christ, in turn, is linked to Solomon, David, and Adam. No matter how distant the relation, Galahad, "the last of his line," represents a vestige of all that has preceded: a part of Solomon passed to and remains embedded in Galahad, just as a part of Adam passed to Solomon, and, by implication, a part of God to Adam. In the sequential play of identity and difference, sameness engenders sameness; and the integral tie to an origin is preserved.

The decision to begin with the tree which preserves an attachment to origin, and which binds within a single nexus both semiology and kinship, is hardly innocent. For the *lignum* so enmeshed with the ideas of lineage and language also serves to define the terms and parameters of our discussion. The series of objects waiting for the Grail Knights are paradigmatic of issues which the text signals to its own progeny of readers. And the passage directly preceding the achievement of the Grail Quest (which is, after all, a quest for meaning) merely defines more succinctly than any other a series of fields of inquiry relevant, even crucial, to our understanding of a much broader textual corpus—virtually the breadth of Old French literature. Through the link which the prose romance establishes between signification and family structure it teaches us from within how to make that exceedingly difficult leap toward that which conditions it from without. Ultimately, it points in the direction of an anthropology of the High Middle Ages based upon the increasingly important discursive practice of the literary performance. In what may seem like a paradox to many historians, the reversal of a natural order of knowledge, the literary work can show us how to begin to read as an interconnected range of symbolic activities the seemingly diverse domains of language theory, kinship, economics, and intellectual and social history. But first to the issues which *La Queste* raises and which will occupy us for the remainder of the chapter. These are: early medieval historical linguistics, internal grammar, sacramental theology, and the determining role of all these in the articulation of an ideal model of the family and a vision of the past.

Genealogy and General Sign Theory

Galahad's family tree is rooted in the primal locus par excellence, and it is implicated in the original inscription of meaning upon the world. More important, the notion of meaning was, throughout the period in question, itself couched in genealogical terms. *La Queste del Saint Graal* merely suggests what was a pervasive association operative at all levels of culture and as close as one may come to a "mental structure" of the age. So widespread, in fact, was the identification of signification and generation that we begin only somewhat arbitrarily with the monumental figures of Augustine, Jerome, and Isidore of Seville.

Augustine's position at the juncture of late Classical and medieval culture makes it easy to idealize his role as the "founder" of medieval sign theory; yet such a title is justified. The depth of his reflection upon signs, which is evident in almost all of the major works, is unequaled by any Latin writer before the time of Abelard or Aquinas. It is, in distinction to the reams of gloss of even the most important encyclopedists of late Antiquity, the last attempt before the High Middle Ages to formulate personally—as well as logically and theologically—a comprehensive semiological theory. This is why Augustine's concentration upon the relation between meaning and procreation is especially telling. "How," he asks, in seeking to distinguish between sense perception and intellectual apprehension, "can the phrase 'to increase and multiply,' which seems to refer only to man, also refer to the offspring of water?" If the words are interpreted according to "the actual nature of things," then they cannot be applied to things "not begotten from seed." But if we interpret them figuratively, "we find multitudes among spiritual and among corporeal things."[9] In the first instance, our senses are deceived by the illusory nature of signs; and in the second, that illusion is corrected by an act of intellection revealing their true meaning. Generation is thus conceived as a problem of interpretation:

> In his omnibus nanciscimur multitudines et ubertates et incrementa; sed quod ita crescat et multiplicetur, ut una res multis modis enuntietur et una enuntiatio multis modis intellegatur, non inuenimus nisi in signis corporaliter editis et rebus intellegibiliter excogitatis.[10]

> In all these instances we meet with multitudes, fertility, and increase. But as to what may in such wise increase and multiply that a single thing may be stated in many ways and a single statement may be understood in

many ways, this we find only in signs corporeally expressed and in things intelligibly conceived.

For Augustine, there can be no distinction between the propagation of men—their increase and dispersion—and the propagation of meaning. A single thing stated multiply, or a single statement understood multiply, participate in the degeneration of signification that accompanied the multiplication of mankind.

The place of Babel as a dispersion of men and of tongues is, of course, paramount in the linguistic mythology of the Christian West.[11] What I am suggesting, however, is that the medieval reception of the Babel myth was itself part of a broader dynamic in which generation and signification are implicated in each other. Genealogy conceived along linguistic lines and language conceived along family lines represent two facets of a more general problematics of the sign prevalent in the thought of many of the most powerful intellectual figures from Augustine to the Renaissance. This connection is evident, for example, in the patristic fascination with the proximity of Adam's engendering of Eve and his naming of her. According to Augustine, the act of naming the earthly things precedes the engendering of Eve and indeed seems to cause it: " . . . iam uideamus, quare sit factum, quod adductae sunt ad Adam omnes bestiae agri et omnia uolatilia caeli, ut eis nomina inponeret, atque ita uelut necessitas oreretur creandi ei feminam ex eius latere. . . . "[12] The creation of the first woman and her designation are simultaneous gestures, as Saint Jerome also makes clear in separate versions of the primal eponymic moment. In the first, Eve is called *Virago*, "quia de viro suo sumpta est"; and in the second, she is called *hissa*, since in Hebrew "vir quippe vocatur *his* et mulier *hissa*."[13] In both cases, a derivation occurring purely within the realm of the referent–"Et dixit Adam: Hunc nunc os ex ossibus meis, et caro de carne mea"—is coterminous with linguistic derivation.

This imbrication of signification and generation is most fully explored within the Alexandrian exegetical tradition, where it becomes practically synonymous with a certain fetishism regarding Hebrew proper names. For Jerome, in particular, the derivation of a divinely given name becomes genetically prescriptive. He maintains that a proper appellation is equivalent to a genealogical program, and its alteration is tantamount to a prophetic rewriting of the future. When, for instance, Abram's name ("quod interpretatus pater excelsus") is changed to Abraham ("pater multarum [gentium]"), his abundant progeny is both understood from the new name and prospectively inscribed in history. Similarly, Sarah's late motherhood entails an altered name which reflects the same rich genealogy:

> Sarai igitur primum uocata est per sin res ioth: sublato ergo ioth, id est I elemento, addita est he litera, quae per A legitur, et uocata est Saraa.

> Causa autem ita nominis immutati haec est, quod antea dicebatur princeps
> mea, unius tantum modo domus mater familiae, postea uero dicitur abso-
> lute princeps, id est ἄρχουσα.[14]

> Therefore she was first called Sarai from "sin," "res," "ioth"; then when
> "ioth," that is the element for I, was removed, the letter "he," which we
> read as A, was added, and she was called Saraa. However, the reason for
> such a change in her name is this, that previously she was called "my
> ancestor" while she was the maternal head of only one household; but
> afterward she is called "absolute ancestor," that is ἄρχουσα, the originator.

Jerome believes not only in the original propriety of Hebrew names but in
the grounding of Hebrew roots in eternal truth. The name "Israel," for
instance, is composed of the triple root for "man" ("uir ex tribus literis
scribatur, 'aleph' 'iod' 'sin,' ut dicatur *'eis'*"), the triple root for "seeing"
("uidens ex tribus, 'res' 'aleph' 'he,' et dicatur *'raha'*"), plus the combined
letter *el* from "aleph" and "lamed" and meaning "God without luck."
Thus "Israel" means "one who sees God or the mind seeing God" ("uir
uidens deum siue mens uidens deum"). Jerome's interpretation is,
moreover, the product of a theological rather than a strictly philological
gesture since, as he maintains, "we are guided more by the scriptures and
angels or by God, who named Israel, than by any secular learning."[15]

Augustine too participates in the mysticism of proper names; and the
program of human history that he conceptualizes according to discrete
evolution of moral and family lines is contained in the names of the
founding fathers of the two cities.[16] But no one comprehended better than
Isidore the close relation between generation and appellation. "Sem," he
tells us, "means *named*, since the name is understood through a perception of future generations" ("Sem dicitur nominatus, quod nomen ex
praesagio posteritatis accepit" [*Etym.*, 7:vi, xvi]). Isidore seems to be
aware that the Hebrew שֵׁם (Shem) means "name." Yet he also plays
somewhat gratuitously on the resemblance between seed (*semen*) and
sign (Greek *sema*, Latin *semanticus*); and such play reveals the extent to
which genealogy is encoded in the name that is "borne out"—understood—through genealogically conceived time: "Ex ipso (Sem) enim patriarchae et apostoli et populus Dei. Ex eius quoque stirpe et Christus,
cuius ab ortu solis usque ad occasum magnum est nomen in gentibus."[17]
For the Bishop of Seville, there is no distinction between the name
"Sem," the engendering of his line, and its meaning; nor can these
elements—Sem, insemination, and semantics—be distinguished from
their culmination in the dissemination through Christ, "whose name is
greatly on the lips of men," of the Word (see below, pp. 60–61).

Thus, naming, reproduction, understanding, and preaching are bound
within an essentially verbal epistemology based upon a deep faith in the
mediatory power of signs. As Augustine affirms, prophecy, promise, and
progeny are all allied:

Non est itaque dubitandum, quoniam haec facta sunt et stulta esse non possunt, ob aliquid significandum esse facta, fructum futuri saeculi ab ipso iam primordio generis humani Deo praescio in ipsis suis operibus misericorditer praedicante, ut certo tempore seruis suis siue per hominum successiones siue per suum spiritum uel angelorum ministerium reuelata atque conscripta et promittendis rebus futuris et recognoscendis inpletis testimonium perhiberent: quod magis magisque in consequentibus adparebit.[18]

Of this there can be no doubt, since these are real facts which cannot be divested of meaning (and these facts are intended to mean something), and since from the very beginning of the human race, God, in his prescience, graciously inscribed in his works that which would come to fruition in centuries hence; he wanted for these things, revealed and written down at the opportune time—whether by the succession of men, or by his Spirit, or by the ministry of angels—to bear witness to those who serve him of the promise of future events and of the knowledge of their completion.

Names, as signs, bear prospectively the mark both of their meaning and of their historical effects; understood through time, they fulfill the promise—complete the genealogy—that they contain.[19] Language constitutes, in this respect, a kind of genetic code in which the future in germ is inscribed but which remains indecipherable until its genesis has become historically realized.

Linguistics and History

The question of historical realization cannot, in fact, be divorced from the implication of signification and generation in each other or from the model of Christian history which it implies. This is evident from the beginning in the writing of Eusebius of Caesarea, who can be said to be the father of Christian historical writing. Not only did the *Historia Ecclesiastica* represent the point of departure for subsequent Church histories, but the *Chronographia* preserved in Jerome's Latin translation stood as the dominant paradigm of world history for over a thousand years. The radical nature of Eusebius's break with tradition lay in an expansion of the geographical and temporal scope of history from local accounts of wars, towns, even dynasties, to the history of all mankind from Creation to the present (A.D. 324); in the recasting of history in essentially linear instead of cyclical "long year" terms; and in the assimilation of the Graeco-Roman model of history as a series of empires to a vision of the past more in keeping with the Old Testament pattern of genealogical succession.

From the fourth century on, the defining mode of universal history was that of genealogy. Just as there was in ancient Hebrew no distinction between the word for history and generation (תרכבות), there is in the Eusebius-Jerome world chronicle no way of separating the sequence of events from paternal succession. With fathers the prime subject of historical enunciation and children its object, the Latin *genere* becomes the binding thread of historical narrative:

Enos vero cum jam esset nonagenarius genuit Cainam: deinde alios filios et filias. Fuerunt autem anni ejus DCCCCV. Cainam vero cum esset septuagenarius genuit Malaleel: deinde alios filios et filias. Fuerunt omnes anni ejus DCCCCX. Malaleel quadragenarius genuit Jareth: deinde alios filios et filias.[20]

Indeed, when Enos was already ninety years old he engendered Cain, and after him other sons and daughters. In fact, his life span was nine hundred and five years. Indeed, when Cain was seventy years old he engendered Malaleel, and after him other sons and daughters. His entire life span was nine hundred and ten years. When Malaleel was forty years old he engendered Jareth, and after him other sons and daughters.

History as procreation is, in its broad outlines, an extension of Creation, its direction a lineage from Adam—through Noah, Abraham, David, and Solomon—to Christ. In the margins of the central sacred line stand the races of men ("alios filios et filias"). Humanity evolves according to a process of accretion, beginning with a single set of parents and moving toward separate branches of the original family, and, eventually, whole tribes.

The Eusebius genealogical model will be modified throughout the period in question. It is possible, even, to speak of an identity between the external history of historical writing and its internal mode; for those whose works are organized genealogically themselves constitute a genealogy no less cumulatively disposed than the original prototype. The medieval historian's task was, in fact, largely conceived as the completion or updating of Eusebius's "paternal" text. And the lineage of the *Chronographia*—its continuators and their continuators—stretches from one end of the Middle Ages to the other.

In addition to translating the *Chronographia*, Jerome updated it to A.D. 379, Augustine to the sacking of Rome, his pupil Orosius to 417.[21] Our knowledge of the early history of Gaul is enhanced by the *Chronicorum Libri II* of Sulpicius Severus who extended Eusebius's text to 403, and by Prosper of Aquitaine's *Chronicon* which terminates in 455. Similarly, Idatius's *Chronicon*, which supplements ancient universal history with an account of the period between 379 and 468, remains the basis of early Visigothic history in Spain.

In the sixth century, Marcellanus, chancellor of the Emperor Justinian, expanded Eusebius to 534; Victor, Bishop of Tunis, to 566; and John of Bisclaro, inspired by Idatius and Victor, to 590. Fulgentius's *De Aetatibus Mundi* is a universal history along the lines of Eusebius's founding vision, as are Cassiodorus's chronicle (ca. 519) and Gregory of Tours's grafting of Frankish history onto that of the world since Creation. Isidore assimilated the *Chronographia* in the seventh century, Bede in the eighth, Frecult of Lisieux and Ado of Vienne in the late Carolingian period. Though several world chronicles appeared during the first century of Capetian rule (e.g., those of Herman of Reichenau, Lambert of Hersfeld, and Marianus Scotus), the second great era of universal history did not begin until the time of the First Crusade. Indeed, the twelfth century witnessed the *Chronographia* of Sigebert of Gembloux and his continuators, that of Hugh of Flavigny and of Ekhard of Aura; these in addition to Hugh of Fleury's *Historia Ecclesiastica* and Otto of Freising's *Historia de Duabus Civitatibus*. The most illustrious world chronicles of the thirteenth century are Robert of Auxerre's *Chronographia* and Vincent of Beauvais's *Speculum Historiale*. In the late Middle Ages, Ranulf Higden's *Polychronicon*, along with its supplements to the first quarter of the fifteenth century, stood as the last vestige of a heritage of historical writing that had dominated for over a millennium.

More important than the history of historical writing, however, is the fact that Eusebius's grounding of humanity in an original order of the world and his genealogical model of evolution cannot be separated from contemporaneous linguistic theory—that is, the grounding of words in an original moment of signification. According to the early medieval sense of history, a primary instance of signification—the moment against which Babel as a dissemination of men and of meaning will be measured—occurred in the Garden of Eden. Adam is said to be the first to speak and the inventor of names: "omne enim quod vocavit Adam animae viventis ipsum est nomen eius."[22] Hebrew, the original language, is sacred because it is as close as any tongue can be to the thoughts of God at the time of Creation, and, as Philo of Alexandria asserts, to the matter of Creation: "with Moses the names assigned are manifest images of the things, so that the name and thing are inevitably the same from the first, and the name and that to which the name is given differ not a whit."[23]

Philo's affirmation of the initial coincidence of words and things is by no means an isolated example. On the contrary, we find the belief in the integrity of a primeval language—an *Ursprache* similar to the Indo-European of the comparative philologist—for as long as the model of universal history seems to prevail. Augustine posits the existence of an original single tongue but hesitates about what to call it, maintaining only that "if the language that Adam once spoke still survives today, it contains the sounds with which the first man named the earthly animals and the birds."[24] Isidore follows the tradition of Alexandrian Judaism according to which "words are the indices of things," and Hebrew "the mother of all tongues."[25] John of Salisbury refers to Hebrew as the tongue "mother nature gave our first parents." Brunetto Latini considers it the "original natural language."[26] Dante's search for beginnings leads him back through "the form of speech created by God together with the first

Adam naming the animals. Ms. 24 Aberdeen University Library, Scotland. (Printed with the permission of the Court of Aberdeen University.)

soul" to the first Hebrew word (see below, pp. 42–43). And the four-teenth-century grammarian Henri de Crissey traces the roots of Latin back through Greek and Hebrew to the "sounds given by God": "Hebrei vero voces multas imposuerunt, mediantibus vocibus datis a Deo."[27]

The first namer (whether Adam, or, as in other originary myths, a grammarian or philosopher) imposed upon things names adequate to express—or *proper to*—their nature. This founding linguistic moment constitutes, in fact, a primary instance of the proper, as the propriety of beginnings is stressed over and over again by theologians, grammarians, and rhetoricians. Cicero, for example, claims that "the proper and defi-nite designations of things were born almost at the same time as the things themselves." Quintilian asserts that "words are proper when they bear their original meaning." Augustine maintains that "signs are proper when they are used to designate the objects for which they have been created."[28] And, as we shall see, the determination of property (what a word is) along with difference (what it is not) constitutes a subbranch of the language arts whose role is to undo the dislocations of sense caused by poetry and use, and thus to restore to each altered articulation its proper—that is, original—meaning.

The initial fixing in language of the properties of things, or adequation between the properties of things and of words, was, in turn, passed on, inherited, along linguistic lines that are also family lines. This is more than a case of assimilating metaphors of the family to those of grammar. On the contrary, language seems to function in a family way. To be more precise, the basic conceptual framework for the evolution of language is one of biological reproduction. And if medieval linguists remain highly conscious of the degenerative nature of verbal signs, of their constant devolution from the proper, they also conceive of this process in terms of familial accretion. Varro, for example, maintains gender to be a function of generation: "*Genera* 'genders' are named from *generare* 'to generate.' For whatever *gignit* 'begets' or *gignitur* 'is begotten,' that can be called a *genus* and can produce a *genus*."[29] Priscian too assimilates linguistic and biological reproduction in the development of nouns: "Genera enim dicuntur a generando proprie quae generare possunt, quae sunt masculinum et femininum."[30] And according to Isidore, word classes procreate because they are sexually defined; letters replicate within words to "engender" or alter their significance: "Genera verborum ideo dicta, quia gignant. Nam activo adicis 'R' et gignit passivum; rursum passivo adimis 'R' et parit activum."[31]

The association of linguistic and genealogical reproduction is, however, nowhere more evident than in the area of patronymics, which serves, at least for Varro, as the basic model of nominal genesis:

> Ut in hominibus quaedam sunt agnationes ac gentilitates, sic in verbis: ut enim ab Aemilio homines orti Aemilii ac gentiles, sic ab Aemilii nomine declinatae voces in gentilitate nominali: ab eo enim, quod est impositum recto casu Aemilius, orta Aemilii, Aemilium, Aemilios, Aemiliorum et sic reliquae eiusdem quae sunt stirpis. [Varro, p. 372]

> As among men there are certain kinships, some through the males, others through the clan, so there are among words. For as from Aemilius were sprung the men named Aemilius, and the clan-members of the name, so from the name of "Aemilius" were inflected the words in the noun-clan: for from that name which was imposed in the nominal case as "Aemilius" were made "Aemilii," "Aemilium," "Aemilios," "Aemiliorum," and in this way also all the other words which are of this same line.

In the name of the father lies the origin of names, and in fact, pure origin. As the grammarian explains, if Jupiter was once called *Diovis* and *Diespater* ("Father Day"), "they who come from him are called *dei* 'deities' and *dius* 'god' and *divum* 'sky' . . . " (Varro, p. 63).

Priscian, in discussing the ways in which secondary words are derived from words of first imposition, begins with the patronym.[32] And not only is the name of the father the principle of derivation appropriate to proper names, but it is deeply rooted in the proper, that is to say, both in a particularized relation between the things designated (derived from each other) and in a singular and exclusive relation between the word and its meaning. In contrast to derivation according to the principle of possession, which from common nouns yields all manner and gender of things, patronymic derivation from a proper noun is appropriate only to men and only to those in a direct line of descent.[33]

Priscian's association of patronyms, the proper, masculinity, and linearity poses the possibility within grammatical theory of something resembling the rule of primogeniture, an idea restricted neither to the area of nominal derivation, nor to late Latinity, nor, as we shall see in relation to the history of medieval families, to linguistics. Isidore betrays a similar associative nexus in his search for the first roots of words (*primogenia*) as well as in the analogy which he establishes between the way fathers and sons are related and the way they are named: "Quattor etiam modis filii appellantur: natura, imitatione, adoptione, doctrina" (*Etym.*, 9:v, xv). Finally, as late as the fourteenth century, the author of the Provençal *Leys D'Amors* offers an even more systematic elaboration of the link between the modes of paternity and lexical derivation. Words are related, he maintains, by sound and meaning, by sound alone, or by meaning alone. If by sound and meaning (e.g., *amors* from *amar*), "this is the equivalent of a natural and legitimate son born within the bounds of legal wedlock." If by sound alone (e.g., *contrafar* from *contrari* and *far*), "this is the equivalent of a natural son, otherwise called a 'bastard.'" And if by meaning alone (e.g., *huey* from *jorn*), "this is equivalent to an adopted son."[34]

If the prime model of linguistic derivation is that of paternity, that of historical linguistics is also one of genealogical succession. Jerome insists upon the coevolution of families and of tongues.[35] Augustine, in dealing with the problem of continuity despite the linguistic catastrophe of Babel, associates "the House of Heber in which the primitive language of the race survived" and Hebrew.[36] Isidore, evoking a false etymology, renders the name "Heber" synonymous with inheritance:

> Heber transitus. Etymologia eius mystica est, quod ab eius stirpe transiret Deus, nec perseveraret in eis, tralata in gentibus gratia. Ex ipso enim sunt exorti Hebraei. [*Etym.*, 7:vi, xxiii]

> Heber means passage. Its etymology is mystical, since through his lineage passes God; nor does it adhere in them, but is transmitted to the chosen people. From that one comes the Hebrews.

Not only is Heber's family the essential link to the truth of an original past but it is indistinguishable from an original language of the prophets and of the sacred text.[37] Linguistic continuity insures genealogical continuity, as language determines race: " . . . ex linguis gentes, non gentibus linguae exortae sunt."[38] For Isidore, the history of mankind is essentially that of its diverse tongues. From Hebrew stem Greek and Latin; from Greek, the five divisions of common, Attic, Doric, Ionic, and Aeolic; from Latin, the four subspecies of early, true, Roman, and corrupted (*Etym.*, 9:i, v–vi). And from corrupted, we can only posit, as did Dante, the diverse vernacular tongues.

It is, in fact, in Dante's *De Vulgari Eloquentia* that we find the most complete model of historical linguistics. The Florentine poet's search for the original language carries him back to the first word and beyond words to the sound *El*, "which is neither question nor answer."[39] This primal moment of signification and of origin is thus removed from all semantic function. Meaning everything and excluding nothing, it is both divine presence and a potential mirror of the created world—an undifferentiated utterance whose subsequent division into syllables, words, parts of speech, languages, regional tongues, city dialects, and intramunicipal patois serves as a reminder that language breeds and that its history parallels that of humanity. Not only parallels it, but is itself inscribed within an unbroken chain of paternal relations, since for Dante the rapport between the illustrious vernacular and other more particular tongues is that of father to son:

> Nam, sicut totum hostium cardinem sequitur, ut, quo cardo vertitur, versetur et ipsum, seu introrsum seu extrorsum flectatur, sic et universus municipalium vulgarium grex vertitur et revertitur, movetur et pausat, secundum quod istud, quod quidem vere paterfamilias esse videtur.[40]

> For as the whole door follows its hinge, so that whither the hinge turns the door may also turn, whether in or out, in like manner also the whole head of municipal dialects turns and returns, moves and pauses according as this illustrious language does, which really seems to be the father of the family.

The history of human language is that of genealogical succession: from the first universal syllable, the name of God, to the most particular patois; and from God the universal father to the last sons of his line.

The homologous endomorphic pattern of universal history and external linguistics is further sustained by the internal organization of grammar itself. Donatus and Priscian structure their presentations incrementally. Both the *Ars Grammatica* and the *Institutiones Grammaticae* move from the definition of sound (*vox*) and letters to a discussion of syllables, parts of speech, syntactic construction, and errors of diction, which, when intentional, constitute rhetorical figures. The *Instituta Artium* of Probus proceeds similarly, as do Isidore's grammatical chapters, which, as in Dante, imply a continuous progression between the genesis of an original language—the development of the *partes orationis* from undifferentiated sound—and the evolution of languages from a single fully constituted tongue. Medieval language theory, historical linguistics, and history seem to mirror each other. And if the Eusebius-Jerome model functions according to a process of genealogical accretion, it merely reproduces an identical ontogenetic movement within the realm of grammar. The expansion of humanity—from a single set of parents to families and nations—parallels the extension of language from sound, letters, and words of first imposition to derived words, word groups, figures of speech, and complete tongues.

The development of linguistics and of history are connatural not only in their common accretional pattern but in their direction as well. Eusebius expanded the scope of history, endowed it with linearity, and traced its movement through the principle of genealogy; and he also recast history in essentially degenerative terms. The "short-wave" regenerative cycles of ancient history cede in the *Chronographia* to a long-range course of decline. Christian history is, especially from the time of Augustine's elaboration of Eusebius, a process of continual erosion according to specific time periods—the *articuli temporum sive aetatum*—prior to a final redemption at the end of human time. Here again, generation and signification meet in the antinomic connection between degeneration and the interruption of meaning. Just as, according to the Eusebian model, men evolve through time away from God, words devolve—through use, catastrophe, translation, and poetry (especially pagan verse)—away from Adam's primal act of naming. From an original univocal signification stems the multiplicity of tongues; and from the unity of the original couple stems the multiplicity of the races of men. Both history and grammar are bound by a common sense of loss and dispersion, by a common nostalgic longing for beginnings, and by a set of ontologically similar strategies of return.

Origins

The primacy of origins is an important, indeed, the defining, characteristic of early medieval grammar. And yet, it is not as simple a matter as it seems.[41] The dominant attitude toward the question of beginnings was, in fact, one of anguished ambiguity provoked by a deep split between what medieval writers *knew* about verbal signs and what they *desired* to believe about them—a split evident in the easy copresence of what seem like mutually exclusive explanations of linguistic origin (natural versus conventional) as well as in an even more pervasive dichotomy between semiological theory and practice. The wish to begin again, to return to the "time before Babel," shapes early medieval sign theory. It accounts for the identification of linguistics with semantics and for a certain nostalgic "theology of words." Thus, the grammar of the period between Priscian and his twelfth-century commentators was dominated by the concepts of signification and definition—by emphasis of the object of meaning over

its mode; by insistence upon "real" definition based upon physical property; and, where grammar and theology coincide, by a certain overdetermined belief in the transparency of signs.

Any attempt to come to grips with the question of beginnings must
itself begin with the distinction between the ontological status of Adam's
founding gesture and what we shall refer to throughout as the various
medieval "strategies of origin." More precisely, for those who speculated
about language in an age ruled by the dream of uniting the divine Word
with words of human intention, Adam's naming of the "earthly animals
and the birds" was necessarily an ambiguous act involving a seemingly
unresolvable paradox: that is, if names are essential to the cognition of
things and "without them," as Isidore asserts, "things would perish,"
how could the first namer have enjoyed a perception of physical objects
sufficient to their proper designation?

The paradox of the first namer is expressed differently according to the
diverse modes of medieval knowledge. It is conceived simultaneously as
a theological, a grammatical, and a logical issue. Even within a single
intellectual discourse, it is subject to a diversity of formulations and
resolutions. The exegetical tradition of Alexandrian Judaism is perhaps
the most radical in its refusal to pose the dilemma as an inherently
linguistic question and in its relegation of the problem of first names to
the orthodoxy of doctrine. Philo Judaeus, for example, considers the first
man to have been "superior to men born many generations later when
the race had lost its vigor." Adam is a divinely inspired namer who
perceived "bodies and objects in their sheer reality."[42] Along the same
lines, Origen too claims that the names imposed by Adam "are not
concerned with ordinary created things, but with a certain mysterious
divine science that is related to the Creator of the universe." When used
properly, that is to say, when "pronounced in a particular sequence
natural to them," they have the power to affect nature; when abused,
they are dangerous to those who degrade "certain mysterious principles
of language" coterminous with an original and sacred order of the
world.[43]

We have seen the results of the Alexandrian solution in connection
with the exegetical tradition it spawned—that is, the medieval cult of
Hebrew proper names (see above, pp. 35–37). Let us note, then, in
passing, that the theological probity of this consecration of the first
namer also assured its wide assimilation and long duration. Thierry of
Chartres, over a century later, still insists that Adam's naming of things
took place in the divine intellect: " . . . hoc totum in mente divina factum
est."[44]

Among late Latin and medieval grammarians the problem of first
names is indissociable from the debate about whether human language is

of natural or of conventional (socially determined) origin. Indeed, the conflict between those who believe words to be the necessary emanations of things and those who believe them to have been "imposed" upon things is at least as old as Western philosophy. Scholars interested in its history have traced it back to Plato's *Cratylus*, exposed its pride of place in Pythagorean, Epicurian, Stoic, Alexandrian, and Aristotelian traditions, and, most recently, have insisted upon its relevance for the understanding of poetry since Mallarmé.[45]

Medieval attitudes toward the issue of naturalism versus conventionalism represent a distillation of conflicting earlier views, but a distillation that is neither adequately synthesized nor, because of abiding hesitations on both sides, fully resolved. There is, for instance, little in late Classical or medieval linguistic theory to sustain the full implications of the naturalist position, certainly nothing equivalent to the Stoic attempt to root the elements of language (letters) in the human body as if nature, unmediated, might somehow speak for itself.[46] On the other hand, we do not find unqualified belief in the purely undetermined nature of human speech, nothing as radical, say, as Saussure's "arbitraire du signe." Here is where the dichotomy referred to earlier becomes most visible: those who theorized about language, from the late Latin grammarians to the speculative grammarians of the fourteenth century, rejected the notion of words as physical extensions of things and accepted the fact of their imposition. In accordance with the Aristotelian precept (passed through Boethius) that "words are sounds having meaning established by convention alone," there was general agreement that verbal signs are socially, not naturally, determined.[47] And yet, a profound resistance to breaking entirely with the wish for continuity between language and matter along with a radical denial of the practical consequences of such a rupture are evident in almost every attempt to confront the complex nature of verbal signs; indeed, together they constitute the most salient features of early medieval linguistics.

Of the Latin grammarians, Varro offers the most sustained consideration of primary word formation, and his position in the *De Lingua Latina* is among the most "naturalist" available to the Middle Ages. The grammarian of the first century B.C. divides all of reality into four universal categories—body, place, time, and action—which correspond to the four essential classes of words. And though he does not specifically designate a first namer, Varro does maintain that nature served as a "guide" to the original imposition of names: "ea (natura) enim dux fuit ad vocabula imponenda homini" (Varro, p. 174). Likewise, Priscian, whose *Institutiones Grammaticae* served to shape much of medieval grammatical thought, had a clear sense of the purely human origin of linguistic signs. Yet he too remains unable to free himself from the notion of the sign as physically rooted. Letters maintain the "appearance of elements of the world": " . . . literas autem etiam elementorum vocabulo nuncupaverunt ad similitudinem mundi elementorum" (Priscian, p. 6).

The "naturalist" strains of Latin grammar and of Alexandrian hermeneutics meet in the monumental figure of Isidore, who believed some letters to be grounded in universal human experience. The Greek "Y," for example, signifies—by resemblance—the life of man ("'Y' litteram Pythagoras Samius ad exemplum vitae humanae"). Other graphic forms, however, signify by custom. "θ" traditionally means death, "for the judges used to affix that same letter 'θ' to the names of those they condemned."[48] According to Isidore, letters have three characteristics: a name; a figure, "by which its character or shape is signified" and which exists either by the nature of its sound or arbitrarily; and a power (*potestas*), "which nature gives" (*Etym.*, 1:iv, xvii–xviii).[49] Where names are concerned, a similar duality prevails. Some are imposed by convention and others in accordance with nature: "Non autem omnia nomina a veteribus secundum naturam inposita sunt, sed quaedam et secundum placitum."[50] Isidore's hesitation with respect to the original formation of words is, moreover, obscured by an uncompromising reverence for etymology. It is almost as if the obsessiveness with which he seeks meaning through origin belies—or causes him to forget—the deeper consequences of his own ambivalence toward primal appellation (see below, pp. 55–56).

A similar ambivalence toward the question of origin is evident in Augustine's assimilation of widely divergent views about the nature of language in general. He displays, for example, a certain trust in the ability of sensible signs to denote reality and thus to serve as inferential tools along the soul's path to higher truth.[51] Augustine does not hesitate to use etymologies to make a point. He indulges in a certain cratylism of Hebrew proper names (see above, pp. 36–37) and is fascinated by natural language, which he associates in the *Confessions* with the immediately comprehensible bodily gestures common to all men. But Augustine also betrays a pervasive distrust of words, which, he emphasizes repeatedly, are hopelessly bound to the contingent, mutable, temporal realm of the senses. Language remains an imperfect medium because of the "corporeal matter of verbal signs."[52] Conventional speech (and all human utterance falls within this domain) at best serves the limited function of indicating to others that which is already and always present in the mind of the speaker.[53] Words are not productive of knowledge in the first instance; on the contrary, Truth, for the Bishop of Hippo, lies beyond the realm of the senses. Intelligible truth, the truth toward which the signs of the perceptible world guide (through memory and illumination) the human soul, hovers in the silence which fascinates Augustine in the *Confessions* and shines forth in the moments of understanding that he associates elsewhere with "listening with the inner ear," or "speaking with the heart."[54] Though conventional linguistic signs may facilitate human understanding, their function within the Augustinian ontology is decidedly pedestrian. Natural signs are situated relatively higher on the ontological scale, but, unlike their verbal equivalents, they are accessible only to the intelligence. Thus, while Augustine accepts the linguistic mythology surrounding Adam's naming of "the earthly animals and the birds," he problematizes this founding semantic gesture. The names which are originally imposed are the proper designations of earthly things, and in this they come as close as is possible to a pristine natural language. Their relation to the spiritual truth beyond words remains, however, only approximate.

The notion of approximation characterizes the sign theory of the later Middle Ages. Abelard maintains that "words imitate things": "voces sunt emulae rerum."[55] Though the *vox* is a natural phenomenon, its meaning has been invented or constituted by human intention in order to signify; and that signification is conventional. Here, as elsewhere, however, intellectual awareness of the socially determined nature of language is accompanied by an unwillingness to dispense with linguistic determinism. According to Abelard, "the one who originally composed names followed the nature of things."[56]

The theme of imitation can also be found in the most comprehensive twelfth-century reflection on the language arts, John of Salisbury's *Metalogicon*. So succinct, in fact, is John's articulation of the problem that it is worth quoting at some length:

> Artium uero matrem superius collectum est esse naturam; sed licet hec aliquatenus, immo ex maxima parte ab hominum institutione processerit, naturam tamen imitatur, et pro parte ab ipsa originem ducit, eique in omnibus, quantum potest, studet esse conformis. . . . Ipsa quoque nominum impositio aliarumque dictionum, etsi arbitrio humano processerit, nature quodammodo obnoxia est, quam pro modulo suo probabiliter imitatur. Homo enim ad exequendum diuine dispensationis effectum et ad instituendum inter homines uerbi commercium rebus his primo uocabula indidit, que preiacebant, nature manu formate, et quas illa uel ex quattuor elementis uel ex materia et forma compegerat et distinxerat, ut rationalis creature possent sensibus obici, earumque diuersitas, sicut proprietatibus, sic et uocabulis insigniri. [*Metalogicon*, p. 32]

> We have already seen that nature is the mother of the arts. While grammar has developed to some extent, and indeed mainly, as an invention of man, still it imitates nature, from which it partly derives its origin. Furthermore, it tends, as far as possible, to conform to nature in all respects. . . . The very application of names, and the use of various expressions, although such depends on the will of man, is in a way subject to nature, which it probably imitates (at least) to some modest extent. In accordance with the divine plan, and in order to provide verbal intercourse in human society, man first of all named those things which lay before him, formed and

fashioned by nature's hand out of the four elements or from matter and form, and so distinguished that they could be designated by names as well as properties.

Abelard and John of Salisbury neither endow the primal namer with superhuman powers nor stress the ontological impossibility of the process of naming. They opt instead for an adequation between things and their original designation. Divested of divine trappings, the first namer is both philosopher and grammarian—"one," as Michel de Marbais maintains, "who must have cognition both of things signified and of the sounds to be applied to them."[57]

Abelard's and John of Salisbury's moderate conventionalism is in many respects typical of medieval sign theory, that is, ideas or mental concepts are considered to signify naturally (and universally), but are themselves signified by convention, or by social institution. Language may be flawed by the roundabout nature of all human intention, but the original namer of "the earthly animals and the birds" was nonetheless guided by the properties of things.

This brings us to a second major characteristic of early medieval grammar, a privileging of the object of reference over its mode, which even assumes metaphysical proportions. According to Augustine, the study of language is essential because all signs work to mediate the relation between man and God. Yet neither such a study nor its object holds any intrinsic value except insofar as they can be of service in orienting the potential believer toward the truth which lies beyond them. In the *De Magistro* Augustine enjoins his interlocutor to "esteem the things signified more than their signs";[58] and to the objection that the word "coenum" (filth) is superior both to its referent and its meaning, he replies that a knowledge of "coenum" is superior both to the word and the thing itself. Words are functional: they exist either to designate that to which they refer or to provide knowledge of their reference. The signifier depends in some fundamental way upon the signified, which is why, Augustine insists, "it is necessary to accord words less value than the objects for which we employ them."[59] More important still, language in the absence of reference is conceived as incomplete and empty: "Words merely teach us other words, less than that, a sound and a simple voiced noise. . . . "[60] It is a knowledge of things that completes the knowledge of words.

Not only are objects to be valued more than their signs, but excessive emphasis upon words constitutes a sin. "To mistake signs for things" is a "pitiful servitude" that prevents the soul from attaining "divine light."[61] Augustine condemns both the dialecticians, "who seek beauties of expression more than appropriate to the gravity of thought," and the rhetoricians, "who seek not to make truth triumph, but the means of making their discourse preferred to that of their adversaries."[62] As in the Pauline dictum, overattachment to the form of expression, as opposed to its substance, has doctrinal consequences: it is the equivalent of an act of concupiscence—a love of the letter (body) to the detriment of the spirit (soul)—in which everything corporeal, temporal, and contingent is implicated. To love words or to become overly involved with them is to defer the knowledge of God.

It is as if language, for Augustine, were transparent because its eternally subsistent object always draws words to their natural mark. Put another way, the role of signs is merely to activate other modes of knowing—memory or intellection; and they point inevitably to the same predetermined truth. Tongues may vary and the means of verbal expression may be hopelessly rooted in material reality, yet all language is about God and leads to God.[63] The theologian insists that it makes no difference whether God's name is written in gold or ink, since "the former would be more precious, the latter more worthless, but the thing signified would be the same."[64] And despite the rhetorical exaggeration, the comparison is perfectly paradigmatic of the extent to which meaning overshadows expression. Words have no specific opacity of their own. On the contrary, they refer "only to other words," as language effaces itself before that which lies beyond it and to which it is naturally drawn.

The Augustinian transparency of the sign finds a corollary among grammarians, rhetoricians, and philosophers in the trend toward what W. and M. Kneale call "real definition," that is, in the impulse to "look at the thing" rather than to its sign in order to determine meaning.[65] We have seen that both Abelard and John of Salisbury, echoing a formulation that dates at least to the *Rhetorica ad Herennium*, affirm that names imitate nature. But, more generally, the classificatory apparatus of early medieval grammar is heavily weighted in favor of the signified. Donatus and Priscian, in rejecting Aristotle's two-part as well as the Stoic five-part classification of the *partes orationis*, opt for a system of word class based primarily on meaning. For Donatus, a noun is "a part of speech which signifies with a case a person or a thing"; a verb is "a part of speech with tense and person but without case, signifying 'to perform some action,' or 'to suffer,' or neither."[66] One of the important assumptions underlying early medieval grammar is that *what* rather than *how* a word signifies determines its linguistic status.

The question of *what*, which is essentially that of how to assess physical property, was traditionally the domain of philosophers and logicians. According to Aristotle, Porphyry, Boethius (and even Cicero and Quintilian), everything has a property, which is the inessential quality differentiating it from all others in its species; or, if a species, from all others in its genus.[67] The determination of property (what a thing is) together with the determination of difference (what it is not) constituted the science of definition invoked by philosophers as the first step in the construction of a syllogistic argument. Definition engaged in the service of dialectics was thus intended to demarcate the differences between things. Its philosophical status was, however, always somewhat fluid precisely because of the Adamic paradox—the difficulty of separating completely the discreteness of things from their linguistic designation. From the beginning, Aristotle, whose categories served as the basis for all such classification, links the practice of definition to that of predication. Property is that which is predicated of an individual or of a species, "for the species is to the genus as subject is to predicate, since the genus is predicated of the species, whereas the species cannot be predicated of the genus."[68]

By the time of Cassiodorus (sixth century A.D.) a shift of focus has occurred such that definition represents "a short statement of a thing's essential nature which separates it from others in its class by determining its proper signification."[69] The definition by difference of the philosophers is no longer seen to represent a relation in nature but has become a phenomenon of language, a statement. The distinctness of things is synonymous with their physical property, which is the equivalent of a "proper signification." Isidore, who follows the schema of the categories of the real of Porphyry's *Introduction to Aristotle* (the *Isagoge*), claims that "the nature of anything whatever is made clear by the unfailing definition of its substance" and that such a definition is the first principle of philosophy. Nonetheless, his outline of the procedure for arriving at a proper definition terminates, like that of Cassiodorus, in a proper meaning:

> Nam posito primo genere, deinde species et alia, quae vicina esse possunt, subiungimus ac discretis communionibus separamus, tamdiu interponentes differentias, quousque ad proprium eius de quo quaerimus signata eius expressione perveniamus, ut puta: Homo est animal rationale, mortale, terrenum, bipes, risu capax. [*Etym.*, 2:xxv, ii]

> For once we have first set down the genus, we then subjoin the species and the other things that are possibly related; then by setting aside the common qualities we make distinctions, continually interpreting differences until we arrive at the proper quality of that which we are examining, its meaning being made definite, as for example: Man is a rational, mortal, biped animal, capable of laughter.

What had begun as a technique for the substantive determination of the nature of things has become, by the time of Isidore, a grammatical strategy by which the meaning of names becomes ascertainable through the principle of physical property.[70] Property is the "reason" or "cause" of the imposition of names ("Nomina sunt consequentia rerum"); and, as an anonymous thirteenth-century grammarian maintains, "Nature is repulsed by a name that does not respect its referent": "Nec est gramatica pure a voce hominis; sed regulatur impositor a proprietatibus rerum, ut non possit significare rem ipsam sub modis significandi qui repugnant proprietatibus ipsius rei" (*Notices*, p. 123).

Definition represents, then, an important point of convergence between the language arts and the physical sciences. For language, which, to a much greater extent than today, was considered an integral part of the physical universe, also shares in the properties of things. Words and word classes themselves have properties, as Priscian makes clear in his definition of the principal parts of speech: "Proprium est nominis substantiam et qualitatem significare. . . . Proprium est verbi actionem . . . significare. . . . Proprium est pronominis. . . . Proprium est adverbii . . . " (Priscian, p. 55). The ninth-century grammarian Remigius of Auxerre will turn the process of definition by difference upon the *partes orationis*.[71] And, by the time of Hugh of Saint-Victor, property rules even syntax. The notion of the proper has become the equivalent of all that is correct: "Igitur proprietas est que regulam sequitur" (*Notices*, p. 83). Not only is the property of a thing the key to verbal imposition ("illo a quo nomen imponitur") and the guiding principle of approximation, but the proper is synonymous with a following of rules, with rectitude.

Here we hit upon the property—the unique quality—of grammar itself, which is that of straightness. Martianus Capella maintains that the Greeks used Γραμματική "since γραμμή means 'line' and γράμματα means 'letters,' and the attribute of letters is to make straight (*lineare*) the forms according to properties."[72] Isidore adopts a similar derivation ("grammatica autem a litteris nomen accepit") as well as the conventional definition of grammar as "the science of correct or straight speech" ("grammatica est scientia recte loquendi" [*Etym.*, 1:v, i]). Isidore also insists upon the connection between the straightness of letters and of roads ("Litterae autem dictae quasi legiterae, quod iter legentibus praestent" [ibid., 1:iii, iii]), which will become a theme of the High Middle Ages. John of Salisbury, for example, maintains that grammar is a highway from which a certain amount of distance constitutes the field of rhetorical figure, and which, when abandoned altogether, is tantamount to a loss of intelligibility.[73] Grammar is not only the art of straight speech and writing (*recte loquendi scribendique*), but the science of literal meaning:

> *Grama* enim littera uel linea est, et inde litteralis, eo quod litteras doceat; quo nomine tam simplicium uocum figure quam elementa, id est uoces figurarum, intelliguntur; aut etiam linearis est. . . . [*Metalogicon*, p. 31]

> *Grama* means a letter or line, and as a result grammar is "literal," in that it teaches letters, namely both the symbols which stand for simple sounds, and the elementary sounds represented by the symbols. It is also [in a way] linear.

The function of early medieval grammar is thus the delineation of straight paths, the creation of linear links between symbols, sounds, and letters as well as between words and the physical properties of things.

If grammar is conceived as the science of the literal and the straight—of orthography (literally "straight writing"), rectitude, and regularity, this linearity is defined more by the field of semantics than by that of syntax. Here lies another important feature of the linguistics of this early period. Before the twelfth century, grammarians were primarily concerned with the status of the individual word and with its relation to that which it represents. Grammar was in this respect heavily oriented toward problems of signification and of lexicon. Donatus, for example, maintains that words belong to grammarians ("ad grammaticos lexos"), while figures of speech and of sense belong to rhetoricians.[74] And as late as the turn of the thirteenth century, Alexander of Villedieu stakes out for rhetoric the domain of eloquence, for logic that of truth, and for grammar that of signification: "Si ordinetur [sermo] ad significandum, sic est gramatica" (*Notices*, p. 470). He invests the Donatian dictum with a logical ring:

> Scema lexeos primo et principaliter et per se est de consideratione gramatici, qui primo et per se intendit sermonem rectum in scribendo et proferendo ad manifestandum intellectum. . . . [*Notices*, p. 471]

> A verbal figure is first, chiefly and by its very nature, the subject of the grammarian's examination, for by his own very nature his primary aim is to lead correct speech in writing and oral delivery toward the clarification of meaning. . . .

Within the grammar of the early Middle Ages, a word is more important in relation to its nonlinguistic point of reference than in relation to other words. It is classified according to meaning and the reason of its invention (*causa inpositionis*) and not according to syntactic function: "Non enim sunt iudicande uoces secundum actum constructionis, sed secundum propriam naturam inuentionis."[75] This may seem like a subtle distinction; it should nonetheless be borne in mind, since the full implications of such an "atomistic" emphasis upon semantics and property will become increasingly apparent when compared to the "holistic" grammar of the later Middle Ages, and, further, when both are assimilated to the modes of kinship characteristic of the postfeudal era.

Strategies of Return

We began the preceding section with an allusion to a fundamental split between what medieval philosophers knew about the nature of verbal signs and what they desired to believe about them. More precisely, we saw how the linguistics of this early period was dominated by the myth of a prescient first namer and by the primacy of beginnings; this despite certainty of the conventional or socially determined origin of all human discourse. Grammarians stress the originality—the determining efficiency—of the signified over its signifier. The notions of property and of propriety are, among the rhetoricians, synonymous with an original meaning. And the logician's technique of definition, transformed into the handmaiden of grammar, makes it possible to locate through language the proper significations that are rooted in (determined by) the properties of things. To signify properly is, within the recuperative, semantically oriented grammar of the period between Donatus and Abelard, to recapture the essence of things before the Fall. The science of straight connections enables those who practice it to undo the dislocations—obliquities, circumlocutions, distortions—of sense that characterize the history of human speech, and hence to restore to each altered articulation its proper or original meaning. This is why the practice of etymology is so important and, in fact, constitutes a branch of scientific knowledge until the fourteenth century.

Etymology

In Classical rhetoric, etymology is one of the intrinsic arguments or topics developed out of the meaning of a word and translated from Greek to Latin by *veriloquium* (true speech) because, in the phrase of Cicero and Quintilian, "words are the tokens [*notae*] of things."[76] Here, both the notion of intrinsic and that of topic are crucial. All arguments are, for the rhetorician, intended to persuade within the context of judicial dispute. But an intrinsic plea is one which is not dependent upon outside authority. As in the example of Biblical names, the word is considered to contain the sign of its own force. The notion of topic (*topos*), which Cicero inherited from Aristotle, denotes a proper place from which to speak, or a place from which arguments can be made. Rhetoric is the topology of the various arguments which found or ground speech.[77] The *topos* defines the final product of the etymological process. End point of the attempt to reverse linguistic chronology—the loss of the proper and dispersion of meaning, it implies a place where arguments end, where sound gives way to silence, motion to rest, and where words begin to border on meaning and meaning on things.

The positing of a place at which words and things both meet and come to a standstill serves to transform etymology—the history of words through time—into geography, a series of spatially defined relations between fixed meanings; and it accounts for the disproportionate role which geography plays in early etymologies. Varro, in whom the principle of etymology reaches it Classical apogee, depicts the rooting of words in things in terms of territorial relations between neighboring properties:

Sed qua cognatio eius erit verbi quae radices egerit extra fines suas, perse-
quemur. Saepe enim ad limitem arboris radices sub vicini prodierunt
segetem. [Varro, p. 13]

We shall follow them [etymologies] to wherever the kin of a word under
discussion is, even if it has driven its roots beyond its own territory. For
often the roots of a tree which is close to the line of the property have
gone out under the neighbor's field.

Elsewhere, the history of words is coterminous with the geography of the
ancient world. Varro insists, for example, that since the source (*caput*) of
the river Tiber lies outside of Latinium and "the name as well flows from
there into our language, it does not concern the Latin etymologist."[78]

The majority of the derivations contained in the surviving fragments of
the *De Lingua Latina* involve the names of places, the *loci*, which Varro
associates with the first property of things, location. The notion of a
verbal typology is subsumed by that of *locus*, the first of the four truly
subsistent universal categories of the real equated with physical fixation:
"*Locus* is where something can be *locatum* 'placed,' or as they say nowa-
days, *collocatum* 'established.' . . . Where anything comes to a standstill,
is a *locus* 'place.'"[79] Speech is thus rooted in the zone where all movement
toward a source comes to a rest, where meaning is immutable—"*Loqui*
'to talk' is said from *locus* 'place'"; and "he who speaks [*loquitur*] with
understanding puts each word in its own place. . . ."[80] Varro's convic-
tion that words are spatially rooted, and meaning therefore *collocatum* or
established, accounts for his reliance upon etymology as the touchstone
of grammar. And if the tedium of reading his Latin roots is matched only
by that attached to Jerome's alphabetical catalogue of Hebrew names,
small compensation lies in the fact that so many of the etymologies
contained in the *De Lingua Latina* border on the delirious, as well as in the
fact that Varro goes as far as anyone before Isidore in establishing a purely
verbal epistemology based upon the principle of etymological return.[81]

In the *Etymologiarum sive originum libri XX*, etymology becomes the
defining principle of both grammar and rhetoric, the basis of all practical
knowledge of the world, and, in the phrase of P. Zumthor, "the exclusive
source of an entire learned culture."[82] Isidore pushes the technique
beyond what it had represented to philosophers, a grammatical means of
assessing the propriety of terms; he pushes it beyond the ken of most
grammarians and rhetoricians, for whom it stood as a means of assessing
the correctness of expression. J. Fontaine claims that Stoic and medieval
exegetical traditions culminate in Isidore, since only the former's rooting
of the elements of speech in the body and only the latter's implicit faith in
Hebrew roots can compare with the Bishop of Seville's search for the
primordial forms of language, its absolute beginning.[83] Like Cicero's

notion of *topos* or Varro's concept of *locus*, Isidore seeks—whether in letters, word classes, or literary genres—the places where language comes to a standstill, where meaning becomes intrinsic, where, to adopt his own phrase, the first parts of language, the *primogenia*, "do not draw their origin from somewhere else."[84]

Isidore's definition of etymology as "origo vocabulorum, cum vis verbi vel nominis per interpretationem colligitur" is traditional;[85] he himself equates it with Aristotle's σύμβολον and Cicero's "nota" (*Etym.*, 1:xxix, i). The distinction that Isidore draws between natural and conventional etymologies is the necessary extension of the belief that some names were originally imposed according to the qualities of things, others according to whim (see above, pp. 45–47). Thus the strategies for uncovering etymologies include all that we have seen—reference to property (the cause of imposition), origin, logical contrariety, nominal derivation, and sound.[86] What is remarkable in Isidore's concept of etymology is, in fact, the equation of the qualities of things and their origin, the conflation of logical and chronological categories (a tendency attested throughout the *Etymologiae* by the numerous causal connectives *causa, ratio, quia, quod* used interchangeably alongside of the prepositions *ex, a, ab*). Relations assumed to exist in nature (e.g., that man springs from earth) become the equivalent of those which are a function of language (e.g., the derivation of *prudens* from *prudentia*), and even of language's lowest common denominator, sound (e.g., an etymology *ex vocibus*). Such a mixture is the product neither of a confused mind nor of inattention to traditionally important categories of thought. On the contrary, for Isidore there can be no distinction between speech and its referent, between the arts of language and the physical sciences. His ontology is essentially an ontology of words. Things come into being with names, and without them consciousness would vanish: "Nisi enim nomen scieris, cognitio rerum perit" (*Etym.*, 1:vii, i).[87]

Whether or not Isidore's faith in the essentially verbal nature of cognition represents an extreme (and ample evidence for such a belief can be found throughout the Middle Ages), the fact remains that in an age which believed words to represent a merely tarnished mirror of the universe, knowledge of the world is essentially lexical. The more we know about the sources of words, the faster we can penetrate the nature of things ("Nam dum videris unde ortum est nomen, citius vim eis intelligis" [*Etym.*, 1:xxix, ii]). Etymology represents a basis for the intelligibility of the earthly realm and the defining principle of all scientific inquiry. As a tool of inference its domain is by no means restricted to the disciplines of grammar and rhetoric but extends virtually everywhere—to metallurgy, geography, gardening, law, the arts of war, navigation, and agriculture. Even astronomy is ruled by etymology according to Isidore's practice of a mode of knowledge in which the causes of physical events matter less

than the cause of their designation: "Nam Astronomia caeli conver-
sionem, ortus, obitus motusque siderum continet, vel qua ex causa ita
vocentur."[88] As P. Zumthor points out, the great etymologist and ency-
clopedist is oriented toward the practical rather than the speculative
sciences. His discourse is more descriptive than analytic, "richer in
'hows' than in 'whys.'"[89] Nonetheless, such a lack of conformity to the
norms of post-Renaissance scientific criteria should not blind us to the
radical effects of Isidore's intellectual temper; nor should it lead us to
mistake his monumental importance for the later Middle Ages. The
ultimate consequence of the *Etymologiarum sive originum libri XX* is the
recuperation of all philosophy by grammar, and even by a lexicology
which takes on metaphysical proportions. Isidore's role as the transmitter
of practically all that was known scientifically (though not theologically)
from the late Classical to the medieval world places his verbal epistemology, based upon lexical derivation, at the threshold of at least five centuries of culture sometimes considered a dark and derivative age.[90]

We will have occasion to examine in some detail the shift in the status
and concept of etymology that accompanied the reemergence in the
twelfth century of philosophy alongside of theology and the privileging
of dialectics over both rhetoric and grammar. Let it suffice for the moment
merely to emphasize the tenacity with which Isidore's reliance upon the
history of words survives even as the principle of temporal priority cedes
to that of logic in the construction of etymological explanations. The
twelfth-century grammarian Peter Helias demonstrates a belief in the
primacy of chronology in his definition of etymology as "true speech,
because he who finds the true etymology, that is the first, can point to the
original word."[91] The first utterance, once discovered, stands as a point of
organic conjunction between the properties of things and the appearance
of letters.[92] John of Salisbury equates etymology with eloquence and with
control over verbal intention.[93]

Among the Latin poets of the High Middle Ages, etymology is treated
as a figure of speech and represents a constant source of fascination.
Mathew of Vendome, in the *Ars Versificatoria*, includes "argumentum
sive locus a nomine" among the epithets appropriate to the description of
people and offers examples from Ovid.[94] Marbod dabbles in the mysticism of letters, finding *mors*, for example, a harsh sound because death is
harsh, and *vita* pleasant because of its meaning.[95] Both Marbod and
Hildebert maintain that truth is to be found in the name of things:
"Nomen enim verum dat definitio rerum."[96] Sigebert, Acerbus Morena,
Henry of Avranches, and Richard of Venosa all indulge in the most
outlandish etymological speculation, which can be found in Goliardic
verse as well.[97] Even Dante, who repeats the traditional dictum "Nomina
sunt consequentia rerum," infers in the *Vita Nuova* that Beatrice's name
corresponds, "for those who do not know her," to the truth of her being.

One final example from the fourteenth-century *Leys D'Amors* is irres-istible in its extravagance. The author of this compilation of the rules of language and love explains that etymologies are based either on letters or on syllables according to the individual example ("segon la natura de la cauza"). If by letters, each written character represents a word:

> *Femna.* per. *f. fenestra.* per. *e. enverenada.* per. *m. mortz.* per. *n. nostra.* per. *a. aparelhada* o *ayzinada.* et en ayssi *femna. fenestra enverenada. mortz nostra. ayzinada* o *aparelhada.* E si voletz far ethimologia per la mayre de Dieu. podetz dire. *fenestra ellumenada mayres nostra advocada.*[98]

> In *femna,* one understands by *f, fenestra* [window]; by *e, enverenada* [poisoned]; by *m, mortz* [death]; by *n, nostra* [our]; by *a, aparelhada* or *ayzi-nada* [bringing]. Thus *femna* signifies *poisoned window bringing our death.* If, however, you want to make this etymology work for the mother of God, you must say *fenestra ellumenada mayres nostra advocada* [shining window, mother our defender].

Though Molinier may pretend to imitate the exegetical practice of sacred etymologies, he recognizes implicitly a certain ironic arbitrariness in the imposition of proper names. The same word, depending upon its refer-ent, can have radically different etymologies, as interpretation seems to depend more on the person named than on ontologically and historically grounded Hebrew roots. The proper is purely a function of the signified and expresses neither, as for Jerome, an original and fixed relation be-tween words and things nor, as for Isidore, the preestablished relations in language that are the equivalents of things. Derivation is displaced by "understanding." And yet, the significance of a passage like that found above lies in the fact that long after the basic assumptions governing etymology have given way to the playfulness of pastiche, a nostalgia for the letter joined to meaning is complemented by a formal strategy of etymological return.

Sacramental Theology

Among the early Church Fathers, attitudes toward the practice of etymology are necessarily ambiguous because of conflicting attitudes toward language in general. Origen, for example, correctly situates the source of etymological thinking in Stoic doctrine, and he summarizes succinctly the relation between linguistic determinism and etymology: "The problem is whether, as Aristotle thinks, names were given by arbitrary determinations; or, as the Stoics hold, by nature, the first utter-ances being imitations of the things described and becoming their names (in accordance with which they introduced certain etymological princi-ples). . . ."[99] Augustine's position is attenuated by his distrust of all verbal signs; yet he distinguishes between a belief in the continuity of linguistic evolution and the originally motivated quality of signs. Words change according to regular laws of resemblance (analogy), proximity (metonymy), and contrariety (antinomy). And though it is not always possible to retrace their history, to arrive at the "resemblance of sound to things," such a quest can, in the best of cases, lead to a fuller knowledge of the earthly realm.[100]

It is, once again, within the realm of Biblical exegesis that the conflict between a knowledge of the degraded and illusory status of verbal signs as opposed to the regularity of their development along with the existence of an original text "sprung from a single tongue"[101] will partially be resolved. According to Augustine, the solution to the dilemma of the loss of intelligibility lies in a limited recourse to philology. The exegete, "armed with the science of languages," becomes capable of restoring the diminutions of sense implicit to translation and thus of discovering the proper meaning of the divine will inherent to Biblical discourse:

> Contra ignota signa propria magnum remedium est linguarum cognitio. Et latinae quidem linguae homines, quos nunc instruendos suscepimus, duabus aliis ad Scripturarum divinarum cognitionem opus habent, hebraea scilicet et graeca; ut ad exemplaria praecedentia recurratur, si quam dubitationem attulerit latinorum interpretum infinita varietas.[102]

> The great remedy against ignorance of proper signs is a knowledge of languages. In fact, those of the Latin tongue, whom I have undertaken to instruct, need two other languages in order to understand the holy Scriptures, namely Greek and Hebrew. These will permit them to appeal to older examples in cases where the infinite variety of Latin translators places them in doubt.

Books 2 and 3 of the *De Doctrina Christiana* contain a series of philological principles by which to distinguish literal from figural expression and thus recuperate Biblical allegory within the realm of the proper. And if Augustine's immediate goal in interpreting *Genesis* is, as he states, "to understand all these passages not in their figural but in their proper sense," his final aim is a recuperation—through philology—of the laws of linguistic evolution, a reversal—through charity—of the history of humanity, and, ultimately, a restoration of man to God (see below, pp. 60–62).

Augustine remains keenly aware of the impropriety of Biblical translation—an alienation of sense implying an estrangement from God. It is, however, Jerome, the translator, who most systematically exploits etymology as a principle of exegesis. Jerome announces at the beginning of the *Hebraicae Quaestiones in Libros Geneseos* that his purpose in writing is to restore the lost (translated) truth, hence the authority, of the Bible; and this through a study of the sources of things, names, and places:

> Studii ergo nostri erit uel eorum, qui in libris hebraicis uaria suspicantur, errores refellere uel ea, quae in latinis et graecis codicibus scatere uidentur, auctoritati suae reddere, etymologias quoque rerum, nominum atque re-

gionum, quae in nostro sermone non resonant, uernaculae linguae expla-
nare ratione.[103]

Therefore, it will be my task either to prove the errors of those men who
are suspicious of various things in the Hebrew books, or to restore to their
original authority those things which seem to abound in the Latin and
Greek codices; furthermore, to explain by means of the vernacular the etymologies of things, names, and places which are not transparently obvious
in my speech.

Jerome's *Liber Interpretationis Hebraicorum Nominum* is nothing more than
an alphabetical list of the etymologies of Biblical names, which makes it
clear that the search for linguistic beginnings and the mysticism of Hebrew roots are merely two sides of the same coin: in one, meaning is read
through the history of the name; and in the other, the name is read in
terms of the historical genesis it prospectively prescribes.

The etymological search for first words—*primogenia*—is also expressed
theologically in the doctrine of the Incarnation, which, within a Christian
economy of salvation, is experienced as a drama of language and lineage.
There is, first of all, much in Classical sign theory to suggest the interpenetration of paternal and linguistic functions. The notion of the *logos* is
associated with paternity; and, according to a certain hermeneutic tradition, it is Hermes, the son and messenger of the gods, who lends his voice
(ἑρμηνευτικός, *hermeneutikos*) to Zeus, the father (λόγος, *logos*).[104] Furthermore, the Christian notion of the Word is, regardless of variations in
trinitarian doctrine, also conceptualized in genealogical terms. The New
Testament designation of Christ the Son as the Word made flesh is
echoed among the Church Fathers. The Apologist Justin calls the Christian Word the "first-born of God"; Origen's pupil Denys of Alexandria
claims that "the Father, who is divine and universal mind, has primarily
the Son for his Word, his revealer and messenger."[105] Eusebius maintains
that "the Father murmurs in the ear of man by means of his only son."[106]
"*Vox* est Filius Dei, ut in Psalmis: 'Vox Domini super aquas,' quod Filius
Dei in carne locutus est ad homines"—so reads the *Allegoriae in Sacram
Scripturam*.[107] But even more important, it is Christ, the voice of the Father,
who permits a return to pure origin. As the "perfect expression" and
source of knowledge of God, Christ the Word restores man to Him.

The drama of return to the Father through the Son is crucial for Augustine's theology of history, which is indissociable from a theology of
sacramental signs. Augustine thus distinguishes between the undifferentiated, immaterial, divine Word which, "engendered by the Father, is
coeternal with Him," and corporeally articulated human speech. In some
extended sense, however, words always refer to the Word.[108] All language thus harks back to an origin synonymous with the Father who
remains present in the objects of his Creation (see above, pp. 35, 50).

The desire to return to the Father accounts for the centrality of memory and illumination in Augustine's verbal theology. And though, as we have seen, words per se cannot lead to truth in the first instance, memory functions in cognition to bind the individual words perceived separately through time, and thus to create "a kind of artificial simultaneity" resembling God's coeternally present Word.[109] God dwells in memory which is essentially of God. So too, the truth that does not belong formally to memory because it has always been there, the truth accessible only to the intelligence, points to the "Word of God coeternal with the Father." The Augustinian apotheosis—the transcendence of the illusory world of the senses—is, finally, a journey through perception and cognition toward the *intellectio* that he associates with a union between parent and child:

> In hac igitur distributione cum incipimus a specie corporis, et pervenimus usque ad speciem quae fit in contuitu cogitantis, quattuor species reperiuntur quasi gradatim natae altera ex altera; secunda, de prima; tertia, de secunda; quarta, de tertia. A specie quippe corporis quod cernitur, exoritur ea quae fit in sensu cernentis, et ab hac, ea quae fit in memoria; et ab hac, ea quae fit in acie cogitantis. Quapropter voluntas quasi parentem cum prole ter copulat. . . . [110]

> In this arrangement, therefore, when we begin with the species of the body, and finally arrive at the species which is formed in the gaze of the thinker, four species are found; they are born, as it were, step by step, one from the other: the second from the first, the third from the second, and the fourth from the third. For the species of the body, which is perceived, produces the species which arises in the sense of the percipient; this latter gives rise to the species in the memory; finally the species which arises in the gaze of the thinker. Hence, the will thrice unites, as it were, the parent with its offspring. . . .

To transcend the body, to attain the inner truth beyond the temporal and beyond language, is to reverse an ontological genealogy whose highest term is God. It is to reunite the Father with the Son, the Speaker with the Word.

Augustine's goal, which is indistinguishable from the sacrament itself, is a convergence of the form of knowledge with its object, a recuperation of the names which are "the images of things." "Everyone," he affirms, "seeks a certain resemblance in his ways of signifying such that signs themselves reproduce, to the extent to which it is possible, the thing signified."[111] And not only does this doctrine of the Incarnation and of the sacrament justify the identification of etymology with genealogy, but it serves as a guide to Augustine's theological version of the Eusebius-Jerome model of universal history. The will for union between speaker and voice, sign and meaning, is, at bottom, linked to the dream of neutralizing the linguistic dispersion that characterizes the degenerative evolution of mankind. The desire for association between Father and Son represents a nostalgia for origins tied to the hope of undoing genealogical dispersion—to abolish history altogether, or to replace world chronology by eschatology. Though the Bishop of Hippo remains skeptical about the power of words—or of etymology—ever to attain to the higher truth which only the intellect can provide, he nonetheless assimilates a reversal of the laws of language and of lineage that brings man closer to God.

Thus, early medieval history, grammar (both internal and external), and sacramental theology are informed by a common underlying pattern defined by the determining effect of what is considered as an absolute beginning, by the unified nature of that origin with respect to a subsequent multiplicity, and by a relative emphasis upon the organic and continuous relations of the multiple parts to an ontogenetic whole. History, grammar, and theology are, further, conceived in genealogical terms; and, where concept is translated into practice, they also can be said to participate in a global strategy of origins. The universal chronicle traces the lineage of man through successive generations from an original set of parents to the families of man; the assumption being that the long-range, linear history of the race will be redeemed at the end of time by a return to the wholeness of the outset. The dominant internal order of contemporaneous grammatical theory reveals a similar development from sound, to letters, to parts of speech, and to syntax, which, extended to the domain of historical linguistics, assumes a progression from an undifferentiated primal utterance to a maternal language (Hebrew), to, eventually, the most divergent tongues of mankind. Grammar takes as its basic premise a founding act of signification and evolution through Hebrew, Greek, and Latin to the present verbal sign which, though debased, still contains a piece of the original essence of its referent. Here, however, the nostalgia for beginnings can be seen in the fact that the second part of grammar, syntax, is overshadowed by its first part, etymology, which finds its equivalent within exegetical tradition in the mysticism of Hebrew roots. Finally, on the level of doctrine, the longing for the lost wholeness of a lineal and linguistic origin is transformed into a theology of history in which the union of Son and Father is identified with the sacramental union of signifier and signified.

The anthropological dream of wedding the laws of kinship to those of language is thus historically realized in the so-called high culture of the Middle Ages. So pervasive, in fact, is the idealization of the discourses of history, linguistics, and sacramental theology in terms of an essential family type that it is difficult not to identify in the principle of genealogy what M. Foucault might term an "episteme" of this early period. But what is the relation of such a genealogically defined representation of the rules of representation to the historical families whose own permutations are neither fully reflected in nor governed by it? What, in short, is the relation between social structure and ideological superstructure, or between the representation of the family and the family as representation? It is to these questions that we now turn in the chapter that follows.

TWO

Kinship

What, it may be asked, does either the originary, diachronic, and "etymological" grammar of the early Middle Ages or sacramental theology have to do with the constitution of actual families some five to seven centuries later? Apparently little, if we expect to find tangible proof that feudal magnates—heads of household—knew Isidore, Augustine, Priscian, or Donatus. And apparently a great deal, when we begin to examine some of the implicit ways in which grammar, the basic discipline of the early medieval language arts, served to ground a world view expressed in social institutions. More precisely, the connection between linguistic and lineal orders becomes compelling when we seek to understand how such an idealized vision of earthly lineage served to mediate a radical reorganization of the aristocratic family of twelfth-century France. For it can be shown that an essentially verbal model, which lay at the center of a prevailing epistemological mode, worked not only to define the family ideologically but to found a more global pattern of social relations and to bolster a strategy of political hegemony operative until the time of the Revolution. And if the goal of the previous chapter was to demonstrate the degree to which a grammatical model was dominated by a familial one, our purpose at present is to show the extent to which the patterns of late medieval kinship were, in turn, molded by those of grammar.

The question of what "actually" happened in "real" medieval families is one of the most difficult areas of European historiography—difficult, first of all, because of the embryonic state of our knowledge of medieval kinship. Despite the survival of numerous canonical precepts—synodal rulings, papal bulls, and interdictions, we still know relatively little about the composition, living arrangements, and sexual habits of the consanguineal group. We are particularly ill-informed about those families (the so-called quiet communities) whose less-than-aristocratic origin or rural isolation left such a meager trace. Moreover, in the era before the Church's hegemony over family law, this sphere was largely a private affair and, as such, entered only tangentially upon the public stage of history. To this blindness are added the difficulty of assessing the difference between what texts prescribe and what men actually did as well as a number of complicating factors specific both to the historical era and the family as an institution. There is, for example, an enormous variation in the structure of kin groups according to region, period, and social class; and such diversity is compounded by the personality of law in the centuries following the invasions as well as by the overlapping of jurisdictions—ecclesiastical, seigneurial, municipal, royal—when law becomes more territorially defined. We find, in addition, a serious problem of "negativity" haunting all of medieval legal studies—that is, the fact that family history tends to become most explicit only when the standard prescriptions of permissible conduct are transgressed as in cases of prohibited marriages, disputed inheritances, bigamy, incest, and divorce. It is precisely the routinely accepted norms of everyday life that, because they are perceived as natural, pass unnoticed and are in some sense systematically "refused" by history.

Due to a general decline in literacy and the official uses of writing, the period between the collapse of Carolingian sovereignty and the reign of the late Capetians represents an especially obscure point within an already dim field. Nonetheless, the image of the noble family that emerges from this "dark" age is of a legal community reduced to its simplest terms, a conjugal unit sometimes prolonged after the death of the parents by an association of brothers (a *frèrêche*). This loosely defined grouping of relatives and retainers, "friends" and neighbors, gravitated around the residence of a lord, who was, above all, a patron, a distributor of gifts and land, the spoils of war or exchange.[1] Within such an extended relatively undifferentiated crowd of all living family members, there was little distinction between the lineage of husband and wife. Both agnatic and cognatic lines were of equal importance, as were relatives linked by marriage (*propinquii*) and by blood (*consanguinei*).

From what we know about the post-Carolingian kin group, several defining principles are of paramount relevance to the present discussion: (1) The noble family of the ninth and tenth centuries seems to have been articulated "spatially," that is to say, as a "horizontal" grouping, spread out in the present, without fixed or precise limits.[2] Though its members may descend from a common ancestor, the family had little consciousness of itself as a temporally defined entity, a succession of generations, a lineage, or genealogy; nor does it emerge from existing documentation that ancestors were privileged over relatives. Descent was a less potent force of family cohesion than affiliation with living relatives, just as within the economic sphere, benefices (lifetime grants) were more important than fiefs, which were not heritable, and which, theoretically at least, reverted to the lord upon the grantee's death. (2) The noble family of this period had no fixed residence. Though its members may have lived in a common region and held land in common, they had little sense of self-definition in terms of a "family seat." (3) Until the eleventh century the clan had no family name. Individuals had a single Christian name, and indeed certain families seemed to have had proprietary rights over certain of these; but they had no *cognomen* or *surnom* (see below, pp. 78–79). There were no dynastic houses and no patronyms. Evidence shows, in fact, a relative inattentiveness to the mixing of names from either the maternal or the paternal lines. (4) Finally, because the institutions of the Carolingian state were, for a long time after its disintegration, still intact, the family had not yet assumed what would become its role in the keeping of the public peace. This means that the family holding was not yet attached to a system of heritable military tenure and that women, as a rule, enjoyed relative economic independence. In theory, a woman could inherit land, was free to manage her own marriage part, and, if widowed, could pass the property of her deceased husband to the children of a "second bed."[3]

In the light of what we know about the kin groups of the post-Carolingian era, it is difficult not to dramatize the startling transformation in the internal makeup of the noble family beginning in the eleventh century. This change varied according to date, region, and social status. It occurred earlier in the North and the West of France, later in the South; earlier among great feudal magnates (counts and dukes) than among simple knights. And though the causes of such a shift are difficult to assess, there is general agreement among historians of the medieval family that what happened to the aristocratic clan happened in response to its own changing relation to the primary source of wealth in a profoundly agrarian age—land. G. Duby (Mâcon, the North), R. Fossier (Picardy), L. Génicot (Namur), R. Hajdu (Poitou), D. Herlihy (the South), L. Musset (Normandy), and P. Bonnassie (Catalonia) all point to a dispersion of patrimony endemic to the "horizontal" clan.[4] Given the capacity of women to inherit as well as the relative equality of heirs (male and female, older and younger), there was a tendency for familial holdings to become increasingly fragmented. This trend was, in the period under consideration, exacerbated by a resurgence of pious donation, gifts inter vivos which furthered the process of partition by irrevocably channeling considerable amounts of property in the direction of the Church.

The parceling of land through division across successive generations and its cession to the ecclesiastical see (which was not, it must be noted, plagued by partition by inheritance) contributed to the gradual impoverishment of the clan. Nor did the "horizontal family" develop a coherent policy of land management. On the contrary, its *patrimoine* was continually diminished by the centrifugal erosion of territory, which was often distant, scattered, crossed by parcels belonging to others, abandoned, or, in the phrase of one southern witness, "confused."[5] In fact, such a demographic state of affairs had deep social implications, for it is the sign of an infrastructure in which personal ties of dependence between individual men are more important than the rights and duties attached to land. Put another way, the authority of those with the power of command, like the legal institutions at their disposal, were not territorially defined. A local lord might rule those under his protection, he might control those living on his domain; but he did not yet dominate a unified region.

Was their relative newness to the areas settled a factor in the incoherency of family policy? What was the effect of a lack of agricultural and administrative experience on the part of those who had been primarily nomadic warriors? Did the Germanic people lack the notion of full ownership so dear to the Roman legal mind? These hypotheses have been advanced to explain the seeming inconsistency of the clan regarding the management of its lands; and they are to some degree relevant and just. The search for causes is, however, less pertinent to the present discussion than the fact that, beginning in the 1000s, the relation of noble families to land began to shift, and this shift accompanied a fundamental change in the family's definition of itself.

There can be little doubt that time alone favored the sense of geographic stability which characterize the families of what M. Bloch termed the "first feudal age." Implantation on a specific piece of land increasingly regarded as a familial possession, a developing patrilocal sense of the kin group bound by reference to a common residence, a castle and cradle of the paternal *alodium* (free holding)—these were important factors in the passage from personal to territorial control. But, most of all, it was the transformation of the fief into a heriditary right, a phenomenon perhaps linked to feudalism itself, that marked a radical break with the "horizontal" clan. From the second half of the eleventh century on, the family began increasingly to receive its fortune by inheritance rather than from a patron. Access to the holdings which had once depended upon the discretion of a lord became at first automatically renewable and then an integral part of a transmissible *patrimoine*. The knight, in turn, was less a retainer than the heir to a domain, function, and title. Chivalry itself, transformed from a relatively open class into a closed and patroclinous caste, was no longer merely an indication of economic status but a hereditary sign of superiority.[6] Henceforth, nobility represented a quality of birth, and a man was powerful because his ancestors, sometime around the year 1000, were already in command.

Such a shift carried enormous consequences; in particular, the tie to heritable land changed the shape of the family in two important ways:

1. There occurred, first of all, a shrinking of the extended clan. This is a phenomenon that remains hard to measure but that is nonetheless reflected (with an obvious delay with respect to actual practice) in Church doctrine. Before the thirteenth century, the endogamic field within which marriage was officially prohibited extended not only to the seventh canonical degree but included prohibitions against marriage to those whose relationship was defined by secondary and tertiary categories of affinity. For example, the *affinitas secundi generis* produced a diriment impediment up to the third degree of kinship between relatives of the second wife of a widower and those of his deceased wife. It even— *mirabile dictu!*—applied in cases where fornication without marriage had occurred. Thus, when a man successively had sexual relations with two women, the relatives to the third degree of the first could not marry the second. The even more arcane *affinitas tertium genus* provided for the inclusion of relatives of the second marriages of the dead spouses of the affines of the *secundi generis*, which, again, also applied in cases of extra-marital intercourse.[7] What this means is that the legal definition of such a family was inordinately large. This is obvious in the exaggerated calculation of the degrees of paternity within which marriage was prohibited, or within which sexual relations were considered incestuous—the factors, in short, which define the rules of exogamy coterminous with the bounds of the family itself. And—this is essential within the medieval setting—it is also visible in the excessively wide limits within which property could be inherited, within which loyalty in blood feuds was required, and within which the family was responsible economically for each of its

members, and shared, in case of his death, in the distribution of compensatory payment.

The enormous extension of the clan—a breadth beyond the reckoning of most of its members and accessible only to those with canonical training—was severely attenuated by the Lateran Council of 1215. Under the direction of Innocent III, both the *secundum* and the *tertium genus affinitatis* were eliminated along with the rule concerning *suboles ex secundis nuptiis*. Even more important, the degrees of consanguinity within which marriage was prohibited were reduced from seven to four. This may seem like an academic distinction within a marital system whose margins are so broad as to appear hopelessly vague. But here again, it must be remembered that more was at stake than merely the establishment of new conjugal cells. Attenuation of the interdiction against marriage also implied an attenuation of the capacity to inherit and the legal responsibility for military aid. Later in the same century, Beaumanoir, evoking the ancient rule of *auxilium*, will remind his readers that the duty of a kinsman to participate in the wars of another is, like the rule of marriage, now restricted to the fourth degree.[8]

2. Alongside the narrowing of the outer limits of the noble family there occurred an internal restriction whose consequences reached beyond the quantitative extension of the marital prohibition, along with mutual military and economic obligations, toward a substantive redefinition of the concept of family itself. For, beginning in the eleventh century, and at different times in different regions, historians detect the onset of a marked preference for consanguineal over affinal kin. That is, the transformation of fiefs into heritable *patrimoines* was accompanied by a growing consciousness of blood relations in distinction to those by marriage. The kin group as a spatial extension was displaced from within by the notion of the blood group as a diachronic progression: the power of feudal princes, once established geographically, produced a corresponding sense of the family through time. And not just any sense, since the "horizontal" clan, loosely and spatially conceived, took on, through increased emphasis upon time and blood, a necessarily tighter and more "vertical" slant.[9] Nobility became, in the period under consideration, synonymous with race (*sanguine nobilitatis*), as the undifferentiated bilateral mixture of agnatic and cognatic kin ceded to the enhanced prestige of a unilateral descent group.

Here we touch upon the central axiom of twelfth-century aristocracy. For the family, narrowed around its outer edges, temporalized and rendered vertical, also underwent a reorientation, an axial shift, such that its articulation of itself acquired the dimensions of a straight line. Linearity is the defining principle of the noble house, dynasty, and—the partial homonymy is striking—of lineage. Henceforth, nobility was no longer dependent upon the bestowal of function or benefice but was a quality of those whose origin can be traced along a continuum of descent. "To be noble," as G. Duby notes, "is to be able to refer to a genealogy."[10]

From clan to lineage, the phrase is all too facile and broad to account for the characteristic development of specific regions. And yet, regional studies seem not only to confirm—without naming—the timeworn cliché but to suggest something beyond an apparently unconscious, historically determined change in family focus—something that borders on the realm of intention: that is, the radicalness of aristocracy's lineal "reorientation" lies less in the notion of race, dynastic order, or house than in the growing consciousness with which it began to manage what can only be described as a "biopolitics" of lineage.

The Biopolitics of Lineage

1. The genealogical family implies, first of all, the exercise of a certain discipline with respect to marriage, more precisely, the restriction of unions to the minimum necessary to assure the continuity of the family line. This was not always easy given the high rate of infant mortality in such uncertain times. Nonetheless, as Duby has demonstrated for the regions of Mâcon and the Northwest, noble families permitted the establishment of only one or two new households per generation, the rest of the unmarried sons being housed in monasteries and chapters, or simply remaining unattached and disenfranchised.[11] Bonnassie finds the same to be true of Catalonia; and Hajdu calculates that in twelfth-century Poitou the number of married eldest sons exceeds that of their younger brothers by a factor of two.[12] When younger siblings were allowed to marry, the family frequently tried to find a wealthy mate, or, that failing, to protect the familial *patrimoine* by a limited endowment (*droit de viage*). Similarly, the marriage of daughters, part of family policy aimed at the deliberate creation of a "network of alliances," often involved a restriction of inheritance to the dowry or marriage portion (*maritagium*).[13]

2. Implicit to the production of sufficient progeny to insure dynastic continuity without a surplus to deplete its wealth is a model of marriage essential to the transmission of the fief and to the organization of feudal society as a series of alliances between landholders with mutual obligations to each other. Marriage represented, above all, a treaty (*pactum conjugale*) to be negotiated between families; and it has often been said that the chivalric houses of twelfth-century France were so closely connected through common ancestry, matrimony, and collateral relation (not to mention fictive forms of kinship like adoption and participation in certain sacraments) that the nobles of the realm must have seemed like one big family. So complex a web of kinship depended upon careful surveillance of marital ties. More precisely, it assumed a matrimonial system involving early betrothal (often at the age of seven to ten), early

marriage (often at puberty), and, above all, the choice of partners to be made by the family or feudal lord. A marriage was, under normal circumstances, concluded by the head of household (*caput mansi*) or the elders (*seniores*) of the lineage; in their absence, by the relatives—the *amis charnels*—mother, brother, sister, or uncle; and, when the potential spouse was an orphan, by the lord who exercised the right of wardship.[14] Under this "lay aristocratic model of marriage" (Duby), the consent of parties mattered little, while that of parents and guardians was the sine qua non of a legal union. The question of who may marry whom was based upon a certain respect for canonical impediments and upon a careful husbanding of the paternal fief in accordance with an interlocking series of military, political, and social ties.

3. The biopolitics of lineage cannot be separated from a system of property rights and practices designed to insure the integrity of the ancestral domain. These include: the *laudatio parentum*, by which relatives participated in the alienation of family lands; the *proïsme*, an offer to purchase tendered in the first instance to kin; and, eventually, the *retrait lignager* (*redemptio, retractus*) by which a member of the lineage retained the right, even after sale to an outsider had been concluded, to substitute himself for the original purchaser.[15]

A general prohibition against the division of noble fiefs served to reinforce the ties between those whose sense of cohesion was increasingly tied to land. The *Très Ancien Coutumier*, transcribed around 1200 in the region (Normandy) where the force of lineage was stronger than anywhere else, forbids the dismemberment of large holdings: "Ne fiez de hauberc, ne sergenterie qui apartiegne a la segnorie au duc, ne baronie ne sera pas partie."[16] Compiled three-quarters of a century later and in a less seigneurial spirit, the *Etablissements de Saint Louis* displays nonetheless a similar interdiction: "Baronie ne depart mie entre freres. . . . "[17] The trend against division was also reflected in the property arrangements surrounding marriage, for here the economics of the conjugal couple was tailored to affect minimally the rights of lineage. Gifts between spouses were prohibited where inherited property was concerned.[18] Even when specifically sanctioned, as in the case of dowries and marriage offerings, these still retained the qualities of a loan. More important, husband and wife did not inherit from one another. Upon the death of either, the surviving spouse reserved control of the dead partner's marriage portion; but at the time of his or her death, and in the absence of descendants, this property reverted to the lineage of its origin. The devolution of family holdings was, in other words, coterminous with blood, a principle which Beaumanoir puts succinctly as follows:

Se j'ai eritage de par mon pere et mes peres muert et après je muir sans oir de mon cors, mes eritages de par mon pere ne revient pas a ma mere, ainçois eschiet au plus prochien qui m'apartient de par le pere; neis s'il estoit ou quart degre de lignage, car ma mere est estrange de l'eritage qui me vient de par le pere, et aussi est mes peres estranges de l'eritage qui me vient de par ma mere.[19]

If I have an inheritance from my father and my father dies and I die heirless after him, my inheritance from my father does not revert to my mother, for it escheats to my closest relative on my father's side; even if this means going as far as the fourth degree of paternity, since my mother is a stranger to the inheritance that comes to me from my father, and, likewise, is my father a stranger to the inheritance that comes to me from my mother.

Beaumanoir's prescription does not cover goods acquired during the course of marriage, but it does provide categorically that noble property belonging originally to one lineage cannot pass to another. The rule of *paterna paternis, materna maternis* as stated above served, moreover, to stress the ephemeral nature of marriage itself. The conjugal couple represented a temporary coupling of two separate kin groups for the purpose of procreation and did not constitute an independent economic unit.[20]

The rules governing *indivision* and the separation of property would have had little effect if it were not for the inauguration, at about the same time, of the practice of primogeniture. Whether primogeniture represented, as some have suggested, the aristocratic appropriation of a royal model, or, as others have held, a return to Roman notions of property, is less important than the fact that beginning in the eleventh century the privileging of one heir over all others became the law of noble succession.[21] Here again, there is a certain amount of variation according to region—earlier in Mâcon and Normandy than in Poitou and Provence—and according to status—earlier among great feudal chiefs than among lesser knights. In addition, the actual techniques of primogeniture reflected local legal usage—customary in the North and by testament in the romanized South. Be these differences as they may, primogeniture implied inheritance by the oldest male of the most profitable and prestigious domains, usually the castle and the central family fief; this accompanied by the distribution of marginal holdings among younger siblings. The *Très Ancien Coutumier* provides that "li chevaliers ainznez avra le fie de hauberc tout entier"; and this prescription is echoed in the *Grand Coutumier*, whose author elaborates a line of succession by sex and age:

Unde notandum est quod primogenitus filius patri succedit, et omnes ei debent succedere qui primo nati sunt in eadem linea consanguinitatis. . . .[22]

Whence let it be noted that the first born son succeeds to the father, and all should succeed to him in the same blood line by order of birth. . . .

According to Beaumanoir, the oldest son gets the principal manor and two-thirds of all the fiefs, while the rest of the family inheritance is to be divided equally among younger sons and the daughters, who become vassals of their brother. Saint Louis concurs, specifying that, "gentis hom ne puet doner à ses anfans, à ces qui sont puisné que le tiers de son heritaige."[23]

The practice of primogeniture represented the keystone of a familial strategy that did much to foster lineage's vertical, agnatic, patrilinear articulation of itself. Through it property descended in a straight vertical line, "like," in the words of E. Le Roy Ladurie, "sap flowing downward, according to some mysterious force, to nourish the lower limits and offshoots of a tall tree."[24] The stress placed not only upon the uni-dimensionality but upon the unidirectionality of lineage is significant and will seem even more so when we examine other systems of inheritance and other kinds of wealth (see below, pp. 163–174). Paternal property is transferred only in one direction—downward (*quasi ponderosum quid*); in the phrase of a popular adage found in the customary material, "fiefs ne remontent pas."

4. Primogeniture and the law of *paterna paternis, materna maternis* assumes that each piece of property follows, according to origin, its own particular course of descent—has, so to speak, its own genealogy. Here, however, we must not forget that the notion of property refers to a specifically aristocratic mode of wealth and that the rule of primogenital inheritance applies to it alone. Noble property is, above all, immobile, *real* estate, which remains, at least in theory, also unsalable. The vagueness of such an associative nexus is, in fact, itself significant. The term *immeuble*, still reflected in the French word for real estate, is, as customary material makes clear, primarily a *res soli* characterized by its fixity. "We call an immobile possession," states the *Grand Coutumier*, "one that cannot be moved from place to place, as a field, a meadow and all possessions inherent to the soil."[25] And Beaumanoir's definition of "l'immeuble" as fixed ("heritages sont choses qui ne peuvent être mues"), as producing annual income ("qui valent par années"), and as permanent ("heritage ne peut faillir") is telling in two important ways.[26] First, immobile property is considered generally to be inalienable. Creditors could not touch a debtor's *immobilier*; nor could the husband who controlled his wife's dowry arbitrarily divest her of it. Second, and this is but a corollary of the first, the *immeuble*, because of its inalienability, is the equivalent of a "heritage"; and in its association with inheritance, the concept of an immobile good becomes synonymous with the *propre*, or with property itself.

The Barbarian codes had distinguished between marked and un-marked property, which, in Frankish law, amounted to a difference between personal (temporary) and familial (perpetual) modes of possession.[27] To the former category belonged individually owned ac-quisitions (*comparatus, conquisitum*), while to the latter belonged inalienable, unseizable, collectively owned land—*terra paterna* or *proprietas*. The affiliation between the proper and the paternal strikes to the core of the medieval concept of property, for land that is inherited—whether over the course of many generations or only once—becomes a *propre*, the possession of ancestors (*terra aviatica, avitins*).[28] A *propre* is an *immeuble* owned by one partner at the time of marriage, or that is inherited after marriage. It belongs, in essence, to a lineage rather than to the individuals through whom it descends. And not only is the *propre* the equivalent of *heritage*, but it is synonymous with ancestry (nobility) itself. Property and genealogy are superimposed upon each other, as the order of proper descent is identified with the descent of the proper. This is why bastards cannot accede to *propres*—because, as Saint Louis states, "they have no lineage" ("Bastard n'a point de lignage"); and why, as Louis also prescribes, it is sufficient, in order to prove possession by *parage*, merely to "recount one's lineage."[29] The history of the noble family is, at bottom, the history of its land.

The association of paternity and property is nowhere more evident than in the Latinized term *alod* (*alodis, alodium*, OF *alleu*). Whether or not *alod* derives etymologically from the Scandinavian *ódal*—and there has been much discussion—the two words are, as A. Guerevič has convincingly argued, conceptually identical.[30] The root *odal* refers to a family possession or to property which has been transmitted from generation to generation. Old Norwegian texts speak of land that "can trace its genealogy back to the sepulchral grounds and to paganism."[31] The *odal* embodies the combined idea of *pater* or *patria*, the paternal and the geographic locus of origin—a place of birth and of hereditary life. In the Germanic tongues this notion is expressed by the term *epel* (*adal, aepel*), meaning "inheritance," "possession," and "country," from which is derived *aepeling, adaling* (Scand. *arborinn, aettborinn*), meaning "a man born of an ancient clan" or "belonging to high lineage." In any case, from the common radical *Adal*, signifying "father" and "paternal," spreads the family of Icelandic *adal* ("innate quality," "substance," "lineage"); the High German *adal, uodal*; Old Saxon *adal, edili, odil*; and Old English *epel, opel, aepel*. The nuances of each may vary, but the general semantic range includes "nobility of race," "high birth," and "innate quality."

And yet, there is another and even more compelling sense in which the progeny of *odal* is crucial to an understanding of the medieval concept of property, since the term *alod* also contains the notion of "free holding"—full possession. The *alod* designates land which belongs exclusively to the family and which, unlike that held in fief, neither depends on anyone outside the kin group nor incurs obligations of service or dues. By the twelfth century there may be, practically speaking, little difference between the de facto heritability of many fiefs and succession to the autonomous *alod*. But the latter still remains less subject to alienation than other modes of possessory concession—use, benefice, *saisine, viager,* or *parage.* Transmitted along patrilinear lines, the allodial holding stands as the fullest expression of the interpenetration of property and genealogy. The devolution of *terra propria* remains indissociable from that of lineage.

The Aristocratic Practice of Signs

We began from the premise that there occurred, beginning in the eleventh century, a fundamental change in the nature of the family, a change whose ultimate cause may lie beyond the ken of historians in regions as mysterious and as historically undetermined as a long-range shift of climate.[32] Nonetheless, we accepted as a viable—not wholly arbitrary, minimally "grounded"—point of departure the phenomenon of geographic implantation along with the transformation of provisional benefices into heritable fiefs. With the fixation of the noble family upon its own soil came a certain narrowing of its peripheral limits and a reorientation of its conceptual base—from the spatialized "horizontal" clan to the more vertically and temporally conceived lineage. This process represented more than a mere institutional shift; it implied, in fact, an important "prise de conscience" on the part of the aristocratic kin group of the necessity for biopolitical management of its own resources, both human and material. More precisely, it involved: restriction and control of marriage in consonance with social, military, and economic interests; adoption of a system of succession that assured the integral transmission of family holdings; and certain awareness of a specifically aristocratic mode of wealth, real property (*proprietas*), which is connatural—both historically and ideologically—with the primogenital articulation of lineage itself.

These are the symptoms of institutional change and of a change in the consciousness of a caste, if not a class. We would, however, ourselves be guilty of practicing a kind of diachronically descriptive history of "mentalités," and, ultimately, of a lapse of consciousness of our own historical moment were we to fail to realize that the institutional signs of a shift in the limits and internal structure of the clan represented, above all, a shift in its relation to signs. This idea cannot be overstressed. It is really the essence and the keystone of our discussion. Given that much of what a family—any family—is depends upon how it is represented, we must, if we are to understand the evolution of medieval kin groups, look first to their constitution of themselves through certain symbols. More important, we must look to the various modes and strategies of symbolic production—to what might be termed the family's "practice of signs." For then it becomes increasingly evident that when the noble family of the twelfth century became conscious of itself as a sign-producing organism, it did so *around* the notion of dynasty or lineage as well as *through* the mediatory semiotic fields of heraldry, patronymics, the plastic arts, and historical narrative. Above all, the organization of family lines coincides with the appropriation of vernacular literary forms.

Heraldry

The phenomenon of heraldry or blazonry is the most obvious European example of a universal totemic activity by which a particular sign or logos is, within a differentiated system of similar interrelated symbols, associated with a particular family or clan. But such generalizations, despite the convincing anthropological identification of totemism and cultural order, remain too broad and ahistorical for this stage of an already historically engaged discussion. More germane is the fact that before the twelfth century there is little evidence of systematic heraldic display. In fact, much of what we know about the use of military insignias points to the contrary. The banners that appear in the Bayeux Tapestry, for example, resemble crude armorials, yet none can be identified with post-Conquest bearings; and a seemingly internal incoherence in their attribution shows even the same warrior carrying different devices in different embroidered sequences. There is, in other words, no necessary "totemic" link between a particular figure and his heraldic sign, much less between his coat of arms and family.

This begins to change in the 1100s as shown by the inventory of the Norman seals and numerous other examples from high princely and royal courts.[33] John of Marmoustier's description of the marriage of Geoffrey of Anjou (died 1151) and Maude the Empress, daughter of Henry I, speaks of the king's having suspended around his son-in-law's neck a shield of golden "lioncels." This is significant because we know, from his tomb at Salisbury, that Henry II's bastard son (and Geoffrey's grandson) William with the Long Sword bore arms of six golden lions in a blue field. We also know that the arms of the King of France consisted of a blue shield with scattered fleurs-de-lis. Louis VII, at the crowning of Philip Augustus, is supposed to have ordered the young prince clad in a blue dalmatic and blue shoes, sewn with golden "Fleurs-de-Loys," the floral name playing upon his own epithetic name of "Florus." Among the great feudal magnates, Philip of Alsace, Count of Flanders, is said to have been the first to bear family arms (1164). And there is from the twelfth century, also in a playful vein, the example of Enguerrand of Candavène, Count of Saint Pol, whose shield shows a horseman uncharged and sheaves of oats, symbols which, perhaps because of the pun involved, become the bearing of the Candavènes when that house came to display arms.

It is worth recalling that the heraldic signs of this period were, above all, personal devices that had not developed into full armorial charges.

Nonetheless, they demonstrate a close, even a necessary, connection between the individual and his insignia. We are tempted even to speak of property or propriety in the relation of figures like Philip Augustus or Enguerrand and the devices unique to them alone; and here the logician's concept of physical property as that which distinguishes an object from all others in its class along with the rhetorician's notion of correct imposition are both pertinent to the particularized relation between the prince, his family, and its singular sign. The propriety of heraldic signs will become even more elaborate in the thirteenth century when the system of ordinaries, tinctures, and identifying objects (still referred to in French as "meubles") became so refined as to offer to each household, each family attached to a piece of property, its own distinctive—proper—design.

These early armorial examples also show that the family insignia, like its land, was, from about 1150 on, transmitted lineally; and in this it constituted an integral part of the primogenital *patrimoine*. First used for military purposes, in tournaments and battles, and first connected only loosely to individuals, certain banners and pennants came to belong exclusively to certain families and to represent, as Duby notes, "a memory of common agnatic origin."[34] The inherited heraldic sign was an important expression of the continuity of lineage—of its origin in property, attachment to a distinct locus, and to a logos that was the sign of place. And if, as we have seen, rhetoric is the science of *topoi*, or of proper places from which to speak, heraldry constituted the rhetoric of aristocratic possession—a differential system of signs guaranteeing the propriety (discreteness) of the family in relation to similar groups, in relation to its land, and even in relation to its separate subbranches.

The diachronic heraldic progression by agnation within the context of a more synchronic pattern of difference among identically constituted lineages was doubled by a system of armorial signs internal to the family and indicative of its most basic inner relations. Thus, only the primogenital heir had the right to the "whole coat," the undifferenced "full" arms, which were, in turn, inherited in toto by his eldest son. The insignias of younger brothers and their (cadet) lines were "differed" by a change in color, a variation in the number of charges, a bend over the shield, a border, etc. The difference customarily reserved for illegitimate sons was a "baston," a stripe whose homonymy with the civil status of its bearer could not have escaped the eye of even the least playful heraldist. Then too, once the use of armorial signs had generalized beyond its original military function, the case of women's bearings became especially intricate. Sometimes an heiress, for example, bore the undifferenced shield of her father. A married woman often adopted a parted or "impaled" double shield to express both her consanguineal origin and her marital affiliation. And, in some exaggerated instances, a woman who had been married more than once might display, as in the late English example of Beatrice Stafford (1404), a shield charged with her ancestral arms between those of both her husbands. Finally, the practice of marshaling by quarters, increasingly popular from the time of Edward I on, reflected in the separate quadrants of the shield a complete pedigree. Isabel of France, wife of Edward II, took as her seal a shield in whose four quarters were placed the arms of England, France, Navarre, and Champagne. The history of the family, which remains inseparable from the history of its feudal holdings, is in this way inscribed in the logos that was a kind of map—a grammar—both of lineage and of land.[35]

Patronymics

The aristocratic family's constitution of itself through certain representational practices goes hand in hand with a grouping around a family name, a *cognomen*. In the era preceding the formation of the great feudal lineages, there were no formal patronyms. The usual single baptismal or Christian name did not function as a designator of the kin group; and although Carolingian onomastics, for example, showed dynastic and tribal preferences for certain names, these were, even at the upper levels of society, only loosely hereditary.[36] Nor do historians of this "middle period" of the Middle Ages detect a marked preference for the privileged names of the paternal over the maternal line; the single name seems to have been taken indiscriminately from the most prestigious side.[37]

The process of patronymic doubling, like that of the formation of lineages itself, occurred at different times according to region and social status—earlier in the South than in Picardy, and earlier among high aristocrats than among the squireen. Most of all, however, it occurred in different ways according to what can only be characterized as the discrete social spaces of city and countryside, which, in the French case, corresponds maximally to class. And whereas in urban areas family names were often derived from town or country of origin, profession, or nickname, the aristocratic *surnom* represented an unmistakable marker of genealogical and territorial attachment. As early as in the last decade of the tenth century, certain southern charters contain patronyms (e.g., Rainaldus filius Novilongi [979], Isanarus filius Rangardae [989]); and the practice will in the succeeding century generalize throughout the Midi, spreading also to the North. Often too, and again first in the region of Roman occupation, filiation is expressed by suppression of the *filius* in the formation *ille filius illius* and by the adoption of the genitive of paternity (e.g., Ingelbertus Pitacis, Guillelmus Hibrini, Hugo Bardulfi).[38]

Alongside of the patronymic (or matronymic) *cognomen* indicating genealogical filiation stood the toponymic *cognomen* which served to fuse metonymically the family name with its hereditary property rights.[39]

Much of the research in this particular area of onomastics pertains to the region of Allemania. The group around K. Schmid, in particular, has convincingly shown the degree to which "Staufen" and other aristocratic names derive from what Schmid calls the "house seat" (*Stammsitz*).[40] Within the French setting there is also much evidence to indicate that adoption of a family name identical to the name of the paternal castle or fief was prevalent among the chatelains of the South as early as the last decade of the tenth century and that the practice spread throughout the Norman nobility in the eleventh. Duby maintains that in twelfth-century Mâcon 90 percent of noble family names were identical to that of the castle. R. Fossier makes a similar claim for Picardy, showing how between 1050 and 1110 those with the power of the ban, which was practically synonymous with possession of a castle, took surnames.[41] These oscillated between the names of fiefs and of alods but were fixed sometime between 1125 and 1175, by which time even simple knights bore patronyms, titles attached directly to a baptismal name without any necessary link to the function of the chatelain.

What is to be retained from such a cursory glance at onomastic trends of the High Middle Ages? Above all, that the noble family name passed from a title of possession and dominance, the name of a geographically rooted place and a fixed locus of power, to a designator of lineage which, along with the castle, land, and heraldic sign, formed part of the noble *patrimoine*. In this passage from topology to genealogy the aristocratic *cognomen* came to constitute a central symbol of the unity of lineage, an indicator of race, and a mnemonic key to genealogical consciousness.

Genealogical Narrative

If the noble *cognomen* produced heightened awareness of the family as an eponymically unified group, the integral transmission of patronym and title contributed to its articulation as a transtemporal continuum—a linear series of homonymic figures at whose source the name of the father (*pater*) fuses with that of the land (*patria, proprietas*). Nor is it possible to separate the eruption of the family *into* history from the early accounts of titular progression, the genealogical records of a succession of names which form its early history. I am referring to the numerous genealogies edited at the time great lineages came to power and stemming no doubt from a general effort to preserve the memory of ancestors also expressed in the organization of ancestral burial grounds and renewed interest in epitaphs. The family chronicles which began to appear as early as the tenth century were first written by domestic clerics in the high princely courts or private monasteries of northern and western France. But like the heraldic sign and the *cognomen*, they too gradually permeated all echelons of aristocracy as the twelfth century drew to a close. Included among these early family histories are: a tenth-century genealogy of the Count of Flanders, Arnoul le Grand, composed by Vuitgerius between 951 and 959; a notice concerning the ascendance of Arnoul le Jeune edited in the monastery of Saint-Pierre-au-Mont-Bertin, a genealogy of the counts of Vendome, one of the counts of Boulogne, and six of the counts of Anjou, all produced between the mid-eleventh century and 1109; two new genealogies (first third of the twelfth century) of the counts of Flanders, one composed at Saint Bertin and the other inserted by Lambert de Saint Omer in the *Liber Floridus*, along with the earliest-preserved *Geste* of the counts of Anjou attributed to Thomas of Loches; a revision (ca. 1160) of the Flemish and Angevine genealogies (e.g., *Flandria generosa*), a reworking of the *Gesta consulum andegavorum*, two new ancestral sketches composed at Saint Aubin d'Angers, and, in this flowering period of genealogical production, texts dedicated to the sires d'Amboise, the counts of Angoulême and of Nevers, these in addition to numerous local histories whose authors are increasingly attentive to family questions.[42] Finally, two texts from the end of the twelfth century are exemplary in their genealogical focus—Lambert de Wattrelos's *Genealogia antecessorum parentum meorum* and Lambert d'Ardres's *Historia comitum Ghisnensium* (History of the Counts of Guines).

What these early chronicles show is that when aristocratic families began to write their own history, they did so, first of all, in terms of a heroic foundation in a mythic past. The invention of ancestral heroes increased the prestige of the lineage and was the sine qua non of genealogical consciousness which took the shape of "a tree rooted in the person of the founding ancestor."[43] Moreover, there is a tendency in these in-house fabrications of houses not only to push back the moment of origin as far as possible (sometimes through successive revisions) but to equate social status with antiquity. As Duby observes, the genealogical memory of small aristocrats does not go back beyond the mid-eleventh century, that of chatelains reaches as far as the first third of the eleventh, and that of counts extends in some instances all the way to the Carolingian period.[44]

The second notable characteristic of these private family histories is that of attachment to land and castle, a rooting of the family tree in its own soil. In fact, this aspect of family fiction is related to the myth of foundation since the progenitor of the line is often also the captor of the land and the builder of the castle. In any case, both serve as structuring principles of genealogical memory, which crystallizes concretely around family real estate. "The origin of the lineage coincides exactly with the institution of autonomous power around a fortress with the titles and rights incumbent upon owning a castle."[45]

Finally, aristocracy's representation of itself confirms what we have already deduced from other sources concerning the importance of the family *cognomen*, which is also the name of the land and castle, and concerning the biopolitics of lineage. For here the noble family is depicted as a linear progression along a vertical axis. The early family chronicles organize the kin group, and are themselves organized, according to a pattern of primogenital inheritance and according to the straightforward narrative presentation of a series of successions.[46] The image that emerges from these private histories is of a family which, geographically implanted, begins to temporalize itself in terms of a lineal descent from the founding ancestor—the original possessor of land, castle, and name— toward the present holder of all three.

What the family chronicle tells us about lineage is elaborated within the more "literary" genealogical works from the same period, or a little later. In these the invention of ancestors takes the guise of pseudohistorical fantasy, and fanciful genealogies doubly defy the imagination. Nonetheless, the implicit discursive strategy remains the same: to establish the most ancient ancestry possible and to create the most coherent continuity between this mythic beginning and the present. As early as Nennius's compilation grouped under the heading of the *Historia Brittonum* (seventh to mid-ninth century), it is possible to detect a turning away from universal ecclesiastical history and a tendency to situate the origin of Britain within the secular context of the Graeco-Roman as well as the Judaic past. The *Historia Brittonum* is filled with genealogies—of the Britons, Saxons, and Welsh. Manuscript MN2 even contains a section entitled "De origine Brittonum de Romanis et Grecis trahunt ethimologiam" (Concerning the origin of the Britons, who derive their origin from the Romans and Greeks).[47] This chapter traces the lineage of Brutus, one of the founders of Rome and the conqueror of Britain, to Trous, the builder of Troy. Geoffrey of Monmouth presents, in the *Historia regum Britanniae*, an even more secular vision of history than that of the *Historia Brittonum*, dispensing entirely with Nennius's Biblical trappings in favor of Trojan origins. In fact, Geoffrey's account of Brutus's arrival in Albion (Britain) offers as fine an illustration as can be found of the eponymic fusion of names, land, and language:

> Agros colere incipiunt, domos aedificare, *ita ut brevi tempore terram ab aevo habitatam censeres. Denique Brutus de nomine suo insulam Britanniam, sociosque suos Britones appellat*; volebat enim ex derivatione nominis memoriam habere perpetuam. Unde postmodum loquela gentis, quae prius Trojana sive curvum Graecum nuncupabatur, Britannica dicta est.[48]

> They began to till the fields, and to build houses in such a way that after a brief time you might have thought it inhabited from the beginning. Then,

at last Brutus called the island Britain, and his companions Britons, after his own name, for he was insistent that his memory should be preserved in the derivation of the name. Whence afterward the country speech, which had been called Trojan or crooked Greek, was called British.

The *Historia regum Britanniae* can only be understood within a nationalist context, since there is little doubt that it was intended to serve the ideological interests of the Angevine monarchy as against the kings of France. And yet, even here, what remains most important, especially in a passage like that above, lies beyond the specifics of a struggle between opposing dynastic houses. It resides in the region of a deep, though historically determined, mental structure that assumed power to be legitimated through recourse to origins.

This originary principle is equally evident in Wace's translation of Geoffrey (*Le Roman de Brut*) and in his *Roman de Rou*, the first part of which contains a chronologically reversed genealogy from Henry II, through William the Conqueror, all the way back to William Long Sword, the son of Rou (Rollo) and the heroic originator of the lineage:

> Guillaume fu fiz Rou, au bon conquereour
> au vassal, au hardi, au bon combateour
> qui fist mainte bataille et souffri maint estour;
> de lignage le claimment le chief et la flour.[49]

> William was the son of Rollo, the great conqueror
> the brave, hardy, and great warrior
> who fought many a battle and settled many a score;
> and whom they claim as head of the lineage and its flower.

The rest of the *Roman de Rou* is a chronological telling of a tale of successions, as the order of lineage determines the order of the text.

The *Chronique des ducs de Normandie* is, in many ways, the most striking twelfth-century example of literary chronicle—all the more so since Benoît de Sainte Maure explicitly recognizes the role of Isidore's etymologies in the generation of his own story:

> Qui cuidera que bien ne die
> Si lise en l'etimologie
> Que fait Ysidorus, li proz,
> Qui plus en parla bel sor toz.[50]

> He who believes I am telling lies
> Can read it in the etymologies
> Of Isidore, the wise,
> Who told the truth about all.

Following the model of universal history, Benoît traces the lineage of mankind from Creation to the early Germanic ancestors of the Normans; he even links the etymology of "Germania" to the act of generation:

De ce nos dit Isidorus
—Qu'autor n'en fait a creire plus—
Que por si fait engendrement
Est dit Jermaine dreitement,
Et d'enjendrer Jermaine est dite,
Eisi mo dit la letre escrite.[51]

This is what Isidore tells us
—And no author is more worthy of trust—
That for such copious generation
Was named the Germanic nation,
And from engendering was Germania proclaimed,
As the written letter does maintain.

What remains most significant, however, is not so much Isidore's status as the guarantor of truth but that this truth, like the mythic ancestors of the private chronicle, is itself invented. In the *Etymologiae* the name "Germania" is derived from "the immoderate body size and frigid climate of this people" (*Etym.*, 9:ii, iiic). Isidore has, in other words, come to play for Benoît that founding role which the seventh-century bishop had reserved for sacred scripture and for Adam himself. The authority of a false etymology is assured merely by reference to a prior text (*la letre escrit*), as philological accuracy cedes to a literary strategy of origins.

Grammar and Lineage

Benoît's association of the etymology of racial names and the genealogy of the dukes of Normandy, like Nennius's and Geoffrey's conflation of the origin (*ethimologia*) of the Britons and their tongue, points in the direction that we have been moving all along: and that is, stated simply, that early medieval grammar and lineage are, despite the chronological hiatus which separates them, part and parcel of a common representational model and of a similar set of representational practices, which can be characterized by:

1. *Linearity*. The founding moment of the family, situated in a mythic time beyond memory, is synonymous with attachment to land and castle. The kin group is unified by the property which establishes it both *at* a place and *as* a place within a differential typology of similarly grounded groups. Each family has its proper locus, its own territory, which remains indissociable from its proper name and from its proper place within the social hierarchy. Property is, moreover, transmitted patrilinearly from the original possessor of land, castle, and name to their present bearer. Thus a linear contiguity is preserved in the succession of family chiefs— the firstborn of the line—and in the metonymic relation of lineage to the symbols of traditional power. For just as the current heir retains metonymically a part of the essence of his original ancestor, both name and heraldic emblem, integral parts of the noble patrimony, are the synec-

dochic expressions of race and of land. The individual member of the continuous descendance maintains a genetic, organic, and participatory relation both to the property that passes through him and to its sacred signs.

Early medieval grammar is, as its exponents are quick to note and its name implies, the science of the straight—of letters (lines), rectitude (correctness), and literal (true) interpretation. Here again, a founding linguistic moment is posited in *illo tempore*. And whether this primal eponymous event is conceived to have been the result of Adam's divine inspiration or of the acumen of an original *impositor*, it is both determined by and expresses an adequation between words and the physical properties of things. Through it meaning is established, or, as in the phrase of rhetoricians and grammarians, a proper place (*locus*, *topos*) from which to speak is identified. From such places words then evolve lineally—by catastrophe, translation, poetry, and use, through Hebrew, Greek, and Latin—to the present set of terms which is bound metonymically both to meaning and to source. Despite change, the verbal sign still retains a part of the essence of that to which it refers; and, through time, it conserves something of the elements (semblance) of the original word from which it derives.

2. *Temporality*. Consciousness of lineage implies an awareness of the family as a diachronic sequence of relations as opposed to the less temporalized notion of a clan extended in space. Ancestry supersedes affiliation within the noble kin group articulated as a series of successions, a race of heirs with a common past. In fact, antiquity is lineage's chief claim to legitimacy; and the older the genealogy, the more prestigious and powerful that claim becomes.

Similarly, the grammar of the early Middle Ages represents a diachronic system in which the roots of words, their etymology, authorizes meaning. The further back one can trace the history of a particular lexical term, the closer one gets to the primal linguistic elements whose sense borders on the stuff of things. And while internal grammar is characterized by emphasis upon the sources of words (etymology) and the causes of their imposition (definition), external grammar is dominated by a genealogically defined historical linguistics that subtends the dominant model of history itself.

3. *Verticality*. A corollary of the emphasis upon temporal definition is a tendency to stress the autonomy of each lineal strand. Blood ties are more important than affinal relations within a system of kinship which privileges descent—and even the consanguineal bonds between oldest males—while precluding any broader sense of horizontal integration. The verticality of the noble family is especially visible in the range of

customs—*laudatio parentum, maritagium, retrait lignager*—which assure the independence of property within marriage. According to the general rule of *paterna paternis, materna maternis*, the patrimony descended from a common ancestor is programmed to devolve exclusively to those who are genetically related. Property, like blood, flows downward in a straight line.

To the economic autonomy of noble *proprietas* corresponds the lexical independence of the individual term within a semantically oriented grammar centered more upon words and classes than their interrelation. Not only is the study of syntax obscured by an insistence upon etymology, the history of single words, but even within the field of semantics we can detect an insistence upon extrinsic meaning (the relation of a word to its extralinguistic referent) as opposed to contextual definition (the modalized relation of words to other words).

4. *Fixity*. Along with the linearity, temporality, and verticality of lineage is a general sense of fixity both in the family's relation to property and in relation to other families. A dynasty or house is rooted in the soil of its ancestral home; it is grounded by a sacred bond to the land and castle which define it as a cohesive group, provide a source of income, and afford the means of strategic domination. The organic, inalienable quality of the tie to the family *patrimoine* is reflected in the terms "alod," designating both paternity and property, and "immeuble," the immutable *real* estate that constitutes the ancestral holding. Thus fixed once and for all, property rights remain relatively stable despite the introduction through marriage of some "new men." Social relations between various dynastic houses as well as between aristocracy and other levels of society tend to be perceived as inflexible, "grounded," permanent.[52] Within the confines of such a fixed hierarchy, those with access to the sole source of power—*immobile* wealth—govern because their ancestors have always governed. Social movement is reduced to a minimum, and nobility, not mobility, is the defining social rule.

In early medieval grammar the truth of words is assumed to have been fixed once and for all in a primal instance of signification. The proper meaning is both the true and original one, as the status of words—literally their establishment or foundation—is equated with the ontological status—the existence—of things. An original order of language expressed an original order of the world and continues, despite linguistic change, to reflect it. What this means is that language does not so much determine as uncover the earthly reality it transmits. As a tool used primarily in the quest for first meanings, grammar retains a somewhat passive character more suited to the chronological restoration of a lost and ontologically fixed origin than to the creation of meaning through logical deduction.

5. *Continuity*. The lineal family model is predicated upon the principles of partial resemblance, contiguity, and, above all, continuity. Thus the son reproduces the father, accedes to the paternal name, title, heraldic sign, and land. He represents an essential link in a genealogical chain, each part of which shares certain common traits with all others, and which, at least in theory if not in practice, remains unbroken from the first ancestor to the current heir.

Likewise, early medieval grammar functions according to an assumed continuity not only between the original properties of things and of words but between the components of original words and their successive phonetic and morphological stages. Such an assumption lies at the center of etymological thought, for without the survival of some recognizable element through each lexical change it would be impossible to retrace the history of a word. The importance of at least partial identity also accounts for the insistence upon analogy both as a principle of linguistic evolution and as a technique of definition. The attempt to move by resemblance from that which is certain to that which is less certain, and thus to arrive at the proper definition of things and of words, is, in a very real sense, the cornerstone of etymological grammar. A true etymology is the equivalent of a correct definition; and any break in the etymological chain linking a term to its origin threatens to upset the entire process.

6. *Inherence of value*. One consequence of our argument is that within the lineal family social value remains a quality internal to those who have it. Nobility becomes, in the centuries during which lineages were formed, a relatively closed caste. Aristocrats are born, and noble status is, by definition, inherited; it cannot, in principle, be earned or acquired. "To be noble," again, "is to be able to refer to a genealogy"; and to be able to refer to a genealogy is to affirm automatically one's place in the upper echelons of a highly hierarchized social network.

Like the social worth of the aristocrat, semantic value remains, within a system of grammar based upon etymology as well as an exegetical tradition based upon the mysticism of Hebrew names, an inherent quality of the word itself. It is, in fact, the inherence of meaning in its sign that allows etymology to function as an epistemological tool: the word abstracted from its referent represents the primary vehicle and the agent of first recourse in the recuperation of the meaning of the physical world. Even the end product of the search for etymological roots transmits the specifically political sense of domination, since, as Isidore asserts, "the more we know about the source of words, the faster we can understand the 'nature' or 'force' (*vim*) of things" (*Etym.*, 1:xxix, ii).

But what is the relation of genealogy as a means of naturalizing lineage to etymology as a means of naturalizing language? Where can we locate this relation? And what do we call it? Social infrastructure? Global homology? Subconscious crystallization? Collective unconscious? Mental structure?

I am not convinced that we can situate it in the sense of the early medieval *locus*, a place where speech stops. Nor is it possible to identify positively such a conjunction. There is no recognizable point of which we can assert the coincidence of the laws of kinship and of language—no medieval grammarian who has treated consciously the family, no canonist who deals with family matters in explicitly grammatical terms. What seems certain is that the discourse of the family and the discourse governing discourse meet somewhere deep in the zone where language, etched in grammatical reflex, shapes perception, and where ties of kinship, inscribed in something resembling taboo, program the social attitudes that become manifest in institutions. Here the term "manifest" is crucial, for all we possess of such a relation are the external symptoms that point like vectors to a point of convergence where more direct connection becomes elusive. Or, can it be that we have conceptualized only partially the problem of location, looked too directly to linguistics and to family history for answers that are to be found elsewhere? I think a rapid look at another kind of manifestation may serve to clarify our phrasing of the question, and, ultimately, may steer us toward the locus of mediation par excellence, which lies neither in the realm of grammar nor of kinship, but in that of poetry.

The Tree of Jesse

One area in which representation of the family as lineage makes a startling appearance in the late eleventh and twelfth centuries is that of religious art.[53] I am referring to the numerous stained glass and manuscript illustrations of the Tree of Jesse, which was also the subject of sculptural and dramatic treatment. The original reference of all of these is the passage from Isaiah 11:1–3, in which it is prophesied "that there shall come forth a rod (*uirga*) out of the stem of Jesse (*radice Iesse*), and a branch shall grow out of its roots. And the spirit of the Lord shall rest upon him. . . . "[54] From Isaiah's prophecy or signification of what was interpreted to be the Incarnation stems a long exegetical tradition. According to Eusebius, Ambrose, Jerome, and Rabanus Maurus, for example, the lineage of Christ stretches from Jesse through David to Mary. The word "uirga" was even taken to be the equivalent of the Virgin; and some commentators point to the homonymic resemblance of "Jesse" and its diminutive "Jesus" as combined proof of etymological and genealogical connection.

The descendance of Jesse constituted a virtual topos alongside of other genealogical forms of late Antiquity and the early Middle Ages—the Roman *stemma*, Arabic tables of consanguinity, and the canonical *arbor*

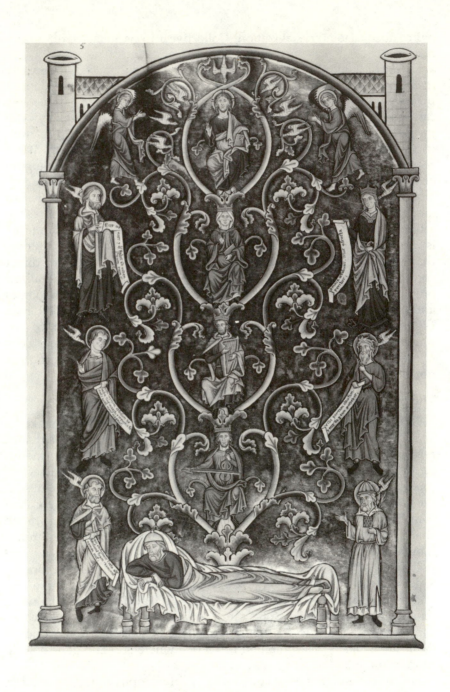

Tree of Jesse from the Ingeborg Psalter.
Ms. 1695 Musée Condé, Chantilly, France. (Printed with permission.)

iuris. But the idealized family trees that began to appear around the time of the organization of France's feudal lineages betray a remarkable change in focus, which is, as A. Watson claims, best understood by reference to a Carolingian text. The ninth-century poem *De Septem Liberalibus Artibus in quadam Pictura depictis* by Theodolph of Orleans portrays a disk out of which grows a tree: "Discus erat tereti formatus imagine mundi, / Arboris unius quem decorabat opus."[55] At the base of the tree stands the figure of Grammar:

> Huius Grammatica ingens in radice sedebat,
> > Gignere eam semet seu retinere monens.
> Omnis ab hac ideo procedere cernitur arbos,
> > Ars quia proferri hac sine nulla ualet.[56]

> Mighty Grammar was sitting at its root,
> > Counseling it to produce and yet to keep her, Grammar, fast.
> Thus every tree is seen to grow from Grammar,
> > Because no art has the strength to arise without her.

The central position of Grammar within an allegory of learning was no doubt inspired by Martianus Capella and again attests to the interpenetration of genealogy and etymology. Yet, Theodolph's originality consists in the modification of the paradigm of the liberal arts into a progression from the most basic toward the highest. As articulated by the motif of the tree, the *De Septem Liberalibus Artibus* (which was intended as a guide for painters) transforms the linguistic and practical disciplines into a graded scale. "It only remained," as A. K. Porter notes, "to substitute Jesse for Grammar, the Kings of Judah and the Virgin for the other arts."[57]

This is exactly what happened in the trees of the High Middle Ages, which include: several doubtful identifications like the Canterbury Candelabrum, the Tree of the University of Prague (Vy šehrad MS xiv), and a twelfth-century copy of Jerome's *Explanatio in Isaiam* (Dijon MS 129); a number of simple trees depicting David and Solomon, for example, that of a Premonstratensian Missal (Bibliothèque nationale MS Lat. 833), that of a mid-twelfth-century *Psalter* in Latin and French from Winchester Cathedral (British Museum MS Nero C. iv), the *Huntingfield Psalter* (Morgan MS 43), and a Bible of Saint Bertin de Saint Omer (Bibliothèque nationale MS Lat. 16746); and, finally, complete illustrations of the descendance of Jesse—through David, Solomon, and other kings—toward Mary and Christ. These full-blown Trees of Jesse, including the famous windows at Saint Denis and Chartres as well as the elaborate ceiling of Saint Michaels, Hildesheim, portray kinship (and kingship) as a complex and complete genealogical series. History is thus inscribed in the Tree of Jesse, which, unlike Theodolph's allegory of the Arts, transforms paternity into a pictorial narrative in which story line and family line coincide. Also, unlike the spatially organized Roman and canonical tables of consanguinity, which are paradigms of possible relation to be used to determine who may marry whom and who may inherit what, the Tree of Jesse stands as the iconographic equivalent of the lineal family and an idealized representation of lineage: it organizes visual space such that the eye is forced to read paternity through time. Based upon a contiguous relation of ancestor to heir, it is, again unlike the *tabula consanguinitatis*, an organic tree ordered vertically from the roots up as a graded continuity of being, a participation of elements within an ascending whole.

Art historians have posed a number of probing questions in relation to the historical status of the Tree of Jesse. At what point, for instance, does a diagram become a tree? Did Suger invent the genre in its final form? Do the series of conjoined figures refer in the first instance to a Biblical succession or to the line of Capetian monarchs? And yet, no art historian to my knowledge has attempted to associate the Tree of Jesse with the contemporaneous articulation of the noble family as lineage; nor has anyone posed the question that led us to it in the first place—namely, the problem of situating the mediatory locus between grammar and the lineal kin group.

Indeed, the *uirga Iesse* raises an issue that responds in part to our original inquiry. For the portrayal of Jesse's line did not, in its fullest expression, originate in the family circles that produced the genealogical chronicle or even the "literary" genealogy. It was not intended explicitly to serve in the invention of ancestors and hence in the legitimation of family power; nor did its Biblical roots encourage those who saw it to experience anything but a temporally distant, mythically removed vision of the family surrounded by the trappings of legend. No particular dynasty, with the possible exception of the kings of France, could identify with the line of Christ. This is because the Tree of Jesse remains, above all, a model, an idealization, that, unlike both the wholly specific private chronicle and the wholly abstract *arbor iuris*, tells a story of paternity with no direct relation to the noble houses of feudal France. It narrates lineage without narrating a definite lineage. Neither paradigm nor event, the *uirga Iesse* retains the ambiguous status of fact cloaked in fiction and of fiction grounded in fact. It is, moreover, precisely this equivocal position between form devoid of content and pure manifestation that speaks to the issue of convergence. What we are suggesting is that early medieval grammar, the formal discourse on discourse, and family structure, a set of formalized precepts governing marriage and inheritance, coincide most intensely in the area of cultural superstructure, of which the Tree of Jesse is but one relatively minor example. This amounts to asserting that the two poles that have dominated our discussion up until now, language theory and paternity, meet neither in the social infrastructure nor in any deep "mentalité," but in the forms of expression ruled by grammar which also served, as we shall see in the following chapter, to articulate the elementary laws of kinship—that is to say, in the poetic forms whose appearance coincided almost exactly with the advent of lineage.

THREE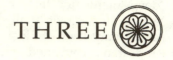

Literature and Lineage

In the preceding chapter we traced what might be described broadly as
the constitution of lineage as a principle of noble family order in eleventh-
and twelfth-century France. This movement away from the horizontally
and spatially defined kin group toward the notion of dynasty or house
was sparked internally by the menacing dispersion of family lands alienated by division and pious donation; and it was catalyzed by geographic
implantation along with the transformation of benefices (fiefs by concession) into hereditary rights. Where the boundaries of kinship are concerned, the clan underwent a process of "narrowing" visible in a relaxa-
tion of the extremely wide impediments to marriage of an earlier age and
in a shift of focus away from affinal and toward consanguineal relations.
The organization of noble family lines was inseparable from a biopolitics
of lineage: a restriction and control of marriages, a husbanding of family
property through such practices as the *laudatio parentum*, the *retrait lignager*, and *indivision*. Then too, lineage was practically synonymous with

specifically aristocratic modes of wealth (the *immeuble*, real estate, *propre*) and of inheritance (primogeniture).

We also saw that such a transformation was furthered by a change in the relation of noble lineages to the signs of nobility. In particular, the family's appropriation of a heraldic emblem, a patronymic name, and a historical discourse by which to articulate its own genealogical past served to mediate the thrust toward lineal arrangement. And alongside the shift in legal, economic, and social institutions there occurred a less visible but equally important shift in the nature of certain key familial symbols as well as in their practice. Such a transformation would not have been so significant, however, were it not for the fact that it also represented, as we saw in Chapter 1, the assimilation of an essentially grammatical model implying an epistemological one as well. Early medieval grammar, based upon the principle of etymology, and lineage, predicated upon that of genealogy, participate in a common representational paradigm characterized by linearity, temporality, verticality, fixity, continuity, and the inherence of semantic and social value. The attempt to locate this rapport remains, however, problematic, since linguistic and paternal models converge neither in the realm of linguistics nor in that of the family. Rather, we hypothesized after a consideration of contemporaneous figurations of the Tree of Jesse that the most promising line of inquiry lies in the area of cultural superstructure; and for that reason, it is to poetry that we now turn.

The Epic

France's earliest epic literature is deeply implicated in the strategy of linguistic and familial origins that we have outlined thus far. In the *chanson de geste* more than anywhere else lineage serves to organize an entire literary mode. Not only are these heroic poems (which Duby thinks may have served as sources of inspiration for family chronicles) filled with catalogues of noble families whose origins are fixed in the Carolingian past, but they are themselves disposed in groups according to the nature of dynastic association:

> A Seint Denis, en la mestre abaïe,
> trovon escrit, de ce ne doute mie,
> dedanz un livre de grant encesorie,
> n'ot que trois gestes en France la garnie.[1]

> At Saint Denis, in the great abbey,
> we find written, in a book of high ancestry,
> of this there can be no doubt or chance,
> that there are only three *gestes* in richest France.

Thus the author of *Girart de Vienne* lays the foundation for classification of the epic into separate cycles by reason of family relation. The term "geste" refers generally to events or deeds, to the family and to the chronicle of family deeds (e.g., the *geste Francor* of the *Chanson de Roland*);[2] and here it designates specifically the three main houses of France as well as the series of legends surrounding each. Nor can the legitimating antiquity of the *livre de grant encesorie*, like Benoît's reliance upon *la letre escrit*, be divorced from the authority conferred by ancestors (see above, pp. 82–83). Family relations are coterminous with literary relations; the songs of the deeds of Charlemagne, Doon de Maience, or Garin de Monglane engender poems about the other members of their lineages, as even Ganelon becomes the focus of a family *geste*:

> Et ausin furent li parant Ganelon,
> qui tant estoient riche et de grant renon,
> se il ne fussent si plain de traïson
> De ce lingnaje, qui ne fist se mal non,
>   fu la seconde geste.[3]

> And thus were the relatives of Ganelon,
> who were so rich and of great renown,
> if they had not been so full of treason.
> Of this lineage which only had evil done,
>   was the second *geste*.

Lineage and *geste* are synonymous, as the epic cycle constitutes itself according to a pattern of affiliation between families of heroes and families of poems.

The close connection of genealogy and poetic groupings can partially be explained by the technique of elaboration of the *chansons de geste*, which were, like the private chronicle, composed in keeping with a reverse chronology pointed always toward the origin of the family line. This is another way of saying that the thematic sequence that links the various separate texts of what seems often like a simple enormous cyclical poem is the opposite of the sequence of composition of its interrelated parts. The earlier a character or event can be situated chronologically within the global cycle, the later, generally speaking, the date of its addition to the whole. This is true even of the more biographically organized *gestes* such as the Cycle of Charlemagne or of the King. The *Chanson de Roland*, a saga of old age, can be dated approximately a century and three-quarters before Adenet le Roi's *Berte aus grans piés* (ca. 1275), which contains the story of the emperor's youth and parents; two other poems which form a kind of minicycle of the "Enfances Charlemagne"— the *Chanson de Mainet* and the *Chanson de Basin* (only known in a Scandinavian version)—also belong to this later period. The composition of the stories about the emperor's mature exploits as narrated in the *Pèlerinage de Charlemagne* and *Aspremont* fall chronologically in between those of the deeds of his youth and old age.

The Cycle of Garin de Monglane or of William offers, in many respects, the most complete assimilation of genealogy and intertextuality. Here, however, the question of cyclical extension is complicated by the simultaneous development of direct and lateral familial and textual branches. The earliest work in the direct group is the *Chanson de Guillaume*, which is roughly contemporaneous with the *Roland*. From *Guillaume* the order of composition stretches back to poems about William's parents, grandfather, and great-grandfather, Garin, the founding ancestor and originator of the line. Where William's affines are concerned, the order of textual elaboration follows a natural chronology: *La Chanson de Renier*, which narrates the deeds of the grandson of William's brother-in-law (Rainouart), was composed at about the same time as the poems attached to Garin.

Altogether the Cycle of William comprehends seven generations, including both consanguineal and affinal relations; and the lineage whose history it recounts remains indissociable from a series of literary successions. Thus, *Garin de Monglane* and the *Enfances Garin* deal with the early history of the family, Garin's father and mother, as well as the capture of the fief of Monglane. The next poem in the generational sequence, *Girart de Vienne*, tells of the exploits of Garin's four sons who leave the paternal castle in search of their own lands, and, in particular, of the war of Garin's lineage against that of Charlemagne. A third epic, *Aymeri de Narbonne*, narrates the capture of Narbonne by Garin's grandson, his marriage, and battles against Saracen invaders. Two other texts in the group attached to Aymeri are particularly significant: the dramatic interest of *Les Narbonnais* is generated by the father's privileging of one heir (in this case the youngest) and the struggle of the disinherited sons to obtain their own holdings; *La Mort Aymeri de Narbonne* depicts the hero's final exploits and death.

As we move to the texts associated with the fourth generation of Garin's lineage, the field thickens. Two works each portray the deeds of Aymeri's sons Beuve (*Le Siege de Barbastre, Beuvon de Commarchis*) and Guibert (*Guibert d'Andresnas, La Prise de Cordres et de Sebille*). No less than six epics recount the life of their brother William (*Les Enfances Guillaume, Le Couronnement Louis, Le Charroi de Nîmes, La Prise d'Orange, La Chanson de Guillaume, Le Moniage Guillaume*). There are, in addition, three works attached collaterally to William's nephew Vivien (*Les Enfances Vivien, La Chevalerie Vivien, Aliscans*); these in addition to the poems based upon the life of his affinal kin (*La Bataille Loquifer, Le Moniage Rainouart, La Chanson de Renier*). The Cycle of Garin de Monglane thus appears, from the perspective of the literary historian, as an enormous reverse genealogy in which, to quote J. Frappier, "sons have engendered fathers."[4] On the level of theme, and certain manuscript collections specify the thematic rapport between texts, the reconstructed narrative gives the impression of a continuous series of intertextual relations determined by an unbroken genealogical chain.[5]

The antiheroic traitors of the *geste* of Doon de Maience belonged, according to the author of *Girart de Vienne*, to the "family of Ganelon." And though such a claim is not justified by a pattern of textual interrelation as comprehensive as that of the Cycle of William, it is nonetheless indicative of the degree to which action, within this more loosely linked body of poems, is a function of familial affiliation. Here, as elsewhere, lineage functions as a principle of internal organization. The hero's situation, along with the limits of his freedom, are determined by duty to clan; even character seems to be inherited. The numerous wars chronicled in the Cycle of the Rebellious Barons are fought strictly along family lines, sometimes across several generations. In *Raoul de Cambrai*, for example, an initial quarrel over the heritability of fiefs devolving to a minor erupts into a full-scale conflict between Raoul's lineage and the sons of Herbert de Vermandois.[6] Despite numerous truces, an expiatory pilgrimage, and even marriage between the two kin groups, the great-grandsons of Herbert continue to battle their own maternal grandfather, Raoul's uncle Guerri. In *Renaut de Montauban* the sons of Aymon de Dordogne are pitted against the forces of Charlemagne as Aymon himself, like Bernier of *Raoul de Cambrai*, is obliged to choose between loyalty to lord and to family. Other works of this series present less elaborate portrayals of kinship, but the law of affiliation remains the same. *La Chevalerie Ogier* depicts an extended series of encounters between Charlemagne and Ogier over the death of the latter's son; *Girart de Roussillon* narrates the wars between Charles Martel and the hero whose *geste* (family and poem) bears his name.[7]

What is to be learned from such a long litany of *chansons de geste*? Not simply that a model of the family as lineage determines a textual genealogy. Nor that lineage is an important thematic component of epic poetry. These are already commonplaces of medieval literary studies. What has been less explored—or ill-defined—is the relation which our discussion of language theory, family, and poetic cycle suggests between genealogical succession and narrative structure. For if the disposition of epic families of poems functions according to the paradigm of human generation, it is because the epic is, at bottom, a genre which breeds according to the nature of narrative itself. Rather, the Old French *chanson de geste* conforms, in its broad macrostructure, to what was considered throughout the Middle Ages to constitute a historical or natural order of events; and such an order, as we shall see, remains indistinguishable from that of lineage.

Classical rhetoricians distinguished generally between a natural exposition (*ordo naturalis*) in which an argument follows the prescribed
order of presentation (*exordium, narratio, partes argumentationis, peroratio*),
and an artificial one (*ordo artificialis*) in which the traditional arrangement
is altered to suit a particular purpose. This distinction focused, in turn,
exclusively upon the *narratio* or statement of facts. Cicero, for example,
defines the narrative as "an exposition of events that have occurred or
that are supposed to have occurred"; and he further discriminates between its three types—*fabula, argumentum,* and *historia,* the last of which is
characterized as "gesta res, ab aetatis nostrae memoria remota."[8] Quintilian distinguishes between "fictitious narrative . . . which is not merely
not true but which has little resemblance to the truth," "realistic narrative
. . . which has a certain verisimilitude," and "historical narrative, which
is an exposition of actual fact" ("historiam, in qua est gestae rei
expositio").[9] Priscian too separates *narratio fictilis,* "the stuff of tragedies
or comedies," and *narratio historica,* "which pertains to events" ("ad res
gestas exponendas").[10] But it was really with the Carolingian grammarian
Alcuin that the conformity of presentation to what is perceived as a
natural historical order, and not the order of rhetorical argument or the
verisimilitude of discourse, determines the status of narrative: "Omnis
ordo naturalis aut artificilis est. Naturalis ordo est si quis narret rem
ordine quo gesta est."[11] A natural narrative order is, then, one that
corresponds to the "order of events."

Alcuin's distinction was adopted by rhetoricians and even philosophers of the High Middle Ages. Conrad of Hirschau (1070–1150) claims
that, "naturalem noveris ordinem cum liber juxta gestae rei seriem
incipitur."[12] In the tradition of Virgil's medieval commentators, he also
cites as an example of artificial order the placement of the fall of Troy in
the second book of the *Aeneid* instead of at the beginning where it belongs
according to the natural course of historical events. Hugh of Saint-Victor
maintains that:

> Ordo . . . attenditur . . . in narratione secundum dispositionem, quae du-
> plex est: naturalis, scilicet quando res eo refertur ordine quo gesta est, et
> artificialis, id est quando in quod postea gestum est prius narratur, et quod
> prius postmodum dicitur. . . . [13]

> Order . . . is determined . . . in narration according to disposition, which is
> double: natural, that is to say when an affair is presented in the order in
> which it happened, and artificial, that is, when a subsequent event is nar-
> rated first, and a previous event is narrated after . . . .

The thirteenth-century rhetorician Geoffrey of Vinsauf concurs. The
order of presentation, he claims, is a "double path": sometimes artificial,
othertimes "it follows the way of nature" ("Tum sequitur stratam na-

turae"). In this case "an extended line serves as guide, since the thing and words follow the same course" ("Linea stratae est ibi dux, ubi res et verba sequuntur eumdem cursum"); "nor does language veer from the order of things" ("nec sermo declinat ab ordine rerum").[14]

This extraordinary conjunction of nature, narrative, linearity, and history is significant for our understanding of the discourse of the epic. Not only does the *chanson de geste* stand as the presentation of historical events, but the sequence of such a presentation follows a natural—that is, chronologically consecutive—order. In its overall design the epic pursues Geoffrey's "path of nature" and is the literary equivalent of a straight line along which "things and words follow the same course." As a genre of origins always situated in historical time, the Old French heroic poem thus assumes, as a condition of its own possibility, a discursive progression in which the literary text and history function side by side; and, further, in which both are implicated in the discourse of the noble family. *Narratio (ordo) naturalis*, the natural sequence of events (*gestae rei*), and the order of familial succession converge in the *chanson de geste*, which is the poetic form of family history. Like the Tree of Jesse, however, the epic only vaguely narrates the genealogy of any historically identifiable clan; rather, it provides a global model of the type of kinship we associate with dynastic order. And if the linearity of its own poetic process rests on a chronological connection of supposedly factual events that remains inseparable from the sequential linking of ancestors, it is because the epic stands both as the poetic transposition of a straight line and the literary equivalent of lineage.

Here we touch upon another rich and revealing semantic nexus alongside the term "geste." In fact, to the extent to which *geste*—family, deeds, and the story of family deeds—came to mean the straightforward narrative presentation of events, it also tended to fuse with the word "estoire," which, as Zumthor points out, represented a generic marker of diverse narrative types, including those later classified under the separate headings of history and fiction.[15] There was, for example, no distinction until the fourteenth century between "estoire" and "roman." But, more important, this last term also enjoyed the resonance—and indeed was employed as a synonym—of "lineage." *Geste* refers to deeds, the natural order of their presentation, family and the family of heroic poems, while its analogue *estoire* captures much of the same semantic field. When, for instance, Wace seeks to "recount and record the *geste* of Rou" ("La geste voil de Rou et des Normanz cunter / Lur faiz et lur proesce dei iço bien recorder"), he conflates the reference to Rollo's ancestors, their story, and his own narrative. Nor does the Anglo-Norman poet distinguish between *geste* and *estoire*: "Longue est la geste des Normanz . . . / Se l'on demande qui ço dist, / Qui ceste estoire en romanz mist."[16] Ancestry, deeds, history, and narrative are allied as Wace makes clear from the very beginning of the *Roman de Rou*. Such an association is even the defining goal of poetic performance:

> Por remembrer des *ancesurs*
> les *feiz* e les diz e les mors . . .
> deit l'um les livres e les *gestes*
> e les *estoires* lire a festes.[17]

> To remember our *ancestors* of days gone by
> One must read at holiday time
> What the book and the *geste* and the *history* say
> About their *deeds* and their sayings and their ways.

Wace's investment of the synonyms *geste* and *estoire* with the double meaning of *narratio* and family is hardly unique. The Turin manuscript of *Richard li biaus* ("Dist la dame: je ne puis croire / Que chilz ne soit de haute estoire"), *Aye d'Avignon* ("Ganor li Arrabi fu de moult grant estoire"), *Les Loherains* ("Doz li venerez fu molt de bone estoire"), and the *Life of Saint Margaret* ("D'aveir sor icels la victoire / qui sont de la dïable estoire") all underscore—and this is essential—the imbrication of history, narrative, and lineage.[18] Just as the epic cycle seems to breed—to proliferate—genealogically, even primogenitally, the individual *chanson de geste* is generated according to a discursive pattern in which dynastic and textual order are combined.

And yet, there is still another and even more compelling sense in which the associative proximity—even the identity—of a lineal definition of family and epic discourse is manifest. It can be found in the final resonance of the term *geste*, which also refers to "action," "deed," or "event," and whose tenor of "factuality" functions, again, to link kinship to grammatical theory and to the manifestation of theory in poetic practice. What I am suggesting is that France's earliest heroic poetry can be situated precisely at the point of convergence between a model of the noble family, whose legitimacy is rooted in the soil and is perceived to be part of an immutable social order, and a model of representation implicit to early medieval grammar and according to which language is assumed to be grounded in an original order of things. Here lies the crux of the matter: the *chanson de geste* is a genre which, despite the exaggeration that is its hallmark, maintains at least the illusion of its own powers of reference. The epic pretends to reproduce in language something outside of language that is taken, in keeping with the Classical definition of historical narrative, for an "exposition of actual fact" ("in qua est gestae rei expositio" [Quintilian]). As in the medieval "science of the straight," where verbal signs lead through etymological (and genealogical) ascent toward a primal moment of meaning to the essence of things, the "genre of the straight" both presents events in their natural (chronological) order and maintains always an assumed continuity between words and their referent—or between language and the possibility of representation. It is, in fact, this epistemological integrity that simultaneously legitimates a strategy of origins and permits narration. For not only is the epic filled with relics, but its characteristic discourse functions according to a "reliquary" presence of things in signs that works to join genealogy to overall narrative design.

Recent studies of the technique of epic composition tend to substantiate the implicit thrust toward congruity of the poetic sign and its meaning. M. Parry, J. Rychner, A. Lord, S. Nichols, and J. Duggan have demonstrated with considerable rigor the extent to which the Old French *chanson de geste* consists of a discrete set of narrative formulas, the formula here defined as "a group of words which is regularly employed under the same metrical conditions to express a given, essential idea."[19] A. Parry and E. Vance, inspired possibly by E. Auerbach's essay on *Roland*, have used the work of their predecessors (though J. Duggan's book is chronologically later) to explore the very special world view which such a mode of elaboration implies.[20] What they show is that texts constructed out of a limited number of linguistic formulas are based upon the assumptions that language is an epistemologically adequate vehicle, that a finite set of word groups is sufficient to describe reality as all men commonly perceive it, and that words, in fact, are linked in some rigid—even participatory— way to that which they represent. The early *chanson de geste* in particular implies a great communality of experience and social interest subtended by the pervading presence of an essentially uncontested linguistic field. Even one-word formulas like the Christian and pagan battle cries (e.g., "Muntjoie" and "Precieuse") affirm not only the unity of the group but the integrity of all linguistic expression. In a poem like the *Chanson de Roland*, as in Homer, there is little effort to look beyond appearances, to explore the gap between illusion and reality, to quibble about the meaning of words, much less about the limits of language as a referential system. On the contrary, the *chanson de geste* pretends to reproduce the subsistent world beyond the text and to reproduce it accurately. Within this universe of the collective and the integral, words are assumed to mean what they say and the world to be as it seems.

This referential integrity also accounts for the fragmented quality of a poem like the *Chanson de Roland*. For not only is *Roland* divided into autonomous units of narration, or strophes, but, as Auerbach observes, an "assonant strophic pattern gives every line the appearance of an independent unit, . . . as though sticks or spears of equal length and with similar points were bundled together."[21] Within the individual line we also find a notable independence of formulaic units joined, as Auerbach insists, primarily by the conjunction *et*. One consequence of such a "paratactic" style is, as J. Rychner has shown and as I have also maintained elsewhere, the low expressivity of logical causality at the level of syntax.[22] In a poem like *Roland*, juxtaposition functions in the absence of subordination to preserve the autonomy of the basic narrative units that are only weakly conjoined. When added to the considerable mass of utterances, which, like war cries, have no syntactic context, or whose context is, like the catalogues of proper names, battle ranks, or insults, severely attenuated, the overall effect is one of extreme discreteness, even atomism. What this means is that the representational universe of *Roland* is one in which the independent relation of autonomous elements to their external referents is stressed above the interrelation of conjoined parts. Again like the lexically defined grammar of the early Middle Ages, the importance of signification—meaning determined by the fixed relation between words or stock phrases and their extralinguistic attribute—overshadows the contextually defined production of meaning through the surface play of self-signifying terms. For the *Roland* poet, mannerism is not an operative principle. Ambiguity, where present, appears unintentional, ascribable to the conditions of oral performance, scribal error, or manuscript corruption. The only exception occurs at the very end of the poem where the issue of multiple meaning—whether the word "vengeance" or "treason" is proper to describe Ganelon's misdeed—is debated in the course of trial.[23] And here, the poet's solution seems to be the collective expulsion of those who contest the power of words to signify univocally that which—beyond language—is experienced as a single event. Even metaphor within this "vertically" pitched world of isolated presences is reduced to the barest minimum. There are only two in its entire 4,002 verses. The epic is, then, more than merely a genre of origins, a historical narrative of "events (*gesta res*) removed from our time" (Cicero). It is the literary form of the proper—of individual ("special" in the etymological sense of pertaining only to one) and appropriate relation between things and their signs.

This is not to suggest that the improper use of linguistic signs is not an important characteristic of the Old French *chanson de geste*. On the contrary, verbal impropriety abounds and seems often to spark dramatic interest. Sacrilegious oaths (e.g., Isembart's apostasy), exaggeration (e.g., Aalais's curse of Raoul), blasphemy (e.g., Raoul's boast that even God could not save him), broken promises (e.g., Charles Martel's grant of an *alod* to Girart de Roussillon), impossible situations (e.g., Louis's bestowal of the Vermandois fief upon Raoul, the expiatory ordeal which Charlemagne imposes upon Huon de Bordeaux), lies (e.g., Ganelon's report of the Algalife's departure, his false interpretation of Roland's horn), and jokes (e.g., the *gabs* of the *Pèlerinage*) all serve as catalysts to thematic development. The "straight" narratives generated by such dislocations of the proper constitute, in fact, potent dramas of language. Yet despite the detachment of words from meaning through blasphemy, boasts, lies, and jokes, the inherent contradiction of representing such linguistic transgression is never really explored. Impropriety is expressed at the level of theme, but it is not experienced as a crisis of representation itself. And though the epic poet may periodically assert his superiority to other composers or jongleurs, he does not question the premises or the limits either of narration or of reference. Where language seems to break down we find instead a strong desire for recuperation, a certain quantitative stretching of prescribed poetic bounds, and an uneasiness about the future which can, as we shall see, be understood in specifically linguistic terms.

Recounted from the unassailable, supposedly objective perspective of a detached third party, the implicit discursive mode of the epic is one of linguistic integrity. That failing (and again such failures are only manifest upon the level of theme) the dominant strategy is essentially recuperative—an attempt to recover that which has been lost, or to translate improper words into proper deeds and thus to restore their propriety (e.g., Isembart's punishment, Girart's and Raoul's struggles to regain their lands, Charlemagne's vengeance, his voyage to the Middle East, Huon's exaggerated quest). In this respect, the epic stands midway between the genealogical chronicle, where such varied possibilities of disjunction are not explored at all, and the romance, where they become a defining principle. Transgression of the proper is, within the assumed universe of epic discourse, an abundant source of dramatic tension; but it does not produce—as in both the novel and the lyric—true dialectical structure.

In the absence of formal transgression—a transcendence of limits generative of form, we do find a tendency toward the quantitative stretching of poetic boundaries, which, again, is best understood by comparison with the family chronicle or "literary" genealogy. In the genealogical history, family and story line coincide to such a degree that the uninterrupted sequence of ancestors compels the uninterrupted transcription of the tale.[24] K. Schmid even suggests that the essential formula of paternal succession (e.g., "Fredericus genuit Fredericum de Buren, Fredericus de Buren genuit ducem Fredericum, qui Stophen condidit") prescribes through its progressive nature a consciousness both of race and of historical process.[25] Then too, there is in the chronicles discussed by Duby a definite sense that an order of consanguineal relations—a primogenital series—determines the order of narrative sequence, which is another way of saying that a linear and continuous model of inheritance serves to define a linear textual mode. In the epic, however, the straight narrative economy that is equivalent to, and even synonymous with, lineage is problematized; and this primarily through repetition. The repetition of geographic and climatic formulas, catalogues of families, arms and armies, rhetorical questions, and even whole laisses serves to slow the pace of narration and thus to threaten the progression both of the text and of lineal family. Yet, such a quantitative fetishizing of language is never completely disruptive of poetic sequence, genealogy, or, ultimately, of representation. Here the central issue is really that of continuity: narrative continuity that, despite repetition, still preserves what is conceived to be the natural order of events; and representational continuity that, despite the thematization of rupture, fails to transform the problem of referentiality into form.

The most tangible sign of an underlying tension in the narratively sequential and representationally integral universe of the epic is to be found in a certain closure to its own posterity. Indeed, so wholly fixated upon the past is the Old French *chanson de geste* as to produce a blindness to (repression of?) any possibility of the future. The hint of such an exclusion is present from the very beginning. It is significant, for example, that the incident in the *Chanson de Roland* which most threatens to interrupt the narrative—that is to say, Roland's initial refusal to blow his horn and thus to engender the second half of the poem—is also the moment that precludes any future for his lineage: "Par ceste meie barbe, / Se puis veeir ma gente sorur Alde, / Ne jerreiez ja mais entra sa brace!" says Olivier to his ex-future-brother-in-law.[26] And it is a meditation upon Roland's only legacy, his sword, that serves to articulate explicitly the problem of succession:

> Rollant ferit en une perre bise
> Plus en abat que jo ne vos sai dire.
> L'espee cruist, ne fruiset ne se brise,
> Cuntre ciel amunt est resortie.
> Quant veit li quens que ne la freindrat mie,
> Mult dulcement la pleinst a sei meïsme:
> "E Durendal, cum es bele e seintisme!
> En l'oriet punt asez i ad reliques,
> La dent seint Perre e del sanc seint Basilie
> E des chevels mun seignor seint Denise;
> Del vestement i ad seinte Marie:
> Il n'en est dreiz que paiens te baillisent;
> De chrestiens devez estre servie.
> Ne vos ait hume ki facet cuardie!
> Mult larges teres de vus avrai cunquises,

> Que Carles tent, ki la barbe ad flurie.
> Et li empereres en est ber e riches."
>
> [*Roland*, v. 2338]

> Roland struck a dark stone,
> He whacks off more than I can say.
> The sword grates, but neither shatters nor breaks,
> It rebounds upward toward heaven.
> The Count, seeing that he cannot smash it,
> Laments over it softly to himself:
> "O Durendal, how beautiful you are and how very holy!
> Your golden pommel is full of relics,
> Saint Peter's tooth, some of Saint Basil's blood,
> Some of my lord Saint Denis's hair,
> Some of Saint Mary's clothing.
> It is not right for the pagans to own you,
> You must be served by Christians.
> May no coward ever possess you!
> With you I conquered many vast lands
> Over which white-bearded Charlemagne rules,
> And the Emperor is powerful and mighty as a consequence."[27]

The above passage, perhaps better than any other contained in the early epic, demonstrates how early medieval sign theory is translated into poetic practice—more precisely, how a mode of symbolizing, a way of representing, becomes more important than the symbols themselves or that which is represented.

Saint Peter's tooth, Saint Basil's blood, Saint Denis's hair, and Saint Mary's robe all bear a vestigial relation to the sacred history which is subsumed in Roland, who is, by extension, also a vestige, relic—or heir—of those whose body parts and clothing are imbedded in his sword. Roland's thought is, in fact, *about* such continuities, about the ways in which Biblical history prefigures the present within a Christian economy of salvation, and about the way in which the New Testament legacy contained in his sword might constitute a proper succession. The relic, vestigially linked to an origin that authorizes because it is original, stands at the source of a doubly constituted lineage of objects and of men; and the anxiety that Roland expresses concerning the interruption of this line is also an anxiety about human genealogy. The sword, whose inwrought parts link it to sacred history and whose only past parallels that of the hero, rhetorically fuses his own ancestry with that of Roland. It represents the hero's only legacy, and its future is his only bequest.

Roland's sword thus functions metonymically in the legitimation of Christian history and of the hero's own relation to the metonymized past. Each relic maintains a contiguous relation not only to the saint whose body part it contains but to the weapon in its entirety; it represents part of a preexisting corporeal whole and is contained in the existing total object.

Durendal, in turn, maintains a rapport of propriety with respect to Roland. As the sign which here expresses his essence, it functions as a totemic projection of his soul. It is, in fact, this proper relation to the hero which prevents it from belonging to anyone else. Such a transfer, as Roland's fear of loss betrays, would constitute precisely what we have defined linguistically as a lack of appropriateness—an inadequation between a word and the property of the thing it alone signifies. Moreover, both the hero and his sword are bound through the fetishized object to a point of origin at which reified body parts become the real men whose participation in the founding events of Christian history was, through prefiguration, both a repetition of all that had preceded (Old Testament history) and a legitimation of that which was to follow. Roland's spiritual genealogy stretches, then, not only back to Christ, whose martyrdom he repeats analogically and metonymically, but to Mary, and, according to the lineage of Jesus through Jesse, back to David and Adam. No matter how distant and precarious the tie, Roland represents a vestige of all who have gone before, just as his sword is the vestigial reminder of its illustrious (because original) ancestry.

The richness of Roland's heritage, of the heritage of his property, and of the propriety of his relation to it, should not, however, blind us to the fact that he remains a terminal figure. Childless, a hero so thoroughly defined by the past that both he and his sword are excluded from the future, Roland embodies the fear that haunted France's feudal aristocracy—that is to say, the prospect of interruption. Ironically, the consequences of such a genealogical break are not evident until the very end of the poem. There the emergence of Thierry, a man not only delicate, even graceful, in build, but refined in his handling of the emperor's legal defense, drives home the point that Roland's champion and spiritual heir is as unlike him as Ganelon himself. Further, the poem concludes with two subtle but significant linguistic events which bear directly upon the termination of Roland's family line. The first, the baptism of Marsilie's wife Bramimonde, takes as its emblem the change of a name: "As banz ad Ais mult sunt granz les c. . . . / La baptizent le reïne d'Espaigne: / Truve li unt le num de Juliane."[28] The imposition of a name, as opposed to its inheritance, not only raises the specter of a voluntary change in family status but carries the possibility of a certain linguistic mobility as well.

More important, Bramimonde's conversion and the loosening of the proper attached to her name and to her status as queen are eclipsed by the final strophe in which the limits of the linguistic universe of *Roland* are in some definitive sense transgressed:

> Quant l'emperere ad faite sa justice
> E esclargiez est la sue grant ire,
> En Bramidonie ad chrestientet mise,

Passet li jurz, la nuit est aserie.
Culcez s'est li reis en sa cambre voltice.
Seint Gabriel de part Deu li vint dire:
"Carles, sumun les oz de tun emperie!
Par force iras en la tere de Bire,
Reis Vivien si succuras en Imphe,
A la citet que paien unt asise:
Li chrestien te recleiment e crient."
Li emperere n'i volsist aler mie:
"Deus", dist li reis, "si penuse est ma vie!"
Pluret des oilz, sa barbe blanche tiret.
Ci falt la geste que Turoldus declinet.

[Roland, v. 3988]

When the Emperor has dispensed his justice,
And his great wrath has been appeased,
He has Bramimonde christened.
The daylight fades away, night has fallen,
The King has gone to bed in his vaulted room.
Saint Gabriel came from God to tell him:
Charles, summon the armies of your Empire!
You shall invade the land of Bire,
You shall aid King Vivien at Imphe,
The city the pagans have besieged,
The Christians implore and cry out for you."
The Emperor would rather not go there:
"God!" said the King, "my life is so full of suffering!"
His eyes are brimming with tears, he tugs his white beard.
Here ends the story that Turoldus tells.[29]

As we saw above (pp. 100–102), the language of the epic—its vocabulary, metrical form, and texture—serves to affirm the shared values of the community of warrior knights, and even to crystallize the aspirations of an entire class. The formulaic discourse of the early *chanson de geste* in particular was ideally suited to express the unity of the group. With the possible exception of Ganelon's clever use of words to betray and the certain exception of Charlemagne's final complaint, there is, in a work like *Roland*, no genuine discourse of interiority to legitimize, or even to render public, the experience of the individual. Two notable moments of iconographic individuation are not accompanied by a corresponding linguistic individuation: (1) Roland, alone before death, addresses the field of dead knights as if they were still alive; he eulogizes Durendal as if his sword were an animate and interested listener. The language of Roland's solitary last stand thus retains an essentially communicative function. (2) The Charlemagne of the four previous dreams attains iconographic individuation through sleep, but he remains incapable of responding to Gabriel's earlier prophecy of future battles. The visual isolation of the sleeping dreamer produces no verbal response comparable to that of the final strophe.

The Charlemagne of laisse 291 uses language not as a communicative or ritualistic tool—to affirm the unity of the community—but to express a profound disharmony between the individual and the external forces brought to bear upon him. Stated simply, he pronounces what remains the only wholly private verbal utterance within the poem. He inaugurates a discourse intended for no one but himself. In the meeting with Gabriel, Charles initiates a seemingly personal dialogue with the self, the subtle start of an inner monologue, which violates the premises of the universe of which he seems—alone at the end—to be the sole survivor. And though the outcome of this inner struggle is apparent, the emperor is henceforth a divided being, aware, like Ganelon of the first part of the poem, of conflicting commitments to himself and to an imperative outside of the self.

Charlemagne's removal of language from its public status is tantamount to the isolation of the individual from the group. The conclusion of *Roland* thus constitutes a relation between terms unlike any that has preceded: the keenly felt tension between war-weariness and the prospect of further crusade sets in opposition a sensing consciousness perceived as inner and personal, on the one hand, and an external order perceived as objective and distinct, on the other. Moreover, the suggestion of a loss of the proper, symptomized by the appropriation of a language of the self (self-contained and self-directed), and by the struggle of individual and community, signals an interruption analogous to Roland's lack of progeny. Both preclude any future for the linguistically and socially integral world of the *chanson de geste*. Put another way, the early epic possesses no discourse by which to assimilate the meaning either of Charles's verbally determined experience of isolation or of the termination of Roland's family line.[30]

The foregoing discussion changes somewhat our original designation of the epic as the literary form of linguistic and genealogical continuity. More precisely, the *chanson de geste* represents from its inception the disruption of an essentially continuous past. Just as Roland, deprived of offspring, can only meditate upon his heritage, the earliest heroic poems are so completely turned toward the past that their sequels can only reverse historical chronology, engendering ancestry and moving backward through time. Even the oldest text begins with the extinction of a family line and of a linguistic order. Nor is *La Chanson de Roland* unique in the impossibility of its own future. The *chanson de geste* is a virtual home for the aged childless, just as the novel will become a school for orphans. Charlemagne loses not only his spiritual son at Roncevaux, but his sons Bertolai and Lohier are killed in *Renaut de Montauban*, his son Charlot in *Huon de Bordeaux*. Ogier's son Baudoinet is murdered in *La Chevalerie Ogier*, as are Girart's two sons in *Girart de Roussillon*. The childless William witnesses his nephew Vivien's death in *La Chanson de Guillaume*; and

Raoul de Taillefer's direct line is ended with the death of his son, Raoul de Cambrai. The Old French epic is the genre of the continuous but only in the sense of a negative progression. Genealogically sterile because of an almost universal lack of progeny, it proliferates continuously in the direction of ancestry; linguistically sterile because of the formal impossibility of assimilating the loss of the proper, it mobilizes none of the playful potential of such a loss.[31] On the contrary, it remains obsessively obedient to the recuperation—through narrative and representational continuity—of verbal *proprietas*.

Thus, we are faced with a significant conjunction of narrative poetry, early medieval linguistics, and the economics of the lineal family. It is difficult, if not impossible, to separate literary discourse from grammatical theory and from the biopolitics of lineage. These three areas of symbolic activity and social practice all imply a special relation to the idea of property, an investment in the principle of continuity, and a deep ideological attachment to origins. Early medieval grammar, founded upon the notion of a proper relation between words and the properties of things, also assumes a continuous evolution of signs which permits the etymological recovery of an original order of language and being. Similarly, the noble family is predicated upon a sacred attachment to property which is transmitted by uninterrupted primogenital succession; like the metadiscourse of language theory, lineage derives its own legitimacy from an abiding connection to origins. In the epic an assumed (though violable) linguistic propriety combines with a realized narrative coherence to produce the somewhat unidimensional universe which proliferates, according to a genealogical model, in the direction of ancestry. There can be no distinction between the narrative and referential continuity of the epic, the biological continuity of lineage, or the economic continuity of noble family property. The "science of the literal" (straight), the linear family, and the literary genre of the continuous are, furthermore, united by a common conservative streak. Implicit to an etymological grammar is the assumption that linguistic change can only represent corruption, a further distancing from the proper. Latent in the (unconscious?) political strategy of nobility is the presupposition that only ancestry legitimates and that social change transgresses this natural law of antiquity. And, finally, underlying the epic exclusion of the future is the premise that no present can rival the past.

The Poetics of Disruption

If the association of early medieval grammar, lineage, and epic verse seems too neat, too globally comprehensive and contained, it is because up until now we have focused somewhat narrowly upon a much broader cultural whole. As we have defined them, these three fields of discursive practice represent but one dimension of a more complicated nexus of symbolic and social relations, the other dimensions of which can no longer be ignored. We have thus reached the midpoint of our investigation, a watershed that permits—even solicits—what may seem like a curious reversal of the logic of presentation, henceforth the opposite of our beginning. Since, in addition, it is no longer necessary to justify the connection between language theory, kinship, and poetry, we will move from literary form to family structure and linguistics with the understanding that the difficulty of distinguishing internal from external causality renders the primacy of poetic discourse increasingly apparent.

The Love Lyric

Among the lyric poets of the twelfth century none is more concerned with lineage and language than the troubadour Marcabru, who is obsessed by family trees of a particular sort:

> Cossiros suy d'un gran vergier
> Ont a de belhs plansos mans lucs;
> Gent sont l'empeut e·l frugs bacucs,
> Selh qu'esser degran sordegier
> Fuelhs e flors paron de pomier,
> Son al fruchar sautz' e saucs,
> E pus lo caps es ba[da]lucs,
> Dolen(s) son li membr' estremier.
>
> Mort(z) son li bon arbre primier,
> E·l(s) viu(s) son ramils e festucs, . . .
> Doncx no pairejon li derrier;
> En totz bos sens ab los faducs. . . .
>
> [Marcabru, p. 9]

I dream of an orchard where there are beautiful shrubby trees in many places; the graftings are large and the pulpy fruit smells sweet to those of low degree. One expects apple leaves and flowers; but when the fruit comes it is only willow and elder. And given that the head is empty, the members are sorrowful at their extremities.

Dead are the good old trees, and those that live are only branches and sticks. . . . Thus the most recent (living trees) do not resemble their fathers in all the good ways.

As we have seen from the beginning, the tree was a potent symbol or structuring vehicle of genealogy in the High Middle Ages. What is special about Macabru's presentation, however, is that the family tree, never whole, is always grafted. The "good old trees," or the "good old days," which he associates elsewhere with the positive values of *valor, pretz, joven,* and *joia,* have been supplanted at their upper extremities by sorrow: "Dolen(s) son li membr' estremier." What has been broken, in fact, is a paternal series; and the apple tree which yields willow and elder refers to a world in which sons no longer resemble fathers: "Non cuich que·l segles dar gaire / Segon qu'escriptura di / Qu'eras faill lo fills al paire / E·l pair' al fill atressi" (Marcabru, p. 71).[32]

There can be no doubt concerning the cause of grafted trees and broken genealogies:

> Moillerat, ab sen cabri
> Atal paratz lo coissi
> Don lo cons esdeven laire;
> Que tals ditz: "Mos fills me ri"
> Que anc ren no·i ac a faire:
> Gardatz sen ben bedoï
>
> > [Marcabru, p. 73]
>
> Car el n'a la clau segonda
> Per qe·l segner, so·us afin,
> Porta capel cornut conin,
> C'ab sol un empeu[t] *redonda*
> Si donz, lo ditz Marcabrus.
>
> > [Marcabru, p. 50]

Married people, in the lascivious sense of goats, you prepare the cushion in such a way that the cunt becomes a rascal. And such a one says: "My son laughs at me," who never had anything to do with his birth.

There is a second key; that is why the lord (husband), I assure you, wears a horned hat coming from the cunt [lit. "of rabbit fur"]. For it is only through a grafting that his wife becomes round (pregnant), according to Marcabru.

Lineage is disrupted by the deleterious effects of adulterous desire, which reaches epidemic proportions; and this in two ways. First, husbands participate in their own cuckoldry through a generalized exchange of wives, "for he who rubs the cunt belonging to another sends his own to market, and he who wants to feel one that does not belong to him makes others covetous of the one that does and he places it in the public domain."[33] And, alongside of the "wife-swapping," the "common folly" that Marcabru equates with widespread civil chaos, stands the cuckoldry of great lords "from below" by those who are supposed to serve them:

> D'autra manieira cogossos,
> Hi a rics homes e baros
> Qui las enserron dinz maios
> Qu'estrains non i posca intrar
> E tenon guirbautz als tisos
> Cui las comandon a gardar.
>
> E segon que ditz Salamos,
> Non podon cill pejors lairos
> Acuillir d'aquels compaignos

> Qui fant la noirim cogular,
> Et aplanon los guirbaudos
> E cujon lor fills piadar.
> > [Marcabru, p. 135; see also pp. 147–148]

There are some powerful and great barons who imprison their wives in houses so that no stranger can enter, and who at the same time entertain the rogues to whom they give the orders to guard them.

But according to the wisdom of Solomon these lords could not offer hospitality to worse thieves than this bunch that bastardizes the race; and the husbands caress little rogues thinking they are covering their sons with affection.

If the "horizontal" exchange of wives within the ranks of nobility obscures genealogy and makes fathers say of their sons, "I think he is mine," the "vertical" disappropriation of paternity produces a bastardization of the race indissociable from a general decline in courtly values— the withering of great family trees at their upper extremities.

What remains significant in Marcabru's obsession is not so much the poet's awareness of the biological consequences of extramarital intercourse as the fact that adultery, whose effects involve a hiding of lineage, cannot be separated from the deceptive effects of poetic language. First of all, the lies that adultery entails seem to produce misconceptions leading directly to conception: "Ladies for their part are deceptive, and they know how to trick and lie; this is why they provide for and nourish the children of others."[34] Furthermore, the bastardization of the race that Marcabru laments repeatedly and in varying modes remains virtually indistinguishable from the poet's role as a defiler of language.

Much has been written about Marcabru's status as a troubadour of the "closed," "dark," "difficult," or "obscure" style, and the debate concerning the roots of the medieval hermetic tradition is of special interest to the literary historian. Here, however, sources are of less importance than the fact that for Marcabru poetry implies the obfuscation of meaning. "My fief," he claims, "is so well protected that no one except I have access to it . . . I am gifted and filled with an infinity of artifices, with a hundred means of achieving my goal (or harming). On the one side, I carry fire, and on the other, I carry the water to put it out."[35] The poet, like the adulterer, is a deceiver, a disrupter of linguistic lines alongside the usurpers of noble family lines:

> Per savi·l tenc ses doptanssa
> Cel qui de mon chant devina
> So que chascus motz declina,
> Si cum la razos despleia,
> Qu'ieu mezeis sui en erranssa
> D'esclarzir paraul' escura.

> Trobador, ab sen d'enfanssa,
> Movon als pros atahina,
> E tornon en disciplina
> So que veritatz autreia,
> E fant los motz, per esmanssa,
> Entrebeschatz de fraichura.
>
> [Marcabru, p. 178]

I consider to be wise the one who can decipher what each word in my song means, how its theme develops, because I myself am subject to error when it comes to explaining an obscure word.

Troubadours with childish minds cause trouble for those of great worth, turn into difficulty what truth grants, and purposefully make words full of breaks.

The poet is a "mixer of words," of meanings, and, by implication, an obscurer of etymologies through the dislocation of linguistic property. Similarly, the adulterer is a mixer of races, of noble fortunes, an obscurer of genealogy through the dislocation of family property. Semantic and genealogical discontinuity go hand in hand. And the disruption of meaning that the love lyric occasions, a "making of words full of breaks," is, ultimately, the same as the disruption of lineage inherent to adulterous desire.

Marcabru's love lyrics contain the most conscious and sustained treatment of the relation between erotic and poetic deception. He is not, however, alone in the association of poetry, adultery, and bastardy. Raimbaut d'Aurenga, for instance, claims to be capable of "making a little poem easy to sing," but he prefers "to make it so it hides its meaning, . . . since love must be hidden."[36] Elsewhere he brags of "intertwining rare, dark, and obscure words" ("Cars, bruns et tenhz motz entrebesc!"), and, like Marcabru, he links such lies to genealogical disruption.[37] Raimbaut offers, further, what stands as an emblematic recognition of the affinity between paternal and poetic dislocation:

> Tal cug'esser cortes entiers
> Qu'es vilans dels quatre ladriers,
> Et a·l cor dins mal ensenhat;
> Plus que feutres sembla sendat
> Ni cuers de bou escarlata
> Non sabon mais que n'an trobat—
> E quecx quo's pot calafata.[38]

One thinks he is a perfect gentleman who is baseborn on all four sides (of his family) and who has a churlish heart within him; no more than felt resembles taffeta or ox-hide good scarlet woolen cloth do they (the scandal mongers) know anything except what they have invented about it, and each one caulks (fills in) as best he can.

In a false perception of filiation lies the beginning of fiction. The *losengiers* or spreaders of scandal misperceive true genealogy; and this misperception—an invention synonymous with the troubadour's art ("Non sabon mais que n'an trobat")—creates the conditions of the possibility of poetry itself. The love lyric or *canso* is a "caulking" of an unbridgeable gap in "true" paternity, a "filling-in" of an irrecuperable distance between language and meaning.

The troubadour Bernart Marti also boasts of "breaking lines" and of "mixing words" ("C'aisi vauc entrebescant / Los motz e·l so afinant"); and he equates the confusion of tongues—linguistic and lingual—with the interpenetration of a kiss ("Lengu'entrebescada / Es en la baizada"). Inspired possibly by Marcabru, he too underscores the link between verbal obfuscation and the bastardization of noble family lines.[39] Bernart Marti equates, in fact, the lies of the slanderers with the disinheritance of rightful heirs:

> Mas fezautat fan carzir,
> Quar no volon lo ver dir
> Tant si fizon en l'auzir
> De caitius desheretar. . . .
> Lengua forquat traversan,
> Si·l metetz deniers denan,
> Far vos a de gossa can
> E d'eyssa guiza levar
> Lo dia tro l'endeman,
> Tan son savi del mesclar.[40]

But they (the slanderers) raise the price of faithfulness with their lies. They are so confident in their reputation that they even dare to disinherit the unfortunate. . . .

A forked lying tongue, if you offer it money, will transform a bitch into a sire and in the same way will raise today until tomorrow (?), so crafty are they in the art of mixing things.

Bernart's "art of mixing things" (*mesclar*) is the equivalent of Raimbaut's "motz entrebesc" and Marcabru's "motz entrebeschatz de fraichura." All three phrases are, within the semantic field of the early *vers*, used in opposition to *lassar* (to link). Each assumes, moreover, that the intertwining of words, their isolation from fixed, received categories of meaning, occasions a jumbling of reality—"a world upside down,"[41] in Bernart's phrase, in which the natural difference between genders (bitch and sire) as well as the natural law of time (today and tomorrow) are reversed. This linguistic rupture and loss of discreteness is associated with a break in an uninterrupted sequence of paternity: bastardy, or the dislocation of a genealogical line, combined with disinheritance, or the dislocation of property.

Thus we find among lyric poets of the difficult style, like Marcabru, Bernart Marti, or Raimbaut d'Aurenga, a discourse which seems not only to refuse any representational function but to revel in such a refusal. The assumed linguistic universe of the early *trobar clus* is, as its name implies, closed upon itself, self-referential, disruptive of linguistic integrity—a world which, to cite Zumthor, "is its own subject without object."[42] Raimbaut is characterized by his biographer as a poet gifted in making rich and closed rhymes ("caras rimas e clusas"). Peire d'Alvernha claims to enjoy singing "tight and closed words" ("motz alqus serratz e clus"). The troubadour Marcoat brags of creating a poem out of "los motz cluz" and of being able to insert into his contradictory verses ("vers contra-dizentz") "three words of different meanings" ("tres motz de divers sens").[43] Nor is the phenomenon of linguistic closure restricted to those poets traditionally characterized as *trobar clus*. When William IX, the first troubadour, proposes "to compose a poem about nothing," he is, in effect, denying the purchase of language upon the world.[44] From the beginning the *vers* represents a symbolic closure of language upon itself, its substitution for action and constitution as event.

Though William IX is not among the poets who, like Marcabru, pretend continually to expose the generalization of adultery, along with the loss of linguistic integrity, he establishes the framework for such an association. In the poem "Campanho, faray un vers . . . covinen" William sets as his announced goal the mixing of meanings: "I will put in it (my *vers*) more folly than wisdom, and one will find there mixed pêle-mêle love, joy, and youth" ("Et er totz mesclatz d'amor e de joy e de joven" [William IX, p. 1]). William's intentional jumbling of words expresses implicitly a certain arbitrariness of verbal signs. The interpretative possibilities of such a doctrine lead, moreover, not only to his oft-remarked social exclusivity but to sexual confusion as well: "E tenguatz lo per vilan qui no l'enten / O dins son cor voluntiers [qui] non l'apren; / Greu partir si fa d'amor qui la trob'a son talen" (ibid.).[45] The loss of directness in speech, of linguistic property, is the result of poetic "mixing"; and it becomes the equivalent of sexual indiscretion. The refusal of univocal meaning is tantamount to a condemnation of monogamy:

> Dos cavalhs ai a ma selha ben e gen;
> Bon son e adreg per armas e valen;
> Mas no·ls puesc amdos tener que l'us l'autre non cossen.
> [Ibid.]

I have for my saddle two horses, and this is well and good; both are good, well trained for combat, and valiant; but I cannot have them both together, because one cannot stand the other.

Even the thinly veiled equestrian metaphor captures the movement of William's doctrine of language and love. A plurality of meanings, irrecon-cilable with each other except within the confines of the *vers*, are iden-tified with the balance of mutually exclusive erotic preferences. Linguistic infidelity, the failure to choose words whose meaning is plain and distinct, cannot be divorced from sexual infidelity, as the coterminous presence of "folly and sense" which marks the poem's beginning is echoed in the closing inability "to choose between Agnes and Arsen": "Ges non sai ab qual mi tengua de N'Agnes o de N'Arsen" (ibid., p. 2).[46]

A similar expression of the relation between language and sexuality can be found in William's problematic "Poem of the Red Cat," which opens with a comparable linguistic gratuity: "I will make a *vers* since I am asleep, and walking, and standing in the sun" ("Farai un vers, pos mi sonelh, / E·m vauc e m'estauc al solelh" [William IX, p. 8]). The initial affirmation of a logical impossibility is in this instance, however, accompanied by the degeneration of language beyond the point of recognition; for when the wives of Sir Garin and Sir Bernard try to get the poet to speak, he responds with nonsense syllables: "I didn't say but or bat to them, didn't mention a stick or a tool, but only this: 'Babariol, babariol, babarian.' "[47] In William's babble ("Babariol"), sound is detached entirely from meaning (except for the homophonic resonance with barbarism), which is precisely what, in this drama of refused language, permits fornication:

> So diz n'Agnes a n'Ermessen:
> "Trobat avem que anam queren.
> Sor, per amor Deu, l'alberguem,
>   Qe ben es mutz,
> E ja per lui nostre conselh
>   Non er saubutz."
>   [William IX, p. 10]

Then Agnes said to Ermessen: "We've found what we are looking for. Sister, for the love of God let us take him in, he is really mute; with this one our conduct will never be known.

Thus, it is not only—as in Marcabru, Bernart, and Raimbaut—the "mixing of words," the concealment of meaning, that fosters adultery, but silence, the abolition of both terms of the semiological equation: "I fucked them, as you shall hear, one hundred and eighty-eight times" ("Tant las fotei com auzirets: / Cen e quatre vint e ueit vetz" [ibid., p. 12]).

Metaphor and the "Closed" Style

William is, of course, excessive in his transgression both of semantic and sexual bounds. But this exaggerated parable of secrecy and seduction points to a more general resistance on the part of the *trobar clus* not so much to speech as to the idea of linguistic property. Alongside of a concealed—because socially inappropriate—polygamous desire stands a polysemous play with words, a fornicating with language that stretches meaning to its limits, and sometimes beyond. Whether such a testing of poetic discourse is expressed as a "mixing of words," a "making of words full of breaks," or silence, it represents, for the poet of the "difficult style," a refusal of the proper.

Here lies an important difference between the *chanson de geste* and the love lyric. For while the discourse of the epic serves either to affirm or to recuperate linguistic property, that of the "closed" *canso* radically denies property, functioning instead according to a more contextually defined poetic model. Where one is originary, historical, governed by a temporal law of contiguity, combination, and sequence, the other is disruptive of sequence, ahistorical, and governed by a more spatially organized law of juxtaposition, similarity and dissimilarity, and supplementarity. If the first depends upon a metonymic grounding of language in things (words in the proper), the second is ruled by a freer game of metaphoric substitutions. This polarity is crucial, since the opposite of a proper signification was, throughout the period in question, a metaphoric one.

Late Classical and early medieval rhetoricians distinguished between: simple linguistic abuse, unintentional errors of diction, vices (*vitii*) like barbarism and solecism; metaplasms, or changes in a word for the sake of ornament; schemes, figures of diction or thought; catachresis, "the inexact use of a like and kindred word in the place of a precise and proper one" (Cicero); and tropes, an expression intentionally altered from its usual signification. The author of the *Rhetorica ad Herennium* claims, for example, that "metaphor" occurs when a word applying to one thing is transferred to another, because the similarity seems to justify this transference." Quintilian specifies that "a trope means the artistic alteration of a word or phrase from its proper meaning to another." The notion of deviation from the norm of conventional meaning is assimilated by Augustine, who equates metaphor with verbal usurpation: "Translata sunt (signa), cum et ipsae res quas propriis verbis significamus, ad aliud aliquid significandum usurpantur. . . ."[48] Isidore concurs in the standard definition of a trope ("Fiunt autem a propria significatione ad non propriam similitudinem" *Etym.*, l:xxxvii, i), which is passed on to the rhetoricians and poets of the High Middle Ages.

The idea of metaphor connotes alienation, denaturalization, translocation, or usurpation of linguistic property. But is also serves as a principle of stylistic elaboration. And the opposition between the proper and the metaphoric is doubled by that between the proper and the ornate. The late Classical grammarian Diomedes, for example, distinguishes—under the rubric of *virtutes orationis generales*—between "property, which is a straight kind of speech" associated with proportion and brevity, and "ornate speech," which includes tropes.[49] The Carolingian grammarian Notker Labeo discriminates between plain or simple discourse (*plane dicere, locutio simplex*), which "accords the proper words to things" (*pro-*

pria verba rebus dare), and ornate or figurative discourse (*locutio figurata*), which, as for Diomedes, consists of word figures (*compositio artificiosa*) as well as figures of thought and tropes (*significatio aliena*).⁵⁰ The anonymous author of a rhetoric written sometime prior to the year 1000 adopts the Classical theory of three styles (Cicero, Horace) according to the degree of elaboration. Thus the humble mode of speech "uses the word itself" ("proprio nomine nominavit"), the middle "casts light upon its subject," and the heavy style casts its subject in a "golden light" ("aureos lychnos").⁵¹ In the second half of the eleventh century, Albert of Monte Cassino distinguishes between *stilus simplex* and *stilus mixtus*, and he extends the concept of property beyond the use of the individual word to cover the correctness of the *copulatio verborum*.⁵² It is, however, only among the rhetoricians of the thirteenth century that the opposition between simple and difficult style receives systematic treatment.⁵³

Simple style implies, as Geoffrey of Vinsauf specifies in the *Poetria Nova*, use of colors of rhetoric: either "figures of words" involving a play on the morphological structure of a single verbal term (e.g., *repetitio, annominatio, conversio, exclamatio*), or "figures of thought," which seem to involve both logical and lexical alteration (e.g., *diminutio* [litote], *accumulatio* [heaping of praise or blame], *demonstratio* [vivid description]). *Ornatus difficilis*, on the other hand, implies the use of tropes, which, as we have seen, means the transfer (*translatio, transsumptio*) of a proper meaning toward a figurative, but nonetheless recognizable, one.⁵⁴ Mathew of Vendome, John of Garland, and Evrard the German all follow roughly the same line of thought with regard to the question of stylistic elaboration.

There are difficulties attached to the equation of the so-called dark, obscure, or covered style of the *trobar clus* and the rhetorical category of *ornatus difficilis*. Moreover, the association of poetic practice and rhetorical theory is by no means intended to imply logical (or even chronological) priority. But even so brief an excursion into medieval manuals of poetry offers as contemporaneous as possible a framework for the understanding of the "difficult" lyric. And before we move on to a consideration of the "easy" or "light" *canso* and to the social implications of both "open" and "closed" verse, it might prove worthwhile to summarize and to situate the question of poetic closure within the context of the issues that have concerned us up until now. For not only does the *ornatus difficilis*, or poetry characterized by the extensive use of tropes, serve to negate linguistic property, but it throws radically into question many of the fundamental principles of early medieval grammar; and this in the following terms:

1. *Spatial*. The *loci* or proper places of speech associated with a grounding of words in the physical properties of things are, in metaphoric discourse, geographically displaced toward a foreign or alien *locus*. Geof-

frey of Vinsauf even associates such a shift with a change of residence: "Noli semper concedere verbo / In proprio residere loco: residentia talis / Dedecus est ipsi verbo; loca propria vitet / Et peregrinetur alibi sedemque placentem / Fundet in alterius fundo: sit ibi novus hospes."[55] Thus the trope implies a verbal dislocation (displacement of locus) conceived still in spatial terms.

2. *Temporal.* The place to which speech is displaced—a figure of speech—can itself constitute a proper *locus* as long as the similitude of the elements conjoined is preserved. At a secondary level there are, then, proper figures—those, as Peter Helias states, "where the transfer of a word from a proper signification to an alien one is appropriate"—and improper ones in which the place to which meaning is transferred is inappropriate ("Vitiosa est locutio ubi est translatio inconveniens").[56] In neither case, however, is the metaphoric expression an original one in the first instance. "Words," as Quintilian states, "are proper when they bear their original meaning, metaphorical when they are used in a sense different from their natural meaning."[57] It is the pristine quality of first words that endows them with the qualities of naturalness and wholeness; and metaphor represents always a less than, newer than, original instance of meaning. This is a point of paramount importance since through tropes language is cut loose from an overweening dependence upon the propriety of origins.[58] Unlike the futureless discourse of the proper as typified by the *Chanson de Roland*, the metaphoric discourse of the *trobar clus* both severs (through novel use) and affirms (through similitude) its attachment to the past.

3. *Linear.* Early medieval grammar is, as we have seen, the "science of the literal"—of straight and correct locution. The use of tropes, however, is synonymous with "circular speech" or circumlocution. We have already seen that John of Salisbury associates grammar with a highway or straight path and that errors of speech are the equivalent of "forsaking the proper thoroughfare" (see above, pp. 52–53). Among the rhetoricians and grammarians of the thirteenth century, it is impossible to separate the *ornatus difficilis* from the general technique of amplification by periphrase, which Geoffrey characterizes as follows: "In order to make a work longer, do not use the name of things; but use other signifiers. Do not show a thing openly, but indicate it by small details. Do not let your discourse go directly to the thing, but circumscribe with *long circling phrases* that which you could say briefly. . . ."[59] Elaborate poetic ornament is thus equated not with "straight writing" (orthography) but with "circular writing" (circumscription). Alexander of Villedieu is even more explicitly geometrical in his definition of metaphor, which, he claims, combines the rectilinearity (rectitude) of proper speech with the curvature of a dislocated meaning:

Item dicitur quod figura sumitur hic ad similitudinem figure semicircularis super dyametralem lineam vel rectam determinate disposite tali modo, quoniam, sicut in tali figura est aliquid rectum, sicut est dyametralis linea, . . . et aliquid est ibi oblicum, sicut est circonferentia cum semicirculo . . . , sic est in omni sermone figurativo aliquid rectum, et hoc est intrinsecus respiciendo ad intellectum, et aliud oblicum, et hoc est extrinsecus respiciendo ad vocem vel ad primum contextum dictionum vel ad primam significationem. [*Notices*, p. 460]

Likewise a figure is said to have a dual likeness here, that of a semicircular figure over a diagonal or straight line, arranged in such a way since, as in this figure, the diagonal line corresponds to the straight part, and the circumference with the semicircle corresponds to the curved part there . . . , so in all figurative speech there is a straight part which is seen to lie within when one looks toward the basic meaning, and there is a curved part which is seen to lie outside when one looks toward the sound or the primary context of the words or their initial signification.

Alexander's highly geometric comparison assumes the mind's ability to judge independently (intrinsically) a straight or literal meaning, and it takes for granted the deviation (extrinsic) of the voiced expression from its original sense (*primam significationem*). But, more important, it accounts for figural speech as a semicircle superimposed upon a diagonal straight line. The Janus-faced trope seems both to respect and to transgress the linearity of its own origin. As Albert of Monte Cassino specifies, metaphor is a means of speech turned away from property in such a way as to innovate: ". . . est metaphorae modum locutionis a proprietate sui quasi detorquere, detorquendo quadammodo innovare. . . ."[60]

"Easy Verse"

The *trobar clus* offers the most striking example of a radical break with all that we associate with early medieval grammar, and, in particular, with the notion of linguistic property. Such a departure is achieved through a spatially conceived translocation, a temporally conceived denial of origins, and a distortion of the geometrically conceived linear attachment of words to things. In this, however, the "difficult" Provençal lyric represents only one aspect of a broader pattern of disruption that is also evident in poetry of the "open" or "light" style. And if the *trobar clus* produces an obfuscation of sense through the interruption of intelligibility, the poet of "easy verse" achieves a similar effect through an insistence upon contradictory clear meanings. What the *trobar leu* repeatedly presents, in fact, are spatially organized paradigms of feeling between which the poet oscillates because of the impossibility of progression. The "easy" love song exists as a static map of conflicting images, emotions, and states held in constant tension with each other, but without the prospect of resolution. The numerous individual poems that often seem indistinguishable because of the homogeneity of self-canceling opposites function according to a rhetoric of contradiction: joy/pain, good/evil, life/death, laughter/tears, sweetness/bitterness, consolation/anguish, hope/despair, rest/movement, sanity/insanity, wisdom/folly, gain/loss, sleep/waking, courage/timidity (cowardice), strength/weakness, freedom/enslavement, intelligence/stupidity, sight/blindness, silence/speech, right/wrong, abundance/dearth, wealth/poverty, etc.

It would, of course, be impossible within the confines of the present study to analyze adequately each of the above contradictory clusters. I am not even sure that such an analysis would prove useful, consisting as it would of little more than a catalogue of polarities. Nor does it seem more feasible to attempt to treat a large number of individual texts each of which participates only partially in the poetics of opposition; such an endeavor poses the prospect of mere summary next to the already unsatisfactory possibility of concordance. What I propose instead is a close look at one lyric by the master of contradiction, Bernard de Ventadorn, for whom the type of vacillation of which we are speaking is so persistent as to render the choice of *canso* almost arbitrary (see Appendix A for translation):

I

En cossirer et en esmai
sui d'un' amor que·m lass' e·m te,
que tan no vau ni sai ni lai
qu'ilh ades no·m tenh' en so fre,
c'aras m'a dat cor e talen
  qu'eu enqueses si podia
  tal que se·l reis l'enqueria
auria faih gran ardimen.

II

Ai las, chaitius, e que·m farai
ni cal cosselh penrai de me?
Qu'ela no sap lo mal qu'eu trai
ni eu no·lh aus clamar merce.
Fol nesci, ben as pauc de sen,
  qu'ela nonca t'amaria
  per nom que per drudaria
c'ans no·t laisses levar al ven.

III

E doncs pois atressi·m morrai
dirai li l'afan que m'en ve?
Vers es c'ades lo li dirai—
no farai a la mia fe
si sabia c'a un tenen
  en fos tot' Espanha mia;
  mais volh morir de feunia
car anc me venc en pessamen.

IV
Ja per me no sabra qu'eu m'ai
ni autre no l'en dira re.
Amic no volh ad aquest plai,
ans perda Deu qui pro m'en te,
qu'eu no·n volh cozi ni paren;
  que mout m'es grans cortezia
  c'amors per midons m'aucia,
mais a leis non estara gen.

V
E doncs ela cal tort m'i fai
qu'ilh no sap, per que s'esdeve?
Deus devinar degra oimai
qu'eu mor per s'amor, et a que?
Al meu nesci chaptenemen
  et a la gran vilania
  per que·lh lenga m'entrelia
can eu denan leis me prezen.

VI
Negus jois al meu no s'eschai
can ma domna·m garda ni·m ve,
que·l seus bels douz semblans me vai
al cor, que m'adous' e·m reve.
E si·m durava lonjamen
  sobre sainhz li juraria
  qu'el mon mais nulhs jois no sia.
Mais al partir art et encen.

VII
Pois messatger no·lh trametrai
ni a me dire no·s cove,
negu cosselh de me no sai.
Mais d'una re me conort be:
ela sap letras et enten
  et agrada·m qu'eu escria
  los motz, e s'a leis plazia
legis los al meu sauvamen.

VIII
E s'a leis autre dols no·n pren,
  per Deu e per merce·lh sia
  que·l bel solatz que m'avia
no·m tolha ni·l seu parlar gen.[61]

Like many of Bernart's *cansos*, "En cossirer et en esmai" takes as its central axis the polarity of pain (II) and joy (VI).[62] Within the confines of the negative and positive sensations, which frame the poem at beginning and end, stand a series of secondary oppositional pairs between which the poet oscillates freely and seemingly without end: for example, invisibility, "she does not know" (II) versus visibility, "No joy matches mine when my lady looks at me or sees me" (VI); fear, "I dare not" (II), "great cowardice" (V) versus courage, "Yes, I shall tell her at once" (III); hesitation, "Yes, I shall . . . No, I shall not" (III) versus resolve, "She will never learn [it] from me" (IV) (and which is broken by the contradictory resolution of the end of VII); hope, "heart and desire to court" (I), "And if she stayed with me a long time" (VI) versus despair, "I take fire and burn" (VI), "I see no help for myself" (VII), "She will never love you" (II); despair versus consolation, "she knows and understands letters" (VII); communication, "It pleases me to write the words" (VII) versus silence or confusion, "foolish behavior and a great cowardice which binds my tongue" (V); kindness of the lady (VIII) versus her cruelty, "she does not know what wrong she does me" (V); and, finally, death, "I could die of chagrin" (III), "I am dying for her love" (V) versus resurrection, "her fair sweet image . . . refreshes me" (VI).[63]

The impact of such an accumulation of self-negating polarities is reinforced by the overall weakness of the *canso*'s verbal system. Bernart draws heavily upon a series of verbs designating: mental or emotional state (perplex, confuse, burn, console, dare, love); perception or cognition (understand, realize, learn, look, see); communication (read, tell, request, swear, speak, write); possession (have, want). "En cossirer et en esmai" contains, however, no verbs expressive of strong action; and those that do signify events are as mildly actantial as possible (help, please, befall; the clusters bind, allow, confine, hold; give, take, send; enter, depart). The most operative verb by far is the copulative "to be," which only reinforces the static general effect. When added to the high density of passive constructions of which the poet is an object and the numerous reflexive forms, the overall impression is one of extreme stillness and fixity—a heightened awareness of the present ("now," "at once") on the part of a mind in dialogue with itself. Here lies the key to Bernart's *canso*, which presents the wholly internal struggle of a psyche so in conflict that all possibility of action is denied. The sole hint of resolution is, in fact, the poem itself ("It pleases me to write the words" [VII]), which, ironically, also stands both as a vehicle of seduction ("let her read them for my deliverance" [VII]) and as a sign of poetic closure.

The syntax of "En cossirer et en esmai" again confirms what its verbal system suggests. For not only does Bernart punctuate this drama of immobility with numerous questions, but the internal logic of his affirmative phrases adds to the pervasive atmosphere of passivity. Despite the presence of many logical terms (of hypothesis and condition), these remain wholly nominal, more descriptive than deductive. Sentences like "*if* she stayed with me a long time, I would swear . . . " (VI); "*Since* I will not send a messenger to her, and *since* for me to speak is not fitting, I see no help for myself. *But* I console myself . . . " (VII); "*if* it pleases her, let her read them [my words] for my deliverance" (VII) all give the impression of logical coordination which, in fact, represents more a juxtaposition of surface phenomena than the reflection of logical process.[64] The "sinces" and "but" are constative rather than causal; the "if" is symptomatic of temporal sequence and not of hypothesis.

Even more revealing than Bernart's pliant syntax, which again works to transform the poet into the object of an on-going course of mental events beyond his control, is the poem's strophic disposition. The order of strophes of "En cossirer et en esmai"—and this is essential—remains wholly arbitrary. The macrometric units of the *canso* are interchangeable. Just as there can be no resolution of permanently conflictual states, there is, with the exception of the poet's parting decision to commit himself to the words that we have just read, no progression. The final strophe only solicits a return to the beginning whose message has to do precisely with confinement and the impossibility of movement: "I am perplexed and confused about a love which binds me and confines me so that there is no place I can go . . . " (I).

Thus a poem of the *trobar leu* style like "En cossirer et en esmai" is in its own way as hermetically sealed as any of the so-called closed love lyrics. It is, however, shut off from that which is assumed to exist outside the text not by the disruption of signification, of intelligibility, but by the creation of a system of meaning that is purely contextual. Bernart's *canso* refers only indeterminately to the lady who is never named, to the ill-defined *amor* which tortures him, or to the vague fiascos of meeting and parting. We cannot say that the meaning of the poem depends upon the strength of such external references. Rather, it lies, if anywhere, in the interplay of the polarities discussed above and in the copresence of oppositional elements whose juxtaposition generates meaning. "En cossirer" can be said to signify only insofar as its key constituent terms—joy/pain, hope/despair, resolve/hesitation, courage/fear, etc.—consignify each other. The *trobar leu* does not effect a dislocation of the "vertical" bonds of language and meaning. It does not disrupt the proper but works instead to strip poetry of meaning by a "horizontal" textualizing of its traditional terms. The "easy" style takes as its point of departure not the "making of new words full of breaks" but the overconventionalizing of a familiar and limited vocabulary—words like *amor, cor, talen, merce, cortezia, jois, solatz* which, within the individual *canso*, are self-referential and serve, at their outer semantic limits, only to situate the poem within a broader intertextual spectrum of similar terms.

What this means is that the love lyric's self-contained system for the production of sense is, in effect, its deepest meaning. Poetic closure and psychic closure work hand in hand to create a pervasive atmosphere of entrapment, which Bernart expresses so succinctly elsewhere: "The better off I am, the worse I feel" ("On melhs m'estai, et eu peihz trai").[65] The psychological "double bind" of "En cossirer" depends, finally, upon a series of contradictions whose most radical consequence is the freeing of language from reference. And the end point of such a detachment is an interpretative license—as Bernart says, "One can put the wrong interpretation on anything"—that breeds paranoia:[66]

> Garit m'agra si m'aucizes,
> c'adoncs n'agra faih son voler;
> mas eu no cre qu'ela fezes
> re c'a me tornes a plazer.
> Agra·n esglai e penedera s'en?
> ja no creirai no m'am cubertamen
> mas cela s'en vas me per plan essai.[67]

She would have cured me if she had killed me, for then she would have accomplished her will. But I do not believe that she would do anything that would bring me pleasure. Would she be afraid and would she repent of it? I shall never believe that she does not secretly love me, but she hides it from me simply to test me.

The passivity of the poetic personality is the logical outcome of a language suspended by contradiction. Trapped by its own inability ever to achieve unpolarized—proper—meaning, the singing voice remains incapable of knowing, and hence of acting within a universe in which song is the only form of action and even time is denied:

> Lo tems vai e ven e vire
> per jorns, per mes e per ans,
> et eu, las, no·n sai que dire,
> c'ades es us mos talans.
> Ades es us e no·s muda,
> c'una·n volh e·n ai volguda
> don anc non aic jauzimen.[68]

Time comes and goes returning through days, through months, and through years, and I, alas, know not what to say, for my longing is ever one. It is ever one and does not change, for I want and have wanted one woman, from whom I have never had joy.

Just as the order of strophes is irrelevant to the meaning of the *canso*, the succession of days, months, and years does nothing to change the poet's desire, which is coterminous with the regularity of his singing. Without origin or terminus, the love lyric begins and ends at random points along a uniform chronological—but only vaguely biographical—scale. Thus, the scrambling of time among the *trobar clus*—for example, Bernart Marti's "raising today until tomorrow"—finds its analogue in the homogenization of time on the part of the *trobar leu*.

If our analysis of the lyric has focused upon the South, it is because the appearance of Provençal verse roughly coincided with that of the earliest epics and because it demonstrates so explicitly the contrast between contemporaneous literary discourses. Such a choice is not intended to suggest that the problematics of language and love developed among the troubadours is geographically limited to the region of Languedoc and Poitou. On the contrary, practically all of the elements that we have traced with respect to the *canso* are also to be found in the *chansons* of the trouvères.[69] There is little need, in fact, to belabor the relation of the southern and northern lyric, which, when posed in general terms, tends to short-circuit history through poetics, and, when posed in terms of specific influence, tends to ignore poetics in favor of historical anecdote. More interesting are the questions of how they differ, of how their resemblance relates to the epic, and of how such a juxtaposition of concurrent poetic forms ties in to the broader issues of linguistics, poetics, and the family.

Where the love lyric of the troubadours and that of the trouvères resemble each other the least is in the consciousness among the southern poets of the process of verse-making itself. The explicitness with which the *trobar clus* in particular speculates about the relation between language and poetry seems lacking in the North. Where they are most similar, however, is in a common opposition to all that we have associated with the Old French *chanson de geste*. Both the "open" and "closed" styles, both the troubadours and the trouvères are united in their subversion of the representational, narrative, historical, originary, genealogical—and essentially aristocratic—discourse of the epic.

The radicalness of the *trobar clus* lies in a refusal of linguistic property which also posits the possibility of an alienation of the real property specific to nobility. Here there is no more telling document than the debate between Raimbaut d'Aurenga and Girart de Bornelh over the relative merits of "closed" and "open" verse:

> Giraut, sol que·l miels appareil
> E·l dig'ades e·l trag'enan,
> Mi non cal sitot non s'espan,
> C'anc granz viutaz
> Non fon denhtatz;
> Per so prez'om mais aur que sal,
> E de tot chant es atretal.
>
> Lingnaura, fort de bon conseill
> Es fis amans contrarïan!

> E pero si·m val mais d'affan
> Mos sos levatz,
> C'us enraumatz
> Lo·m deissazec e.l diga mal!
> Que no·l deing ad home sesal.[70]

Giraut, only provided that I prepare what's best, express it there and then, and bring it forth, I'm not concerned if it's not spread far and wide, for a thing of great cheapness was never a dainty morsel; that's why one prizes gold more than salt, and with any song it's just the same.

Lignaura, of right good advice is the argumentative noble lover! And yet if my piping tune costs me any more effort, then let some croaker garble and sing it badly! for I deem it not fit for a man of property.

In this *tenso* dominated by the parallel closed economies of price and poetic expression, Girart uses the word "sesal" to designate property. Moreover, he grasps the bivalent significance of such a term and the consequences of its transgression. The interruption of meaning through "garbling" and the interruption of real property (and, by extension, of lineage) are equated. As Girart affirms, the difficult lyric associated elsewhere with bastardy and disinheritance is, in its disruptive disregard for linguistic property, ill-suited for men of noble birth.

We will have occasion later to return to the relationship in this period between real property and the advent of an economy of exchange (see below, pp. 161–170). Let it suffice for the present merely to signal the close connection between the nominalizing lyric based upon a never-ending series of metaphoric substitutions and the type of conversion implicit to money, or metaphoric property. The word *translatio*, as M. Shell has pointed out, can be applied both linguistically to the act of translation or economically to that of exchange.[71] Geoffrey of Vinsauf sums up the metaphoric potential of words by the term *convertibilitas*, their potential for semantic conversion. And Albert of Monte Cassino, in a passage already quoted in part (see above, p. 119), adds to the resonances of dislocation and innovation attached to metaphor those of price and sale:

Suum autem est metaphorae modum locutionis a proprietate sui quasi detorquere, detorquando quadammodo innovare, innovando quasi nuptiali amictu tegere, tegendo quasi praecio dignitatis vendere.[72]

However, it is the function of metaphor to twist, so to speak, its mode of speech from its property; by twisting, to make some innovation; by innovating, to clothe, as it were, in nuptial garb; and by clothing, to sell, apparently, at a decent price.

There can be little doubt that the love lyric, "the making of words full of breaks," represents a disjunction of the linguistic property that we have associated both with the epic and with early medieval grammar. Nor can such a disengagement of words from their conventional and proper meaning be separated from the disruption that the reintroduction of money within the circuit of human affairs represented for the great lineages, the "men of property," of twelfth-century France. The social, economic, linguistic, philosophical, and theological dimensions of that disruption, which thus far we have read only through poetry, constitute the subject of the chapters which follow.

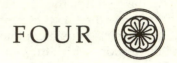

FOUR

Poetry, Philosophy, and Desire

In the preceding chapter we explored some of the ways in which the Provençal love lyric can be said to stand in opposition to the discourse of the Old French epic and thus the ways in which it seems to undermine an essentially agnatic and aristocratic family model. The *trobar clus* creates a breach in the continuity of lineage through a break in the continuity of language, a severance with both economic and linguistic property. The *trobar leu* achieves a similar subversive effect through the creation of a static, taxonomic theater of the self which prescribes oscillation between conflicting states, but which at the same time precludes action, denies time, renders futile narration and history, and implicitly obstructs a continuous genealogical progression. If the *trobar clus* fornicates with words, extending their semantic range to the point of illegitimacy, the *trobar leu* provokes an incestuous relativizing of meaning through the closure of language upon itself. Both undercut in different ways the patrilineal discourse of the noble *geste*—the family and the songs that are sung about it.

And yet, there is another sense in which the subversiveness of the lyric is even more compelling. We spoke earlier of a biopolitics of lineage based upon the close surveillance of family marriage policy (see above pp. 70–75). The question of who may marry whom is, at bottom, that of the future of the paternal fief, of lineal *proprietas* and the propriety of lineage. This is why anything resembling the notion of romantic love—of desire belonging exclusively to an individual—represented such a threat. The prospect of individuals loving freely implies the possibility of their marrying freely; and this eventuality entails a concept of marriage in which the future of great family fortunes is increasingly removed from direct family control. Desire, hypostatized, constitutes a menace to the aristocratic houses of feudal France; and the *canso/chanson* is the genre of pure desire.

To present fully the crucial question of the relative importance of nature versus culture in the determination of social status would be to risk an unnecessary detour in our discussion; all the more so since this subject has been masterfully summarized by E. Köhler.[1] Let us pass, then, to the poets and "theoreticians" of courtly love for whom the socially disruptive effects of sexual desire are directly linked to the destruction of genealogy. It is here that the notion of autonomous desire is linked to an implied equalization of social difference, and hence, where desire might lead to marriage, to the disruption of lineage. Andreas Capellanus, for example, senses, even revels in, this threat in the *De Amore*, which takes as its basic premise the equality of all who serve in "Love's army":

> Nam quum omnes homines uno sumus ab initio stipite derivati unamque secundum naturam originem traximus omnes, non forma, non corporis cultus, non etiam opulentia rerum, sed sola fuit morum probitas, quae primitus nobilitate distinxit homines ac generis induxit differentiam.

> Cognosco igitur manifeste, quod amor non consuevit homines discretionis stilo discernere, sed omnes pariter angit in suo, id est, amoris exercitu militare, non excipiens formam, non genus, neque sexum, neque sanguinis inaequalitatem distinguens, sed hoc solum discernens, an aliquis sit aptus ad amoris arma ferenda.[2]

> For since all of us human beings are derived originally from the same stock and all naturally claim the same ancestor, it was not beauty or care of the body or even abundance of possessions, but excellence of character alone which made a distinction of nobility among men and led to differences of class.

> Therefore I am confident that love is not in the habit of differentiating men with titles of distinction, but he obligates all equally to serve in his army,

making no exceptions for beauty or birth and making no distinctions of sex or of inequality of family, but considering only this, whether a person is fit to bear the arms of love.

The second of the two above examples occurs within the rhetorical context of a middle-class man's attempt to seduce a woman of the nobility. Nonetheless, even the possibility of such a seduction serves to subvert what for the early Middle Ages was conceived as a natural historical—and genealogical—model. It suggests, in fact, an inversion of the Eusebius-Jerome conception of world history such that the original unity of mankind becomes an argument in favor of sexual equality as opposed to the fixity of rank. Whether or not he actually believed it, Andreas here articulates the superiority of an acquirable nobility of soul—spiritual nobility—over nobility of birth. I say "articulates" because the issue of the authorship of the *De Amore* is far from resolved. But the question of the person to whom the "he" actually refers is less significant than the fact that the *De Amore* is dominated by the question of the appropriateness of love between those of different classes (cf. the dialogues between men and women of nobility, high nobility, and middle class).[3] And the decisions of the supposed Court of Love turn more often than not around the disputed claims of those who, because of the equality that love allows, become capable of desiring the same thing.

Among the lyric poets, love is no less a leveler of the human condition. Bernart de Ventadorn observes that love "makes poor and rich of the same rank." And he claims to have personal experience in that domain: "Beautiful and graceful, she made me into a rich man from nothing."[4] Conon de Béthune takes up the same problem in a debate between a younger, lesser knight and an older and nobler woman, who has refused his love in the past but who now seeks it. To the belated attempt at seduction, based upon riches and race, the uninterested lover replies: "On n'aime pas dame por parenté, / Mais cant ele est bele et cortoise et sage. Vos en savrés par tens la verité!"[5] This consciousness of the equalizing effects of love is expressed at its most extreme as an inversion of social status and the ability to love. The troubadour Guilhem de Montanhagol, for example, asks his lady to love not because of his exalted rank but because of his low condition, "for the poorer one is, the more worthy."[6] The famous *partimen* between Girart de Bornelh and Alphonse II even seems to imply that the powerful are incapable of *fin' amors*:

> Senher, molt pren gran mal domneis,
> Can pert la cud' e·l bon esper;
> Que trop val enan del jazer
> L'afars del fin entendedor,
> Mas vos, ric, car etz plus maior,

> Demandatz lo jazer primer
> E domn' a·l cor sobreleuger
> C'ama celui que no·i enten.[7]

Lord, the service of ladies suffers a great wrong whenever it loses patience and good hope; since before the nuptials are concluded noble suitors of great worth request, as they are powerful, their pleasure first; and the lady who loves he who does not woo her has a frivolous heart.

Girart's affirmation, which poses the interesting issue of the relation between deferral of sexual gratification and social status, also attests to the fact that, within the increasingly differentiated levels of aristocracy (and even within the middle class), love offers at least the illusion of a meritocracy. As the rhetorician Mathew of Vendome, citing Claudianus, notes, "we are distinguished by virtue, not blood; and nobility of soul is the only virtue."[8]

Rhetoric and Desire

This leads to the question of the relation between rhetoric and desire. We have seen that where desire is adulterous it tends to falsify genealogy—to obscure true paternity—just as "difficult" language tends to hide meaning (as well as to incite desire). More important, the desire of those who are as yet unmarried opens almost infinite possibilities of recombination, of (mis)match. It represents an even greater threat to the aristocratic family through the abrogation by a desiring individual of the choice that once belonged to—and assured the integrity of—lineage. Thus romantic love as it was invented in the twelfth century introduces a potential obliqueness of family line that remains intimately tied to the process of linguistic deflection. Rhetoric, which by this period had shed its original epideictic function and had come to embrace the art of poetry, constitutes, in fact, the map of such potential digressions.

The connection between desire and figurative language is nowhere more apparent than in the *Leys D'Amors*, a manual of rhetoric and love. Here the doubly ambivalent status of the poetic figure and of illusory descent—Alexander of Villedieu's "semicircle imposed upon a diagonal line" (see p. 119) and John of Salisbury's "wandering from the straight grammatical path" (see p. 52)—is presented through a highly ambiguous genealogy occasioned by a series of mock-epic wars between the three kings of linguistic vice (Barbarism, Solecism, and Allebolus) and the three queens of rectitude (Diction, Oration, and Sentence). After much fighting, hostilities are finally ended by Lady Rhetoric who arranges marriages between the three kings and the sisters of the three queens:

> En tan que Barbarismes hac per molher Na Methaplasmus sor de Na Dictio.

E Soloecismes hac per molher Na Scema estiers dicha Alleotheca, sor de na Oratio.

Et Allebolus hac per molher Na Tropus, sor de Na Sentensa.[9]

Barbarism marries Metaplasm, sister of Diction.

Solecism takes as a wife Schematismus, otherwise known as Alleotheca, sister of Oration.

Allebolus weds Trope, sister of Sentence.

From the offspring of the three couples begins the genesis of the entire range of rhetorical figures, that is, "Barbarism had with his wife Meta-plasmus fourteen daughters: Prothesis, Epitimesis, Paragoge, Augerese (?), Syncope, Apocope, Extasis, Systole, etc. . . . Solecism had with his wife Schematismus twenty-two daughters: Prolepsis, Zeugma, Hypozeuxis, Syllepsis, Anadiplosis, Anaphora, Epizeuxis, Paronomasia, etc. . . . Allebolus had with his wife Trope thirteen daughters: Metaphor, Catachresis, Metalepsis, Metonymy, Autonomasia, Epithet, Synec-doche, Onomatopoeia, Periphrasis, Hyperbaton, Hyperbole, Allegory, Omozeuxis."[10]

Nor does the tedious, cacophonous genealogy end there, but stretches instead across several generations. "Three of these daughters," we are told, "married": "Hyperbole married Trouble [?] and they had five daughters: Hysterologia, Anastrophe, Parenthesis. . . . Allegory wed Alexis, which means 'foreign language,' and they had seven daughters: Irony, Antiphrasis, Enigma, Sarcasm. . . . Omozeuxis married Clarity from whom came three daughters: Icon [Image], Parable, and Paradigm. And since Allebolus was always on good terms with his wife Trope . . . , Lady Rhetoric blessed some of their daughters and grand-daughters with the flowers [of rhetoric] of diverse colors gathered in her garden."[11]

What is striking about the above passage is not only the dissonance of the rhetorical catalogue but the fact that the lineage of rhetoric, in defiance of all genetic probability, consists entirely of females. In what must have seemed a nightmare for the aristocratic family of the High Middle Ages—the production of nothing but daughters, the descendance of the flowers of rhetoric poses the specter of a massive interruption of primogenital sequence. Just as the figure of speech disrupts "normal and proper usage," to invoke once again John of Salisbury's phrase, the reign of daughters disrupts the normal devolution of family property. Put another way, the lack of a male heir forces a transfer of the paternal holding by affiliation as opposed to filiation and thus serves to destabilize that which was heretofore considered to be sacred, inalienable, and immobile (see above, pp. 73–75). At the same time, the use of poetic figure works to detach language from fixed meaning, its fixation in the proper, and thus to mobilize—through the very kind of alliances contained in the *Leys D'Amors*—its playful potential.[12]

Poetry and Perversion: Alain de Lille

No one is more aware of the close connection between adultery, false genealogy, and poetry than Alain de Lille, whose *De Planctu Naturae* reads like a virtual casebook of all that has concerned us up until now.[13] Alain thus associates the "lawful path of sure descent" with Nature, who in turn delegates the task of assuring genealogical continuity. "I stationed Venus," Nature confesses, "so that she . . . might weave together the line of the human race in unwearied continuation, to the end that it should not suffer violent sundering at the hands of the Fates."[14] Venus's path is "the straight way," and the means of achieving her ends bespeaks linearity. Nature has endowed her handmaiden with two instruments of rectitude—*ortho*graphy, or straight writing, and *ortho*dox coition, or straight sexuality:

> Incudum etiam nobiles officinas ejusdem artificio deputavi, praecipiens ut eisdem eosdem malleos adaptando rerum effigiationi fideliter indulgeret, ne ab incudibus malleos aliqua exorbitatione peregrinari permitteret. Ad officium etiam scripturae calamum praepotentem eisdem fueram elargita, ut in competentibus schedulis ejusdem calami scripturam poscentibus, quarum meae largitionis beneficio fuerat compotita juxta meae orthographiae normulam, rerum genera figuraret, ne a propriae descriptionis semita in falsigraphiae devia eundem devagari minime sustineret. Sed cum ipsa genialis concubitus regula, ordinatis complexionibus, res diversorum sexuum oppositione dissimiles ad exequendam rerum propaginem connectere teneretur. . . . [*De Planctu*, p. 475]

> Also, I appointed for her work anvils, noble instruments, with a command that she would apply these same hammers to them, and faithfully give herself up to the forming of things, not permitting the hammers to become strangers to the anvils. For the office of writing I provided her with an especially potent reed-pen, in order that, on suitable leaves that desire the writing of the pen and that she had taken possession of thanks to my generosity, she might, according to the rules of my orthography, trace the nature of things, and might not suffer the pen to stray at all in the trackless diversion of false style away from the path of proper description. But since for the production of progeny the rule of marital coition, with its lawful embraces, was to connect things unlike in their opposition of sexes. . . .

Licit intercourse thus preserves the continuity of lineage and is indissociable from correct writing, or grammar, which excludes diversion from "the path of proper description," that is to say, the proper. Nouns and adjectives copulate according to the rules of heterosexual combination;[15] and people conjugate according to the precepts of regular construction:

> Praeter hoc adjunxi, ne Dyonea conjunctio in transitivae constructionis habitum uniformem, vel informem, vel reciprocationis circulum, vel retran-

sitionis anfractum reciperet, solius transitionis recta directione
contenta. . . . [*De Planctu*, p. 477]

Besides this, I added that the Dionean conjugation should not admit into
its uniform use of transitive construction either a defective use, or the circuity of reflexiveness, or the crookedness of double conjugation since it is
content with the direct course of single conjugation. . . .

Alain's veiled references to masturbation, "the circuity of reflexiveness,"
and to adultery, "double conjugation," raise the combined possibility of
linguistic deviation and sexual derogation. He mythologizes, in fact, the
former in terms of the latter. For Venus, bored with licit intercourse with
her husband Hymen (marriage), seduces Antigamus (Antimarriage) and
conceives Jocus, or Mirth.[16] In this way the satirist envisages two types of
language coterminous with two principles of descent. The first is natural
and correct, since Nature, Hymen's brother, is the guardian of grammar,
the proper, and the paternal; the second, in contrast, transgresses the
rule of natural genealogy and of grammatical rectitude. It poses the
possibility of a discourse divorced from property, and, as its name suggests, inscribed in the illegitimacy of play. According to Alain, then,
adultery is both a sexual and a linguistic act: Venus, "destroying herself in
grammatical constructions, and perverting herself in dialectical conversion, changes her art by the gaudy ornament of rhetoric into artifice, and
her artifice into viciousness."[17]

Grammatical deflection and marital derogation are further subsumed
in the principle of sexual deviation. And if adultery or fornication with
words represents both a genetic and a verbal illegitimacy, it remains the
least serious of sexual and linguistic transgressions. All rhetoric is, for
Alain, the equivalent of deviance:

Sicut autem quasdam grammaticae dialecticaeque observantias inimicantis-
simae hostilitatis incursus volui a Veneris anathematizare gymnasiis; sic
metonymicas rhetorum positiones, quas in suae amplitudinis gremio rhetorica mater amplectens, multis suas orationes afflat honoribus, Cypridis
artificiis interdixi, ne si nimis durae translationis excursu, a suo reclamante
subjecto, praedicamentum alienet in aliud, in facinus facetia, in rusticitatem
urbanitas, tropus in vitium, in decolorationem color nimis convertatur. [*De
Planctu*, p. 478]

Furthermore, just as it has been my purpose to attack with bitter hostility
certain practices of grammar and logic, and exclude them from the schools
of Venus, so I have forbidden to the arts of Cypris those metonymic pos-
tures of rhetoricians which Mother Rhetoric embraces in her wide bosom,
thereby gracing her speeches with many fine touches; for I feared lest if, in
the pursuit of too strained a metaphor, she should change the predicate
from its protesting subject into something wholly foreign, cleverness would
be too far converted into a blemish, refinement into grossness, a trope into
a fault, ornament into a show.

Grammatical and sexual prohibitions work hand in hand to prevent the use of "too strained a metaphor," which is the equivalent of verbal and moral vice. Viciousness, which, it will be recalled, is also a rhetorical concept designating incorrect usage (barbarism and solecism), carries the bivalent resonance of a confusion of active and passive functions—a "retaining under the letters of the passive the nature of the active," that is, "an assumption of the law of the deponent"—and a confusion of genders. The homosexual, for example, is thus "both predicate and subject, he becomes likewise of two declensions, he pushes the laws of grammar too far. He barbarously denies that he is a man. Art does not please him, but rather artifice; even that artificiality cannot be called metaphor; rather it sinks into vice."[18] The association of sophistry—linguistic artifice, excessive ornament, show—and sodomy lies at the core of Alain's own tricky (because satirical) thought; and it leads syllogistically to the identification of poetry with perversion. Those who "push the laws of grammar too far" and defy Nature's rule of straightness find themselves, as in Dante's placement of Brunetto Latini, among the sodomites.[19] The poet belongs to the line of Jocus, those who embrace—through simulacrum instead of rectitude—the art of *gai saber*.

Even here, however, it seems that Alain is more perturbed by the notion of irregularity than by any specific linguistic or sexual derogation:

> Eorum siquidem hominum qui Veneris profitentur grammaticam, alii solummodo masculinum, alii femininum, alii commune, sive genus promiscuum, familiariter amplexantur. Quidam vero, quasi heterocliti genere, per hiemem in feminino, per aestatem in masculino genere, irregulariter declinantur. Sunt qui, in Veneris logica disputantes, in conclusionibus suis subjectionis praedicationisque legem relatione mutua sortiuntur. Sunt qui vicem gerentes suppositi, praedicari non norunt. Sunt qui solummodo praedicantes, subjecti termini subjectionem legitimam non attendunt. Alii etiam Diones regiam ingredi dedignantes, sub ejusdem vestibulo ludum lacrimabilem commentantur. [*De Planctu*, p. 463]

> Of such of these men as profess the grammar of love, some embrace only the masculine gender, some the feminine, others the common or indiscriminate. Indeed, some, as if of heteroclite gender, are declined irregularly, through the winter in the feminine, through the summer in the masculine. Some, in the pursuit of the logic of love, establish in their conclusions the law of the subject and the predicate in proper relation. Some who have the place of the subject have not learned how to form a predicate. Some only predicate and do not await the proper addition of the subject's end. Others, scorning to enter into the court of Dione, devise a miserable sport below its vestibule.

As in our analysis of the *Leys D'Amors*, it is, ultimately, the mobility of poetic language and of sexual identity ("the heteroclite gender") that represents for Nature the most potent threat to the *straight*ness—*correct-*

ness, *regularity, orthodoxy*—of *grammar* and to the continuity of *lineage*. The lack of definition—and it will be remembered that the grammar of this early period is based upon the search for *recti*tude of definition—is tantamount to the dissolution of paternal relations, the transgression of Nature's and of society's most sacred law.[20] To the modern dictum "Nature abhors a vacuum" the Doctor Universalis might have preferred "Natura abhorret hermaphroditos," with the understanding that the poet is himself the polyvalent figure who, in the words of Bernart Marti, "will transform a bitch into a sire and raise today until tomorrow" (see above, p. 113).

For Alain, undefined sexuality or hermaphroditism represents an extreme form of the sterile perversions (masturbation, homosexuality, sodomy) as well as the fecund but transgressive diversion of adultery. Nor can marital infidelity be separated from adulterated language—words which do not respect the rules of definition, of class, conjugation, gender, the "law of subject and predicate," or the limits of ornamental expression. Here, in fact, the twelfth-century satirist seems to articulate theoretically that which the lyric poets express more implicitly: that desire—free-floating, indiscriminate, and disruptive of hierarchy—and poetic ambiguity—the mixing of meanings and the break with intelligibility—are coterminous principles which effect coevally the subversion of a traditional semantic and social order. The most apparent manifestation of this loss of linguistic and genealogical determinacy is the unbounded and directionless proliferation of verbal discourse and of family.

In the *Leys D'Amors* each rhetorical marriage, instead of producing one male heir and thus guaranteeing primogenital continuity, gives rise to a cacophonous plethora of offspring—a surfeit of figures of speech which replicate geometrically. Each new combination, according to the catalytic potential of rhetoric for making heretofore unanticipated connections (verbal marriages), only multiplies the seemingly limitless possibilities of semantic "conversion." In the *De Planctu Naturae*, the disruption of social order through the transgression of marriage, literally the cuckolding of Hymen, produces the boundless free play of Jocus—game, artifice, simulacrum, the discourse of fiction. And in the courtly lyric, whether of the "open" or "closed" style, Alain's allegorical Jocus is made flesh through the circular practice of self-reflexive word play, poetry as a game and as the endless repetition of an unchanging drama of suffering and joy. Thus, in each case, a dispersion of seed—against the grain of the biopolitics of lineage—implies and is implicated in semantic dispersion. The dispersion of family line parallels the dissemination of meaning in a nexus which sets linguistic and genealogical continuity (affirmation of the proper and of legitimate generation through coition in marriage) against sexual impropriety and the diffusion—strewing, radiation, dissipation, uncontrolled distribution—of genealogy inherent to poetry and rhetoric.

Poetry and Castration: Jean de Meun

Among the vernacular allegorists, none is more aware of the relation between poetry, desire, procreation, and signification than Jean de Meun, who derives much from Alain. Jean's Nature, like that of the *De Planctu*, is the earthly agent of generational continuity, the guarantor of the species despite the death of individuals.[21] Nature's confessor, Genius, is the "god and master of places and of property."[22] If Nature assures the survival of the human race, its continuity, her vicar preserves the proper places (*leus*) of speech or the order of representation itself. Genius embodies the figure of the writer, the scribe of that arch-text of the Middle Ages—the Book of Nature:

> Devant Nature la deesse,
> Li prestres, qui bien s'acordoit,
> En audience recordoit
> Les figures representables
> De toutes choses corrumpables,
> Qu'il ot escrites en son livre,
> Si cum Nature les li livre.
> > [*Rose*, v. 16278]

Sitting in audience before Goddess Nature, the willing priest recorded the images (representational figures) of all corruptible things, which he had written in his book, as Nature gave them to him.

Proper writing (the discreteness of place) and proper generation (the uninterrupted devolution of things according to their nature or property) are, through Nature and Genius, combined.

Nature remains, however, an ambiguous figure as her role as "forger" suggests: the measure of which she is the guarantor is itself a forgery, the product of an always already operative corruption.[23] And in what amounts to an exemplary adaptation of a Classical theme to the medieval concern with signs, Jean recasts the story of the end of the Golden Age in the mold of contemporaneous language theory. He participates, along with his traditional sources (Hesiod through Ovid, Claudian, Macrobius), in the myth of the prelapsarian era before the existence of desire, private property, social difference, or the linguistic difference brought about by Reason's imposition of names on things.[24] Jean's version of the fall from an original unity into multiplicity involves neither perversion nor marital diversion but a family drama emphasizing the connection of semiotics, economics, social status, and sexual desire:

> Justice qui jadis regnoit
> Au temps que Saturnus vivoit,
> Cui Jupiter copa les coilles
> Son fis, cum ce fussent andoilles,
> Puis les geta dedens la mer,
> (Mout ot ci dur filz et amer)

> Dont Venus la deesse issi,
> Car li livres le dit issi. . . .
>
> [*Rose*, v. 5535]

Justice used to reign in the age of Saturn whose balls were cut off by his son Jupiter as if they were sausages; then he threw them into the sea, this cruel and bitter son, from which Goddess Venus sprang forth, as the book recounts. . . .

Thus the break in genealogy that castration implies, the physiological disruption of the continuity of lineage, is directly associated with a radical problematizing of the nature of verbal signification. In Saturn's loss the dismemberment of the family becomes synonymous not only with the birth of desire—Venus issued from the foam around the father's discarded member—but with the dismemberment of meaning.

Jean is obsessed by the question of how properly to name that which Saturn lost at the time of his castration. The debate between Reason and the Lover, itself set within a drama of desire and seduction, focuses explicitly upon the issue of linguistic propriety, as Amant reproaches his seductress her directness of speech:

> Si ne vous tienz pas a cortoise
> Que ci m'avés coilles nomees,
> Qui ne sont pas bien renomees
> En bouche a cortoise pucele.
> Vous, qui tant estes sage et bele,
> Ne sai comment nommer l'osates,
> Au mains que le mot ne glosates
> Par quelque cortoise parole,
> Si cum prodefame parole.
>
> [Ibid., v. 6928]

I do not hold you to be courteous because you have just used the word "balls" which are not of good repute in the mouth of a courtly maid. I do not know how you, who are so wise and beautiful, dare name them without at least glossing the word with some more courteous expression as a noble woman should speak.

Here, the playful hint of nonreproductive sexuality (oral copulation)—which Jean, unlike Alain, seems to encourage rather than proscribe—is linked to nondirect language or gloss ("Au mains que le mot ne glosates"). What is more, the charge of impropriety tied to Reason's use of direct speech is countered by a general defense of linguistic property:[25] since everything in God's creation partakes of his divinity, there can be no harm in the designation of a created object by its proper name:

> Se je nomme les nobles choses
> Par plain texte, sanz metre gloses,
> Que mes peres en paradis
> Fist de ses propres mains jadis,

Et touz les autres instrumens
Qui sont piliers et argumens
A soutenir nature humainne,
Qui fust sans eus et casse et vainne.
Car volentiers, non pas envis,
Mist Diex en coilles et en vis
Force de generacion
Par merveillouse entencion,
Por l'espece avoir toute vive
Par renouvelance naÿve,
Par quoi Diex les fait tant durer
Que la mort ne puet endurer.

[*Rose*, v. 6957]

If I call noble things by their proper name, without glossing, it is because my father in heaven once made them with his own hands, along with all the other instruments which serve as pillars and arguments to sustain human nature, which without them would be broken and vain. For willingly, not begrudgingly, did God with marvelous understanding place in balls and in prick the force of generation in order that the species might survive through innocent renewal, through which God made them live so that death might not triumph.

The above example points as poignantly as any to the close identification of the directness of a proper appellation and the continuity of generation. The nominative "balls" possesses grammatical rectitude and is the very instrument of generation; the straightness of proper signification and of linear descent are conjoined. Further, just as human genealogy would collapse without sexual organs (the "force of generation in balls and prick"), human nature—that which is proper to man, or Reason itself—would dissolve in the absence of proper speech. The linearity of logic ("argumens") would literally be broken ("casse et vainne") were it not for straight speech ("plain texte").

Thus we are faced with a potent paradox: through castration both genealogy and meaning are interrupted; yet through the severed member and the word which names it the integrity of lineage and of language are restored. This contradiction is only resolvable if we bear in mind that Reason is herself a highly ambiguous figure. On the one hand, she affirms the importance of linguistic property: "Comment, por le cors saint Homer! / N'oseré je mie nomer / Proprement les euvres mon pere?" And, on the other hand, she maintains the contingent nature of all verbal signs: "Que, tout ait Diex faites les choses, / Au mains ne fist il pas le non."[26] It is a matter of habit, then, whether "balls" are called "coilles" or "reliques."[27] Reason, the namer, thus simultaneously espouses both a doctrine of property and what looks like that of pure convention:

Se fames nes nomment en France,
Ce n'est fors de acoustumance.

> Car le propre non lor pleüst,
> Qui acoustumé lor eüst. . . .
> Chascune qui les va nommant
> Les apelle ne sai comment,
> Borces, hernois, riens, piches, pines. . . .
>
> > [*Rose*, v. 7131]

If women never say such words in France, it is by lack of habit. For the proper name which was customary pleased them. But they run about naming them I don't know what—pouches, harnesses, nothings, pots, apples. . . .

Reason's nature, in contrast with the consistency of logic, is that of a paradox. She incarnates both abstinence and desire, encouraging the Lover to renounce love while at the same time attempting to seduce him. In the linguistic quarrel she supports both the primacy of the proper and the arbitrariness of signs. She is, in short, a contradictory figure, the very opposite of a fixed, univocal, even obsessional, allegorical sign. The inconsistency of her behavior and her thought raises, in fact, the horrifying specter, so dear to Alain, of the indeterminate—the hermaphroditic simulation of the true sign whose extreme expression in *Le Roman de la rose* is Faux-Semblant: "Je sai bien mon habit changier, / Prendre l'un et l'autre estrangier. / . . . Or sui princes et or sui pages, / Or sai parler tretouz langages."[28] In the loss of a proper language and the refusal of a single identity, Faux-Semblant exploits the social consequences of Reason's linguistic theory—that is, the close connection between the rejection of property, antisocial desire, and, ultimately, of poetry. He/She completes the cycle of linguistic, familial, and poetic dissemination beginning with castration and terminating in the *Roman* itself.

Saturn's mutilation entails a break in genealogical continuity, a disruption of lineage, that is indissociable from semiological dispersion, a break with the fixity of signs implying, in turn: (1) the breakdown of character and even logic (e.g., Reason acting incoherently and desiring what she denounces); (2) indiscriminate sexuality, manifested in Jean's portion of the poem in the constant denunciation of the insatiable lust of women (first that of seductive Reason and later that of Nature, whose role is supposedly the preservation of the propriety [linearity] of descent); (3) indeterminate sexuality, embodied in the figure of Faux-Semblant who keeps as his/her companion Lady Abstinence Constraint, in order to seduce more freely; (4) and, finally, the allegorical poem itself.

The proliferation of desire inherent in the dissemination of proper meaning is articulated poetically as a break with the hierarchical order of true allegory (i.e., Guillaume's portion of the *Rose*), implying a refusal of the univocity of the true allegorical sign. Problematizing simultaneously the notions of proper signification and of proper genealogical succession,

Jean's poem ultimately transgresses its own familial or generic form. The second half of the *Roman de la rose* is a directionless, never-ending, ever-supplemental, seemingly tumorous, multiform, "hermaphroditic" text that, like Faux-Semblant, is difficult to pin down because it incarnates the very undefined principle of semiotic and sexual indeterminacy, free-floating desire, the abrogation of the rule of family and of poetic form.

Philosophy and the Family: Abelard

The great medieval drama of letters and castration is, of course, that of Abelard, whose mutilation, unlike that of Saturn, does not give birth to desire but stems it. Actually, the cycle of Abelard's calamities is more complicated still, since letters produce pride, and pride engenders desire. It is, in fact, the act of regarding himself "as the only philosopher remaining in the whole world" that leads Abelard, in his own phrase, "to loosen the reins on his desires," despite a lifetime of continence.[29] Desire, in turn, is augmented by letters, which become the vehicle of seduction:

> Que cum per faciem non esset infima, per habundantiam litterarum erat suprema. . . . Tanto autem facilius hanc mihi puellam consensuram credidi, quanto amplius eam litterarum scientiam et habere et diligere noveram; nosque etiam absentes scriptis internuntiis invicem liceret presentare. . . . [*Historia*, p. 71]

> Of no mean beauty, she stood out above all by reason of her abundant knowledge of letters. . . . The more I came to recognize that she lovingly possessed a knowledge of letters, the more easily nonetheless I believed that this girl would be at one with me; so, even if we were parted, we might yet be together in thought with the aid of written messages.

The instrument of passion is the book which, as Abelard admits, represents a deflection of letters: "Our speech was more of love than of the books which lay open before us; our kisses far outnumbered our reasoned words. Our hands sought less the book than each other's bosoms; love drew our eyes together far more than the lesson drew them to the pages of our text."[30] An overattachment to the formal principles of language associated with rhetoric was, since the early Church Fathers, couched in the essentially erotic terms of a fixation upon the flesh. And the Middle Ages are filled with lovers whose desire is crystallized—mediated—through books.[31] But, with the possible exception of Augustine, no one more than Abelard explores the consequences of such a fetishizing of the letter (or the body) to the detriment of its spirit. For desire, pushed beyond the mediatory capacity of signs, leads to the immediacy of fulfillment; fulfillment leads to castration, castration to philosophy ("a devotion to the study of letters in freedom from the snares of the flesh"), and philosophy, finally, to another kind of book: "Accidit autem mihi ut ad ipsum fidei nostre fundamentum humane rationis similitudinibus dis-

mus nobis qui misericordo   urus nec potint nominare

Scene of Castration, from the Customal of Toulouse, Bibliothèque Nationale, ms. lat. 9187. (Printed with permission.)

serendum primo me applicarem, et quendam theologie tractatum 'De Unitate et Trinitate divina' scolaribus nostris componerem.''[32]

Like his own truncated psychic, moral, and philosophical development, the Abelardian biographical circle—from pride in philosophy to philosophy, and from letters to letters—is informed by the principle of closure. Despite its narrative structure, the *Historia Calamitatum* fails to enunciate any progression other than its own genesis; it is, in this respect, a castrated story—*Historia "castrata."* Even the book of philosophy contained in the autobiography suggests such a reading. Offering to the faculty of understanding "rational and philosophical explanations" instead of obeisance to authority, the *De Unitate et Trinitate divina* mentioned in the passage above is both occasioned by castration and itself castrates an entire theological tradition. In it Abelard's appeal to reason—"human understanding"—poses the possibility of interpretation independent not only of the exegetical past, but of doctrine itself. The book on the Trinity, based upon explanation rather than tradition, constitutes a heresy of reading; and when, in the trial which follows its publication, Abelard offers "to explain," his accuser, Albert of Rheims, pretends to "care nothing for human explanation or reasoning in such matters, but only for the words of authority."[33] The essence of Abelard's heresy is, then, the substitution of the "logic of words" for authority. Rather, the setting of one authority against another implicit to the *Sic et Non* opens a Pandora's box by which doctrine is no longer the product of a long, uncontested, received tradition but of a self-generating, dynamic, and relative process creative of its own value and truth. Through dialectic Abelard manages to liberate theology from blind obedience to the past—from an overwhelming attachment to origins—as well as to make it accessible to all who can read and reason. Such a liberation, like that of the poetic sign, signals the heretical possibility of a doctrinal proliferation (analogous to the *Roman de la rose*) which will find its own form in the scholastic *summa*.

Abelard's disruption of an exegetical line, the heritage of a theology for which theology was heritage, becomes even more compelling in light of the book which is condemned. For if the appeal to reason, understanding, or the "logic of words" served to castrate the authority of preexisting doctrine, the actual treatment of the Trinity contained in the heretical tract sustains a similar conclusion. Abelard is, in fact, tried for denying that "although God had begotten God, He had begotten Himself, since there is only one God."[34]

The Trinity was, throughout the Middle Ages, the archetype of the ideal family whose metaphysical terms offered an abstract—universal and eternal—representation of human kinship. As we have seen, Augustine's expression of the trinitarian desire of the Son for the Father betrays a deep-seated wish to escape not only time but the contingency inherent to paternity—in fine, to escape difference (see above, pp. 58–62). And while Abelard pretends to follow Augustine's teachings on the Trinity, he nonetheless inserts into its internal dynamic a profound shift that is not without significance for the present discussion. His insistence upon the oneness of God serves to collapse the Trinity as a genealogical grouping—a genetic relation of engenderer and engendered. Abelard minimizes the etiology of the paternal rapport through a denial of the possibility of the parturition of the One and a rejection of the objective or substantial diversity of any tripartite division. This is another way of saying that he formulates trinitarian doctrine in terms of a grammatical problem, and not merely in the line of the Augustinian attempt to escape verbal and genealogical difference, which ultimately preserves the hierarchy of paternity in both linguistic and familial domains, but more in the mold of Anselm's search for a proper name for God.[35]

Abelard reasons elsewhere that the diversity of the three persons of the Trinity must exist either in language or in that to which the word *persona* refers.[36] If in language, then the Trinity cannot be eternal since words exist only by human imposition and since, in that case, the Trinity would be infinite because of the infinity of names applicable to God. If, on the other hand, triune diversity exists substantially, then God is not one. Abelard's eventual solution provides for diversity according neither to substance nor to number, but according to definition or property. God does not represent three separate essences; rather, he is triune with respect to persons. This is comparable to saying, for example, that man is also one with respect to the uniquely human properties, for example, capacity for laughter, for philosophy, or for grammar (see above, pp. 50–51). At the same time it poses the problem of what it means to predicate a property of a subject. For Abelard, the *tres* and *personae* of the Trinity are joined in an accidental predication which, in fact, escapes the determination of the dialecticians. The names "Father," "Son," and "Holy Ghost" express only approximately the internal relation of the substantially and numerically identical parts of a *unique res*. By way of example, Abelard invokes the common metaphor of the Trinity as a seal (*signum*) consisting of the bronze which seals, the image in wax, and the seal itself.

Thus Abelard seems to abstract the Trinity from a genetic or genealogical rapport; he defamiliarizes family difference—paternity, or even the logical priority of engenderer over engendered. In this his trinitarian doctrine is, once again, of a piece with the biographical narrative, for the conflation of genealogy inherent to the Abelardian Trinity is the doctrinal reproduction of the drama of interrupted lineage central to the *Historia*. Here we should bear in mind that the philosopher-lover is castrated not so much because of desire, seduction, or even his subsequent marriage, but for removing Heloïse from her family.[37] His sin is less one of concupiscence than of having bastardized a noble line, having tampered with the biopolitics of lineage.

Abelard is at once the one whose genealogy has been irrevocably interrupted and the archetypal interrupter. Even the name which he chooses for his son—Astrolabe—represents a curiously scientific break with theology and with philosophy.[38] And the lack of attention paid to this progeny of illicit desire suggests something even more basic to the constitution of the *persona* presented in the *Historia Calamitatum*: namely, that Abelard, irrespective of his mutilation, remains incapable of playing the role of father. This is abundantly clear during the course of his abbacy at Saint Gildas, portrayed in terms of a violent generational struggle:

> . . . et multo periculosior et crebrior persecutio filiorum adversum me sevit quam hostium. Istos quippe semper presentes habeo, et eorum insidias jugiter sustineo. Hostium violentiam in corporis mei periculum video, si a claustro procedam; in claustro autem filiorum, id est monachorum, mihi tanquam abbati, hoc est patri, commissorum, tam violenta quam dolosa incessanter sustineo machinamenta. [*Historia*, p. 105]

> . . . for the persecution carried on by my sons rages against me more perilously and continuously than that of my open enemies, for my sons I have always with me, and I am ever exposed to their treacheries. The violence of my enemies I see in the danger to my body if I leave the cloister; but

within it I am compelled incessantly to endure the crafty machinations as well as the open violence of those monks who are called my sons, and who are entrusted to me as their abbot, which is to say their father.

If Abelard suppresses (castrates?) through neglect his genetic offspring, he is in turn overwhelmed by the spiritual sons who put poison in his chalice and "bribe bandits," as he contends, "to waylay and kill him." The monk who in the beginning functions well as a brother among brethren, then as a lover, and eventually as a guide to the nuns of the Paraclet, fails utterly to experience paternity as anything other than absolute rupture. Abelard represents, at bottom, a profound disruption of the continuity of lineage.

Abelard's status as the arch-interrupter of genealogy is obvious in the association with castration, in his attitude toward authority, in his doctrine of the Trinity, and both in his refusal of and difficulty with actual paternity. And yet, it surfaces in other ways as well: in, for instance, his highly personalized notion of sin and penance stressing the primacy of individual responsibility and remorse rather than the heritability of original sin and of collective guilt[39]; in his choice of the biographical genre which, in view of its relative rarity in the twelfth century, served to valorize the events of an individual life—a self not unlike the *je* of the troubadours and later Guillaume de Lorris—in isolation from either ancestry or progeny; and, finally, in the practice of philosophy itself.

One of the constant themes of the *Historia* is the incompatibility of philosophy and paternity:

> Que enim conventio scolarium ad pedissequas, scriptoriorum ad cunabula, librorum sive tabularum ad colos, stilorum sive calamorum ad fusos? Quis denique sacris vel philosophicis meditationibus intentus, pueriles vagitus, nutricum que hos mittigant nenias, tumultuosam familie tam in viris quam in feminis turbam sustinere poterit? [P. 76]

> What possible concord could there be between scholars and domestics, between scriptoria and cradles, between books or tablets and distaffs, between the stylus or the pen and the spindle? What man, intent on his religious or philosophical meditations, can possibly endure the whining of children, the lullabies of the nurse seeking to quiet them, or the noisy confusion of family life?

The perfect philosopher is thus the castrato, he who, because he is beyond desire, escapes the contingent and illusory world of the senses. All of which changes somewhat Abelard's own relation to the narrative of his misfortunes. It makes him appear, in fact, less the mutilated victim of his own lust than the heroic mutilator of a long exegetical, doctrinal, discursive, and, most of all, semiological tradition.

Abelard's rejection of a paternally present *auctoritas* in favor of dialectics, his conflation of the Trinity, legitimation of biography, and refusal of family are the most apparent gestures of a life conceived from the outset as a saga of interruption. What remains less apparent, however, is the extent to which the Abelardian drama, which will haunt the High and late Middle Ages, is itself determined by a radicalized sign theory. The language arts are central to his philosophical vision—so much so that the deeper one delves, the more difficult it becomes to distinguish biography, linguistics, and theology. For here, perhaps more than anywhere else, the legendary castrato severs his own attachment not only to an intellectual past but to a philosophy of signs based upon origins.

Abelard's departure from the originary grammar of the early Middle Ages can be seen, first of all, in his skepticism toward etymology. Names, he maintains, are imposed upon things according to physical property, but a given appellation only expresses one essential aspect of a more complex reality; the etymology of the word leads therefore to a partial perception of the thing. To be made of earth (*humo*), to take the example dear to Isidore, reflects only part of what it is to be a man (*homo*). Hence the fractional nature of even a proper etymology makes it dangerous to generalize on that basis; as Abelard notes, not all Bretons are brutes as their name implies, "even though the majority are."[40] Then, too, just as the character expressed by an etymology may not be present in all of its referents, it may not be reserved exclusively for the beings designated by the name. This inadequation between signs and signified in fact can prevent the etymology from revealing true *proprietas*, since a *propre* is by definition attributable to the whole of the species. According to Abelard, language and the ontological categories of the real are no longer coterminous principles, and the etymological effort to arrive at the nature even of physical reality is severely compromised. In contrast to Isidore's faith that "knowledge of the source of names leads more quickly to an understanding of things," Abelard is convinced that such knowledge reveals more about "the composition of the name than about the substance of the thing."[41] Etymology cannot, therefore, be used to demonstrate propositions having to do with the real: "Huiusmodi interpretatio, quia solius nominis compositionem sequitur nec rei potius proprietatem exprimit, nullam probabilitatem exigit."[42]

Abelard's distrust of etymology has far-reaching implications for the essentially verbal epistemology of the early Middle Ages. More precisely, the attenuation of faith in the power of etymological thought to recuperate an original order of the world relegates to the realm of the contingent, relative, and historically determined that which once partook of the necessary, absolute, and eternal. Through the castrated castrator, language is, as J. Jolivet observes, "deprived of that ontological foundation which less enlightened, or more mystical, ages accorded it."[43] Abelard incarnates the drama both of Eden and of Babel in an archetypal cycle of desire, satisfaction, and exile which ends in a fall from linguistic grace.

Abelard's break with the linguistic past, which implies a break in the semantic integrity of the individual word, also extends to larger grammatical constructions. And just as the noun whose function is to signify substance with a quality can signify a nonqualified substance, more than one substance, or an accident instead of substance, the *constructio* of the phrase or proposition based upon such an appellation does not conform to the apparent reality of things. The rules of language do not necessarily follow the laws of nature; and in misrepresenting dialectical truth, grammar also betrays that which dialectics acknowledges to be true. But beyond the appellative anomaly and syntactic imperfection lies a more pervasive, systemic inadequation: that is to say, words never designate things in the first instance; they refer instead to a third set of terms (*sermones*) or intellections, which again do not always parallel the verbal *constructio*. The same intellection can be the object of different expressions as in the example of "running" and "he runs" (*cursus* and *currit*). The mind, in addition, can conceive of absence, inexistence, or intellections without objects (e.g., "rational stones"). Language is, then, always mediated by the meaning of words which, bearing an immediate rapport only with human intelligence and not with reality, offer a more faithful image of the psyche than of the world.[44] For Abelard, linguistics and psychology are intertwined to such a degree that the notion of mental structure—language as a map of the mind—supplants the supposedly objective and universal categories of the real.

In the question of the status of universals, sign theory and ontology seem to merge; and it is here more than anywhere else that Abelard's disruptive presence makes itself felt. He grants that exemplary forms exist in divine understanding, and he acknowledges the resemblance of things in nature; but he denies the claim of universals or ideas to independent existence—to substance, since such a claim contradicts physics (i.e., if the individual members of a same species express a common nature that is external to them and if the distinction between them is merely accidental, then there is, in the example dear to the philosopher, no way of proving as real the difference between Socrates and Plato, or between Plato and an ass). More important, Abelard shifts the question of the reality, the subsistence, of universals toward a general theory of signs, with the result that the ontological family model of genres and species passed from Aristotle to the Middle Ages through Porphyry and Boethius fuses with the discipline of grammar. Abelard transforms Porphyry's three questions concerning the independence, the corporeality, and the inherence of universals into an essentially linguistic problem. What, he asks, for example, does a word like "man" have to signify in order to be joined to an individual like Socrates by the verb "to be"? When one asserts that both Socrates and Plato are men, where and what is the nature of such a conjunction?

Abelard's solution to the problem of universals focuses, in keeping with the grammatical distinction between proper and common nouns, upon the general terms which alone are endowed with universal status: "restat ut huiusmodi universalitatem solis vocibus adscribamus."[45] *Vox*, *sermo*, or *nomen*, the universal is a sign and a word, and, as such, it can be inserted into the grammatical model of predication. Abelard is even more precise: "The universal is a word [*vocabulum*] which has been formed for the purpose of serving as a predicate to several terms taken individually, as, for example, the noun 'man,' which one can connect to the names of particular men according to the nature of the subjects [*subjectarum rerum*] to which it is imposed."[46] A genre, then, is a word to which one can join other words to express, ultimately, the particular, which, in Abelard's view, is alone endowed with existence. For the independence which is attributed to things denies the thingness of universals; a thing is entirely and only itself and cannot be invested with the universality reserved for words or common terms. This is the same as saying that genres and species designate the same thing and that each designates the same as the individual. A collective category is essentially coextensive with its constituent parts, and the difference between them merely verbal. To the question of where two men like Socrates and Plato meet in order for us to call them both *homo*, Abelard responds that it is in their status as men, "which is not a real thing, but is the common cause of the imposition of the same name to each one taken separately."[47]

Thus, linguistics offers both a paradigmatic and syntagmatic solution to the central ontological issues of a profoundly metaphysical age: the status of universal categories and of general nominal terms. The common *vox*, identical to a common intellection as a statue is to a stone, is less the product of a subsistent third entity between words and things than of a socially determined gesture of verbal imposition reflecting observable resemblances in nature. The relation between such *voces* is that of a more universal category predicated of a less universal one. Semantics and syntax are for Abelard more "real"—more satisfactory tools of explanation—than blind faith in the genres and species of early medieval Realism. Even here, however, the relation of nouns and verbs enjoys only approximate status, since verbal propositions, as he emphasizes, remain rooted in contingent and not subsistent reality. The chain of intellections corresponding to the *copula* of noun and verb expresses "the comportment of things among themselves, that is to say, whether they agree or not" rather than any necessary objective rapport. The value of the proposition is more logical than ontological. As Jolivet again notes, the closest modern equivalent is the phenomenological term "Sachverhalt," a "state of things" corresponding to Abelard's "quidam rerum modus habendi se."[48]

If I have insisted upon Abelard's denial of the reality of universals and his redirection of metaphysics toward problems of signification, it is because this aspect of his thought is of a piece with the legend of his castration; and it points, once again, to the monumental role of the philosopher whose genealogy is supposedly disrupted in the disruption of an intellectual genealogy itself predicated on such linguistic and ontological continuities. He to whom paternity is denied, and who becomes the central symbol of such a denial, is, ironically, the one whose ruptured heritage—heritage of rupture—will prevail. For Abelard's theory of signs points in the direction of, and in fact sets the tone for, the radical reorientation of linguistics of the High Middle Ages.

Nominalist and Modal Grammar

The first manifestation of this break appeared with the early if somewhat isolated articulation of Nominalism by Roscelin of Compiegne, whose thought, known primarily through Anselm and Abelard, was more extreme than that of any of his successors before the fourteenth century. Roscelin asserted the nonexistence of universals, which represent for him mere names (*nomina*) and even "empty noises" (*flatus vocis*). He is unwilling to grant even a loose, approximate relation between the resemblances observable in nature and general linguistic terms, which represent only arbitrary meanings. This position will be modified throughout the period in question: by Abelard who, as we have seen, considers universal grammatical expressions to be "confused general images" extrapolated from particular things; by Thomas Aquinas for whom the order of language no longer transmits directly the order of the world, since words as conventional signs refer in the first instance to concepts (mental abstractions); by William of Ockham in whom Nominalism will, two and a half centuries after Roscelin, reach its apogee.

Ockham takes up many of the central issues of Abelard's theory of signs, but his Nominalism is more extreme. Thus, he too, in seeking to rescue an independent conceptual order from confusion with that which exists only in the mind, substitutes logic for metaphysics. For Ockham, cognition comes first in the order of being; and there is little difference, he maintains, between intellect and cognition. The multilayered distinctions that give his writing the appearance of a spectacular hall of logical mirrors are, moreover, oriented toward marking the difference between knowledge and being. Different ways of signifying being do not necessarily connote different levels of being, whether the mode of reference is, like that of Aquinas's version of Aristotle's categories, defined in terms of actuality versus potentiality, or in terms of the Augustinian opposition between immaterial essences and their determinate states.[49] Rather, they constitute terms that may in propositions be substituted for each other. In fact, the question of *suppositio*, how the terms of logic and grammar may stand for each other as cognates, constitutes the crux of Ockham's thought. Hence, the distinctions: between terms taken significantly and nonsignificantly; between natural and conventional signs; between terms of first intention (a natural sign that does not stand for another sign) and of second intention (signs of signs or of concepts such as genus and species); between terms of first imposition (conventional signs for all terms of first and second intention, i.e., the names of natural signs) and of second imposition (names imposed to signify conventional signs, i.e., grammatical categories like "noun," "verb," etc.); between terms having real definition (an absolute term standing for a real thing completely and individually) and nominal definition (a connotative term having only indirect, relative, or negative signification); between concrete terms encountered through direct cognition (e.g., white, hot) and abstract terms requiring real or nominal definition. Such categories for understanding the terms which may be substituted for each other are, further, merely a necessary prelude to the categories of actual supposition. In the substitution of one term of a proposition for another, Ockham also discriminates between: personal supposition (when a term stands for what is signified) in the affirmation of an ontological truth; simple supposition (when a term stands for a concept but not significantly) in the affirmation of a conceptual truth; and material supposition (when a term stands grammatically for another term) in the affirmation of a semantic truth. Within personal supposition, Ockham further distinguishes discrete supposition (when a proper name or demonstrative pronoun is signified) from common supposition (when an appellative stands as the subject of a proposition); and within common supposition, he separates determinate from confused supposition, etc.

These diverse classes of terms and modes of supposition are aimed at establishing the proper conditions for a supplemental exchange within the confines of a logical proposition. And lest their complexity seem gratuitous, it must be remembered that Ockham's ultimate goal is a precision synonymous with unity. He seeks, first of all, perceptual simplicity; and this by shifting what in the early Middle Ages was taken for real distinction emanating from differences in nature or kind toward logical distinction between terms. To this end, he detaches what is considered to be a false perception of real property—the investment of abstractions with objective status—from the conditions or properties of words and signs. The reductive thrust of such a strategy also tends to simplify the referent. For if different terms do not signify substantially different entities, then they must signify the same entity in different ways, or under different aspects. (We will return shortly to this modalization of truth.) Finally, Ockham's terminist linguistics simplifies the realist ontology of an earlier era by eliminating the mediatory role of ideas between the universe of perception and of being. Ockham does away with the need for anything even resembling a species between the knowing conscience and the object known. Abstract knowledge, he grants, does require something beyond the intellect and knowledge, but that supplement or excess represents a mental habit (*habitus*) with no claim to subsistence. General ideas are mere *ficta*, constructions (but not fictions), abstracted from the individual things which alone exist. While the universal is a concept, the natural sign of an act of real knowledge and an object known in the mind, it is not the essence of another substance in which it inheres, at once distinct from individual things and from other universals. The genera and species of Porphyry's ontological tree can be defined only by virtue of their greater or lesser universality in signifying more or fewer particular things.[50] Thus, the categories of the real which Abelard castrates by reduction to more or less general predicable intellections are further mutilated—yea, eliminated—by Ockham's mentalist, empirical, nominalist "razor."[51]

The second radical break with and redefinition of traditional medieval grammar occurred in the second part of the thirteenth century and throughout the fourteenth among the *modistae* or speculative grammarians for whom the object of grammar is expanded to universal—even cosmic—proportions.[52] For thinkers like John and Martin of Dacia, Michel de Marbais, Siger de Courtrai, and Thomas of Erfurt, the goal of language study is the establishment of general linguistic laws. Up until the thirteenth century there were as many grammars as there were languages. The lack of a means of distinguishing between the function of a sign and its origin in a founding moment of imposition precluded any discourse on language abstracted from particular tongues; and it meant that linguistics and historical linguistics were indissociably allied (see above, pp. 37–44). As early as the second half of the twelfth century, however, the distinction began to be drawn between individual languages and the rules of language. Dominicus Gundissalinus (died after 1180) divides grammar into two parts, the "science of observing and considering that which one speech means among the people whose language it is, and the science of observing the rules of those words."[53] And while the former, determined by usage, can only lead to the particular, "according to the diversity of tongues," the latter is "the same among all peoples according to the similarity of rules."[54] A universal grammar, made possible by "immutable and identical conditions and based upon immutable principles" (Nicholas of Paris), comes increasingly to characterize the grammar of the later Middle Ages.[55]

What happened, in fact, is that the universality which had been considered to exist separately in the subsistent world of things was displaced toward the mind and could be located more specifically in grammar. Grammar, which formerly dealt only with contingent entities (*voces* or material sounds), is transformed into a metalanguage as comprehensive in its abstraction as it once was limited in its specificity. By the 1200s it had passed from an auxiliary pedagogical art preparatory to the study of Classical or Biblical texts to an independent branch of speculative philosophy.

Grammar's elevation to the status of universal method was, in fact, a symptom of its merger with logic. We have already seen the degree to which Ockham's attempt to distinguish various types of word use for the purpose of supposition represents a permeation of grammar by dialectic. Among the *modistae* a reliance upon scholastic principles is also much in evidence. The rapport between grammar and language, for example, is conceived variously as analogous to the relation of substance to accident, matter to difference, potentiality to actuality, the general idea to its particular manifestation. Hence the diverse tongues of mankind are to the rules of grammar as individual features—and concrete instances—of speech to formal principle.[56] The speculative grammarian assumes that since the nature of things and of intelligibles are the same to all men, their modes of signifying—that is, the basic categories of speech—must be the same. Where difference exists, it is accidental, nonsignificant; in the words of Robert Kilwardby, "it is not the proper subject of grammar."[57] Grammar discovers through logic unified and eternally true laws. It is disengaged from the vicissitudes of time and, in fact, constitutes itself, as Kilwardby maintains, in terms of an abstract—universally applicable, immaterial—science equivalent in rigor to geometry:

> Dicendum quod sicut geometria non est de magnitudine linee neque de magnitudine enee neque de aliqua contracta ad materiam specialem, sed de magnitudine simpliciter, ut abstrahit ab unaquaque tali, sic gramatica simpliciter non est de oratione congrua secundum quod concernit linguam latinam vel grecam et huiusmodi, sed hoc accidit; ymo est de constructione congrua secundum quod abstrahit ab omni lingua speciali. [*Notices*, p. 127]

> Just as we can say that geometry does not consist of the greatness of a line or the greatness of a weight or of anything limited to a specific substance, but consists simply of greatness disengaged from each of these specifics, so grammar does not consist simply of speech that is fitting because it deals discriminately with the Latin language or Greek and so on, but this is accidental; in truth, it simply consists of a construction that is fitting because it is disengaged from every specific language.

Not only is grammar one, but its laws are necessary and, again like geometric theorems, permit deductive demonstration.[58]

This is because the speculative grammarian believes deeply that though the individual words of a particular tongue may not—because of their accidental nature—reflect reality, the parts of speech considered in abstraction are the correlates of ontological truth.[59] That which is accessible to the intelligence, as Siger de Courtrai claims, can be indicated by the *partes orationis*: "rerum proprietatibus partes orationis invicem distinguuntur."[60] Language, considered categorically and in isolation from concrete expression, stands as a counterpart of that which truly exists or has substance. Thus the two primordial elements of being, stability or permanence (*habitus*) and becoming (*fieri*), are expressed respectively in the noun and pronoun (matter and form of stability) and the verb and participle (matter and form of becoming).

The goal of speculative grammar is to establish a congruity between the mode of being of a thing, the mind's mode of understanding it, and the voice's mode of signifying it. A sign (sound or *vox*), if understood, acquires a *ratio significandi* (power to signify), thereby becoming a *dictio* (word); the *dictio* then acquires from the mind a *modus significandi* by which it in turn is transformed into a *pars orationis*, which, in its ultimate linguistic state, acquires the power to consignify (*ratio consignificandi*) or to enter syntax as a meaningful grammatical unit. A metaphysical series (being, understanding, signifying) exists alongside of a linguistic series (sound, word, part of speech) and serves, where the question of the status of universals is concerned, to place the *modistae* somewhere between the realist and the nominalist: realist or objectivist in that words are not mere figments of the mind with no external correlate; and nominalist to the degree that the word must, in the phrase of R. Bursill-Hall, "pass through the filter of intellectual apprehension" which imparts to it something of the subject.[61] Even here, however, the categories of genre and species endowed by early medieval metaphysics with subsistence are, as Siger notes, equally applicable to general and specific modes of signification: "sicut ad constitutionem speciei concurrent genus et differentia specifica, sic ad constitutionem partis concurrent modus significandi generalis et specificus."[62]

Both the nominalists and the *modistae* in different ways displace the question of origins from the center of grammatical speculation and hence disrupt the assumed continuity between words and things characteristic of early medieval linguistics. This break is situated for the nominalist between the word and its intellection, since, in Ockham's precept, "the concept, or movement of the soul, signifies naturally [essentially] all that it signifies, but the spoken or written term only signifies as a result of willful convention."[63] Among the *modistae*, language, thought, and being exist parallel to but not contiguous with each other. Each linguistic, psychological, and ontological stage is self-contained and complete, as word classes, intellections, and things, despite their homologous relation, remain hermetically sealed from one another. Nor do any of their constituent elements manifest themselves adequately in words or sounds. Speculative grammar is analogical, taxonomic, and paradigmatic to such an extent that it deals only with universal categories with no material expression in any actual tongue.[64] Once again, there is no way of passing from an instance of speech to the original and necessary order of the world.

The diminishing importance of origins in late medieval linguistics can be seen in a turning away from philology, from grammar as mere explanation or gloss of preexisting texts, and, along with the rediscovery of Aristotle, in a triumph of logic over both Biblical exegesis and the *auctores* of Classical and late Roman Antiquity. Within the economy of the medieval language arts, dialect comes to dominate both rhetoric, which passes into the field of poetics, and grammar, which becomes progressively localized. Such a trend is, of course, important for a general history of linguistics and of ideas; but it has special relevance for the originary, participatory, and metonymic grammar of the early Middle Ages—and, in particular, for the concept and role of etymology, which, like the notion of origin itself, is rendered increasingly marginal.

We have seen that Abelard considers etymology to represent a partial truth and rejects it as a principle of argument in the establishment of syllogistic propositions (see above, p. 146). More important, beginning in the second half of the twelfth century, etymologies are defined less and less by the chronological history of a word; and they are increasingly motivated by logical connection. Witness the explanation by one of the glossators of Priscian, associated with the school of Ralph of Beauvais, of the words "formosus" and "morosus":

> Item invenitur quod dictio, que deberet significare plenitudinem rei significate a qua sumitur dictio, non notat nisi plenitudinem rei illius quod est inferius, ut formosus dicitur non qui habet formam, sed qui bonam habet formam, et morosus non qui mores habet, sed qui malos habet mores.[65]

> Likewise we find that a word which ought to signify the full meaning of that thing from which it is derived does not mark apart from the full meaning of that thing anything that diminishes its scope; for example, "shapely" does not mean having a shape, but having a handsome shape, and "willful" does not mean having a will but having an evil will.

Among the *modistae* logical analysis takes precedence over lexical evolution. Thomas of Erfurt, for example, justifies a derivation of the word "albus" from "albedo" on the basis of the logical priority of the latter over the former term. "Whiteness," he reasons, "must exist before the quality 'white' can be obtained."[66]

This shift from diachronic to synchronic or logical etymological criteria was accompanied by a general movement away from the first part of grammar—*etymologia*—toward *diasynthetica* or syntax.[67] The key to such a trend lies in the changing status—limits and power—of the parts of speech. In Classical grammar, word classes were defined as *partes orationis*, and syntax played the role merely of clarifying the division of parts within the unit of the sentence. Accordingly, the grammarian sought merely to identify the group to which each *pars* belonged in order to define its proper role in the *dispositio* of the phrase. The *modistae*, however, consider the *partes orationis* with their synthetic function included as a latent factor. More than isolated words or even word classes, they are the potential *constructibilia* of sentences. Grammar too can no longer be defined as "the art of speaking and writing correctly," but, according to Siger, "grammatica . . . est propter expressionem conceptus mentis per sermonem congruum."[68]

In effect, the speculative grammarians found grammatical analysis upon synthetic criteria instead of upon the autonomous relation of the individual word to that which it signifies. This preference for the *pars orationis* over the *dictio* and for the *sermo congruus* over the *sermo significativus* amounts to an obscuring of the early medieval identification of grammar and semantics or simple signification. For, in the phrase of Bursill-Hall, the word comes to have "not only a notational or semantic meaning which will be linked to its essence and is thus its essential meaning, but also a syntactic meaning which enables it to function by means of a substantial, verbal or other meaning which will derive from its essence."[69] Concerned less with the origin of words than with their relation within a universal grammar which parallels a universal cognition, which, in turn, parallels reality, the *modistae* conceive of the word less as part of a greater thing than as part of a relation in language that reproduces a similar relation in the mind and in the world. And if their grammar can no longer be defined as "the art of speaking and writing correctly," neither can it be said to be synonymous with etymology, definition, or rectitude in the imposition of names. The individual word, cut off from its autonomous power to signify, is rendered powerless; it is "castrated," as the isolating verticality of early medieval grammar has been supplanted by a more horizontal textualizing of terms. What this means is that linguistic value is not a function of an inherent rapport between words and things but of the *dictio* relative to other similar units of meaning. The semantic links that once were conceived to have been established by an original moment of verbal foundation or by the prescience of a knowledgeable namer can no longer guarantee the meaning of the contextually determined signifier. Among the *modistae*, even the basic word categories are reduced to the status of an accident whose mode—not essence—depends upon their relative function within the phrase.

This valorization of consignification or syntax over signification or semantics served to dissipate what appeared in this earlier period as an overemphasis of object over subject. Such a tendency is to be found in a confusion of the categories of meaning and being, and in the subservience of the signifier to the physical property of the thing signified; it is expressed, in Augustinian semiotics, as a certain transparency of signs, a tendency for language, regardless of its particular form, to find automatically the unique object of meaning, which is God (see above, pp. 49–50). In this manner the specificity of language is either overdetermined or radically denied in favor of that to which it refers. Among the nominalists, however, the signifier has no necessary connection to the signified; and for the *modistae* that relation is attenuated by an emphasis upon the modes of verbal signification as opposed to its object. Meaning derives from a part of the word and constitutes a property belonging to it rather than to its referent.

Actually, the distinction between that which a word signifies and the way in which it signifies had become an important concern from the mid-1100s on. Abelard wonders, for example, if tense, which constitutes the specific difference of the verb, does not also apply to nouns: "quod itaque tempus verbis accidit, hoc etiam nominibus congruit . . . ?" And he concludes that the verb differs from the noun less in its designation of time than in its mode of reference: "Non tam igitur in significatione temporis nomen a verbo recedere videtur quam in modo significandi."[70] In keeping with such a theoretical distinction Abelard will also differentiate the verbal form *currit* from the nominal form *cursus* according to diverse conceptual modes (*diversus modus concipiendi*): "*cursus* is designated in its being, *currit* in its adjunction with a subject and with distinction of time."[71] In the generation following Abelard, Peter Helias shifts the traditional definitions of the parts of speech in a similar direction, that is, away from meaning perceived as objective or essential and toward its modalization. A noun, for instance, not only designates substance with a quality, but it is "unus modus significandi in locutione significare substantiam cum qualitate"; and a verb is "alius modus significandi significare actionem vel passionem."[72] Robert Kilwardby, still later, maintains that "the *partes orationis* are not distinguished according to the distinctness of things, but according to the distinctness of the modes of signification."[73]

For the *modistae*, it matters less *what* a word signifies than *how* it signifies. An object may possess several properties which elicit multiple modes of reference.[74] Words with different *consignificatio* may have the same meaning, just as different consignifications of the same word may signify the same object with different accidental qualities. Thomas of Erfurt offers, in his *Grammatica speculativa*, an excellent example of such modalization: the *dictiones* "albedo" and "dealbo" possess the same root *alb-*, but separate accidental possibilities (*rationes*) of consignification.

They have, therefore, not different essential meanings, but diverse essential modes of meaning, that is, a mode of permanent being (*modus entis permanentis*) for "albedo" and a mode of becoming and flux (*modus esse et fluxus*) for "dealbo." Despite their common signification, the two terms display different consignifications because they signify different properties by means of modes of signifying that are essential to different *partes orationis*.[75]

In Thomas's emphasis upon the role of the mind in the determination of meaning according to how its object is understood (*consideretur*), the knowing intelligence is freed from the fixed—perceived as external, universal, and permanent—categories of early medieval grammar (and philosophy). More generally, this deviation away from origins and toward logic produced, along with an investment of the subject *with* meaning and with a responsibility *for* meaning, a corresponding liberation from the monolithic stability (and passivity) of a grammar considered merely to reflect an original ontological order and, in addition, to represent the product of a continual process of linguistic erosion. Grammar was, through nominalist and modalist thought, transformed into an energetic tool of analysis, constitutive as well as reflective of reality. It was, in a word, mobilized—charged with an active role in the creation of a system of value and truth at once inclusive, relative, and dynamic. Unlike the "passive" sign theory prevalent until the twelfth century, the linguistics of this subsequent period represented an aggressive, even imperialistic, science generative of its own arguments—a dynamic model capable of integrating any of its constituent parts.

These elements, again in contrast to the fixed categories subserviently glossed since late Antiquity and in consonance with any genuine meta-discourse, are articulated in such a way as to be interchangeable. The modalized, accidental, and mobile properties of the *partes orationis* are considered less as unidirectional global projections of the stable properties of things than as transposable semiological categories divested of positive meaning. Their hylomorphism is expressed among the nominalists in the theory of *suppositio* and among the *modistae* in the doctrine of *consignificatio*. In both cases, linguistics takes as its central project the identification and classification of common terms favoring the reduction of any element of such a closed system to any other. Essentially commutative and multidimensional, terminist and modal grammar assume the currency of their discrete parts; valorize a constant verbal reciprocity; work, in fact, to maximize the possibilities of substitution and exchange. They stand as mobile models of conversion whose dynamism is, of course, not only contemporaneous with but permeated by late medieval dialectics. Like the scholastic method generally, they represent totalizing systems aimed at creating the isomorphic logical distinctions by which concepts can engage with—be converted into—one another. And, as we shall see in the following chapter, they are also the linguistic equivalents of a closed monetized economy in which substitution is catalyzed by the mediatory presence of a modalized measure to which the value of goods and services can be referred—and for which they can be exchanged.

FIVE

The Economics of Romance

In the preceding chapters we traced the copresence of two seemingly contrary grammatical discourses. The first, inherited from late Roman grammarians and encyclopedists, was transmitted through Carolingian commentators to the glossators of the postfeudal age. It can be characterized in terms of the rhetorical principle of metonymy, though this is merely an insufficient abbreviation for a grammar defined by: a privileging of the notion of temporality, diachronic word evolution or etymology, and more generally, of origins; an assumed attachment of the meaningful units of language—words and word classes—to physical property and thus a deep investment in the propriety of terms (i.e., insistence upon definition and signification as well as upon the continuity and isolated verticality of linear semantic relations); a valorization of the object of reference to the detriment of formal principle, which appears, as a result, unidimensional, fixed, and "passive." The second grammatical discourse, initially articulated by Roscelin and Abelard, was later refined by

Peter Helias, Priscian's twelfth-century commentators, nominalist philosophers, and, in particular, the speculative grammarians of the thirteenth and fourteenth centuries. For the sake of contrast, this body of grammatical thought can be rhetoricized in terms of metaphor, though here again the label represents only partially a linguistics that is: spatially—even geometrically—organized around synchronic categories; more committed to logical distinctions than to chronological sequence, continuity, and origins; less oriented toward the "verticality" of the single word—etymology or definition—than toward "horizontal" problems of syntax and consignification; disruptive of any naturalized attachment of word to physical property (and tending, therefore, toward a supplemental play of substitutions); and, finally, this second principle of grammar proffers a linguistics in which the relativizing mobility of the subject, which has become the arbiter of semantic value, gives the impression of a multidimensional dynamic verbal model.

In terms of literary types we have identified metonymic grammar with the epic. As a genre of origins always set in historical time, the *chanson de geste* demonstrates a narrative linearity, a representational contiguity, a paratactic independence of discursive and dramatic units, a diminished interiority of the subject, and a fixity of objectified values that are thoroughly consonant with the grammar of the early Middle Ages. The troubadour lyric, on the other hand, maintains an analogous relation to a nominalist or modal grammar. Situated in an eternal present outside of temporality or events, the *canso* in particular consists of spatially conceived taxonomies of joy and pain that serve not only to delineate but to valorize a self-creating subject. The language of the lyric has lost its purchase upon the world. And if the *trobar clus* affects a semantic rupture equivalent in its underlying assumptions to the nominalist assertion of the arbitrariness of signs, the *trobar leu* functions according to a mode of textualization equivalent to the modist insistence upon consignification. Nonrepresentational or confusing, the lyric refuses to signify or scrambles meaning by maintaining its own distance, under the regime of rhetoric itself, from linguistic property.

Where kinship is concerned, we have equated metonymic grammar and the epic with the family conceived as lineage. Here the seemingly organic attachment of words to things finds its analogue in the noble kin group's attachment to land, castle, and patronym; and the etymological devolution toward the current term finds a parallel in the genealogical devolution of a family *patrimoine* toward the present scion of the house. Both language and lineage are articulated as transtemporal models whose function is the preservation of the continuity between each of its elements—morphological and biological—and a mythologized origin. To the isolating verticality of a grammar fixated at the level of the word (semantics, definition) corresponds the verticality of lineage with its discreteness not only of maternal and paternal lines but of every line in relation to all others.

Household

The copresence of radically different literary types alongside of contrasting models of the discourse on discourse, or grammar, would have less meaning were it not for the existence of a similar opposition between the aristocratic family conceived genealogically and a contemporaneous notion of kinship closer to what we think of as the conjugal unit. For the genealogical paradigm was, throughout the period in question, threatened by a pattern of family relations which may have been a vestige of the way nobility once pictured itself (as a spatially ordered grouping of relatives, see above, p. 66), but which coincides more readily with the notion of household or *ménage* as opposed to lineage or *maison*. This second model of kinship, more in keeping with the living arrangements of a nascent urban class, is characterized by:

1. A concept of marriage closer to ecclesiastical doctrine according to which the consent of partners and not the decision of family or feudal lord makes a legal conjugal bond.[1] Actually, the importance of the consent of the parties involved can be traced back to the Roman prescription "Nuptias non cucubitus sed consensus facit" (*Digest* 35, 1, 15) and to some of the early patristic thinkers, for example, Augustine but not Jerome. It is not until the twelfth century, however, that the Church, in extending its jurisdiction over all issues having to do with marriage, also asserted the power of partners to choose; and this in two distinct ways associated again both with different ecclesiastical discourses and with distinct geographical loci.

In the discourse of theology as it developed in the region of Paris, there appeared a marked preference for what might best be described as a doctrine of "pure consensualism," that is to say, for the belief that nothing other than the assent of parties is necessary to a valid bond. "Efficiens autem causa matrimonii est consensus"—so states Peter Lombard, who also stipulates that the words of consent must be stated in the present tense ("nec futuro sed de praesenti") because marriage is, above all, an "obligation of words."[2] The agreement of parents is not required either at the time of the betrothal or at the time of the actual wedding.

Alongside of the theological fixation upon consent there developed at Bologna—in the discourse of canon law and especially in the writings of Gratian—a doctrine according to which both consent and consummation are required to make a matrimonial tie.[3] Here the model invoked is that of the sacrament; the union of Christ with the Church, as applied to the domain of matrimony, is not complete without both free choice and physical *unitas carnis*. In reality, what Gratian meant was not that consent did not make a marriage, since he states explicitly that "the consent of those between whom the marriage is made is sufficient according to the law," but that the bond only became indissoluble once the *commixtio sexuum* had occurred.[4] Here we enter the realm of the scholasticism "avant la lettre" of the difference between a valid and a wholly licit tie, which for Gratian resides in the difference between nuptials (*conjugium initiatum*) and their confirmation in the *conjugium consummatum* or *ratum*. Only in the mingling of the flesh is the contract transformed into a bond whose sacramental status cannot be revoked.

Much of the debate about what constitutes a marriage culminated in the so-called Alexandrian synthesis of 1163.[5] According to Pope Alexander III, as long as a vow is pronounced in the present tense (*per verba de praesenti*) or in the future tense (*per verba de futuro*) followed by a consummation, it is legally binding. Even a marriage contracted in the absence of witnesses takes precedence over a subsequent one celebrated publicly and with progeny. Alexander's ruling thus subordinates everything—the approval of parents, the formal request and negotiations between families, the betrothal, publishing of the bans, dowry, intercourse, ecclesiastical ceremony—to what F. Pollock and F. Maitland so elegantly term "a formless exchange of words."[6] This priority of consent over contract will lead, of course, to the legendary abuses of clandestine marriage which, both before and after their prohibition at the Council of Trent (1575), were a source of interest to dramatists like Shakespeare and Webster as well as to novelists as recent as Thomas Hardy.[7]

The social implications of consensualism were profound indeed. From the perspective of the persistent medieval struggle between secular and ecclesiastical power, Alexander's ruling tended to extend the jurisdiction of the Church and the canonical courts as against that of local lords and the feudal judiciary. Seen in generational terms, it bolstered the claims of children against parents. And where the noble family was concerned, it signaled a catastrophic short-circuiting of the biopolitics of lineage. The choice of partners was, for the aristocratic families of feudal France, a collective matter, since it carried with it a host of military, social, and economic considerations: obligations to vengeance and to armed service, political alliance, legal and financial responsibility. But, as we have seen, the question of who may marry whom was synonymous with the question of the future of the fief; and its removal from the hands of those whose role it was to husband the family *patrimoine* represented a threat to the noble lineage's economic strength which cannot be separated from nobility's definition of itself. More precisely, the displacement of the marriage decision away from those invested with the maintenance of genealogy, its continuity free from interruption or the cumbersome dispersion of lateral branches, meant that the family could no longer constitute itself with the same minimal economy—one male heir per generation—as a line. Instead, the autonomy of the individual to determine the biological course of lineage, which remained coterminous with its economic course, posed the possibility of overmultiplication and division—fragmentation and diffusion of race as well as of lands.

2. The notion of household assumes a system of inheritance in which goods are divided more or less equally among heirs as opposed to a system of strict agnatic succession or primogeniture.[8] This represents one of the most complicated areas of medieval family history—complicated because much of what we know about nonfeudal inheritance patterns is culled from late customary material and because even these fourteenth- and fifteenth-century records of practice are marked by enormous regional, demographic, and class differences. There is, nonetheless, a tendency to distinguish between: the customs of the Romanized South, the West, and what E. Le Roy Ladurie refers to as the "Capetian open field area"; the law of towns and that of the countryside, and, above all, between noble holdings and "fiefs roturiers."[9] As we have seen, inequality of inheritance (generally a preference for firstborn sons) was the rule for transfer of the aristocratic central holdings—the castle and chief paternal fief or *alod* (see above, pp. 73–75). Even in southern France, where the eldest male was not as strictly favored, testamentary practice still reinforces the superiority of one descendent over his (or her) siblings. This is not the case, however, for nonnoble possessions for which the rule was that of equality among heirs.

The modes of such equality again vary greatly, and it has only been in the last fifteen or so years that, thanks to the monumental work of J. Yver, we have been able systematically to detect regional patterns.[10] Thus Normandy (and the West in general) is characterized as a region of "strict equality" since, where nonnoble or lesser noble holdings were concerned, an equal division took place at the time of the death of the parents. This meant that married sons and daughters were not excluded from inheritance and, in fact, "brought back" their dowries to the paternal estate which was then redistributed, even against paternal stipulation, in equal portions. "Se li peres depart en sa vie les parties a ses emfanz e chascuns a tenue sa part longuement e en pes el vivant au pere, les parties ne seront pas tenables après sa mort"—so prescribes the *Très Ancien Coutumier de Normandie*.[11] The rule of "rappel" also meant that children whose parents predeceased them before themselves inheriting were eligible to inherit from their grandparents. This preference for direct descendants over collaterals, sometimes referred to as the "rule of infinite representation," again points to the emphasis in the western area upon the maximum distribution of the family *patrimoine* to all members of the same lineage. Lineal, egalitarian, and highly partible, the law of Normandy tended to stress, among nonnobles and nobles alike, bonds of consanguinity over alliance: to wit, even after a marriage had been concluded, the property relations it entailed remained fluid—subject to renegotiation—until the death of the parents.[12] The departure of a son or daughter represented more of a temporary arrangement than a definitive economic break with the household of his or her birth; one was, in other words, not fully married until his parents were dead.

Norman practice contrasts with that of the South, where the stability of wills and of limited *inter vivos* gifts permitted a degree of inequality, as well as with that of the Paris-Orleans basin, where the firmness of dotal exclusions had a similar effect. But, most of all, it differs from the couple-oriented practices of the urbanized North, for example, the customs of Artois, Arras, the Cambresis and Hainaut, French Flanders, Wallon, Lille, Douai, and Tournai.[13] In these centers of demographic density household was stressed over lineage. Not only did children participate in the management of family property, but, more important, that which belonged to the group was conceived to represent a genuine community of goods. Once a marriage had been concluded, a fundamentally new *patrimoine* was created. The alienations on both sides became stable in such a manner that the newly formed conjugal couple, definitively separated from the lineage of birth, was free to dispose of them without fear of a "rappel" for redivision at the time of their parents' death. Furthermore, children of successive marriages inherited according to the "bed of birth," and husband and wife could inherit from each other. This is a fact of considerable significance, since it will be remembered that the rule of aristocratic inheritance, in accordance with the biopolitics of lineage, provided for a strict agnatic autonomy of maternal and paternal lines. Within the space of the town, however, the precept of discreteness—*materna maternis, paterna paternis*—is abrogated so as to effect the continual cognatic alienation of that which, among nobles, was considered the inalienable right, the proper, of dynastic succession. Thus the household cannot be defined "vertically" as those through whom ancestral property devolves but consists of a more "horizontal" fusion of only temporarily independent lines. The urban family, as to some degree the peasant household, represents a genuine economic entity and not merely the coupling of descent groups for the purpose of procreation.

3. The household presupposes a mode of property which, because of the necessity of division, is necessarily more partible. Such property—alienable, personal, salable, constitutive of the principle of exchange itself—corresponds to the reintroduction into the circuit of human affairs of the mobile form of wealth par excellence: money.

Money

Economic historians have, since the nineteenth century, characterized the "first feudal age" as a natural or closed economy as opposed to the monetized, market economy of a later era. More recent studies have shown, however, that even during this earlier period the exchange of goods and services for money did not cease altogether; it merely slowed. In any case, it is not our purpose here to summarize or to try to negotiate between the excellent social and institutional histories of what was surely a formative era in the development of the early modern economy. What concerns us more directly is the fact that medieval economics—how men thought about money in distinction to what or how efficiently actual money may have circulated—is, from all that we have learned about linguistics, assimilable to a general theory of signs. This is an intellectual gesture that is by no means given. Accustomed as we are to the dynamic economic models that have dominated since the eighteenth century, we think of money as a sign only in the narrow sense of its relation to goods, other currencies, and itself. That is, money maintains a symbolic rapport with that which it can be converted into (commodities and services); with other moneys (as well as with the other fixed denominations within a single currency); and, to the degree that the face of a coin stands as a figurative representation of the metal contained therein, with its own constitution. The medievals, on the contrary, had no dynamic economic model, perhaps, it has been suggested, precisely because "problems of money were perceived within the much more comprehensive context of problems of signification."[14]

The subordination of economics to semiotics is fundamental to medieval monetary theory. For while we assume that economics constitutes a metalanguage to which even linguistics is subordinate, those who speculated about money between the time of the Patristics and the Renaissance envisaged such an undertaking as a subcategory of the study of signs. Augustine points out in the *De Ordine* that the birth of letters occurred simultaneously with the discovery of accounting and that both "the art of writers and of calculators together constitute the childhood of grammar."[15] Isidore claims that "money is so called because it warns [*monet*], lest any fraud should enter into its composition or weight. The piece of money is the coin of gold, silver, or bronze, which is called *nomisma* because it bears the imprint of the name [*nomen*], and the likeness of the prince" (*Etym.*, 16: xviii, viii). Though the etymology is false, its repetition by Aquinas and Oresme testifies nonetheless to the recuperation of numismatics by general sign theory.

If economics belongs to the field of semiotics, it is because coins were held to be analogous to verbal symbols. The tendency, especially among theologians of the early Middle Ages, to condemn commerce on doctrinal grounds was, in fact, rooted in a distrust of money in keeping with the suspicion of all earthly—contingent, illusory, corruptible—signs. More generally, the question of how money signifies was articulated along linguistic lines. Albert the Great, for example, incorporated the central issue of language theory, that of nature versus convention, into an explanation of the origin of money; if "numismatics" comes from *nomen*, he maintains, it is because coins, like names, signify by imposition: "non natura est, sed positione; hoc igitur nomisma vocatur."[16] Just as linguists acknowledge that the meaning of words originates by imposition according to the properties of things, coins signify, despite their inherent value, by social convention. Like the verbal terms that are considered to constitute the unity—the common speech or *koiné*—of the community, monetary signs embody the principle of oneness. To invoke another false etymology, again more truthful in its logic than a true etymology in its philological accuracy, Augustine attributes the Latin root of the word "coin" to "co-uneus" instead of to its actual source "cuneus," wedge; and he compares the unifying effects of coinage to the social fabric itself.[17]

Falsifying coinage was, throughout the period in question, a crime against public authority since the right to mint was a princely privilege; counterfeiting and currency manipulation were also, however, crimes against language. Nicholas Oresme, whose *De Moneta* is the most systematic treatise on minting of the Middle Ages, compares such acts to lying; and when "the coin is inscribed with the name of God or of some saint and with the sign of the cross," they become the equivalent of blasphemy:

> Si ergo princeps sub ista inscriptione immutet materiam siue pondus, ipse uidetur tacite mendacium et periurium committere, et falsum testimonium perhibere, ac eciam preuaricator fieri illius legalis precepti quo dicitur: *Non assumes nomen Domini Dei in uanum.*[18]

> If the prince, then, despite this inscription, should change the material or the weight, he would seem to be silently lying and forswearing himself and bearing false witness, and also transgressing that commandment which says: "Thou shalt not take the name of the Lord thy God in vain."

Of the legal means of altering numismatic value Oresme strictly forbids simple changes of denomination because any shift in the name of a coin falsifies its relation to other monetary units, and, above all, because it represents an improper verbal imposition: "For that would be called a pound which really was not a pound, which is, as we have said, improper."[19]

What, it may be asked, constitutes a proper appellation? One, Oresme replies, in which the sign printed on the face of the coin corresponds to its actual weight:

> Quod autem impressio talis instituta sit nummis in signum ueritatis materie et ponderis, manifeste nobis ostendunt antiqua nomina monetarum cognoscibilium ex impressionibus et figuris, cuiusmodi sunt libra, solidus, denarius, obolus, as, sextula et similia, que sunt nomina ponderum appropriata monetis. . . .[20]

And that the stamp on coins was instituted as a guarantee of fineness and weight, is clearly proved by the ancient names of coins distinguishable by their stamp or design, such as pound, shilling, penny, half-penny, *as, sextula*, and the like, which are the names of weights applied to coins. . . .

All other names, Oresme contends, are improper, that is to say, not derived from the essence of the signifier; they are "accidental or denominative."[21] Here it is obvious that monetary theory shares in the key concerns of early medieval grammar, that is, the question of rectitude of imposition and of proper signification. Moreover, it is difficult not to recognize that Oresme's idealized ancient coinage, in which the sign participates in the property of its referent, smacks of an "economic realism" analogous to the linguistic realism of the period between Augustine and, for example, Abelard.

The phrase "economic realism" is not original. E. Bridrey, in a long book on fourteenth-century coinage, maintains—unsuccessfully, as we shall see—that Oresme is a monetary realist living in a nominalist age. M. Bloch refers in his *Esquisse d'une histoire monétaire de l'Europe* to the economic realism of early feudalism as opposed to the economic nominalism of the second feudal age. Within the context of the sign theory of medieval economics the former term applies to:

1. A concept of value that has independent and universal existence regardless of the particular cost of things. Oresme's perfect coin testifies, in fact, to an abiding faith in the subsistence of universal weights and measures which merely inhere in the coins bearing their names. More generally, however, it is worth recalling that until the thirteenth century, when gold was minted for the first time since the Carolingian era, monetary units like the *livre* and the *sou* existed primarily as account or "ghost" moneys—that is to say, as fixed values of which there were no material representations or actual coins.[22] Pure monetary instruments, these monetary "ideas" were used as standard measures of value for payment of taxes, debts, or rent in goods or services. They served to quantify the actual objects of exchange in transactions in which no money actually changed hands; and though obligations might be stipulated in terms of monetary abstractions, they were acquitted in equivalent amounts of commodities or labor. It was assumed, furthermore, that "ghost" denominations were as fixed and eternal as an ideal ontological form. The value of account moneys did not change; rather, the quantity of goods or services varied according to stable monetary criteria (e.g., in a given year one pound might be worth nine bushels of grain and in the next year eleven bushels). Thus, alongside the Platonism of early medieval philosophy and, to a degree, of linguistics, stood a certain economic Platonism determining everyday practice.

2. The expression "economic realism" refers to the fixed relation of account money to the *denier*, which was the only indigenous coin in

circulation until the thirteenth century. The *sou* equaled twelve *deniers*, one pound equaled twenty *sous*; a pound was therefore the equivalent of two hundred and forty *deniers* throughout the period under consideration.

3. Finally, the term "realism" applied to economics implies that the essence of early medieval money was that it contained its own worth. This is especially true of the goods with use value and that were not only exchanged but employed as money, for example, arms, jewelry, serving platters, cloth, food, liturgical objects, etc.; but it is true of metallic money as well. It was assumed that the face value of a coin corresponded to the weight of the metal contained therein. Money represented in this respect a "printed lingot" (M. Bloch) which in times of political order and monetary stability was minted into coins, which in more chaotic times was recast into usable objects, and which, as this fluid circuit between the coin's use and exchange status implies, was frequently put to the test on scales. As a signifying system we can speak, then, of the already abstract notion of early medieval coinage in "realist" terms, or in terms of a relatively direct and fixed rapport between face value and contents. Oresme's hypothetical conformity of volume to denomination is the monetary expression of the wish for union between the signified and its sign, a wish, moreover, thoroughly in keeping with Augustine's desire for semiotic and sacramental union (see above, pp. 60–62).

It was only beginning in the twelfth and thirteenth centuries that we can detect the symptoms of an economic shift of such major proportions as to justify the label of "economic nominalism." In this case, the linguistic analogy indicates the massive appearance of particular pieces of money, which were the manifestation—the realization—of pure monetary ideas and which possessed autonomous value. In short, the individual coin exists, or, to invoke the medieval philosopher's terminology, it "has substance." No longer is money merely an instrument of measure, but it began, against ecclesiastical opposition, to stand as a commodity in its own right. At the same time, the fixity of "ghost" denominations was relaxed, while their relation to articles of exchange was inverted. Henceforth, the value of goods was measured according to variable amounts of money, thus divested of universal value. Money became free to float—a floating signifier—according to prevailing market price. In fact, the question of what constitutes a just price stood at the very center of economic debate among canonists, romanists, and theologians.[23] And in practice not only did money come to constitute a mobile measure displacing the former mobility of goods, but the fixed equivalences between different coins became increasingly mutable from the thirteenth century onward. Such a trend was, of course, attached to the reinsertion of the state into monetary policy, the reconstitution of a public authority with the power to guarantee and deliberately to alter rates of exchange.[24] Finally, this period witnessed a gradual loosening of the relation between the face value and the metallic value of coins. As M. Bloch notes, "the resumption of gold minting, the appearance of large silver coins, and the whittling down of the denier (. . .) succeeded in separating the intrinsic value of money from money of account."[25] The reign of the late Capetians inaugurated the era of monetary mutation—devaluation and revaluation; for this age was marked by the periodic recall of coins and their reissue in equal weight and alloyed substance or in decreased weight despite maintenance of the original face value.[26] Oresme's treatise is, in fact, less a nostalgic attempt to recapture the realism of ancient coinage than a guide to the legal limits—the conditions, techniques, and quantitative bounds—of currency manipulation.

Thus a species can be altered in form alone by the inscription of a new name upon an existing currency which is maintained. Oresme specifies, however, that such "making of new money and demonetizing of the old" is justified only when the prince's money has already been counterfeited or when it has become worn.[27] Money can also be modified by a change in the bimetallic ratio of its denominations, that is, the value of gold coins relative to that of silver ones. Or, it can be manipulated by a shift in name, which requires readjustment of the internal dynamic of the entire system: "It is necessary, then, that if the proportion is to remain unchanged, and one coin changes its denomination, the others should be changed in proportion so that if the first coin is called two pence, the second shall be two shillings and the third two pounds."[28] Similarly, a deviation in weight should be accompanied by a revision of face value, as should any change of material. Oresme even spells out the guidelines to be followed in the making of alloyed pieces:

> Si autem in tali materia sit mixtio, ipsa debet fieri solum in minus precioso metallo per se monetabili, . . . et in nigra moneta, ut cognoscatur purum a mixto. Hec eciam mixtio debet esse secundum certam proporcionem, sicut decem de argento contra unum, uel contra tria de alio metallo. . . .[29]

> But if the material be mixed, it should be so only in the less precious of the metals which are coined pure . . . , and in black money, that the pure may be distinguished from the mixed. And the mixture must be made in fixed proportion, such as ten parts of silver to one, or to three of another metal. . . .

In addition to the simple changes of form, ratio, denomination, weight, and material, any of these may be combined as long as the traditional proportion of the elements of the overall system is preserved.

Historically, the type of mutation that Oresme legitimates by legislation reached its culminating point in the fifteenth century with the issuance of the first paper money—a purely symbolic promise, in the absence of any metal content, to pay what its printed face says. This rivalry of printing press and mint represented, however, the end product of a process begun much earlier: that is to say, the constitution of money as an autonomous commodity to be traded against other species in opposition to the early medieval sense of money as an abstract measure of the value of goods or as a relatively immobile good to be hoarded but not exchanged. Cut off from its roots in physical property or weight, the economic sign was, by the 1300s, conceived to be as much a *flatus vocis* as its verbal equivalent. Oresme simply establishes the modalities of alteration alongside of Ockham who, earlier in the same century, had established the modalities of grammatical substitution. Not only does the articulation of the social institution lag chronologically behind that of its appropriate linguistic model (in this case Nominalism) but economics appears, again, as a subbranch of the *artes sermocinales*.

Oresme's attempt to do for coinage what Ockham did for grammar attests to the penetration of both linguistics and monetary theory by the logical techniques of scholastic analysis. The rise of scholasticism as an integral part of the urban revival of the High Middle Ages was even accompanied by what might be termed a "scholasticism of exchange." Canonists and theologians struggled, against a long anticommercial tradition, to make the kinds of distinctions and connections by which profit could be justified and by which even fraud might be exculpated.[30] As in the areas of sin, penance, and criminal responsibility, intention became the basis of business ethics. And alongside of the plethora of texts devoted to the question of the just price (see above, n. 23, p. 265), there appeared numerous treatments of usury matched in subtlety only by the Jesuitical casuistry of the seventeenth and eighteenth centuries.[31] The application of logic to business served to oil the rusty ideological machinery of a relatively inert economy, to mobilize a system heretofore oriented precisely around the idea of *l'immobilier*. It created, according to a dynamic dialectical model, the conditions under which concepts and techniques essential to effective exchange were naturalized.

To dwell upon the logicization of profit, price, or interest is also to recognize that money is an always already modalized form of property whose purpose is to catalyze substitution—a kind of metalanguage akin to logic itself.[32] Here, in fact, is where late medieval monetary theory and linguistics seem to merge. It will be recalled that we defined nominalist and speculative grammar in terms of a comprehensive, dynamic, and reductive system capable of assimilating any of its integral parts to any other (see above, pp. 150–158). Indeed, such a description of the strategy of the field of logic is equally applicable to any monetary system, as the Aristotelian economics of the scholastics seem to suggest.

According to Aristotle, the unequal division of natural goods and of labor created the necessity of money, a third term by which such inequalities might be measured in order that the diverse sectors of society might interact.[33] Human needs require a scale according to which everything is commensurable; and money, for Aquinas, Bonaventure, and Albert the Great as well as for Aristotle, represents just such a commutative sign capable of rendering naturally dissimilar objects equal. This is why it is properly classified as a subset of justice and why its laws are considered to function in keeping with the natural law of mathematical proportion. All transactions, for example, are governed by a proportionality of value to be arrived at through the ratio of the arithmetic mean. What this means is that the Aristotelian concept of money as uniform measure, a standard of value facilitating exchange, represents an economic version of dialectics. Put otherwise, monetary exchange and dialectics mirror each other. Both are dynamic—one furthering reciprocity through the substitution of a circulating medium for inapposite objects, the other maximizing the substitution of grammatical terms. Both are reductive—one of dissimilar goods, the other of contrasting ideas. (The sale and the syllogism are coequal operations; one oriented toward the reduction of asking price and bid to selling price, and the other toward the reduction of thesis and antithesis to synthesis or sentence.) Finally, both money and logic present themselves as universal systems—one as the quantifier of all commodities (even itself), and the other of all concepts as well as their verbal expression.

Do we then posit money as the economic equivalent of intellectual currency? Or logic as the intellectual equivalent of economic currency? Indeed, they are so implicated in each other that neither can be said truly to be primary. Their equivalence indicates, moreover, that the nominalizing of economic thought by Oresme and its modalization among the scholastics are but secondary (meta-) articulations of the already modalized language of money, articulations that are also coextensive with the identical trends in the logicized science of grammar. Such an assertion suggests that the revival of monetary exchange in the twelfth century stands in relation to the relatively low-keyed rural economy of the early Middle Ages much as a nominalist or modal grammar stands in relation to the fixed grammatical principles of the same earlier period. To the immobile grammar of *proprietas* and an economy of immobile wealth based upon *proprietas* correspond a mobilized grammar of *suppositio* and an economy of exchange.

In fact, not only does money represent modal property but through it real property is also modalized. The history of noble wealth is, from the twelfth century on, one of a gradual conversion of landed estates into money rents. The substitution of payment in species for feudal service and payment in kind was, for all but the most powerful princes, who themselves acquired many alienated holdings, a means of raising the liquid capital necessary to survival in an economy of the marketplace.[34] Such a trend carried with it a depersonalization of possession that ran counter to the very notion of property as we have defined it. For the transformation of the fiefs that were coterminous with ties of personal dependence between particular men into rents emanating from ownership coupled with mortgage divests the once inalienable (unsalable) noble holding of all that is proper—that is to say, unique to it alone (see above, pp. 73–75).

This short-circuiting of the feudal exchange of armed duty for land is also reflected in a corresponding depersonalization of military service. Thus, beginning in the thirteenth century armies were increasingly composed of salaried soldiers—mercenaries—as opposed to enfeoffed knights. Where economic relations were once determined by the agreement of specific individuals (or their heirs), where property, military, and political relations were once indissociable, the monetization of land and defense worked to deny the personality of both function and status. To wit, office becomes more important than the personality of its holder, which is increasingly a matter of indifference; the source of a tax, toll, rent, or salary counts less than the fact of its discharge, since *rentiers*, like *soudoiers*, are interchangeable. The noble's proper name is—through money—detached from its roots in family property precisely at the moment when the word "property" is divested of its proper name.

Historically, in France at least, the importance of money and of its institutional possibilities—long-range trade; a salaried bureaucracy; modalized business techniques such as partnership, banking, double-account bookkeeping, insurance, and credit—constituted a threat to lineage whose social and demographic effects are writ large upon our reconstitution of the High Middle Ages. For the gradual intrusion of a system of mobile wealth alongside of the relatively fixed forms of the early feudal period implies a system of value in which worth is created not so much by origin as by relative position within a more fluid whole. Especially with the revival of towns the question of origins becomes, in fact, less and less the sine qua non of status. The city, as the German proverb attests ("Stadtluft macht frei"), is the locus of personal freedom, the place to which everyone at first comes from somewhere else and the social space in which origin as the determinant of value leaves its least trace. With the advent of money, of seemingly originless fortunes next to those that are inherited, "the clever and the courageous took their place alongside of heirs."[35] Bourgeois property is, in fact, secretive and almost can be defined in terms of goods that escape the view, and therefore the control, of lineage, for example, money, merchandise, jewelry, clothes, linen, serving vessels, lingots, etc. The town is an economic zone in which moveables, chattel, personal property are more important than the immoveable real estate of the countryside, where even *l'immobilier* is salable, and where *propres* are eclipsed by *acquêts*; "nowhere else," as Duby notes, "did inheritance have so little a place."[36] And indeed, nowhere else did the extended kindred, as opposed to the conjugal unit composed of a married couple and their immediate descendants, play less of a role in the management of family fortunes.

The catastrophic effect of monetization upon the noble family is by now a cliché of medieval studies amply discussed elsewhere. Money represented the great disruptor of lineage and of all that a landed aristocracy stood for. Less evident, perhaps, is the degree to which contemporaneous—especially scholastic—economic theory offers ideological confirmation of what the social historian reconstitutes in retrospect as a supposedly "objective" phenomenon. That is, many of the canonical and theological arguments against usury focused upon the fact that interest is, for a variety of reasons, unnatural: it represents the sale of time, which belongs only to God; the usurious transaction both sells and loans the same object; two different values placed upon a single sum runs counter to natural law since money does not multiply or deteriorate; money as an instrument of measure is neither vendable nor consumable. These last two criteria are particularly significant since they are based upon the belief, originating with Aristotle and prevalent throughout the Middle Ages, that money is dead, unproductive, sterile, an unfruitful good incapable of breeding, that is, of yielding profit.[37] "For money," says Aristotle, "was intended to be used in exchange, but not to increase at interest. And this term interest [*tokos*, literally 'offspring'], which means the birth of money from money, is applicable to the breeding of money because the offspring resemble the parent. Wherefore of all modes of getting wealth this is the most unnatural."[38]

Aristotle, who elsewhere contrasts the sterility of money with the organic generation of the fruits of nature, thus specifically couches the question of usury in terms of human reproduction, a setting of the problem that will not be lost upon medieval thinkers. Saint Bonaventure affirms its inherent infertility: "pecunia quantum est de se per seipsam non fructificat." Saints Albert and Aquinas follow Aristotle, insisting upon money's purely formal character; he who seeks its increase commits, in other words, an act against nature. The specialists of the late thirteenth and early fourteenth centuries, Giles of Lessines and Alexander Lombard, adopt the Aristotelian dictum: "nummus non parit nummos." Oresme too claims that the one who employs money other than for exchange "misuses it against the natural institution of money, for he causes money to beget money. And besides, in these changes by which profit accrues it is necessary to call something which is not a penny, a penny, and which is not a pound, a pound."[39]

Oresme's warning participates in a long tradition according to which money is excluded from reproduction. What remains to be articulated, however, is that such an exclusion is tantamount to identifying money with the disruption of genealogy. Because it cannot generate, monetary wealth represents an absolute rupture in the continuity of both fortune and lineage. This point cannot be emphasized enough. Nor can it be divorced from Oresme's equation of the usurious act with grammatical imprecision. To use money as if it were fertile is to risk an improper designation—"to call something which is not a penny, a penny, and which is not a pound, a pound." If money serves to interrupt genealogy, that interruption, once again, implies an analogous break in definition or etymology, the use of a word in a sense other than its proper sense. The usurer is in many ways the colleague of the poet—fellow disruptors of genealogy through monetary and linguistic impropriety, interest, and metaphor.[40]

The Courtly Novel

Seen synchronically, the discourse of the family as lineage stands in relation to that of the family as household as the etymological discourse of early medieval grammar stands in relation to nominalist and modal grammar, and, further, as the genealogical discourse of the epic stands in relation to the lyric disruption of genealogy. Here, however, the example of the *canso*, strategically selected, remains extreme in its refusal of history and of the narrative and representational integrity that we have identified with lineage. The bulk of the literary production of the High Middle Ages does not break so radically with the nexus of ideas and strategies that we have also associated with an epistemology of origins but serves, rather, to problematize that which the *canso* presents as absolute disjunction. It is, in fact, in the earliest *chansons de geste* that the esthetic consequences of the genealogical paradigm are most operative. Many epics from the late twelfth century onward tend both to thematize a certain tension among consanguineal relations and to lose their generic specificity. The Bernier of *Raoul de Cambrai*, for example, is forced to choose between loyalty to family and to lord; and even at the end of several generations of warfare, the great-grandsons of Herbert de Vermandois continue to battle their own maternal grandfather, Raoul's uncle Guerri. The Aymon of *Les Quatre filz Aymon* must choose between his seigneur and his sons. In *Huon de Bordeaux* brothers struggle against each other. More important, the eruption of conflict within the lineal group is accompanied by a tendency for the lineally defined epic to trail off into a *roman d'aventure*, as kinship and poetic form disintegrate reciprocally. In turn, there are many lyric forms (e.g., the *tenso, joc partit, sirventes, alba, pastorela, chanson de croisade, chanson de toile*) that are to varying degrees narratively or historically inclined—that can be situated either in historical time or in repeated daily moments, that narrate a temporally defined "story," and that pretend to represent a reality other than that of the singing voice. The contraposed literary types that we have articulated are, in fact, more often than not implicated in each other. And if the possibility of such a generic mixing seems to exceed the neatness of paradigmatic boundaries, it is precisely such an excess which allows our own critical discourse to function, and which impels it henceforth toward the privileged locus of "contamination"—the romance.

To understand how the novel serves as a point of juncture between contrasting familial, linguistic, economic, and literary principles, we turn to *Aucassin et Nicolette*, a work which in its variegated form both exaggerates and exposes forcefully the ideational tension that has concerned us thus far.[41] The thirteenth-century *chantefable* is eminently "readable" according to the critical apparatus that we have developed, and it works, at the same time, to push our analysis even further toward a mediatory third term between the *canso* and the *chanson de geste*. Thematically, *Aucassin et Nicolette* begins with an expression of anxiety concerning lineage: "Li quens Garins de Biaucaire estoit vix et frales. . . . Il n'avoit nul oir, ne fil ne fille, fors un seul vallet: cil estoit tex con je vos dirai."[42] It is a menace to the continuity of family line ("nul oir") that creates the possibility of a story line ("con je vos dirai"). The imbrication of generation and narration is subtended, moreover, by the archetypal novelistic drama of a marriage imposed against the will of the parties involved. Aucassin loves Nicolette and refuses to defend the paternal castle if he cannot have her: "Ja Dix ne me doinst riens que je li demant . . . se vos ne me donés Nicholete me douce amie que je tant aim." Garin, on the other hand, claims to reserve his son—and the future of his lands—for a richer match: "Et se tu femne vix avoir, je te donrai la file a un roi u a un conte."[43] Dramatically speaking, *Aucassin et Nicolette* turns, then, around a generational conflict—the desire of young lovers versus the menace, in the poem's own terms, of being *desiretés*.

More important, this drama of love against parental sanction is translated into a drama of language that is nowhere more evident than in the passage directly following Nicolette's escape from prison and preceding Aucassin's own flight to join her (see Appendix B for translation):

XVIII. Or Dient et Content et Fabloient

Nicolete se dementa molt, si con vos avés oï; ele se conmanda a Diu, se erra tant qu'ele vint en le forest. Ele n'osa mie parfont entrer por les bestes sauvaces et por le serpentine, si se quatist en un espés buisson; et soumax

li prist, si s'endormi dusqu'au demain a haute prime que li pastorel iscirent
de la vile et jeterent lor bestes entre le bos et la riviere, si se traien d'une
part a une molt bele fontaine qui estoit au cief de la forest, si estendirent
une cape, se missent lor pain sus. Entreusque il mengoient, et Nicolete
s'esveille au cri des oisiax et des pastoriax, si s'enbati sor aus.

"Bel enfant, fait ele, Damedix vos i aït!

— Dix vos benie! fait li uns qui plus fu enparlés des autres.

— Bel enfant, fait ele, conissiés vos Aucassin, le fil le conte Garin de
Biaucaire?

— Oïl, bien le counisçons nos.

— Se Dix vos aït, bel enfant, fait ele, dites li qu'il a une beste en ceste
forest et qu'i viegne cacier, et s'il l'i puet prendre, il n'en donroit mie un
menbre por cent mars d'or, non por cinc cens, ne por nul avoir."

Et cil le regardent, se le virent se bele qu'il en furent tot esmari.

"Je li dirai? fait cil qui plus fu enparlés des autres; dehait ait qui ja en
parlera, ne qui ja li dira! C'est fantosmes que vos dites, qu'il n'a si ciere
beste en ceste forest, ne cerf, ne lion, ne sengler, dont uns des menbres
vaille plus de dex deniers u de trois au plus, et vos parlés de si grant avoir.
Ma dehait qui vos en croit, ne qui ja li dira! Vos estes fee, si n'avons cure
de vo conpaignie, mais tenés vostre voie.

— Ha! bel enfant, fait ele, si ferés. Le beste a tel mecine que Aucassins
ert garis de son mehaing; et j'ai ci cinc sous en me borse: tenés, se li dites;
et dedens trois jors li covient cacier, et se il dens trois jors ne le trove, ja
mais n'iert garis de son mehaig.

— Par foi, fait il, les deniers prenderons nos, et s'il vient ci, nos li
dirons, mais nos ne l'irons ja quere.

— De par Diu! fait ele.

Lor prent congié as pastoriaus, se s'en va. [*Aucassin*, p. 19]

Nicolette's meeting with the shepherds occurs in the margins of distinct
geographic zones: she has just left the town of Beaucaire and is about to
enter the forest. It represents a juxtaposition of discrete social spaces, one
the locus of the law (through a justice that would punish her), and the
other, a realm inhabited by wild animals (*les bestes sauvaces*) where only
the law of the strongest prevails. At an extreme lurk the Wild Men—half
human/half animal, completely unsocialized beings, to which the
ploughman, whom Aucassin later encounters, bears a certain
resemblance.[44] Finally, Nicolette's exchange with the shepherd stands as
a meeting of two social classes and of the discourses appropriate to each.

Nicolette, a captured slave whose noble identity is as yet unknown,
speaks the artificial language of courtly poetry. She uses difficult ornament according, in fact, to Geoffrey of Vinsauf's definition of one kind of
metaphor: "the transfer of the meaning of a word from man to things or
from things to man" (see above, p. 117). In the veiled speech to the
shepherd Nicolette substitutes an animal (*beste*) for herself, a hunt for the
experience of love, Aucassin's sickness or *mehaing* (from Ovidian tradition?) for love-sickness, a cure (*mecine*) for fulfillment in love by joining
her in the forest. The shepherd, on the other hand, rejects Nicolette's

artificial use of language, insisting instead upon the literal meaning of her words: "C'est fantosmes que vos dites, qu'il n'a si ciere beste en ceste forest . . . et vos parlés de si grant avoir."

Nicolette's discussion with the shepherd over the value of words can, in fact, be reduced to a question of the value of value, revolving as it does around the issue of price. And what began as a meeting of distinct social spaces (town and countryside), of distinct classes (noble and nonnoble), and even of distinct languages (an elevated, metaphoric discourse and a simpler, more literal one) ends as a meeting of separate economic orders implicit to disparate linguistic mediums. Nicolette's troped speech nominalizes its referent through, in the rhetorician's phrase, "the transfer of a word from its proper sense to another." And this dislocation of linguistic property can be separated neither from the dislocation of paternal property inherent to Nicolette as the object of Aucassin's desire nor from her inflation of price. Verbal and monetary signs are, for the potentially disruptive affine of Garin's lineage, mutually mobile concepts which, in the light of our discussion of economic nominalism, seem even to entail each other. The shepherd, in contrast, demonstrates a marked distrust of the inflated detachment of value from intrinsic worth, and thus he appears to favor a certain economic realism contrary to Nicolette's manipulation of words and of cost.[45]

Aucassin et Nicolette contains, then, a meeting of geographic zones, of social classes, of discourses appropriate to each, of economic orders, and, finally, of literary genres. In its mixed form the *chantefable* can be classified neither with the epic nor with the lyric. It combines narrative elements subsumed in the act of telling (indicated by the marker "conter") and assimilable to its prose sections, along with lyric elements subsumed in the act of singing (indicated by "chanter") and associated with the verse portions of the whole. This polarity has been statistically substantiated by S. Monsonégo who, in a painstaking study of the vocabulary of *Aucassin et Nicolette*, demonstrates that within such a stylistic dynamic poetry enjoys a wider range of expression than prose.[46] The vocabulary of the verse sections is richer in the area of words occurring only once, a lexical wealth which lies, moreover, in substantives and adjectives and which contrasts with a proportionate strength in verbs and adverbs within the prose passages. What this means is that the verse portions of the *chantefable* "proffer," as E. Vance notes, "a world that is static and removed, where nominalizing language constitutes its own action"; the prose, by comparison, "proffers a world that is temporal and spatial, in which movement and action are compulsory."[47]

In the mixture of generic modes *Aucassin et Nicolette* merely makes explicit that which is less evident, less formally marked, in earlier, more "generically uniform" romances. That is, that the courtly novel repre-

sents a combination of the distinct literary discourses that we have identified with the epic and the *canso,* and, further, that the implications of
such a commingling extend to the social, familial, economic, and grammatical models appropriate to each. To the degree that Aucassin's father
favors an imposed marriage, he stands on the side of aristocracy, lineage,
and real property. He reminds Aucassin repeatedly of the importance of
retaining the family *patrimoine,* urging him at the same time to pursue an
inherited war by "acting" like a hero of a *chanson de geste*:

> Ha! fix, fait il, con par es caitis et maleurox, que tu vois c'on asaut ton cas-
> tel tot le mellor et le plus fort; et saces, se tu le pers, que tu es desiretés.
> Fix, car pren les armes et monte u ceval et defen te tere. . . . [*Aucassin,*
> p. 8]
>
> Ha! son, he said, how unfortunate you are, when you see that your best
> and the strongest castle is attacked; and know that if you lose it, you will
> be disinherited. Son, take up your arms and mount your horse and defend
> your land. . . .

Garin's concern for genealogical continuity and for military vigor situates
him within the thematic field of the epic; and where such concerns are
assimilable to an implicit doctrine of language, it serves to ally him with
the determining possibilities of narration and representation. Most of the
action of *Aucassin et Nicolette* does, in fact, occur in the prose or narrative
sections.

Conversely, to the extent that Aucassin resists the paternal pressure to
enter battle and to continue the family line that might have constituted its
geste, his position is antiaristocratic, disruptive of lineage, and heedless of
inherited family fortunes. Put another way, both Aucassin and
Nicolette—those who desire and sing rather than fight and legitimately
procreate—can be identified with the lyric portions of the *chantefable,*
which tend to interrupt narrative sequence and to reduce representation
to repetition. The spatially and temporally defined tale recounted in the
prose sections is quite literally punctuated by verse interludes reserved
primarily for the expression of the internal states of the protagonists or for
the re-presentation of events that have already occurred. Hence the
self-reflexive status of these "lyric pearls on an epic string" permits not
only the identification with the reflexive natures of the passive young
lovers, as against the paternal invocation to (epic) action, but solicits the
comparison with the similarly static and closed generically independent
love song.

Aucassin et Nicolette stands, then, both as an affirmation and a contesta-
tion of the principles of genealogy and of noble property that are captured
in the *chantefable*'s mixed form. Where the oppositional paradigm seems
most poignant is, furthermore, precisely where the potential tragedy of

an imposed genealogical succession turns into farce. The episode of Torelore is characterized by the fantasy of a kingdom in which men give birth and women lead the wars that have degenerated quite literally into food fights (*Aucassin*, pp. 29–33). With the complete loss of procreative determinacy, narration too is condemned; and the epic integrity of lineal and story line trails off into what looks awfully like some of the more "dadaist" medieval nonsensical genres, for example, the *fatras* or the *resverie*. This may seem like a minor incident within the larger whole, but the episode of Torelore stands nonetheless as a negative proof that the break with reproduction, as we have insisted again and again, entails a concomitant break with representation.

What I am suggesting is not only that contrasting familial, linguistic, and generic modes are contained within a single form, but that their contraposition constitutes a form distinct from both the *canso* and the epic whose traits it shares. This is not true, for example, of the lyric types which may display narrative elements and which seem less hermetic than the *canso*, since that difference is not marked at the level of structure. Even the dialogued *tenso, joc partit, pastorela,* and *débat* remain thoroughly cast within the lyric mold. Epic narrative, on the other hand, may often give the impression of a dissolution of the story line and of a certain poetic closure, for example, in the more static, less actantially defined *laisses similaires* and *juxtaposées*. But even here, despite the slackening of action, the epic only simulates through repetition a certain lyric stasis in the absence of the formal attributes of song. The difference between such passages and the rest of a poem like *La Chanson de Roland* remains purely quantitative. *Aucassin et Nicolette*, however, displays a genuinely dialogic structure whose thematic components (a conflict between love and war) are indissociable from a generic opposition (lyric and narrative) whose separate elements also remain formally distinct. Such a paradigm is rooted in discrete orders of family and, as we shall see, constitutes the very essence of courtly romance.

If called upon to localize a point of origin of the antigenealogical narrative of which the *chantefable* is a shining example, one would have to turn to an unlikely source—the abundance of hagiographic texts dealing specifically with the conflict between a family imposed marriage and the future saint's desire for spiritual purity. Here, the Old French *Vie de Saint Alexis* (second half of the eleventh century) serves as a prime illustration. Thus Alexis's father, like Garin, is haunted by the fear of genealogical interruption, and he also seeks to arrange an appropriate marriage for his only heir:

> Quant veit li pedre que mais n'avrat enfant,
> Mais que cel soul cui il amat tant,

> Donc se porpenset del siecle ad en avant:
> Or vuelt que prenget moillier a son vivant;
> Donc li achetat fille ad un noble franc.[48]

When the father realized he would have no more children other than the
one that he loved so much, he began to think of the future: Now he would
like him to take a wife while he is still alive; and he negotiated for him the
daughter of a noble.

Alexis's own choice of virginity over marriage is, in direct opposition to
the paternal concern for lineal continuity, a willful disruption of the
family line and, in particular, of the family *patrimoine*. His initial refusal
coincides, in fact, with the partial disbursement of family funds—"Tot
son aveir qu'o sei en at portet, / Tot le depart, que giens ne luin remest";
and his death bespeaks, as his father's lament betrays, an absolute interruption of ancestral property: "O filz cui ierent mes granz ereditez, /
Mes larges terres dont jo aveie assez, / Mi grant palais en Rome la citet?"[49] In
keeping with the ecclesiastical model of marriage, Alexis thus chooses
freely, which, in hagiographic literature at least, is synonymous with the
rejection of lineage altogether: "He loved God more," the anonymous
poet tells us, "than all his kinsmen combined."[50]

The election of God over family is a common theme of twelfth- and
thirteenth-century saints' lives. The life of Edward the Confessor, who
marries but preserves his chastity, is known in numerous Latin versions
and in at least one Old French rendering from the *Vita Sancti Edwardi Regis
et Confessoris* by Ailred of Rielvaux. Likewise, Saint Evroul, whose Old
French biography stems from the second part of Orderic Vitalis's *Historia
Ecclesiastica*, resists paternal pressure to marry, just as the orphaned Saint
Gilles, whose life was recounted in nine complete and several abridged
Latin versions as well as in numerous vernacular texts, withstands the
influence of his barons. A thirteenth-century life of Saint Juliane, whose
rejection of marriage received both Anglo-Saxon and Middle English
treatment, is attributed to Nicholas Bozon, the author of the similarly
antigenealogical life of Saint Lucy. Comparable stories of resistance characterize the lives of Saints Osith, Simon of Crecy, and Cecilia. In addition,
a subgenre of these archetypal refusals of family can be found in a series
of works depicting the simultaneous vows of virginity undertaken by
both members of the affianced or married couple (e.g., the lives of Saints
Chrysanthus and Dacia, Henri and Cunegonde, Julian and Basilissa).

The most developed rendering of the refusal motif is the Latin *Life of
Christine of Markyate*. The anonymous author of this text, written, according to its editor, between 1255 and 1265, dramatically "fleshes out" the
Alexis story, recasting it in a contemporaneous setting and providing
elaborate detail concerning both the motivation and the social implications of the withdrawal of a potential heiress from her obligation to

family. In this case, a persistent suitor, in conjunction with the Bishop of Durham, "gained, against Christine's will, the parents' consent for her to be betrothed to Burthred."[51] The bride's subsequent reluctance to consummate the union is not in and of itself unusual in spite of the lengths to which her parents go in order to force her to comply—entreaty, gifts, drink, love potions, and even rape. What remains extraordinary, however, is the explicitness with which her role in what we have termed the "biopolitics" of lineage is articulated:

> Insuper inerat ei tantum acumen in sensu. talis providencia in gerendis. ea efficacia in deliberatis. ut si seculi rebus tota vellet incumbere crederetur non se tantum suamque familiam. sed reliquum genus suum posse diviciis et honoribus ampliare. Huc accessit quod speraverunt ex illa nepotes proles matri non dissimiles. Et hos fructus intendentes vitam ei celibem inviderunt. Quippe si propter Christum casta permaneret. metuebant quod et ipsam et quod per ipsam haberi possent, una perderent.[52]

> Furthermore, she was so intelligent, so prudent in affairs, so efficient in carrying out her plans, that if she had given her mind to worldly pursuits she could have enriched and ennobled not only herself and her family but also her relatives. To this was added the fact that her parents hoped she would have children who would be like her in character. So keen were they on these advantages that they begrudged her a life of virginity. For if she remained chaste they feared that they would lose her and all they could hope to gain through her.

Christine's refusal to marry represents an abrogation of the feudal familial right to "husband" its offspring so as to insure both the continuity of the genealogical line and of the ancestral fief. And nowhere is the hagiographer more conscious of the saint's infidelity to lineage as a class issue than in the *Life of Christine of Markyate*. Her father laments becoming "the laughing stock" of his neighbors; and he fears that his daughter's actions will disgrace all aristocrats: "Why," he asks, "must she depart from tradition? Why should she thus bring dishonor upon her father? Her life of poverty will bring the whole of the nobility into disrepute. Let her do now what we want and she can have all that we possess."[53]

There is little doubt that the archetypal hagiographic reluctance to take one's proper place in a genealogical succession serves to affirm the ecclesiastical over the lay matrimonial model. After all, Alexis dies a saint, and Christine's marriage is, through a second intervention of the bishop, annulled. The investment of the individual with a certain sexual autonomy—as against the biopolitics of lineage—transforms this "virginity cycle" into the direct expression of official doctrine and of a less official strategy aimed at diversion of family fortunes (through the enlistment of family scions) in the direction of the Church. Less apparent perhaps is the resemblance between such possibilities of lineal interruption and the disruptive thrust of the love lyric. This is less a case of superficial similarity of theme and spirit than of a profound identity of effect. For the refusal of sexuality is, in its disruption of the continuity of lineage, as potent a threat to the hegemony of noble families as the antigenealogical proliferation of adulterous desire.

It is, however, not so much in the adulterous *canso* as in the marital romance that the "monstrous" secular reformulation of the principle of free choice defines an entire literary mode. The courtly novel is essentially *about* marriage and seems always to involve a conflict between a consensual attachment and a contractual bond, to problematize succession, and to combine structurally elements both of narrative progression and of lyric closure; and this from the very beginning. The Tristan story, for example, is motivated by Marc's barons' fear of a lateral succession and consequently their insistence upon his marriage to Iseult. In this respect Marc resembles a failed saint, one who gives in to the pressure to marry.[54] Be that as it may, the tension between Tristan and the barons, which serves dramatically to shape the entire poem, can be reduced to a conflict between the two components of the global warrior group—between true paternity, Tristan as nephew, and fictive paternity, or vassalage. Adultery stands merely as the wedge by which the barons share Marc's favor. Each time they manage to convince him of his wife's infidelity, they rise in his estimation; and with each discovery of her faith, Tristan regains the upper hand. Nor can such a cycle of jealousy be separated from the Tristan legend as a drama of signs. For the adulterous usurpation of paternity is predicated upon the necessity of hiding, of lies; and action is defined, within the illusory world of Béroul's text, by the attempt to understand the constantly shifting appearances of a universe of half-truths. This applies, for instance, as Marc descends from the pine tree.[55] It is apparent in the episode of Iseult's exculpation at the Gué Aventuros. But it is especially characteristic of the problematic episode of the sleeping lovers in Morrois Forest. As Marc stumbles upon the apparently adulterous couple he fails to act because he fails to comprehend the copresent signs of both innocence and guilt:

> Quant vit qu'ele avoit sa chemise
> Et q'entre eus deus avoit devise,
> La bouche o l'autre n'ert jostee,
> Et qant il vit la nue espee
> Qui entre eus deus les desevrot,
> Vit les braies que Tristan out:
> "Dex!" dist li rois, "ce que puet estre?
> Or ai veü tant de lor estre,
> Dex! je ne sai que doie faire,
> Ou de l'ocire ou du retraire. . . . "[56]

When he saw that she had her shift and that between them there was a space and their lips did not touch, and when he saw the naked sword separating them and that Tristan was wearing pants, he thought: "God!

What can this mean? Now I have seen enough of how they are together that—my God!—I no longer know what to do, whether to kill them or withdraw. . . . "

Like the reader of the novel itself, Marc is paralyzed by the impossibility of reconciling the hopelessly contradictory message of the lovers' situation versus the attributes of their intentions; and the necessity of interpretation prevents him from achieving the vengeance that was not only his right but, as I have maintained elsewhere, his obligation.[57]

The king's uncertainty about adultery, which is, at bottom, an uncertainty about the integrity of lineage, is directly connected to one kind of narrative disruption characteristic of the romance in general—namely, the inner monologue. For with his inability to read the signs which have lost their determinacy, reflection intrudes upon action, as the exteriorized universe of compulsory activity and objectified events that we have associated with the epic cedes to a more psychologically defined world of compunction and thought. Such a reading is not wholly our own, but was originally suggested by Gottfried von Strassburg's rendering of the Morrois episode (ca. 1205) in which the dilemma of interpretation intimated by Béroul seems to generate a dynamic model of the mind.[58] In both instances, Marc's renunciation of vengeance, which is tantamount to a shedding of his epic or feudal self, serves to constitute a language of the self with all that such a concept entails in the way of genealogical, grammatical, and literary interruption.

The Marc of Béroul's *Tristan* essentially picks up where the Charlemagne of the final strophe of *Roland* leaves off (see above, pp. 105–107); and the overall narrative movement of the early romance is punctuated, like *Aucassin et Nicolette*, by multiple moments of self-reflection, of representational closure, similar to independent lyric pieces. But the mode of interruption most particular to Béroul lies elsewhere—in the fragmentation of his presentation according to a subjectively defined, dovetailed pattern of interlace. Superficially, *Tristan* consists of a series of loosely linked episodes of varying lengths. From the encounter under the pine tree (vv. 1–319), to Frocin's flight (vv. 320–338), to the scene of reconciliation in Iseult's bedroom (vv. 339–380), to the two years of adultery at court (vv. 573–642), these relatively independent dramatic tableaux resemble, except for the use of rhymed couplets instead of assonance, the epic *laisse*. Upon a deeper level of structure, however, the global tableaux are composed of equally independent subunits, some of which contribute to the narrative progression of Béroul's tale and others of which refer either to preceding subunits or anticipate subsequent ones. The scene in Iseult's bedroom, for instance, can be broken down in the following verses:[59]

339–347	The queen returns to her room.
*348–369	Iseult recounts to Brengain what has transpired in the pine tree scene (1–319).

*370–380   Brengain reacts to what she has heard.
*381–384   Tristan recounts the pine tree scene to Governal who comments, in turn, upon what he has heard.
385–387   Marc comes to his wife's bedroom.
388–399   Marc asks Iseult if she has seen Tristan.
*400–458   Iseult recounts the pine tree scene to Marc.
459–468   Reconciliation of Marc and Iseult.
469–475   Marc informs the queen of Frocin's role in the pine tree episode and she asks him if he were present.
*476–492   The king reveals how touched he was by Tristan's meeting with the queen.
493–504   Iseult further justifies her behavior at court.
505–526   Marc sends Brengain to fetch Tristan.
†527–546   Brengain informs Tristan of the exchange between Iseult and Marc.
547–568   Reconciliation of Tristan and Marc.
‡569–572   Evocation of the couple's subsequent life at court.

From the above schematic summary it is evident that we are dealing with a narrative that advances slowly and hesitantly, that both progresses and resists progression. Relatively few new givens are introduced within a long sequence of events: the queen returns to her room, Marc arrives, husband and wife, and then uncle and nephew, are reconciled. All other exchanges either hark back to the previous scene in the royal garden or to a preceding phase of the scene under scrutiny (e.g., vv. 527–546), the only exception being the prefiguration of the two years of adulterous leisure (vv. 569–572). Thus, Béroul's text seems to dissociate itself from a continuous logical development; it moves, as the following diagram indicates, even somewhat gratuitously.

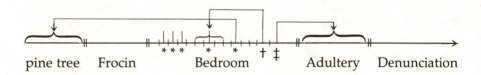

pine tree   Frocin   Bedroom   Adultery   Denunciation

The halting progression of *Tristan* is also evident within the epic where some *laisses* within a single text may contribute to the dramatic action while others may, on the other hand, slow it down. But with two fundamental differences: the repeated epic strophe continues to advance the dramatic action somewhat, even though this progression occurs more slowly than elsewhere. The passages of *Tristan* that recall what has already happened do not promote the telling of the tale except insofar as they function to transmit information to those not originally present. Thus, while the double, triple, or quadruple epic *laisse* may tend toward a moment of lyric stasis within a rapidly moving linear narrative, the novelistic reference to past events fulfills a purely mimetic role. The novel contains the embryonic seeds both of a closed text reflecting at certain points only upon itself and of a world which, unlike the lyric, does not consist exclusively of words but in which words have come to constitute a form of action.

More important, where the epic narrative presents a multiplicity of episodes from a single point of view, Béroul's text presents a limited number of episodes from multiple points of view. The retelling of the encounter in the royal garden is, in this respect, a classic example of shifting group dynamics. For with each repetition of the same event it becomes ever more apparent that the speaker and his listener—Iseult and Brengain, Brengain and Iseult, Tristan and Governal, Governal and Tristan, Iseult and Marc, Marc and Iseult—create successive realities whose re-presentational form is potentially subject to infinite recombination. Here again, we might just as well have selected the scene of the sleeping lovers which serves, in fact, to thematize precisely the process of perceptual dovetailing operative throughout. For Marc's own difficulty comprehending that which he witnesses and his decision to "leave a sign of his presence in the forest" instead of slaying necessitates a second act of reading, or misreading: "He left us in order to betray us," says Tristan upon discovering his uncle's sword in the place of his own; "By this exchange we can see that he wants to deceive us," he adds in observing Marc's ring on Iseult's finger.[60] Tristan's miscalculation, as we have seen, depends neither upon a personal trait of character nor upon any particular situation. Rather, it is of a piece with a universe increasingly defined by a personal language of the self as opposed to the public discourse of the epic. For Béroul, perception becomes a function of who one is, what one knows, and what one wants to believe, as the subject comes to determine the shape of a reality whose fragmented nature also emanates from a narrative built of overlapping partial truths. Not without sacrifice, however; for Béroul's self-creating narrative transforms all who are seduced by it into Marcs and Tristans—that is to say, into misreaders. The final casualty of such an open-ended process of textual elaboration is, from the perspective of the last repetition (that of the poet for his audience), the presumably objective reality toward which each repetition aspires, but which none attains.

If the interruption of narrative continuity seems to determine a definitive rupture with the assumed possibility of perceptual coherence and of ontological totality, it also signals a break with the possibility of representation itself. Indeed, the collective struggles of the epic presented under the impartial guise of authorial omniscience are transformed within the early romance into a struggle of the author against his text.

Thomas, in particular, thematizes the limiting conditions of the poetic act, betraying a constant self-doubt and obsession with the adequacy of his own partial presentation of the tale which he acknowledges to be incomplete, scattered, and "diverse":

> Seignurs, cest cunte est mult divers,
> E pur ço l'uni par mes vers
> E di en tant cum est mester
> E le surplus voil relesser.
> Ne vol pas trop en uni dire:
> Ici diverse la matyre.[61]

Lords, this tale has many parts, and for this reason I have gathered it in my poem and told as much as is necessary, leaving off the rest. I did not want to say too much at once, and so I have divided the material.

The Tristan legend is, then, at once a genealogical and a semiological drama: a tale of lost paternity, of adultery bordering on incest, of an aborted lateral and an impossible direct succession coupled with a scrambling of the narrative sequence and the representational integrity that we have associated with lineage. The poet's effort to assure the progress of the tale that seems, as Thomas admits, to exceed and elude him is mirrored in the struggle of his protagonists to interpret the baffling signs of a world of supplementary half-truths. Both, finally, are identifiable with the desire for genealogical continuity within the archetypal story of adulterous interruption.

Chrétien de Troyes is no less haunted than the Tristan poets by problems of matrimony, desire both within and outside of marriage, and succession. *Cligés* presents itself, in fact, as an "anti-Tristan." Its prologue contains allusions to Ovid and to King Marc; its unhappily married heroine, Fenice, claims to prefer dismemberment to the "solution of Iseult."[62] Of Chrétien's three "matrimonial" romances, poems concerned either with the consummation or with the internal dynamics of marriage, *Cligés* reads like a virtual casebook of medieval marriage. The episode of Fenice's broken betrothal to the Duke of Saxony poses the question of the legal status of the *sponsalia* (vv. 2528–2915). Her legally contracted but unconsummated union with Alis raises the hotly debated contemporaneous issue of intention versus ratification (see above, pp. 161–162). But, most of all, the dramatic interest of *Cligés* turns around a tale of succession and around the conflict between an elective affinity and an imposed contractual obligation. Both Alis and Fenice are forced, respectively by barons and by family, into a marriage that neither desires: Alis, in consonance with the biopolitics of the royal Greek dynasty, has promised never to marry; and Fenice loves Cligés.

The opposition between two models of marriage, seen in the struggle of family (or feudal retinue) against lovers, is formally expressed in *Cligés* as a tension between the dominant story line and the long lyric interludes disruptive of the poem's overall narrative design. And where the mode of textual interference is for Béroul one of dovetailing coupled with a purposefully unresolved jumbling of perception, Chrétien seems to establish discrete textual "zones" that can again be equated with distinct poetic as well as familial principles. *Cligés* is a genealogically determined tale in which, already in the amorous anguish of the hero's parents, love is associated with the inner monologues that become the privileged loci of Fenice's and Cligés's desire.[63] Though they are too long to quote *in extenso*, each of these set pieces serves to dislocate the discursive sequence of an otherwise linear narrative progression. What is more, the inner monologue marks within Chrétien's text a break with referentiality equivalent to the *canso*'s closure of language upon itself or to the reflexivity of the verse portions of *Aucassin et Nicolette*. "A li seule opose et respont"—thus begins Fenice's extended dialogue with herself, which bears, excluding the stanzaic form, all the earmarks of the love lyric:[64]

> Par sa lobe et par sa losenge
> Mes cuers de son ostel s'estrenge,
> Ne ne vialt o moi remenoir,
> Tant het et moi et mon menoir.
> Par foi, donc m'a cil maubaillie
> Qui mon cuer a en sa baillie,
> Ne m'aimme pas, ce sai je bien,
> Qui me desrobe et tost le mien.
> Jel sai? Por coi ploroit il dons?
> Por coi? Ne fu mie an pardons,
> Asez i ot reison de quoi.[65]

By its betrayal and trickery my heart is estranged from its home; nor does it want to remain with me, it so hates both me and my being. By faith, that one has so mistreated me who has my heart in his power; he does not love me, that I know well, the one who robs me and carries it away. Do I know it? Why does he cry then? Why? It is not at all for pardon, for which there is ample cause.

Likewise, Cligés's own *planctus* is couched in a language divested of communicative function, that seems to turn only upon itself:

> M'amie est morte, et je sui vis.
> Ha! dolce amie, vostre amis
> Por coi vit, et morte vos voit?
> Or porroit an dire par droit,
> Quant mortes estes par mon servise,
> Que je vos ai morte et ocise.
> Amie, don sui je la morz,
> Qui morte vos ai—n'est ce torz?—,
> Qui ma vie vos ai tolue,
> Si ai la vostre retenue.[66]

My beloved is dead, and I am alive. Ha! sweet love, why does your friend live who sees you dead? Now one could say rightly that when you died through my service it was I who killed you. Beloved, then I am the dead man who slayed you—Is that not right?—the one who took my life away from you and kept yours.

In the emotive "stations" in the progress of erotic desire, all other action seems suspended, as words become a fetishistic goal in themselves.

E. Vance maintains that such outpourings or "lyric cores" are actually generative of broader narrative structure; and this assertion, substantiated by Dante's preference for poetry over prose, is well-taken.[67] What I am suggesting, however, is that the dialectical relation of the narrative and lyric passages is more important than the issue of primacy; and, further, that the exclamatory and constative components of romance are assimilable thematically as well as formally to the distinct discourses of the *canso* and the epic. *Cligés* combines the themes of love and war proper to the *chanson d'amour* and the *chanson de geste* within a bivalent poetic framework integrating antithetical discursive modes whose copresence permits novelistic development. And if the thrust toward narrative continuity sustains Chrétien's efforts beyond the limits of the relatively short and static love song, it is the monologued lament that endows the extended and objectified narrative of deeds and events with depth sufficient to produce that which is denied in the epic—closure.

The question of how Chrétien's text relates to our two models of family is somewhat tricky. It would appear that the tension between the literary form of genealogy and the antigenealogical lyric also bespeaks a tension between lineage and household. But here we must bear in mind that these early matrimonial romances—*Cligés, Erec et Enide, Yvain*—do end in marriage and that the outpourings of desire indentifiable with the inner monologue lead in that direction. In *Cligés*, moreover, the interruption of lineage is never really a problem, since Alis and Cligés's father are brothers and the union of either would preserve the family line. What is at stake, rather, is the issue of matrimonial models—the right of individual decision—evident in the crucial choice between two members of the same descent group. Fenice recognizes, in fact, that consummation of the marriage to Alis would mean disinheritance of his nephew and the man she loves: "Garder cuide son pucelage / Por lui sauver son heritage."[68] *Cligés*, like the life of Alexis and that of Christine of Markyate, seems, then, to affirm the ecclesiastical model of matrimony. Fenice's preservation of her virginity despite the forced marriage to Alis makes her a "semi-saint." But, more important, it posits the possibility, within a synthetic literary mode, of something akin to an accommodation with feudal family practice. In *Cligés* the threat to lineage is attenuated by the ultimate triumph of an elective affinity thoroughly in keeping with the biopolitics of a dynasty which had originally privileged the line of Alexander over that of Alis. Thus, where the Tristan story and the saint's life stand (in different ways) as parables of absolute interruption, *Cligés* comes down on the side of reconciliation between the claims of lineage and of desire.

Such a reading is also sustained by *Erec et Enide* which takes as its initial premise the consent theory of marriage, but which at the same time explores the difficulties of achieving even within wedlock a viable balance between sexual desire and social obligation. Again, the dialectical relation of the two principles is formally manifested in the tension between opposing discursive modes. So perfect, in fact, is the blend of form and theme that the long inner monologues which punctuate the event-filled narrative tend to mirror the protagonists' dilemma: Erec is a hero at first obsessed by desire to the exclusion of action, then by an unremitting dedication to activity excluding all nonenergetic pursuits, even speech. It is, moreover, in the explicit prohibition of speech that the inner monologue is born (v. 2764). Enide's inability to communicate in the face of grave danger gives rise to the significant interruptions of narrative sequence through which, as in *Cligés*, a static and nominalizing dialogue with the self holds in abeyance a sequence of events.[69] Thus the drama which pits an active self against a desiring (and thinking) self becomes manifest in the tension between a language of action and events and a language serving to disengage the subject from both. The hero's attempt to reconcile the active and passive components of his own nature is reflected in the synthesis of constative (narrative) and exclamatory (lyric) discursive modes. Here, the notion of synthesis is crucial, for Erec, the hero who is initially too passive in his erotic attachment to Enide and then too active in his quest for honor, eventually manages to integrate both; and Enide, excluded at first from action, similarly learns to mobilize a more energetic self.

The resolution of "La Joie de la Cour" is in this respect paradigmatic. Not only is the couple trapped in the marvelous garden related by blood to the central figures of Chrétien's romance (the lady is Enide's cousin), but Maboagrains bears a certain "family resemblance" to Erec's former self. Like the hero, Maboagrains has been overly given to sexual desire and as a result finds himself trapped by a senseless obligation to action. Erec's conquest of his alter ego—first with speech (entreaty) and then by arms—represents an assimilation of both sides of a newly integrated *persona* which also prepares the way for his own succession (v. 6452). For the synthesis of both poles of this psychological dilemma, which coincides with the death of the father, is again duplicated in the fusion of discursive modes: the hero who accedes to the paternal function becomes at the same time the father of the text:

> Quant apeisiez fu li murmures,
> Erec ancomance son conte:

ses avantures li reconte
que nule n'en i antroblie.[70]

When the crowd quieted down, Erec began the tale of his adventures,
which he recounted without forgetting a single one.

Both the inner drama and the distinct modes of its poetic presentation are
resolved in Erec's retelling of his own saga, in the achievement of a
successful consensual union, and, presumably, in the completion of a
continuous genealogical line.

Chrétien's *Yvain* follows a pattern similar both thematically and formally to that of *Erec*. Hence an initial overcommitment to sexual desire
within marriage leads to the recuperative effort to redress the imbalance,
again within the framework of a series of lyric interludes bound by a
strongly narrative story line. And again, though marriage is problematized along the way, it triumphs in the end. *Lancelot* stands, in this regard,
as an exception, since Chrétien, despite the traditional amalgam of constative and exclamatory "zones," seems to opt for a definitive adulterous
interruption, or at least for a lack of resolution comparable, even in its
unfinished state, to the Tristan motif. Finally, Chrétien's last work,
Perceval, presents special interests and difficulties; and we will have
occasion to return to it shortly in discussing the family of Grail romances
(see below, pp. 198–212).

Though Chrétien seems to espouse differing views of the relation
between desire and marriage—and thus to affirm radically opposed matrimonial as well as textual models, the *Lais* of Marie de France demonstrate the most nuanced and sustained exploration of familial issues to be
found in twelfth-century courtly literature. So varied are the situations
and attitudes that she portrays that it is almost impossible to characterize
them generally. Nonetheless, these short pieces offer a glimpse of feudal
marriage practice as it is determined by the same concern for genealogical
continuity that we have encountered elsewhere. Equitan, for example, is
in love with his seneschal's wife, but finds himself pushed to marry by his
followers who are anxious about the royal succession.[71] In *Eliduc* the Lord
of Exeter tries to procure a husband for his daughter because of the lack of
a male heir, just as in *Yonec* the aged Lord of Chepstow marries in order to
insure the future of his "heritage": "Pur ceo k'il ot bon heritage, / Femme
prist pur enfanz aveir, / Qui aprés lui fussent si heir." The dramatic
interest of *Lanval* is sparked by the exclusion of the hero from Arthur's
distribution of wives and land: "Femmes et tere departi / Par tut, fors un
ki l'ot servi."[72] And the issue of parental control is complexly thematized
in *Les Dous Amanz* where a father's capricious fixation upon his daughter
not only prevents her marriage but causes her death.

On balance, parents, old men, and feudal barons appear to prevail
when it comes to the question of whether or not to marry and to the choice

of mate. Where the lay matrimonial model seems to break down is in the everyday reality of conjugal life; and Marie is ultimately more interested in the negative consequences of forced marriages than in the contractual bond itself. This is why the *Lais* give the impression of a virtual gallery of unhappily married women (and sometimes men, e.g., *Eliduc, Le Laustic*) and why adultery occupies such an important place in their thematic unfolding (e.g., *Guigemar, Lanval, Milun, Yonec, Equitan, Eliduc, Bisclavret, Le Laustic, Chevrefoil*). Even here, however, the marital infidelity emanating from arranged marriages is by no means simple, since not all spouses are presented unsympathetically; and a number of these miniromances work out to the favor of the young lovers in the end (e.g., *Milun, Guigemar, Lanval*).

Among the *Lais*, none offers a more impressive picture of the lived experience of an imposed union than *Guigemar*, which also deals explicitly with the role of the literary text in an archetypal drama of marital constraint and adulterous desire. Thus, as Guigemar lies wounded and adrift, the boat which carries him away from home and youth enters a mysterious city whose character is emblematized in the conjugal situation of its lord:

> Li sires ki la mainteneit
> Mult fu velz humme, et femme aveit
> Une dame de haut parage,
> Franche, curteise, bele e sage;
> Gelus esteit a desmesure,
> Kar ceo purporte la nature
> Ke tut li veil seient gelus,
> (Mult hiet chascun ke il seit cous!)[73]

The lord who looked over it was an old man; and he had a wife of great nobility—simple, courteous, beautiful, and wise. He was jealous beyond all bounds, for nature prescribes that all old men are jealous, since no one likes to be cuckolded.

In the effort to prevent adultery, the jealous husband has imprisoned his wife in a tower guarded by his niece and a castrated priest:

> Li sire out fait dedenz le mur,
> Pur mettre sa femme a seür,
> Chaumbre: suz ciel n'aveit plus bele.
> A l'entree fu la chapele,
> La chaumbre ert peinte tut entur;
> Venus, la deuesse d'amur,
> Fu tres bien mise en la peinture:
> Les traiz mustrez e la nature,
> Cument hom deit amur tenir
> E lealment e bien servir.
> Le livre Ovide, ou il enseine
> Comment chascun s'amur estreine. . . .[74]

> The lord had a room built within the wall in order to keep his wife se-
> curely; there was no more beautiful one on earth. At the entrance was a
> chapel. The room was painted all around; and Venus, the goddess of love,
> was well represented: it showed her traits and her nature, and how a man
> should conduct himself in love, by serving loyally. The book of Ovid,
> where it teaches how each one carries on his love affairs. . . .

Dramatically, the family prison bears a certain resemblance to the situation of the frustrated wife and the jealous husband—the *gilos*—of the love
lyric. More interesting, however, is the proximity of the chapel, the locus
of communion, to the tower, the locus of excommunication, as well as the
juxtaposition of the books appropriate to each.

The opposition of the sacred text and the profane book—*le livre Ovide*—
suggests a tension between the universe of love ("Cument hom deit amur
tenir") depicted on the walls and that which the walls are designed to
exclude. In other words, the prison remains insufficient to shut out that
which enters through the images of the book which both undermines the
effectiveness of the walls and thwarts the strategy of an old man's
lineage. *Guigemar* contains perhaps the first vernacular manifestation of
the book intended as a vehicle of allurement. As in Dante's portrayal of
the temptation of Paolo and Francesca by the "Romance of Lancelot" (see
above, p. 141), Marie's lovers are lured by a text which, in refusing a
directly mimetic function, merely reflects a prior text (in this case Ovid)
which itself belongs to a preexisting erotic and literary tradition.

The images on the wall are the opposite of the evangelical book, and
they attest to that moment in which the words of men, subject to a process
of infinite sequential substitution, replace the divine and transcendent
Word of God. Because one book only leads through a process of infinite
regress to another, the book itself becomes a tool of seduction rather than
redemption. Marie thus transforms what looks like a strategy of literary
origins into a complex articulation of the relation between medieval love
poetry, sexual desire, and the threat of desire to lineage that we have
identified all along with the antigenealogical courtly lyric. Moreover,
what remains essential is not so much the poet's consciousness of his or
her own place in a long line of seductions, which includes that of the
reader (listener or viewer), but the fact that in the romance both elements
of our sexual and textual equation are intertwined. The walls designed to
preserve the purity of lineage are also catalysts to its disruption.

Are the images which supposedly reproduce the book also intended to
suggest a pattern of poetic dislocation—a reduction of discursive sequence to spatial (visual) presence—akin to the *canso*? Perhaps. Yet Marie
seems to establish more generally a psychosexual cycle in which the
imposed marriage leads to imprisonment, imprisonment to desire, and
desire to the fantasy which, from the episode of Guigemar's encounter

with the white stag onward, is regularly interfaced with the harshly realistic givens of the heroine's situation. For if Béroul's mode of textual interruption entails a certain narrative scrambling, and if that of Chrétien involves the punctuation of story line by lyric (and descriptive) interludes, Marie achieves an analogous break with representation and with "natural" (linear) presentation through recourse to fantasy. It is impossible in the case at hand to discern whether Guigemar has actually traveled to another land, or whether, in fact, the poetess has merely departed from the inferred logic of her beginning—whether, in other words, the displacement which the text announces has been geographic or ontological. A similar ambiguity characterizes Lanval's daydream (?) of the fairy queen who later materializes, the other-worldly voyage of the frustrated wife in *Yonec*, the metamorphoses of lovers and husbands in *Le Laustic* and *Bisclavret*, and the false death recounted at the end of *Eliduc*. In each case, the constraint of marriage provokes an imagined (or real) break with lineage that is translated poetically into a break with the reader's expectations of the narrowly mimetic text. Through the seductive integration of the marvelous, Marie creates the impression of narrative continuity while at the same time distancing herself from the credible.

Like the epics of the Cycle of the Rebellious Barons, several Anglo-Norman works often grouped under the heading of "ancestral romances" depict the heroic struggle to preserve or to recuperate a lost inheritance and thus to restore the continuity of a threatened lineage (e.g., *Boeve de Haumtone, Gui de Warewic, Waldef, Fouke le Fitz Waryn*).[75] Similarly, a number of Old French verse romances from the late twelfth and thirteenth centuries revolve so wholly around issues of marriage and succession that they seem to constitute an independent matrimonial cycle (e.g., Hue de Roteland's *Ipomedon*, Raoul de Houdenc's *Meraugis de Portlesguez*, Renaut de Beaujeu's *Le Bel Inconnu*, Gautier d'Arras's *Ille et Galeron*, and the anonymous *Partonopeu de Blois* and *Amadas et Ydoine*).[76] These are difficult poems whose length and diffuseness are often disconcerting. Yet they do at times offer important insight into the problematics under discussion. In almost every case, we are privy to the inner workings of the feudal model of marriage; and, in some instances, the kind of conflict between opposing models implicit to Marie's novellas gives way to open debate. In *Ipomedon*, Lafiere's men, like those of King Marc and Equitan, force her to marry, and they even discuss at the highest baronial level the issue of free choice (vv. 1927–2380). The Melior of *Partonopeu* is faced with a similar situation also accompanied by a quarrel over the limits of consent (vv. 1484, 6589); and Partonopeu's mother and uncle attempt to compel him to wed a niece of the King of France (vv. 4040, 4381, 5331). The King Arthur of *Le Bel Inconnu* presses Guiglains to marry Blonde Esmerée despite the hero's passion for La Pucele as Blances Mains

(v. 6168). In *Amadas*, Ydoine's father marries her against her will; and in *Ille et Galeron*, the Duke of Brittany arranges a union for his sister and Ille, just as the Emperor of Rome will later conclude a similar match for his daughter.

. Love notwithstanding, this series of matrimonial romances proffers the general impression of a world filled with matchmakers—vassals, sovereigns, parents, and guardians—who seek to marry off those from whom they hold land, those who hold land from them, or those who will inherit. And yet, even here, where the lay aristocratic model of marriage prevails, it is often tempered by an enlightened seigneurial, baronial, or parental hand; and this both through an exploration of the negative consequences of imposed unions as well as through the assertion of what looks like the principle of meritocracy in the collective determination of conjugal choice. The authors of *Ipomedon*, *Partonopeu*, and *Le Bel Inconnu*, for example, adopt the motif of the tournament in order to demonstrate the true worth of the already beloved hero whose genealogy may be somewhat obscure. Thus they seem to suggest a natural accommodation between desire and descent. As the author of *Partonopeu* maintains, "a good son born in sin is worth more than a bad one conceived in wedlock."[77] Elsewhere, the feudal matrimonial model is condemned outright: Ydoine's father admits his mistake in having married her to a rich but detested spouse (v. 7477); and Galeron gracefully withdraws to a convent in order to allow her husband to marry Ganor, who affirms succinctly the rule of consent: "Grans pecciés est, si con moi samble, / De metre feme et ome ensamble, / Des que on set qu'il s'entreheent."[78]

As we have seen throughout, the question of marriage is, ultimately, indissociable from that of land, of inheritance, and, in particular, of cognatic succession. Here the status of fiefs accruing to women is crucial, for if this group of romances is filled with those anxious for others to marry, those *others* are almost always heiresses (or heirs who have inherited from their mother) who, in some instances, succeed to entire realms. Ipomedon's as well as Lafiere's fiefs come from the distaff side. The daughter of the king of Great Britain inherits his lands (*Meraugis*). Melior is heiress to the Eastern Empire (*Partonopeu*), the Pucele as Blances Mains to L'Ile d'Or (*Le Bel Inconnu*), Ydoine to Burgundy (*Amadas*), Galeron to Brittany, and Ganor to Rome (*Ille et Galeron*). Furthermore, the repeated motifs of the hero's obscure lineage and of marriages contracted below the bride's station, the emphasis upon merit as well as birth, and especially the frequence of cognatic succession all suggest that these are novels of social ascension. To a much greater extent than the romances of Béroul, Chrétien, or Marie, they stand as almost perfect illustrations of what E. Köhler and G. Duby have identified as the historical phenomenon of the *juvenes*: unmarried knights (*bacheliers*), who also may be younger sons, in pursuit, irrespective of the lineages involved, of an advantageous marriage.[79] I say "almost perfect" because of the lack of evidence for the existence of older brothers of these social climbing heroes who seem, if anything, to be only sons, and because of the importance of the holdings which devolve to those who seem—by race, prowess, and love—to deserve them.

One final remark is in order concerning the mode of textual interruption characteristic of the late twelfth- and thirteenth-century matrimonial romance. In fact, these works participate to varying degrees in all of the modes that we have delineated: scrambling, lyric intrusion (description, inner monologue), and the *merveilleux*. And yet they are also characterized by what can best be described as a certain narrative attrition. They are long romances (in some cases over ten thousand lines), and the clarity with which they focus in places upon issues like marriage choice and inheritance is more than undermined by a general loss of narrative coherence. Plots and subplots are complexly intertwined, innumerable secondary characters share the stage with the principal protagonists, action ranges freely over Eastern and Western Europe, thus contributing to a general sense of disorientation. Such narrative confusion, implicating the *estoire* both as story and as lineage, is sometimes thematized as a failure to recognize true genealogy and other times as a search for paternity. In this the matrimonial romance resembles the equally disoriented and disorienting *corpus* of contemporaneous verse and prose romances surrounding Chrétien's *Perceval*.

In concluding this brief overview of the courtly novel, we mention in passing a work so rich as alone to justify a full-length study: *Le Roman de Silence*. This little known poem (thirteenth century) thematizes many of the issues we have encountered in the lyric, epic, and romance—war concluded by marriage, public debate of matrimonial policy, the economics of the *bacheliers*. Its author, who twice identifies himself as Heldris de Cornuälle (vv. 1, 6682), is, moreover, obsessed by the question of inheritance, which not only shapes this "romance of succession" but is linked explicitly to such broader concerns as the relation between nature and culture, poetry, erotic desire, and sexual difference. Superficially, the central dramatic focus of Heldris's text is prepared by an almost incidental subplot in which a quarrel between two counts over which one will marry the eldest of two sisters, and therefore inherit the largest of two holdings (*la maisnee*), results in the death of both and a royal prohibition of cognatic succession. "Never again," proclaims King Ebain, "will a woman inherit in the realm of England, as long as I hold land."[80]

The exclusion of females, which angers those anxious to endow younger sons through affiliation (cf. v. 314), thus lays the foundation for an elaborate biopolitical drama whose resolution occupies the rest of the verse romance. For when King Ebain then seeks to marry off the only daughter of the Duke of Cornwall and to invest the dead duke's son-in-law with the paternal duchy, that investiture, according to Ebain's own decree, depends upon the production of a male heir (vv. 1295, 1455, 1588). The subsequent birth of a daughter to Eufemie and Cador poses the dilemma of absolute interruption, which Heldris conceives simultaneously in genealogical and semiological terms: that is, a lack of primogenital continuity entailing a loss of ancestral property is recuperated by an improper act of naming that itself hides its own occurrence. Cador to Eufemie:

> Sel faisons apieler Scilense. . . .
> Que Jhesus Cris par sa poissance
> Le nos doinst celer et taisir,
> Ensi com lui est a plaizir!
> Mellor consel trover n'i puis.
> Il iert només Scilenscius;
> Et s'il avient par aventure
> Al descovrir de sa nature
> Nos muerons cest -us en -a,
> S'avra a non Scilencia.
> Se nos li tolons dont cest -us,
> Nos li donrons natural us,
> Car cis -us est contre nature,
> Mais l'altres seroit par nature.[81]

We will call her "Silence." . . . Jesus Christ in his infinite power gave us the ability to hide and to remain quiet, as is his pleasure! We will never find a better solution. She will be named "Scilencius"; and if it happens by chance that her true nature is discovered, we will change this *-us* into *-a*, and his name will be "Scilencia." If we remove then this *-us*, we restore to her her natural law; for this *-us* is imposed against nature, but the other is by nature.

The above passage better than any other establishes the complex network of associations that serves as an interpretative key to the whole. Hence, nature is linked to the propriety of names, sexual difference, and the rule of primogenital inheritance; artifice or hiding ("celer et taisir"), on the other hand, is bound to the transgression of grammatical property, sexual inversion, and the deflection of a proper succession. The dramatic structure of *Le Roman de Silence* turns, in fact, around the imbalance introduced within just such a paradigm by the reversal of its terms, that is, a false appellation and a nominal sexual difference maintained in the interest of a true and real inheritance.

How, then, is such a direct series of ideas and their seeming reversal rhetoricized within Heldris's text? Here there can be no simple response, since the particular misnomer which lies at the core of textual elaboration is itself highly problematic. Would not, for instance, the discovery of the impropriety of Silence's name put a quick end to all possibility of further narrative progression? Or is it not, rather, a correct understanding of her name, whose proper is to hide, that motivates a discursive sequence ended precisely by the discovery of the nature (property) of its referent? The impossibility of distinguishing the denotative impropriety of the heroine's name from its connotative propriety is fundamental to this drama of language and lineage; and it points in the direction of Heldris's own identification of such ambiguity with eroticism and with the nature of poetry itself. Earlier, he expressly links writing with desire, which can lead either to interruptive silence (v. 1172), or, if fecund, to Silence, and the narrative prolongation of a tale (v. 984). Even the latter case remains ambiguous, however; for Silence, the monster of generic and linguistic illusion and a perfect illustration of Alain de Lille's principle of sexual and grammatical indeterminancy (see above, pp. 134–136), is drawn to poetic performance and in the end escapes in the company of two jongleurs (v. 3117). More important, as the product of pure artifice, Silence embodies the respresentational order of simulacrum that both Alain and Heldris hold to be the equivalent of tricky and perverse poetic invention. *Le Roman de Silence* reads, in places, like a vernacular version of the *Planctus Naturae* in which it is no longer possible to discern the difference between Nature and Noreture, between "straight writing" and invention, between the sexes, or between the suffixes (*-us* and *-a*) and the customs (*us*) appropriate to each.[82] Ultimately, the poet identifies profoundly with the double nature of silence/Silence: the difficulty attached to "representing" the tale that exceeds him is, at bottom, a difficulty of succession catalyzed by the infinite possibilities of artifice, yet menaced by empty simulation. In the seamless blending of these two poetic principles indissociable from their appropriate laws of property and of inheritance, *Le Roman de Silence* embodies the bivalent, mediatory essence of romance.

SIX

Grail Family and Round Table

No issue in the study of Old French literature has invited greater interpretative license than the question of the sources of Chrétien de Troyes's *Conte du Graal*.[1] Some explanations are indeed difficult to believe. Take the following, for example: that the episode in which Perceval visits a mysterious castle, meets an invalid king, sees a graillike dish and bleeding lance, forgets to ask what they mean, and awakens to find that both castle and king have vanished—that this *aventure* is: part of early Aryan literature, derived from an ancient Babylonian cult, the survival of an archaic Indian vegetation ritual or of an esoteric Islamic initiation ceremony; or, that the mysterious meal is, in reality, a Sephardic Jewish Passover seder, that the old king is a secret emissary of the Cathar faith, a medieval version of the Egyptian god Thoth, or a historical image of Baldwin IV afflicted with elephantiasis; or, finally, that the graillike dish represents a "sex symbol of immemorial antiquity," the pearl of Zoroastrian tradition, a talisman of heretical Albigensians worshipped in caves in the Pyrenees, a secret religious relic originating in Hellenic Greece (and preserved in the medieval *corpus hermeticum*), or a genuine "Great Sapphire" kept in the sacristy of Glastonbury Abbey.[2] And, further, we are asked by the scholarly workers at this building site of Babel to believe that all of the above sources of Chrétien's tale reached the medieval poet without leaving any visible trace.

Such attempts to explain the *obscurus per obscuriorem* seem to err in two directions. They tend either to universalize their object to such an extent that, within the context of assumed thematic archetypes, everything is to be found everywhere and meaningful difference vanishes; or, they tend to be overly genetic, to seek the positive traces of tradition where no evidence exists—to mistake analogy for influence. They point, in any case, to the extreme difficulty of establishing for Chrétien's poem definite origins (which were most likely Celtic and liturgical). More serious perhaps, they are blind to the fact that *Le Conte du Graal*, irrespective of Aryan, Babylonian, Indian, Egyptian, Islamic, Greek, Judaic, Cathar, or Zoroastrian tradition, is about the problem of origins; and this from the very beginning:

> Ki petit semme petit quelt,
> Et qui auques requeillir velt,
> En tel liu sa semence espande
> Que Diex a cent doubles li rande;
> Car en terre qui riens ne valt,
> Bone semence seche et faut.
> Crestïens semme et fait semence
> D'un romans que il encomence. . . .
> [*Perceval*, v. 1]

He who sows little reaps little; and he who wants to harvest well must put his seed in such a place that God will increase it a hundredfold, since in worthless land good seed dries and dies. Chrétien plants and conceives a romance that he begins. . . .

In his insistence upon the homophonic couple *semmer/semence*, Chrétien articulates a nexus of issues, not only germane to the present study but suggestive of a virtual program for the reading of this and other Grail texts.

The first of these, emanating from the Latin root *semino*, "to sow," and *semen*, "seed," plunges us from the outset into the thematics of agricultural production. *Perceval*, like the lyric (cf. in particular the *reverdie*), begins in the spring; and the sowing of seed mirrors the rebirth of nature as well as of the poetic voice:

> Ce fu au tans qu'arbre foillissent
> Que glai et bois et pre verdissent,
> Et cil oisel en lor latin

Cantent doucement au matin
Et tote riens de joie aflamme,
Que li fix a la veve fame
De la gaste forest soutaine
Se leva. . . .
Il pensa que veoir iroit
Herceors que sa mere avoit,
Qui ses avaines li semoient.

[*Perceval*, vv. 69, 80]

It was at the time that trees blossom and flowers and woods and fields turn green, and birds in their tongue sing sweetly in the morning, and the whole world is aflame with joy, that the son of the widow of the distant waste forest awoke. . . . He thought he would go see his mother's farmers, who were sowing seed for her.

The joyous harmony of nature's creatures and of nature and man is, however, double; and the geographic situation of Chrétien's beginning belies its temporal setting. For the seeds of springtime fall on the soil of the waste forest ("la gaste forest soutaine") whose resonance for the medieval audience introduces a tension that will shape not only the rest of the poem but the entire Grail cycle.

The Wasteland

The root *gaste* refers to an isolated, distant, or marginal area; or, to uncultivated woodland as opposed to the arable plain.[3] More important, it means "destroyed" or "ravaged" land. In the *Perlesvaus*, for example, a hermit explains to Perceval the inhospitality of the surrounding countryside in which "there used to be a giant who was so large and cruel and horrible that no one dared to live within the realm; and he so destroyed the land and wasted [*gastoit*] it as you saw today."[4] Distant land, fallow land, destroyed land—the Arthurian Wasteland constitutes a landscape and a relation of men to their natural environment characterized by depopulation, the infertility of nature, and a crisis of social order.

The Wasteland implies, first of all, a shortage of people with respect to a preceding moment of sufficient manpower. In the earliest full-blown rendering of the motif, that found in Geoffrey's *Historia*, Merlin predicts with a Biblical ring that "Death shall snatch away the people and all nations shall be made void." For the author of the *Perlesvaus*, the *terre gaste* is "tot voit de gent." And as the dust settles on the final battle of the Arthurian age, that which pits Arthur against Mordret, the author of *La Mort Artu* laments the decimation of the noble population: "se en remestrent aprés leur mort les terres gastes et essilliees, et soufreteuses de bons seigneurs."[5]

The Wasteland implies, second, the infertility of the countryside, a disruption, as the *Elucidation* poet observes, of natural order, and, in particular, of the cycle of fertility characteristic of springtime in Chrétien's "gaste forest soutaine": "Li roiames si agasti / K'ains puis n'i ot arbre fueilli; / Li pré et les flor(s) essecierent / Et les aiges apeticierent."[6] The author (or authors) of the *Queste del Saint Graal* and the *Estoire del Saint Graal* offer strikingly similar descriptions of nature's failure to produce the fruits by which men are sustained: "li arbre ne porterent fruit, ne en l'eve ne fu trové poisson, se petit non."[7] The theme of nature's sterility is, in fact, almost synonymous with the Wasteland which is, in some versions, coextensive with Arthur's realm:

> Logres est uns nons de dolour,
> Nommés en larmes et en plour.
> Bien doit iestre en dolour nommés,
> Car on n'i seme pois ne blés, . . .
> Ne abres fueille n'i porta,
> Ne nus prés n'i raverdïa,
> Ne nus oysiaus n'i ot naon
> Ne se n'i ot beste faon. . . .[8]

Logres is a name of sorrow, uttered in tears and cries; it is fitting that it be named in sorrow, for here is sown neither peas nor wheat, the trees bear no leaves, the meadows never turn green, no bird bears young there, no beast a foal. . . .

The above passage from the *Sone de Nansay* underscores the extent to which the Wasteland means the disruption of gathering culture ("Ne arbres fueille n'i porta"), of pastoral culture ("Ne nus prés n'i raverdïa"), of hunting culture ("Ne nus oysiaus n'i ot naon"); and yet it also points to a corresponding crisis in the arts of cultivation, the dissolution of agriculture ("Car on n'i seme pois ne blés"), and of animal husbandry ("Ne se n'i ot beste faon"). Both the fruits of the earth and of human labor have become problematic in what amounts to a spiraling process of decline.

If agricultural and reproductive disorder are the symptoms of crisis, they are not its cause, which lies in the transgression of human law, and, more precisely, in the deliberate destruction of the means of production that accompanies war. The campaign which the Brutus of Geoffrey's pseudochronicle leads through Aquitania has all the earmarks of a "scorched-earth policy." And as the Saxon kings of the *Estoire Merlin* invade Arthur's kingdom, they burn, loot, and destroy everything in sight.[9] So too, Chrétien's "gaste forest soutaine" originates in the series of wars following Arthur's father's death. Perceval's mother to her son:

> Vostre peres, si nel savez,
> Fu parmi la jambe navrez
> Si que il mehaigna del cors.
> Sa grant terre, ses grans tresors,
> Que il avoit come preudom,

> Ala tot a perdition,
> Si chaï en grant povreté.
> Apovri et deshireté
> Et escillié furent a tort
> Li gentil home aprés la mort
> Uterpandragon qui rois fu
> Et peres le bon roi Artu.
> Les terres furent escillies
> Et les povres gens avillies,
> Si s'en fuï qui fuïr pot.
>
> [*Perceval*, v. 435]

Your father, if you do not know it, was wounded in the leg so that his whole body suffered. His great lands, his great treasure, that he held as a brave knight were all lost and fell into ruin. After the death of Uterpandragon, who was king and King Arthur's father, noblemen were wrongly impoverished, disinherited, and exiled. So too were the lands wasted and poor people despoiled; those who could flee fled.

Even more important than the theme of war and decline, however, is the fact that the retreat to the Wasteland and the disruption of peace and prosperity is accompanied by a disruption of paternity—first the death of Uterpandragon and then, along with the death of Perceval's two older brothers, the loss of his father as well: "Del doel del fil morut li pere."[10] The lapse of procreation among birds and animals, the infertility of trees and fields, are, ultimately, linked to the interruption of human genealogy, a disinheritance and privation of the paternal function.

Here a second resonance of the root *semme/semence* comes into focus— namely, the cluster of meanings connected to the idea of origin and stemming from the Latin *semino*, "to beget," "engender," "bring forth," or "procreate." Again, the beginning of Chrétien's tale contains a polyvalent series of paternal relations whose rhetorical presentation sets into play an elaborate strategy of reading. For the origin of the tale is itself bound up in the genealogy of a prince ("Cest li quens Phelipes de Flandres, / Qui valt mix ne fist Alixandres") and in the genealogy of a book ("Ce est li Contes del Graal / Dont li quens li bailla le livre / Oëz coment il s'en delivre").[11] There can, in fact, be no distinction between *li contes* and *li quens*, a literary and princely lineage stretching from Alexander to Philip, to Chrétien, and to the reader, since the act of writing, also cast as a sowing, engenders that of reading or reaping: "E si le seme en si bon leu / Qu'il ne puet [estre] sanz grant preu."[12] The Count of Flanders is, above all, a successful reader ("Li quens est teus que il n'escoute / Vilain g[ap] ne parole estoute");[13] and the homonymic identity of his title and the process of narration binds the status of nobility to a determined mode of understanding. To fail to read as Chrétien prescribes (literally "prewrites") is to lack the nobility which is as much a part of the book as it is an attribute of the book's princely patron.

The rhetorical strategy of Chrétien's beginning—and of beginnings—points to the close connection between the dynamics of the tale and a thematics of perception (or of reading), which reveals yet another dimension of the radical *seme*. From the Greek *sēma/semantikōs* (sign [mark] and significant) the couple *semme/semence* elicits a wealth of meanings having to do with understanding and interpretation. For if *Perceval* begins with an association between social status and proper reading, the body of the text is concerned with—even defined by—the hero's attempt to learn to read the signs of knightly culture. Here, our three levels of meaning seem to fuse: *seme* (to sow) calls into question an economics of war versus agriculture; *seme* (to beget) binds the process of destruction and decline to the death of the father; and *seme* (to signify) situates both natural and paternal functions within the context of a drama of meaning.

Grail Quest and the Quest for the Name of the Father

Perceval's youth in the wasted margins of society is, as we have seen, synonymous with a loss of the father that can also be equated with an ignorance of the signs of knighthood. In this his mother stands as the agent of interruption, since her horror of her husband's fate leads her to shield the son from knowledge of the father, who, had he lived, would, as she acknowledges, have preserved the continuity of lineage: "Chevaliers estre deüssiez, / Biax fix, se Damedieu pleüst, / Qui vostre pere vos eüst / Gardé et vos autres amis."[14]

Perceval's first contact with the world of the father is set within the frame of a series of misreadings based not only upon ignorance but upon misinformation:

> Molt se merveille et dist: "Par m'ame,
> Voir se dist ma mere, ma dame,
> Qui me dist que deable sont
> Les plus laides choses del mont;
> Et si dist por moi enseingnier
> Que por aus se doit on seingnier
> Mes cest ensaing desdaignerai,
> Que ja voir ne m'en seignerai."
> [*Perceval*, v. 113]

He marveled greatly and said: "By my soul, it is true that my mother told me that they are devils and the ugliest things in the world. And she told me by way of instruction that one should cross oneself before them; but I will disregard such teaching and will not cross myself."

The neophyte's meeting with the knights underscores the extent to which his mother, in seeking to deny a proper inheritance, also undermines the property of perception, of meaning, and, as the play upon *enseingner, seingnier, ensaing* suggests, the extent to which Perceval's attempt to come to terms with the world of the father is an attempt to assimilate its signs.[15] The gap between the mother's misinformation and the hero's perception accounts for the irony of the passage, that is, the crossing of oneself, a second misreading of the mother's devils (*deables*) as angels, and, finally, their relegation to the status of gods.[16] Nor should Chrétien's ironic intent blind us to the fact that for Perceval knowledge of the world is essentially a knowledge of the names associated with the father—first the name "knight" itself (" 'Qui estes dont?'—'Chevaliers sui' "), then the lexicon of knightly weapons: " 'Que est or che que vos tenez?' . . . 'Sel te dirai, ce est ma lance' "; " 'Escu a non ce que je port'; 'Vallet, c'est mes haubers.' "[17]

Le Conte du Graal is, in effect, an upside-down Bildungsroman, one in which learning is essentially a process of unlearning—an undoing of the obfuscating signs of the mother, her "protective" *sens*, and, eventually, of the teaching of the spiritual father, Gornemanz.[18] Even once Perceval's mother has accepted the inevitable attraction of knighthood, her instructions are no less misleading, no less productive of the series of misreadings that can be said to shape Chrétien's tale. For example, Perceval's "sex education"—the directives to serve women ("Dames et puceles servez"), to kiss them but to "leave off the rest," to accept the gift of a ring (v. 553)—leads directly to the encounter with the mistress of Orgueilleux de la Lande, as Perceval's actions, in keeping with his mother's teachings ("Que ma mere le m'ensaigna," v. 696), only provoke a series of further misunderstandings.[19] Orgueilleux cannot believe any woman capable of "leaving off the rest";[20] and the disfiguring abuse to which he submits his beloved merely confirms this belief, since, when Perceval meets the couple again, he fails to recognize them. Thus we have come full circle. A first misreading (the maternal *enseignement*) gives rise to a second (the initial encounter with the victimized woman), the second to a third (Orgueilleux's misinterpretation), and the third to a fourth (Perceval's failure to recognize his victims because of the disfigurement caused by Orgueilleux's original misprision).

A similar pattern is to be found in Perceval's relation to the substitute father Gornemanz de Gorhaut. The older knight initiates the neophyte to the use of arms and to the chivalric code, thus reversing the maternal preaching. To the mother's warning not to travel with a companion without first learning his name, Gornemanz counters with an injunction against speaking too much.[21] And it is, of course, this rule that leads to Perceval's celebrated lapse of speech in the presence of the Grail mysteries:

> Si s'est de demander tenus
> Coment ceste chose avenoit,
> Que del chasti li sovenoit
> Celui qui chevalier le fist,

Que li ensaigna et aprist
Que de trop parler se gardast.
Et crient, se il le demandast,
Qu'en le tenist a vilonie;
Por che si nel demanda mie.
[*Perceval*, v. 3204][22]

He kept himself from asking how this thing came about, since he remembered the warning of the one who made him a knight and who taught him to refrain from speaking too much. And he feared, if he were to ask, that one would hold him in scorn; and for this reason he asked nothing.

The failure to speak, the interruption of language altogether, stands, then, as the prolongation of the mother's attempted interruption; for, as his cousin later attests, the right question at the right time would have restored the maimed king's health, the prosperity of the Wasteland, and the integrity of lineage. The rest of Chrétien's unfinished text represents, in fact, an attempt to return to the Grail Castle in order to undo the misreading, interpreted through Gornemanz, of the mother's original invocation to speech.

Le Conte du Graal focuses poignantly upon the issue of nature versus culture, which seems to be resolved in favor of a certain genetic continuity. Perceval's mother's effort to shield him from the world of the father is as ineffective against the urge toward knighthood as Silence's parents' attempt to hide her sex (see above, pp. 195–197). And the son's deaf ear to the mother's obfuscation ("Li vallés entent molt petit / A che que sa mere li dist") is transformed, upon contact with the outside world, into a desire for that which has remained hidden ("Molt m'en iroie volentiers / Au roi qui fait les chevaliers").[23] Perceval desires instinctively the inherited—natural—status of the father, as that which is intuitive and innate triumphs over that which is learned. Upon further examination, however, there is in Perceval's assumption of knighthood no contradiction of the principle of culture, for that which impels him naturally is precisely the desire for social status despite the father's death and the mother's attempt at interruption.

What I am suggesting, first of all, is that the socialization that Perceval undergoes is indistinguishable from the process of learning the signs that make him capable of reading knightly culture. To play one's "natural" role in society and to be *sené*, to be endowed with signs, are connatural concepts. And not only is the *ingénu*, referred to initially as "cil qui petit fu senez," equivalent to "one who is ignorant of the law" (" 'Sire, que vos dist cist Galois?' / —'Il ne set pas totes les lois. . . . Que Galois sont tot par nature / Plus fol que bestes en pasture' "), but Chrétien's equation of savagery, ignorance of signs and of the law has deep roots in the etymological connection of *lex* and *lectio*.[24] He who is conversant with the law is essentially a reader, just as he who is mad—*forcené*—remains essentially excluded from the law. To be outside of signs, *insanus*, is to be outside of society (*Perceval*, vv. 319, 933, 4187, 4197).

Second, Perceval's quest for knighthood is, at bottom, a quest for the father that is indistinguishable from a quest initially for the proper names of the father's profession and, ultimately, for his own proper name. The drive toward mastery of the signs of chivalry uncovers bit by bit the traces of a lineage scattered—by the dispersion (the dissemination) associated with the Wasteland itself—throughout the Arthurian countryside. It is, for example, during the meeting with his cousin shortly after the visit to the Grail Castle that Perceval remembers his own name which, merely repressed, inhered in his "lineal subconscious" all along: "Et cil qui son non ne savoit / Devine et dist que il avoit / Perchevax li Galois a non."[25] Later, in the course of another fortuitous encounter, this time with the hermit who will remind him of his (the hermit's) sister (who is also the hero's mother), Perceval learns that the Grail King is his uncle and the Fisher-King his cousin: "Cil qui l'en en sert est mes frere, / Ma suer et soe fu ta mere; Et del riche Pecheor croi / Qu'il est fix a icelui roi."[26] The attempt to return to the Grail Castle becomes, then, an attempt to relocate and thus to restore the integrity of a lineage that is from the beginning unrecognizably fragmented—and, at the same time, to restore a lost plenitude of meaning situated beyond signs. In the quest for union with the lost father lies the wish to unite the signifier with its signified.

What this suggests, finally, is an elaborate textual strategy indissociable from the thematics of paternal and semiological loss. Here again, *Le Conte du Graal* falls within the romance mode of a simultaneous problematization of paternity and of narration. Perceval's origins are shrouded in mystery; he does not know his own name (though he later recalls it); he fails to recognize the cousin with whom he has been raised, just as later he remains ignorant of the identity of his maternal uncles. Even more significant, Perceval is most cut off from a proper reading of familial signs at the very moment that he is closest to his lineage, that is to say, at the Grail Castle and later at the hermitage.[27] The dispersal of his lineage, its loss of property, and of intelligibility, these, along with their attempted recuperation, serve to inform the text to such a degree that there is, finally, no adequate means of differentiating the hero's *estoire*—his genealogy—from Chrétien's *estoire*, or tale. The various paths (*sentiers*) which the fatherless protagonist follows in pursuit of a lost paternal presence associated with chivalric signs, holistic meaning, and health (*enseignement, sens, santé*) are the paths of the tale itself:

> Et tote jor sa voie tint,
> Qu'il n'encontra rien terïene

Ne crestïen ne crestïene
Qui li seüst voie ensaignier.
[*Perceval*, v. 2976]

And all day long he kept on his way such that he encountered no Christian, man or woman, who could instruct him in his way.

The above passage is significant for what it tells us both about the wandering Perceval and about the poet. Just as the hero can find no one to guide him through the disorienting Wasteland (cf. v. 2959), neither is Chrétien ("Christian, man or woman") capable of orienting him anew. The inaccessibility of a straight path, here expressed on the level of theme as an objective spatial disorientation, remains indistinguishable from the poet's inability to recapture a lost narrative continuity. Chrétien, like Perceval, himself seeks a poetic rectitude that is, in the telling of the tale, constantly disseminated—scattered and partial; and that accounts, ultimately, for the increasing incoherence of a bifurcated romance which cannot end. The unfinished state of this last tale of adventure (and the word is itself suggestive of a certain textual erring) can be understood, then, less as the product of biographical anecdote than as the logical consequence of an unresolvable drama of language, lineage, and literary form. *Le Conte du Graal* is the story of a quest within a linear narrative mode for that which—beyond words—is perceived as total or whole but which bears only an asymptotic relation to the process of search. Perceval's own impossible quest for the paternal presence that will restore the integrity of lineage is, finally, doomed by the impossibility of totalizing meaning—of a transcendence identifiable with the Grail itself—within the romance mold.

This mingling of paternal, semiological, and textual issues is even more pronounced in the thirteenth-century Perceval Continuations: the *Perlesvaus*, *Didot-Perceval*, and Vulgate Cycle. Here again, the Grail Quest, which provides both the internal coherence of individual works and their common denominator, represents a desire to return to the father and to reunite a dispersed genealogical grouping, expressed in each instance as a tendency toward (will for) dramatic unity and formal closure within the confines of an increasingly fragmented textual tradition. In the less biographical works the drama of lineal return and semiological transcendence is posited in collective terms. Thus Robert de Boron's *Roman de l'Estoire dou Graal* and the *Estoire del Saint Graal* proffer a genealogy of the Grail family, its successions and transfer to Great Britain, that is belied by the extraordinarily disjointed narrative of the search of the Quest Knights (*La Queste del Saint Graal*) not only for the holy vessel but for each other. Those works bearing Perceval's name and defined by his attempt to rediscover the Grail Castle as well as to recapture his lost inheritance

(especially the *Perlesvaus*) are largely extensions or elaborations of Chrétien's poem.

The prose romances which focus specifically upon Lancelot present a
similar pattern. Like Perceval, Lancelot is, as he explains to the maid of
the "Castel de la Charete," both fatherless and disinherited: "Car iou
perdi en vne matinee mon pere qui moult estoit preudoms . . . et fui
desherites de toute ma terre." Raised by the Lady of the Lake, he remains
uncertain about his own lineage: "Ensi fu lancelos .iij. ans en la garde a la
damoisele a trop grant aise. & bien quidoit pour voir que ele fust sa
meire."[28] The search for his own name along with that of his father
occupies as much of that enormous portion of the Vulgate Cycle known
as the *Lancelot Propre* as the adultery with Guinevere or the forgotten Grail
Quest. In fact, as a messenger of the Lady of the Lake predicts, Lancelot
will learn the name of his parents precisely at the moment that he
recaptures his lost inheritance:

> Lors le trait a vne part a conseil si li dist que sa dame del lac lenuoie a li &
> demain fait ele saurois vostre non. & le non vostre pere & vostre mere. Et
> che sera la sus en chel castel dont vous seres sires ains que vespres soient
> sounees.[29]

> Then she took him aside and told him that her Lady of the Lake sent her
> to him and that tomorrow she would make known your name and the
> name of your father and your mother. And that it will take place up in that
> castle of which you will be lord by vespers time.

And in lifting the tombstone, part of the ritual ordeal of repossession of
the *propre* of "La Douloureuse Garde," Lancelot encounters the sepulchral writing informing him simultaneously of the name of the father and
of his own death: "Et lors voit les lettres qui dient. Chi gerra lancelos del
lac le fiex au roi ban de benoyc. & lors remet la lame ius & bien seit que
chest ses nons qu'il a veu."[30]

Where family relations are concerned, the Grail corpus gives the impression of an immense genealogical confusion emanating not only from
the wealth of Arthurian figures but from a certain (purposeful?) textual
inconsistency as well. Consanguineal ties vary within a single tradition
like that of the Perceval story. The Fisher-King, for example, is at once the
hero's cousin (Chrétien), his maternal uncle (Manessier, *Perlesvaus*),
paternal uncle (second Continuation), grandfather (Robert de Boron,
Didot-Perceval), and father (Bibliothèque nationale MS 768).[31] Even within
an individual text, bonds of kinship may seem fluid or obscure. In the
Lancelot Propre and *La Queste*, for instance, it is almost impossible to
determine the relation between King Pellés, the Fisher-King, the Maimed
King, and Galahad. Galahad speaks of his uncle King Pellés and of his

ancestor (*aiol*) the rich Fisher-King, thus indicating that they are separate individuals and that Pellés is the Fisher-King's son.[32] Yet Bohort has just reminded us that Galahad is the son of Lancelot and the daughter of the "Riche Roi Pescheor," just as later, upon Lancelot's entry into the Castle of Corbenic, Pellés informs him of "the news of his beautiful daughter who was dead, the one in whom Galahad was conceived." In addition, the author(s) of the *Lancelot Propre* speaks of Galahad as the son of "the best knight in the world [Lancelot] and of the daughter of the rich Fisher-King."[33]

The extreme complexity of kinship ties, the lack of stability of paternity where it appears evident, the superimposition of the family of those through whom the Grail descends upon those united by blood—all of these factors have led J. Roubaud to posit a hidden incest within the clan of the Grail Knights, an incest which remains unverifiable, and, moreover, whose obfuscation is the basic function of the text: "Donc, si l'inceste est caché, c'est *par le récit même*."[34] We will have occasion shortly to return to Roubaud's masterful articles on the Grail corpus in relation to the textual strategies of familial scrambling. Let it suffice for now to suggest that Roubaud's own obsession with incest seems to blind him to a range of issues which, within the Perceval and Merlin as well as the Vulgate cycles, pose more broadly the question of the continuity and the limits of lineal affiliation. Incest is a key concern in Arthurian literature, but it is not always hidden. It remains, further, more attached to the notion of finality than to that of mysteriously incestuous origins, Roubaud's "primal Grail scene." Arthur's relationship to his sister stands as the determining cause of the end of Arthurian kinship, of kingship, and of further poetic production: "Adont conut li freres carneument sa serour et porta la dame chelui qui puissedi le traist a mort et mist a destruction et a martyr la terre, dont vous porrés oir viers la fin dou livre."[35] In the incestuous termination of a family line is the end of an era and of a book; for the Wasteland occasioned by war, associated with Perceval's origins and especially the loss of the father, is also connected to the slaying of the father:

> Car a cel tens estoient si desreez genz et si sanz mesure par tout li roiaume de Gales que se li filz trovast le pere gisant en son lit par achaison d'enfermeté, il le tresist hors par la teste ou par les braz et l'oceist errannment, car a viltance li fust atorné se ses peres moreust en son lit. Mes quant il avenoit que li filz ocioit le pere, ou li peres li filz, et toz li parentez moroit d'armes, lors disoient cil del païs qu'il estoient de haut lignage.[36]

> For at the time there were so crazed and lacking in measure throughout the Kingdom of Wales that if a son found his father lying in bed because of some sickness, he pulled him out by his head or arms and killed him on

the spot, for it would have shamed him if his father had died in bed. But when it came about that the son killed the father, or the father the son, and all the great families perished by arms, then they said that those from this land were of high lineage.

Infraction of the incest taboo is, ultimately, responsible for the generalized Oedipal violence that plunges the Arthurian realm into an eternal Wasteland, as both the transgressor and the progeny of transgression transform the law of paternity into a simultaneous patri- and infanticide: "Einsi commença la bataille es pleins de Salebieres, dont li roiaumes de Logres fu tornez a destrucion . . . ; si en remestrent aprés leur mort les terres gastes et essilliees et soufreteuses de bons seigneurs. . . . Einsi ocist li peres le fill, et li filz navra le pere a mort."[37] In the obfuscation of difference within the family lies, then, the prospect of absolute lineal and textual interruption.[38]

If incest or the collapse of the rule of minimal distance within the kin group spells its termination, the consequences of a transgression of its outer limits are hardly milder. Within the Grail corpus bastardy is an even more pressing concern than incest. Lancelot's brother Hector, Bohort's son, the false Guenivere, even Arthur are the illegitimate offspring of adulterous desire. But, more important, Galahad, the "perfect knight," embodies the principle of an interruption implicit to his perfection. As the last member of the line of David, he represents a disruption of lineage extending beyond the paternal confusion of illegitimacy so evident elsewhere. His conception occurs in the absence of sexual desire—Lancelot is drugged, and Pellés daughter "did not do it because of his beauty or out of hotness of flesh."[39] Galahad, alone capable of completing the Grail adventure, has himself transcended desire, since his perfection consists in a chastity precluding even the wish for union.[40] Thus, where Perceval seeks unsuccessfully to find the father, the Grail, and to escape the contingent nature of signs, Galahad, himself the product of an almost immaculate conception and a second Christ in Christ's line, eludes genealogy altogether. His is a faultless self-sufficiency connatural with the identity of engenderer and engendered as well as with the coincidence of signifier and signified. In the achievement of the Grail Quest, Galahad transcends paternal and linguistic difference, penetrating—beyond language—to "that which can neither be thought nor said" ("ce que langue ne porroit descrire ne cuer penser").[41]

The Grail corpus is played out between incest, paternity transgressive of the law of internal difference, and bastardy, paternity transgressive of its outer bounds. This is, so to speak, the anthropological theater or space in which the drama of language and of lineage takes place. Where the textualization of such a dynamic is concerned, we can point, first of all, to a characteristic mixing of proper names equivalent in their homophonic resemblance to the conflation of family difference. Here it is perhaps worth recalling that in Arthurian literature the proper name is synonymous with—a kind of map of—lineage, and there is no more common epithet than its patronymic evocation, for example, "Lancelot, fils de Ban de Benoyc," "Yders, fils de Nut," etc.[42] Hence the significance of seemingly free-floating prefixes and suffixes like *Bran-* (e.g., Brandalēs, Brandus, Brangor, Brangemner, Bron, He[bron]) and the similarity of whole names (e.g., Gauvain's brothers Gaheriet, Guerrehes, and Agravains; Guinevere and the false Guinevere; Yvain, son of King Urien and Yvain li Avoltres; Galehot and Galahad; Nasciens li Hermites, Nascien [Mordrain's brother-in-law], Nascien [son of Narpus]; Mordrain, Mordret; Pellés, Pellinor, Pellehan; Balaain, Balaan; Morgue, Morgain; etc.). The case of Lancelot is, in this respect, particularly revealing. Not only is his mother's name, Elaine, similar to that of her sister, Evaine, but the daughter of Pellés is named Helaine. There is, in other words, no phonic difference between Galahad's mother and grandmother, just as there is none between Lancelot and his grandfather, or between Lancelot and his son. "Lancelot" is merely a nickname, hiding the hero's true baptismal roots: "auoit non lancelos en sournon. mais il auoit non en baptesme galahos."[43] The similarity of family names is even further complicated by the background of nameless kings, knights, and hermits whose ill-defined relation to the named but homophonically enmeshed protagonists as well as to each other makes it impossible to discern with certainty the genealogical lines of the Arthurian corpus. The absence of phonetic definition along with the collapse of phonetic difference is tantamount to a loss of lineal discreteness assimilable, ultimately, to a loss of the proper and of a proper story line.[44]

This incestuous onomastic mixing is also accompanied by a more general formal scrambling practically synonymous with the prose romance's overall narrative design. I am referring to the technique of dovetailing by which the successive episodes of the enormous Lancelot-in-Prose are so thoroughly imbricated in one another as to give the impression of a continually overlapping discursive grid. The mode of interruption within the thirteenth-century prose novel is that of interlace ("entrelacement"), a progressive interpenetration of distinct elements of independent plots that move simultaneously along different narrative fronts and whose components are gradually woven into a whole.[45] Thus, where in Chrétien's *Perceval* the *estoire* that is the equivalent both of lineage and of story stands disrupted by a loss of coherence, and where in the Perceval Continuations this lack of cohesion is compounded by the impossibility of closure, in the prose romance we find an intricately conceived system of overlay by which the main narrative thrust is constantly deferred by the introduction of new elements and the superim-

position of secondary, tertiary, quaternary, quinary, senary, and sep-
tenary subplots upon one another. If the verse Grail works seem to
disorient the reader through a certain narrative inconsistency, the prose
corpus achieves a similar effect through an intricacy of design so complex
as to overwhelm the reader with a finally unassimilable abundance of
finely fitted parts.

What this means is that the text, beyond the lexical confusion of its
proper names, works less to hide an original act of incest, as Roubaud
insists, than to detour consistently the continuity of the story line that we
have identified with genealogical continuity. The Lancelot Prose Cycle,
no less than *Tristan*, Chrétien's romances, or those of Marie, expresses a
tension between directness of narration (and filiation) and its disruption.
And though the mode of interruption differs, marked as it is by a system
of interlace, the conflicting principles of continuous versus discontinuous
paternal and narrative sequence remain the same. Behind Perceval's and
Lancelot's quest for the father and the Arthurian knights' quest for the
Grail stands the author's search for the tale that is the equivalent of
lineage and that constantly eludes him: "Mes a tant se test ore li contes.
. . . Or dist li contes"; "Mes atant lesse ore li contes. . . . Or dit li contes";
"Mes a tant se test ore li contes. . . . Or dit li contes."[46]

Genealogy of the Book and the Book of Genealogy

The Romance is characterized, then, by a constant tension between the
possibility of a certain filial and narrative continuity as against its interruption. Here the body of texts which focus either wholly or in part upon
the figure of Merlin are crucial to an understanding of the relation between paternal and authorial filiation. So explicit, in fact, is the Merlin
legend with which we began that it alone might have served as guide to
the present study; and it is to the Huth manuscript that we now turn for
the light which it sheds on the problem of genealogical and textual
production.

Merlin is, it will be remembered, not only the inventor of writing and
the custodian of letters within the Arthurian world but the god of paternity as well (see above, pp. 1–3). The magician's omnivalent powers are,
in fact, most acute in the area of succession. He is the guardian of
genealogy; and his peregrinations around Great Britain are accompanied
by a series of revelations concerning illusory paternal bonds—first those
of the judge who accuses his (Merlin's) mother of commerce with the
Devil (*Huth*, 1:27); then of the dead child whose true priestly father
officiates at his burial (1:51); of Mordret (1:154); of the peasant Tor (2:112);
and, finally, of Arthur. Merlin's role where fatherhood is concerned is
that of a reformer. His perfect perception of lineal relations allows him to
demystify false kinship and thus to undo the genealogical illusions in-
duced by fornication, adultery, and incest, while serving, simulta-

neously, as a source of dramatic interest. Merlin is a spoiler of family fictions and an embodiment of the principle of fiction itself.

Nor can Merlin's command of paternity be separated from the link which the Huth text establishes between such mastery and writing. Each act of generation is accompanied by an act of transcription suggesting a deeper tie to the process of romance production. The antihero's own birth is no exception. Upon hearing the story of Merlin's conception, his mother's confessor Blaise "is greatly surprised, and he recorded the night and the hour."[47] The boy wizard pleads his mother's defense on the basis of the written record, just as after her disculpation he reveals to the judge's own mother that her lover had "put into writing each time he slept with you out of fear you might sleep with another."[48] Similarly, the mastermind of paternity, who engineers Uter's union with Ygerne, assures him of the exact hour of Arthur's conception: "Et si fai mettre l'eure et la nuit en escrit que tu l'engenras."[49]

If Merlin demonstrates a visionary control of paternal relations, it is because he is an expert at written calculation, a patron saint of letters. He is, moreover, indistinguishable from the author of the text which bears his name. Here is where the magician's relation to writing becomes most interesting. For Merlin's poetic powers are also bound to the issue of his own ancestry. The master-calculator of genealogy has, in reality, two fathers, each of which imparts to him a particular kind of knowledge. From the Devil or physical father Merlin enjoys a perfect vision of the past; and from God, the spiritual father who usurps true paternity after his mother's confession, he gains insight into the future.[50] These two paternal principles are, further, textualized in terms of discrete orders of human discourse each implying the possibility of a book. The two modes of knowledge approriate to Merlin's two fathers—*les choses faites* and *les choses a venir*—are the subjects of separate written accounts.

The first is a book of origins and events dictated at periodic intervals by Merlin to Blaise—a documentary rendering of Arthurian prehistory, the Passion, Grail transfer, and Merlin's own birth:

> Et Merlins dist: "Or quier dont enche et parchemin assés, que je te dirai moult de choses que tu metras en ton livre." Et quant il ot tout quis, si li conta Merlins les amours de Jesucrist et de Joseph tout ensi comme eles avoient esté, et d'Alain et de sa compaignie tout ensi comme il avoit alé, et comment Joseph se dessaisi dou vaissiel et puis devia, et comment dyable(s) après toutes ces choses qui furent avenues prisent conseil qui il avoient perdu lour pooir que il soloient avoir seur les hommes, et se li conte comment li prophete lor avoient mal fait, et pour chou (s')estoient (accordé) ensemble comment il feroient un homme. [*Huth*, 1:31]

> And Merlin said: "Take up now enough ink and parchment so that I might tell you many of the things you will put in your book." And when he had gathered all that was necessary, Merlin recounted to him the passion of Jesus Christ and of Joseph exactly as they took place, and of Alain and his

band and how they went forth, and how Joseph obtained the vessel and then wandered, and how the demons after all that had happened realized that they had lost their power that they used to have over men; and he recounted how the prophets had done them in, and that it was for this reason that they decided they would make a man.

Blaise's chronicle is, as the author of the Huth version suggests, genealogically rooted in Robert de Boron's *Roman dou Graal*; and it is, above all, a book of genealogies: "Si sera Joseph [et li livres des lignies que je t'ai amenteues] avec le tien et le mien."[51]

The historical book supposedly contains a record of that which has occurred—"les choses dites et faites et alees." It stands as the transformation of theme into predicate, events into language, by which we become privy to Arthurian history.[52] Blaise's chronicle is, in essence, a narrative account of human history based upon the generational sequence of Joseph's line, "ses ancisseurs," "ses hoirs," "son lignage" (*Huth*, 1:47). Meaning within it is assumed to be nonproblematical: the transparent words of the dictated text require no interpretation and are held to maintain a direct relation to the world beyond. This is not to suggest that the discourse of human history is necessarily true. On the contrary, because it is grounded in the contingent universe of events, and despite the fact that it can be understood without interpretation, the first book is also subject to corruption, trickery, misrepresentation. Before consenting to transcribe Merlin's words, Blaise elicits a promise not to be deceived: "Je ferai volentiers le livre, mais je te conjure el non del pere et le fil . . . que tu ne me puisses dechevoir ni engingnier." History, as Merlin admits, is the Devil's terrain: "Je sai les choses dites, faites et alees, et [. . .] je le tieng par nature d'anemi."[53]

The second book, Merlin's words transcribed by the counselors at the court of Uter and Pendragon, is composed of a language according to which events will shape themselves.[54] This is a prophetic text whose *oscures paroles*, without explanation, remain empty signs. Its instigation coincides with Merlin's withdrawal from the world of events into that of "covert speech"; and the discourse of this "livre de prophecies" can, in fact, only be understood once the events it foretells have already occurred: "Ne je ne(n) parlerai plus devant le siecle se si oscurement non que il ne saveront que je dirai devant que il le voient."[55] Unlike Blaise's record, the text originating at court is not biographical in nature but stands as a spontaneously generated, autonomous discourse cut off from discernible origins: "ne dist pas chis livres qui Merlins est ne dont il vint."[56] It is composed of a series of speech acts realized as events, of predication transformed into theme. As Merlin assures Arthur, "I will pronounce no obscure word the truth of whose meaning you will not know before passing out of this world."[57] The book without origin is an original book: nonmimetic; beholden to nothing, not even the "text of history"; always true because consistently self-referential. Since it exists independently of external meaning, its self-generating and self-determining language is situated beyond the limits of truth and falsehood. The book of the future contains only words—"il ne metoient en escrit fors que chou que il disoit," words, moreover, whose supposed source is not the Devil, but God: "Et nostre sires qui est poissans sour tout m'a donné sens de savoir toutes choses qui sont a avenir en partie."[58]

Merlin's two books embody the two principal poetic modes which, as we have seen, are associated with conflicting family models. The historical narrative of events, representational and organized internally according to the order of lineal succession, offers a potent illustration of the discourse of the epic, the literary form of genealogy. Structured cyclically according to family groups, the *chanson de geste* is a genre of origins which also preserves a narrative and representational contiguity identifiable with early medieval grammar as well as with the continuity of lineage; this despite its vulnerability, as Blaise suggests, to "trickery and deception" (see above, pp. 97–102). The self-contained and unintelligible book of prophecies is, on the other hand, much closer to the exclamatory discourse of the love lyric. The prophet's "obscure words," comparable to the "closed style" of the *trobar clus*, are disruptive of representation, meaning, and the narrative sequence that we have identified with genealogical progression. Its textualizing thrust is, finally, assimilable to a grammar emphasizing mode over lexical origin and to a model of the family in which alliance is more important than lineage (see above, pp. 109–127).

This juxtaposition of poetic, grammatical, and paternal principles within a single form speaks directly to the issues posed at the outset. That is: the question of the status of the subject at the end of the Dark Ages; the relation of the literary text to the interior—psychological—space that we designate as subjective; and the place of both a changing notion of the subject and its poetic articulation in the social transformation of the twelfth and thirteenth centuries. Here there is no more instructive guide to the reading of culture than *La Queste del Saint Graal* with which we began Chapter 1.

As Bohort wanders aimlessly in search of the Grail, he comes upon one of the numerous hermits whose role as the guardians of a certain kind of knowledge is to explain to those with the power bestowed by lineage—knights—the meaning of the sensible world. Once Bohort has identified himself by revealing his name and paternity ("il dit qu'il a non Boort de Gaunes et fu filz le roi Boort"), the holy man makes an obvious case for the inherence of social worth among those of noble birth:

"Certes, Boort, se la parole de l'Evangile ert en vos sauvee, vos seriez bons chevaliers et verais. Car, si com Nostre Sires dit: 'Li bons arbres fet le bon fruit', vos devez estre bons par droicture, car vos estes le fruit del tres bon arbre. Car vostre peres, li rois Boors, fu uns des meillors homes que je onques veisse, rois piteus et humbles; et vostre mere, la reine Eveine, fu une des meillors dames que je veisse pieça. Cil dui furent un sol arbre et une meisme char par conjonction de mariage. Et puis que vos en estes fruit vos devriez estre bons quant li arbre furent bon."[59]

"Certainly, Boort, if the word of the scripture works to your advantage, you will turn out to be a good and true knight. For since Our Saviour says, 'A good tree gives good fruit,' you should be good by rights; for you are the fruit of a very good tree. Your father, King Boors, was one of the best men whom I ever saw—a pious and humble king; and your mother Queen Eveine was one of the best ladies that I have seen in a long time. These two made a single tree and were of one flesh through marriage. And since you are the fruit of this marriage, you must be good because the trees were good."

Bohort, however, responds by questioning the hermit's assessment of lineage:

"Sire, fet Boors, tout soit li hons estrez de mauvés arbre, ce est de mauvés pere et de mauvese mere, est il muez d'amertume en dolçor si tost come il reçoit le saint cresme, la sainte onction; por ce m'est il avis qu'il ne vet pas as peres ne as meres qu'il soit bons ou mauvés, mes au cuer de l'ome."[60]

"My lord, said Bohort, even though a man may come from a bad tree, that is from a bad father and bad mother, he can be turned from bitterness into sweetness as soon as he receives the holy oil; for this reason, it is my feeling that it is neither a question of father or mother, whether or not a man is good or bad, but of his own heart."

The model of kinship which the hermit espouses is predicated upon the notion of continuity—"li bons arbres fet le bon fruit"—and it serves to legitimate an essentially aristocratic model of power. The claim to hegemony of France's feudal aristocracy rested, as we have seen, upon the claim to an uninterrupted link to the past. Nobility is, in principle, inherited and cannot be acquired. Social hierarchy is thus fixed and mobility extremely limited. The model which Bohort proposes is, in contrast, directly subversive of that proffered by the hermit, questioning as it does the importance of origins. Next to the guiding tenet of inherited aristocratic power, Bohort's rejection of the mother and father in favor of "the heart of a man" affirms what looks like the rule of meritocracy according to which status can be acquired, hierarchy is not fixed, and mobility—as opposed to nobility—is the name of the game.

Neither Bohort's nor the hermit's position can be taken to be representative of secular or ecclesiastical attitudes, since another hermit, contradicting the first, assures Lancelot that "where mortal sins are concerned, the father carries his own and the son his own; the son does not participate in the iniquities of the father, nor the father in those of the son;

but each is rewarded according to what he deserves."[61] There is little doubt that such a doctrine can be traced back to the New Testament rule of personal responsibility. But the question of source remains anecdotal next to the antithesis established between the independence of the individual and the rule of lineal succession. What the author(s) of *La Queste* means by the "cuer de l'ome" as opposed to the order of lineage ("un sol arbre et une meisme char") is precisely that realm of inner intention synonymous with the autonomous subject. The notions of interiority and of genealogy are conceived to be mutually exclusive.

Round Table and the Politics of Intention

The opposition which the text maintains, and which also defines its innermost law, strikes to the very heart of the Arthurian corpus. It implicates both the Grail and the Round Table and poses, ultimately, the question of relation between the individual and the broader social community.

Merlin is alleged by the author(s) of *La Queste* to be the founder of the "third table":

> Vos savez bien que puis l'avenement Jhesucrist a eu trois principaus tables ou monde. La premiere fu la Table Jhesucrist ou li apostre mengierent par plusor foiz. Ce fu la table qui sostenait les cors et les ames de la viande dou Ciel. . . . Aprés cele table fu une autre table en semblance et en remembrance de lui. Ce fu la Table dou Saint Graal. . . . Et il [Joseph] despeça les pains et les mist ça et la et mist ou chief de la table le Saint Graal, par qui venue li douze pain foisonerent si que toz li pueples, dont il avoit bien quatre mile, en furent repeu et rasaziez trop merveilleusement. . . . Aprés cele table fu la Table Reonde par conseil Merlin.[62]

> You know that since the coming of Jesus Christ there have been three principal tables in the world. The first was the Table of Jesus Christ, where the apostles ate several times. This was the table which sustained the body and the soul of the flesh of heaven. . . . After this table came another table like it and in remembrance of it. This was the Table of the Holy Grail. . . . And he [Joseph] cut up the bread and distributed the pieces, and at the head of the table he put the Holy Grail, which caused the twelve loaves to multiply so that all the people, of which there were a good four thousand, were fed and satisfied marvelously well. . . . After this table came the Round Table by the counsel of Merlin.

What stands out in this conflation of apostalic, apocryphal, and Arthurian tables is, first of all, their association with the spontaneous production of food in direct contrast to the mythology of dearth synonymous with the Wasteland (see above, pp. 200–203). The Grail, of course, is portrayed generally as a food-bearing dish. The contents of Chrétien's Grail nourish the invalid king. In Robert de Boron's *Roman dou Graal*, the *Estoire Merlin*, *Estoire del Saint Graal*, and *La Queste*, the Grail has the

Grail Table, from a fourteenth-century *Lancelot del Lac*,
Bibliothèque Nationale, ms. fr. 120. (Printed with permission.)

power to provide food in as abundant a quantity "as the hearts of men may desire." According to Manessier, no one can name a food, however exotic, that it does not contain. And Hélinand de Froidmont's chronicle (1204) describes the Grail as a "wide and somewhat deep dish in which tasty meats in their rich juices are placed by degree, one after the other, according to rank."[63]

Thus both the Grail and the Round Table are associated with the notion of abundance; and, further, Hélinand links the cornucopia motif specifically to that of social order. The hierarchical arrangement of tasty meats in the "wide and somewhat deep dish" mirrors the ranks of society itself, as the Grail and Round Table seem to render apparent that which the Wasteland only suggests: namely, if dearth and famine are the wages of strife, sufficiency can only be recovered through the restoration of peace.

The Arthur of the *Historia Regum Britanniae* is a peacemaker; and yet there is no mention of the Round Table, which first appears in Wace's translation of Geoffrey. Here we are told that Arthur, having conquered Ireland and Iceland, establishes the Round Table to insure domestic peace:

> Pur les nobles baruns qu'il out
> Dunt chescuns mieldre estre quidout,
> Chescuns se teneit al meillur,
> Ne nuls n'en saveit le peiur,
> Fist Artur la Roünde Table

Dunt Bretun dient mainte fable.
Illuec seeient il vassal
Tuit chevalment et tuit egal;
A la table egalement seeient
Et egalment servi esteient
Nul d'els ne se poeit vanter
Qu'il seïst plus halt de sun per,
Tuit esteient assis meain,
Ne n'i aveit nul de forain.[64]

For his noble barons—each of whom believed himself to be outstanding and held himself to be the best, and none of whom would admit to being the worst—Arthur made the Round Table, of which the Bretons tell many a tale. Here sit the vassals, all chivalrous and all equal; at the table they are equally seated and equally served. None of them could boast that he was seated higher than his peer; all were seated hand-in-hand, and none was excluded.

Layamon will expand upon Wace's version, presenting the Round Table, which can feed sixteen hundred, as the architectural solution to a quarrel of precedence. And though this is only inferred in the passage above, it stands nonetheless as an adequate response to the conflicts which bring on the Wasteland. In fact, the Round Table is, in almost every respect, the polar opposite of *la terre gaste*: it represents a food-producing vehicle of plenty around which men eat to satisfaction as part of an innate fellowship whose peace is guaranteed by a healthy king at the height of his ruling powers. It not only serves as a spatial ratification of the *pax arthuriana*, but it points in the direction of a fundamentally new order of relations between individual, king, and state. As the structural embodiment of a social contract according to which "all are equal," "none are excluded," and "all sit hand-in-hand," Arthur's table posits the possibility of a community so radically different from that of an earlier historical era—and reflected most clearly in the epic—that the limits of our conclusion permit only the barest outline.

The community of the Round Table offers, first of all, the possibility of reversing the geographic dispersion characteristic of the Wasteland. At the time of its creation Merlin promises Arthur's father that "those who sit around it will never want to return to their own lands nor leave this place."[65] And if the *terre gaste* means a scattering of men—their isolation throughout the countryside—the Round Table serves as a catalyst to their unification, a coming together for permanent settlement in one place. The "third table" renders feasible a lococentric community, the foundation of a fixed geographic center which implies, in turn, a recuperation of the lost or "wasted" margins:

Car en ce qu'ele est apelee Table Reonde est entendue la reondece del monde et la circonstance des planetes et des elemenz el firmament; . . .

dont len puet dire que en la Table Reonde est li mondes senefiez a droit.
Car vous poez veoir que de toutes terres ou chevalerie repere, soit de cres-
tienté ou de paiennie, viennent a la Table Reonde li chevalier.[66]

For by the Round Table is understood the roundness of the world and the
spheres of the planets and the elements in the firmament; . . . thus one
can say with reason that the Round Table properly signifies the world. For
as you see, knights come to the Round Table from all countries where chivalry is practiced, whether in Christendom or pagandom.

Thus, for the author of *La Queste*, the centripetal attraction of the Round
Table takes on universal and even cosmic proportions.

What this means in terms of family relations is that the Arthurian court,
like the renascent urban centers of the twelfth century, represents a stable
locus toward which men will gravitate. Even more important, it is marked
by the integration of something resembling the nuclear family within the
lococentric community. For not only do knights, once having been
seated, not desire to leave, but they send for their wives and children as
well:

Et quant vint que li baron prisent congié et que il s'en departirent, si vin-
rent as preudommes qui seoient a la table. Et li rois meismes lour demanda
qu'il lour estoit avis. Et il respondirent: "Sire, nous n'avons (jamais) talent
de mouvoir ja mais de chi, ains ferons venir nos femes et nos enfans en
ceste vile, et ensi viverons au plaisir nostre signuor; car teuls est nostres
corages." [*Huth*, 1:97][67]

And when it was time for the barons to take leave of each other and depart, they came to the knights who were sitting at the table. And the king
himself asked them what they wanted to do. And they replied: "Sire, we
have no desire ever to leave this place, but will have our wives and children come to this city and, with the grace of God, will dwell here; for this
is our desire."

The assimilation of the family into a larger political body, in contrast to its
isolation in the wasted countryside, entails a weakening of the autonomy
both of lineage and of vassalage. The Arthurian community of the Round
Table consists of a loose federation of families with reciprocal obligations
to each other as opposed to either kinship ties, or the independently
contracted, personal bonds of allegiance that have for so long been
associated with the phenomenon of European feudalism.

It is by now a commonplace of medieval studies that one of the failures
of feudal institutions was the direct tie between lord and vassal compared
to the relative weakness of lateral social bonds between vassals of the
same lord. That the Arthurian Round Table reverses this equation can be
seen in the texts dealing with its formation, which read like a program for
the consolidation of intervassalic interests. Those who frequent Arthur's

court come, above all, as equals ("Iluec seeient li vassal / Tuit chevalment et egal") and are equally seated and served ("A la table egalement seeient / Et egalement servi esteient"). Such a notion represents a radical departure from anything resembling a vertically organized hierarchical chain of command based, as in the epic, upon precise obligations between vassal and lord or between consanguineal relations. On the contrary, the Arthurian community, at its inception, is predicated upon the depth of feeling that the individual knights experience for each other ("Tuit esteient assis meain / Ne n'i aveit nul de forain"). In contrast with the crisis of difference that plagues the Wasteland—a nondifferentiation that produces even within the family the violent encounter of fathers and sons—the equality of the Round Table implies a purgation of the inclination toward violence along with an assumed affiliation of all the members of the same federated group:

> Et li rois lour demanda: "Signour, avés vous tout tel corage?" Et il respondent tout: "Oïl, si nous esmiervillons moult comment che puet estre. Car il i a de teuls de nous que onques mais ne virent li uns l'autre, et peu i a de nous dont li uns fust acointes de l'autre, et *ore nous entramons autant ou plus comme fieus seut amer pere*. Ne nous ja mais, chu me samble, ne ferons desassamblee ne departirons, se mors ne nous depart." [*Huth*, 1:97]

> And the king asked them: "Sires, do you all have this desire?" And they all responded: "Yes, and we are quite astonished that it is so. For there are some of us who have never seen each other before, and only a few of us were heretofore acquainted, and *now we love each other as much or more than a son should love his father*. And we will never, it seems to me, disband or separate, unless death parts us.

Herein lies the radical nature of the Arthurian state: against the catastrophic struggle of one against all typified in the Wasteland motif, the Round Table structures an equidistant relation of each to each and to an immovable center. Thus it nullifies quarrels of precedence within a society for which the question of difference—of hierarchy—has become problematic.

Lococentric, centralized, and based upon assumed feelings of fellowship, Arthurian polity is also organized according to a radically different principle of integration of the individual within the broader community. Rather, the place of feelings—of interiority in general—becomes the focal point, the binding mediatory thread, of all possible integration. Already in Robert's *Roman dou Graal* the Grail stands not only as a food-producing vessel but as a vehicle for the exposition of inner feelings. In the absence of any external means of distinguishing those who respect the law from those who transgress it, the holy relic functions as a sort of moral divining rod:

Ainsi ha Joseph perceü
Les pecheeurs et conneü
Ce fu par le demoustrement
De Dieu, le roi omnipotent.
Par ce fu li veissiaus amez
Et premierement esprouvez.[68]

In this way Joseph knew and recognized the sinners; this happened through the revelation of God the Almighty. Thus was the vessel loved and first tested.

If "none are excluded" from the Arthurian Table, it is because, as Robert claims, that exclusion has already occurred—"Cil dient: 'Par ce veissel ci / Summes nous de vous departi'"—and because the prime function of the Grail is, as the author(s) of the *Estoire Merlin* concurs, that separation: "Par cel vaissel departi compaignie des boins des maluais."[69]

The Arthurian community of the elect, like the modern state, is organized around the principle of accountability—of the recountability of the "feelings" which the Grail initially elicits and which the Round Table endows with coherence. Joseph's Grail Table inaugurates the rule by which inner states of worth become apparent; the Round Table serves, in turn, to establish the regular mechanism by which the individual becomes periodically accountable to the center of power and of writing at Camelot.

Already in the romances of Chrétien we find a steady cycle of departure from court, quest, and return accompanied by the telling of adventures while away. In the thirteenth-century prose renderings such accounts receive prescriptive formulation and are transformed into a normative system of accountability. The Lancelot Prose Cycle is filled with the transcription by Arthur's clerks of the adventures of the knights who, as the guardians of social order, regularly convert their victories over a chaotic Other World beyond the law (and court) into the tale that we supposedly read, for example, "Et quant il orent mangie. si fist li roys uenir auant ses clers si mist on en escrit les auentures si com lancelot les conta. Et par che lez sauons nous encore."[70] In the *Estoire Merlin* we are told that Arthur "will not sit down to dinner, no matter where he is, until he has heard some tale of adventure"; and he appoints four scribes "to put into writing all that happens to those within."[71] It is, however, in the Huth text that Merlin exposes to Arthur—precisely at the moment of the bestowal of the Round Table—the means by which every knight becomes responsible for himself to an increasingly efficient machine of state:

" . . . il convient, che ses tu bien connoistre les bons des mauvais et hounerer chascun selont chou qu'il est, pour chou te loc jou que si tost que chevaliers se metera en queste des armes que on li fache jurer si tost coume il s'en partira de court qu'il dira voir au revenir de toutes les choses qui li seront avenues et qu'il avra trouvé en sa queste, ou soit s'ounour ou soit sa honte. Et par chou porra on connoistre le proueche de chascun; car je sai bien qu'il ne se parjurront en nulle maniere." "En non Dieu," fais li rois, "Merlins, vous m'avés bien ensegniet. Et je vous creant que ceste coustume sera tenue en mon ostel tant coume je vivrai." [*Huth*, 2:98]

" . . . it is fitting, as you know, to discern the good from the bad and to honor each accordingly; for this I tell you that whenever a knight sets out on a quest of arms, you should have him swear before he leaves that he will tell the truth when he comes back about everything that happens to him and all that he finds on his quest, whether it be to his honor or shame. And in this way, you'll know the prowess of each one, for I know that they will not perjure themselves." "By the name of God," said the king, "Merlin, you have advised me well, and I promise you that this custom will be honored in my house for as long as I live."

The Round Table takes on, then, the function of the Grail—to separate the good from the bad ("il convient . . . connoistre les bons des mauvais"). It is the vehicle by which a hidden truth, the truth concerning that which occurs outside of the direct purview of the court, becomes regularly and infallibly exposed: "il dira voir au revenir . . . ; car je sai bien qu'il ne se parjurront en nulle maniere."

For the feudal oath of unswerving loyalty between vassal and lord—a promise of mutual aid and protection—the Arthurian state substitutes the knight's oath "to tell the truth concerning all that he has found in the course of his quest," that is to say, concerning the private deeds of a private self which is, in the telling, both integrated to and governed more fully by the group. And if all who sit at the Round Table are equal and none are excluded, it is because all have become equally liable to recount a truth that makes them equally accountable to the Arthurian law of accounts.

I have maintained elsewhere that Merlin's power as detailed in the apparatus of governance that he prescribes to Arthur is part of a broader contemporaneous shift of legal institutions.[72] More precisely, the Arthurian quest for adventure, which is always a quest to bring those outside of the law under its pale, exists only insofar as it can be transformed into a periodic narration. And not just any narration. For this sworn deposition of the "truth" of each knight's quest closely resembles the increasingly important thirteenth-century procedure of judicial inquest which stands as the organizational principle of a state of self-governing subjects (and eventually citizens) as opposed to a state consisting primarily of independently contracted feudal rights.

The traditionally positivist thrust of medieval studies has tended to consider any expression of an inner self, like that prescribed by Merlin, within the context of a general legitimation—even "liberation"—of the individual evident across a broad cultural spectrum: in the revival of

Classical studies; renewed interest in autobiography and letter writing; the personalization of portraiture and scupture; altered notions of intention, sin, and penance; the popularity of mystical religious experience; the appearance of the singular heroes of the late epic as well as satirical and courtly forms.[73] What is perhaps less obvious is that this "discovery of the individual," which was an important part of the "renaissance" of the twelfth century, also suited the ideological as well as the long-range political interests both of a nascent urban class and of monarchy.[74]

Monarchic policy during the period under consideration was directed toward the weakening of the power of the feudal clan—the power of lineage—through the destruction of its legal autonomy. Chief among its tactics (conscious or not) was the substitution of direct ties of allegiance between each inhabitant of the royal domain and royalty itself for the intermediate ties binding lord to vassal, or fathers to sons. Beginning in the twelfth century, the individual assumed a distinct economic and legal personality by which he became less and less responsible to family or clan, which was, in turn, less liable to and for him. Where the warrior group was once responsible for defending the rights of each of its members, avenging their deaths, making sure they were not involved in faulty causes, and paying reparation when they were, the individual grew evermore accountable to the state only for himself. The fragmentation of legal responsibility, its focus upon the individual as opposed to his kin group, thus served (intentionally?) to undercut the power of noble families by encouraging loyalty to a more global central authority.

Some of the ecclesiastical signs of this tendency can be seen in the regularization of penitential practice: emphasis upon intention as the basis of ethical theory; the doctrine of Contritionism by which external proof of repentence must become evident in order for penance to be efficient; and, most of all, a shift away from the once-in-a-lifetime solemn confession in extremis toward yearly confession to the same confessor. Here, in fact, is where Merlin the devil, trickster, and enchanter begins to resemble Merlin the prophet with divine powers; for the technique of regular deposition that he prescribes for Arthur's knights resembles so closely the techniques of confession mandated by the Fourth Lateran Council (1215) that there can be no distinction between the sacred and the satanic exercise of a common regulatory power. Within the less strictly canonical sphere, Merlin's advice to those who sit at, venture from, return to, and eventually account for the Round Table can be seen in the renewed historical importance of the notion of self-knowledge, which became one of the dominant themes of the age.[75]

In the legal sphere, the most important manifestations of the trend toward the progressive accountability of the individual to the state include the reserved right of intervention in special judicial cases, the right of appeal to the Parlement de Paris, the individuation of the notion of criminal responsibility, and, in particular, the suppression of aristocracy's traditional prerogative of settling its differences internally through recourse to trial by combat and private war. In the place of the violence of the *champ clos* and the battlefield, monarchy sought to impose the Frankish and canonical procedure of trial by inquest—an inquiry into the circumstances of transgression and judgment of individuals instead of the family as a whole. With the advent of inquest, the dynamic of the judicial encounter shifted from a conflict between opposing families to a contest between individual and the broader body politic.[76] But, more important, it was transformed from a physical match into a more abstract verbal contest based upon investigation, debate, and, as in the Arthurian court, the obligation "to tell the truth." The technology of the inquisitory state not only substituted a battle of wits for armed conflict but placed at the center of the judicial process a system of sworn testimony not unlike Merlin's program for the surveillance of the Round Table Knights. Thus, the institutions that came to characterize an inquisitional and confessional model of social regulation, and which assumed the existence of direct ties between self-governing individuals and an ever-widening and abstract (universal and occulted) political center, stand in direct opposition to the traditional hereditary power of lineage.

The place of the literary text in such a process of global social transformation is analogous to Merlin's own invisible and ubiquitous power. Analogous, first of all, because the rule which the "third table" imposes functions only so long as it cannot itself be seen. Merlin's transparence, his absence and withdrawal into "obscure speech," coincide both with the initiation of the prophetic book and with his role as an active force in the organization of the Arthurian state: "il m'en convient par force, par fies, eskiver de la gent."[77] Similarly, the courtly novel works to obscure its deepest social function, to hide its own effect behind the mythic veil of a temporally distant fairylike king. The text appears always to operate in the margins of genuine political power; it pretends to be irrelevant—frivolous, entertaining, "pleasurable"—precisely when its unrecognized force becomes most valid.

The work of "romance" and Merlin also resemble each other because of the omniscience of a shared universal authorial regard. Under the system of surveillance which the "enchanteor" outlines, nothing escapes the watchful eye of the inquisitory wizard. Merlin's multiple forms, his ability to perceive both outer reality and inner intention, and his ubiquitous presence in every corner of the realm correspond to the specter of an all-powerful, all-seeing authority that, abstracted, becomes inescapable.

Likewise, the courtly text operates to expose and explore every aspect of public and private life—to render it, in direct opposition to the interests of lineage, accessible to an imagined all-encompassing regard of the public sphere. Here it is worth remembering that the genealogical epic, based upon events, deeds, and gesture, also excludes—at least in its earliest examples—interiority; the *chanson de geste* contains no language by which to render public the deeds of a self perceived as inner and personal (see above, pp. 105–107). The love lyric, on the other hand, and this from the very beginning, represents a privileged locus for the articulation of the subject. I have maintained elsewhere that courtliness is in many ways synonymous with a "psychologizing" of social reality—the conversion of a set of reciprocal social relations, sensed as external and objective, into moral qualities, for example, the terms *salaire, saisine, guerredon, heritage, droit, tort, honor, foi, servise, homage, largesce, pretz, valor, joven, courtois,* etc.[78] What I am suggesting at present is that, among the distinct courtly forms, the love lyric can be considered both an authorized forum for the articulation of a dynamic psychological model and the place of its creation. As a kind of map of that which is perceived to be internal and subjective, the *loci* of the mind designated by the *canso* are the very ones outlined earlier in terms of a rhetoric of contradiction: joy, pain, consolation, anguish, hope, despair, timidity, courage, reason, folly, and, in particular, sexual desire (see above, pp. 119–125).[79] More important, the lyric does not merely uncover hypostatized inner states assumed to have always existed but is directly productive—inventive—of them in accordance with an investment of the "courtly" individual with a moral responsibility for the governance of himself in relation to the increasingly "inner-oriented" inquisitory/confessional monarchic state.

If the lyric charts the terrain of what is conceived to be a hidden self, the romance serves as a virtual guide book, a manual of instruction, for its integration within the public sphere. The romance hero is precisely he who, having lived through a series of internal crises, either achieves—like Erec, Yvain, Cligés—a balance between personal desire and social necessity, or who—like Tristan—is excluded from society altogether. The major locus of expression of the autonomy of the chivalric hero is, of course, the inner monologue which we have already associated with the presence of a lyric disruption within the romance narrative (see above, pp. 186–191). But the inner monologue, which is often accompanied by a *prise de conscience* of a social imperative, is more than just the *expression* of interiority. It is symptomatic of an investment of the individual with the necessity of choice in the governance of himself, again in consonance with an inferred pattern of social organization that not only conflicts with the clannish interests of feudal nobility but that is thoroughly consistent with the political strategy of monarchy—that is to say, with the creation of a nation of self-governing citizens responsible for themselves as opposed to a loosely linked federation of lineages accountable only to each other. Both the courtly lyric and the romance can be said to constitute a forum in which the traditional power of genealogy found itself transformed in what was the first in a series of stages in the naturalization of the idea of the self and of the development of the early modern state. It is in this sense that Old French literature can be said to occupy a truly anthropological space within the culture of the High Middle Ages. Medieval poetry served to found a vision of man that will for centuries to come inform his notion of what he is and govern his rapport with others. As the hermit says to Bohort in relation to confession, but which might just as easily be applied to the text itself, "by that door . . . it is necessary to embark upon that Quest and to change the being of each one. . . . "

Appendix A

I

I am perplexed and confused about a love which binds me and confines me so that there is no place I can go where it does not hold me in its reins. For now love has given me the heart and the desire to court, if I might, such a one that courting her, even if the king himself were her suitor, would be an act of great daring.

II

Alas, wretch, what shall I do; and what counsel shall I take for myself, since she does not know the pain I bear, and I dare not cry out for mercy. Ignorant fool, you have little sense, if you have not hanged yourself before now, for she will never love you in name or fact.

III

And so, since I shall die anyway, shall I tell her of the suffering I undergo? Yes, I shall tell her at once. No, I shall not do it, by my faith, even if I knew all Spain would forthwith be mine for the telling. Indeed, I could die of chagrin for having allowed such a thought to cross my mind.

IV

She will never learn from me what is wrong, nor will another tell her anything about it. I want no friend, cousin or kinsman in this affair. May whoever helps me be forever damned. It would seem a very honorable act for love to kill me for my lady's sake, but for her to do it would not be seemly.

V

And since she does not know what wrong she does me, why does it happen? God, she should realize now that I am dying for her love, and why? Because of my foolish behavior and great cowardice which binds my tongue when I am with her.

VI

No joy matches mine when my lady looks at me or sees me. Then her fair sweet image enters my heart and sweetens and refreshes me. And if she stayed with me a long time, I would swear by the saints that there would be no greater joy in the world. But at parting, I take fire and burn.

VII

Since I will not send a messenger to her, and since for me to speak is not fitting, I see no help for myself. But I console myself with one thing: she knows and understands letters. It pleases me to write the words, and if it pleases her, let her read them for my deliverance.

VIII

If no other ill may befall her on that account, for God's sake let her not take away the kindness nor the beautiful words she had for me.

Appendix B

XVIII. Now One Speaks, Tells, and Recounts

Nicolette lamented greatly as you have heard; she commended herself to God and walked so far that she came to the forest. She did not dare penetrate too deeply into it because of the wild beasts and serpents; she hid herself in a thick wood, and sleep overtook her. She slept until 8 o'clock the next morning when young shepherds came out of town and sent their animals to pasture between the woods and the river; they withdrew to one side next to a very beautiful fountain that was at the entrance to the forest; they spread out a large cape and put their bread on it. While they ate Nicolette woke to the cries of birds and the shepherds and fell upon them.

"Dear children, she said, may God be with you.

— And God bless you! said the one who was more articulate than the others.

— Dear children, she said, do you know Aucassin, the son of Count Garin of Beaucaire?

— Yes, we know him well.

— May God be with you, dear children, she said, tell him that in this forest there is an animal that he should come hunt; and if he can take it, he would not sacrifice one of its members for 100 marcs of gold, nor for 500, nor for any price."

And they looked at her and saw her to be so beautiful that they were stunned.

"I tell him that? said the one who was more articulate than the others; a curse on the one would talk to him of it or tell him! What you say is a lie because there is not so expensive an animal in this forest—neither stag, nor lion, nor wild boar—of which one of the limbs is worth more than two deniers or three at the most; and you speak of such great sums. A curse on the one who believes you, or will tell him! You're a fairy, and we do not care for your kind; be gone now.

— Ha! dear children, she said, you will do it. The animal has a medicine such that Aucassin will be cured of his sickness; and I have here five sous in my purse. Take them and tell him; he must go hunting within three days, and if within three days he does not find it, he will never be cured of his ill.

— By faith, he said, we will take the deniers, and if he happens along, we will tell him, but we will never seek him out.

— With God's blessing," she said.

Then she took leave of the young shepherds and withdrew. [*Aucassin*, p. 19]

Notes

Introduction

1. The first several pages of this Introduction appeared under the title "Merlin and the Modes of Medieval Legal Meaning," Colloques de Cerisy, *Archéologie du signe au moyen âge*, ed. E. Vance and L. Brind-Amour (Toronto: Pontifical Institute, 1982).

2. ["And Merlin went to Blaise in Northumberland and told him everything; and Blaise put it into writing, and by his book we know it still"] *Huth*, 1:90.

3. ["And our Lord who is all-powerful gave me the intelligence to understand partially things to come"] Ibid., 1:94.

4. See Geoffrey of Monmouth, *Vita Merlini*, ed. J. J. Parry (Urbana: University of Illinois Press, 1925), p. 62; and *Didot-Perceval*, ed. W. Roach (Philadelphia: University of Pennsylvania Press, 1941), p. 278; P. Zumthor, *Merlin le prophète: un thème de la littérature polémique, de l'historiographie et des romans* (Lausanne: Payot, 1943), p. 166.

5. Cited Zumthor, *Merlin*, p. 58.

6. "ne savoient mie que Merlins peust prendre autre forme que la soie ne autre samblance" (*Huth*, 1:64); "cest gent qui me cuident connoistre ne sevent riens de mon estre" (ibid., 1:68).

7. See R. Bernheimer, *Wild Men in the Middle Ages* (Cambridge: Harvard University Press, 1952), pp. 13–15; P. Haidu, *Aesthetic Distance in Chrétien de Troyes* (Geneva: Droz, 1968), p. 119; J. LeGoff and P. Vidal-Naquet, "Lévi-Strauss en Brocéliande," *Critique* 325 (1974): 541–571; Zumthor, *Merlin*, p. 43.

8. Merlin's rhetorical skill is confirmed when, at the age of two weeks, he conducts a successful courtroom defense of his mother, accused of commerce with Satan (*Huth*, 1:27–29). His mastery of technology is demonstrated in the transportation from Ireland of the monoliths for Pendragon's tomb, whose inscription also falls within his domain (ibid., 1:93). The numerous etchings in stone scattered around Logres mark, like hermes, the boundaries of the Arthurian world along with the thresholds of the lives of its inhabitants. See N. O. Brown, *Hermes the Thief* (New York: Vintage, 1947).

9. See *Huth*, 1:69, 72, 84, 95–97, 109, 138–143; 2:60–65, 122.

10. Merlin, in fact, contrasts conventional power with that afforded by his special kind of knowledge. First, in response to Arthur's accusal of having obtained his gifts from Satan—"'Or ne parlés plus,' fait Merlins, 'de mon savoir; je cuic qu'il vous vaurra encore mieus que toute vostre poesté'" ["'Speak no more,' said Merlin, 'about my knowledge; I think that it will be worth more to you than all your power'"] (ibid., 1:188). And then to Balaain—"'Quels que je soie,' fait Merlins, 'Je vous di qu'il sera plus parlé de mon sens apriès ma mort qu'il ne sera de vostre prouece'" ["'Whatever I am,' said Merlin, 'I assure you that people will talk more after my death of my intelligence than of your prowess'"] (ibid., 1:236).

11. "Quant li clerc oirent chou que li rois leur requeroit [, si disent]: 'Sire, nous n'en savons riens, mais il a chi de teuls clers qui bien le porroient savoir, s'il s'en voloient entremetre [par une art qui a non astronomie]'" ["When the clerks heard what the king asked of them, they said: 'Lord, we know nothing of the matter, but there are those among those here who can know it if they put their mind to it; and this by an art called astronomy'"] (ibid., 1:39).

12. "'et pour chou que je savoie bien que il me queroient me fis jou connoistre a iaus par un enfant que je feri pour chou que il me nommast'" (ibid., 1:45); "'. . . tant voel jou bien que vous sachiés, se vous mentés, je le savrai bien'" (ibid., 1:44).

13. C. Lévi-Strauss, *Tristes Tropiques* (Paris: Plon, 1955), p. 294.

14. J. Derrida, *De la Grammatologie* (Paris: Minuit, 1967), p. 159.

15. See R. Barthes, *Le Plaisir du texte* (Paris: Seuil, 1973); E. Said, *Beginnings* (Baltimore: Johns Hopkins University Press, 1975).

16. The consequences of Derrida's paradise before or beyond difference are not at all clear. R. Girard, for example, maintains that it is precisely the loss of difference that engenders violence (see *La Violence et le sacré* [Paris: Grasset, 1972]). Where the individual case is concerned, Lacan associates it with a "dissociation of the subject's personality": "La Loi primordiale est donc celle qui en réglant l'alliance superpose le règne de la culture au règne de la nature livré à la loi de l'accouplement. . . . Cette loi se fait donc suffisamment connaître comme identique à un ordre de langage. Car nul pouvoir sans les nominations de la parenté n'est à portée d'instituer l'ordre des préférences et des tabous qui nouent et tressent à travers les générations le fil des lignées. Et c'est bien la confusion des générations qui, dans la Bible comme dans toutes les lois traditionnelles, est maudite comme l'abomination du verbe et la désolation du pécheur. Nous savons en effet quel ravage déjà allant jusqu'à la dissociation de la personnalité du sujet peut exercer une filiation falsifiée, quand la contrainte de l'entourage s'emploie à en soutenir le mensonge. Ils peuvent n'être pas moindres quand un homme épousant la mère de la femme dont il a eu un fils, celui-ci aura pour frère un enfant

frère de sa mère. Mais s'il est ensuite,—et le cas n'est pas inventé—, adopté par le ménage compatissant d'une fille d'un mariage antérieur du père, il se trouvera encore une fois demi-frère de sa nouvelle mère, et l'on peut imaginer les sentiments complexes dans lesquels il attendra la naissance d'un enfant qui sera à la fois son frère et son neveu, dans cette situation répétée" (J. Lacan, *Ecrits* [Paris: Seuil, 1966], pp. 277–278).

17. See for example M. Foucault, *Histoire de la folie* (Paris: Plon, 1961); *Les Mots et les choses* (Paris: Gallimard, 1966); *L'Archéologie du savoir* (Paris: Gallimard, 1969); *Surveiller et punir* (Paris: Gallimard, 1975); and *Histoire de la sexualité* (Paris: Gallimard, 1976). For what might be considered an anthropology of the Middle Ages, see J. LeGoff, *Pour un autre moyen âge* (Paris: Gallimard, 1979).

18. See M. de Certeau, *L'Ecriture de l'histoire* (Paris: Gallimard, 1975).

19. Philology is the initiatory voyage of the medievalist, though to posit it as an autonomous branch of knowledge is to imagine the anthropologist who never returns to assess the meaning of his material.

20. P. Zumthor, *Langue et technique poétiques à l'époque romane* (Paris: Klincksieck, 1963); and *Essai de poétique médiévale* (Paris: Seuil, 1972).

21. See H.-R. Jauss, *Alterität und Modernität der Mittelalterlichen Literatur* (Munich: Fink, 1977); and "The Alterity and Modernity of Medieval Literature," *New Literary History* 10 (1979): 181–227. P. Haidu may actually have first applied the term to medieval literature in a review of Zumthor's *Essai* entitled "Making It New in the Middle Ages: Towards a Problematics of Alterity," *Diacritics* 4 (1974): 2–11.

22. See, in particular, M. Baratin and F. Desbordes, "Signification et référence dans l'antiquité et au moyen âge," *Langages* [Special issue] (March 1982); R. Bursill-Hall, *Speculative Grammars of the Middle Ages* (Paris: Mouton, 1971); M. Colish, *The Mirror of Language: A Study in the Medieval Theory of Knowledge* (New Haven: Yale University Press, 1968); J. Jolivet, *Arts du langage et théologie chez Abélard* (Paris: J. Vrin, 1969); G. Leff, *William of Ockham, the Metamorphosis of Scholastic Discourse* (Manchester: Manchester University Press, 1975); J. Murphy, *Rhetoric in the Middle Ages: A History of Rhetorical Theory from Augustine to the Renaissance* (Berkeley: University of California Press, 1974); J. Pinborg, *Die Entwicklung der Sprachtheorie im Mittelalter* (Copenhagen: Arne Frost-Hansen, 1967); E. Vance, "Mervelous Signals: Poetics, Sign Theory, and Politics in Chaucer's Troilus," *New Literary History* 10 (1979): 293–338.

23. Derrida is somewhat conscious of this problem in *De la Grammatologie*; see pp. 186–196.

24. See E. Auerbach, *Literary Language and Its Public in Late Latin Antiquity and in the Middle Ages* (New York: Pantheon, 1965); J. W. Thompson, *The Literacy of the Laity in the Middle Ages* (Berkeley: University of California Press, 1939), pp. 123–141.

25. "Le seul phénomène qui l'ait fidèlement accompagnée est la formation des cités et des empires, c'est-à-dire l'intégration dans un système politique d'un nombre considérable d'individus et leur hiérarchisation en castes et classes" (Lévi-Strauss, *Tristes Tropiques*, p. 318).

26. See A. Adler, *Epische Spekulanten* (Munich: Fink, 1975); and *Rückzug in epischer Parade* (Frankfurt: Klosterman, 1963); E. Köhler, *Ideal and Wirklichkeit in der höfischen Epik* (Tubingen: Max Niemeyer, 1956).

27. The term "generator of public consciousness" is taken from D. Maddox's excellent anthropological study of Chrétien de Troyes's *Erec et Enide* (*Structure and Sacring* [Lexington: French Forum, 1978], p. 26). See also H. Brinkmann, *Zu Wesen und Form mittelalterlicher Dichtung* (Halle: Max Niemeyer, 1928), pp. 18–26; H.

Emmel, *Formprobleme des Artusromans und der Graldichtung* (Bern: Francke, 1951), p. 11; R. Hanning, "The Social Significance of Twelfth-Century Chivalric Romance," *Medievalia et Humanistica* 3 (1972): 13; W. Kellermann, *Aufbaustil und Weltbild Chrestiens von Troyes im Percevalroman* (Halle: Max Niemeyer, 1936), pp. 7, 156, 172; Zumthor, *Essai*, pp. 31–32, 37–44, 112.

28. R. H. Bloch, *Medieval French Literature and Law* (Berkeley: University of California Press, 1977).

29. "Brutescent homines, si concessi dote priuentur eloquii; ipseque urbes uidebuntur potius pecorum quasi septa, quam cetus hominum, nexu quodam societatis federatus, ut participatione officiorum et amica inuicem uicissitudine eodem iure uiuat" (*Metalogicon*, p. 7).

30. Cicero, *De Inventione*, ed. H. M. Hubbel (Cambridge: Harvard University Press, 1976), p. 4.

31. ". . . inscientiam caeca ac temeraria dominatrix animi cupiditas ad se explendam viribus corporis adutebatur . . ." (ibid.). For a medieval version of the same motif see Brunetto Latini, *Li Livres dou tresor*, ed. F. Carmody (Berkeley: University of California Press, 1948), p. 318.

32. "Nec homini homo firmissime sociari posset nisi colloquerentur atque ita sibi mentes suas cogitationesque quasi refunderent, vidit esse imponenda rebus vocabula, id est, significantes quosdam sonos" (Augustine, *De Ordine*, ed. R. Jolivet [Paris: Desclée de Brouwer, 1948], p. 424).

33. "Sed quia homo est animal naturaliter politicum et sociale, necesse fuit quod conceptiones unius hominis innotescerent aliis, quod fit per vocem" (Aquinas, *In peri hermeneias Aristotelis commentaria* [Monograph] [Montreal: Laval University, 1945], p. 4).

34. "Dico originem habet Graecam, quod Graeci δεικνύω. . . . Hinc iudicare, quod tunc ius dicatur; hinc iudex, quod ius dicat. . . ." (Varro, p. 228).

35. See M.-D. Chenu, *Nature, Man and Society in the Twelfth Century* (Chicago: University of Chicago Press, 1968), pp. 27, 33, 115; Colish, *The Mirror of Language*, pp. 138, 221; B. Stock, *Myth and Science in the Twelfth Century* (Princeton: Princeton University Press, 1972), pp. 197, 225; W. Wetherbee, *Platonism and Poetry in the Twelfth Century* (Princeton: Princeton University Press, 1972), p. 75.

36. *The Didascalicon of Hugh of St. Victor*, trans. J. Taylor (New York: Columbia University Press, 1961), p. 145.

37. B. Silvestris, *De Mundi universitate*, ed. C. S. Barach and J. Wrobel (Innsbruck: Bibliotheca Philosophorum, 1876), p. 39; John of Salisbury, *Policraticus*, ed. J. Dickson (New York: Knopf, 1927), p. 65.

38. "Universus enim mundus iste sensibilis quasi quidam liber est scriptus digito Dei" (*PL*, 176: col. 814); "Omnis mundi creatura / Quasi liber, et pictura / Nobis est, et speculum" (ibid., 210: col. 579); "Illic exarata supremi digito dispunctoris textus temporis, fatalis series, dispositio saeculorum" (Silvestris, *De Mundi universitate*, p. 13).

39. See Colish, *Mirror of Language*, chap. 1.

40. M. F. O'Meara, for example, shows the degree to which the resolution of the problem of an original language, and especially the question of whether it is considered to be divinely inspired or of human invention, determines eighteenth-century political ideology. See her "*Le Taureau blanc* and the Activity of Language," *Studies on Voltaire and the Eighteenth Century* 148 (1976): 115–175; also P. Juliard, *Philosophies of Language in Eighteenth Century France* (Hague: Mouton, 1970).

41. J.-J. Rousseau, *Essai sur l'origine des langues* in *Oeuvres complètes*, ed. P. R. Anguis (Paris: Dalibon, 1825), 1: 488.

42. G. Vico, *La Science Nouvelle*, ed. A. Doubine (Paris: Nagel, 1953), p. 20.

43. Ibid., p. 163.

44. See I. Iordan, *An Introduction to Romance Linguistics* (London: Methuen, 1937), chap. 1; R. H. Robins, *Brève Histoire de la linguistique de Platon à Chomsky* (Paris: Seuil, 1976), pp. 139 ff.

45. W. von Humboldt, *Über die Verschiedenheit des menschlichen Sprachbaues* (Berlin: Royal Academy of Science, 1836), p. 41.

46. M. Müller, "The Last Results of the Researches Respecting the Non-Iranian and Non-Semitic Languages of Asia or Europe, or the Turanian Family of Language," in C. C. J. Bunsen, *Outline of the Philosophy of Universal History* (London: Longman, Brown, Green, and Longman, 1854), 1:284; see also M. Müller, *The Science of Language* (Chicago: Open Court, 1899).

47. Müller, "The Last Results," p. 285.

48. Ibid., p. 477.

49. This debate was actually inherited from the naturalists and the antinaturalists about the primacy of sociological versus psychological factors in language formation.

50. F. Boas, *The Mind of Primitive Man* (New York: Macmillan, 1911), p. 154.

51. E. Sapir, *Language* (New York: Harcourt, Brace and World, 1921), pp. 218, 219.

52. B. L. Whorf, "A Linguistic Consideration of Thinking in Primitive Communities," in D. Hymes, *Language in Culture and Society* (New York: Harper and Row, 1964), p. 130. See also *Language, Thought, and Reality*, ed. J. B. Carroll (Cambridge: Massachusetts Institute of Technology Press, 1956), p. 55; N. Struever, "The Study of Language and the Study of History," *Journal of Interdisciplinary History* 3 (1974): 401–415.

53. F. G. Lounsbury, "One Hundred Years of Anthropological Linguistics," in *One Hundred Years of Anthropology*, ed. J. O. Brew (Cambridge: Harvard University Press, 1968), p. 223.

54. A. L. Kroeber, "Classificatory Systems of Relationship," *Journal of the Royal Anthropological Institute of Great Britain* 39 (1909): 77–84; F. de Saussure, *Cours de linguistique générale* (Lausanne: Payot, 1916).

55. F. G. Lounsbury, "A Semantic Analysis of the Pawnee Kinship Usage," *Language* 32 (1956), pp. 191–192. "Thus phonemic description bears the same relation to speech as sounds and behavior that cultural description bears to the material world in general" (W. H. Goodenough, "Cultural Anthropology and Linguistics," in Hymes, *Language in Culture*, p. 37).

56. A. F. C. Wallace and J. Atkins, "The Meaning of Kinship Terms," *American Anthropologist* 62 (1960), p. 60. See also W. H. Goodenough, *Property, Kin, and Community on Truk* (New Haven: Yale University Press, 1951), p. 110.

57. J. H. Greenberg, "The Logical Analysis of Kinship," *Philosophy of Science* 16 (1949), p. 58.

58. Lounsbury, "A Semantic Analysis of the Pawnee Kinship Usage," p. 169.

59. Greenberg, "Logical Analysis," p. 64. The term "cultural grammar" is that of H. C. Conklin, "Ethnogenealogical Method," in W. H. Goodenough, *Explorations in Cultural Anthropology* (New York: McGraw-Hill, 1964), p. 25.

60. G. Murdock, *Social Structure* (New York: Macmillan, 1946), p. 183. As examples of such postulates and theorems: "Postulate 1: The relatives of any two kin-types tend to be called by the same kinship terms, rather than by different terms, in inverse proportion to the number and relative efficacy of (a) the inherent distinctions between them and (b) the social differentials affecting them, and in direct proportion to the number and relative efficacy of the social equalizers

affecting them. . . . Theorem 1: When secondary or tertiary relatives tend to be called by the same kinship term as the daughter of the primary relative, etc." (ibid., pp. 138–139).

61. ". . . the rules of kinship and marriage serve to insure the circulation of women between groups, just as economic rules serve to insure the circulation of goods and services, and linguistic rules the circulation of messages" (C. Lévi-Strauss, *Structural Anthropology* [New York: Doubleday, 1967], p. 82); and ". . . en effet, exogamie et langage ont la même fonction fondamentale: la communication avec autrui, et l'intégration du groupe" (C. Lévi-Strauss, *Structures élémentaires de la parenté* [Hague: Mouton, 1967], p. 565). Lévi-Strauss is also heavily influenced by phonemics as well as by de Saussure: "Malgré ces pressentiments, une seule parmi toutes les sciences sociales, est parvenue au point où l'explication synchronique et l'explication diachronique se confondent. . . . Cette science sociale est la linguistique, conçue comme une étude phonologique. Or, quand nous considérons ses méthodes, et plus encore son objet, nous pouvons nous demander si la sociologie de la famille, telle que nous l'avons conçue au cours de ce travail, porte sur une réalité aussi différente qu'on pourrait croire, et si, par conséquent, elle ne dispose pas des mêmes possibilités" (*Structures élémentaires*, p. 564).

62. Lévi-Strauss, *Structural Anthropology*, p. 62; Lévi-Strauss discusses this system at length under the rubric "general exchange" or "general reciprocity" in *Structures élémentaires*, pp. 270–358.

63. Lévi-Strauss, *Structural Anthropology*, pp. 62–67.

64. A. Schleicher, *Das Darwinsche Theorie und die Sprachwissenschaft* (Weimar: H. Böhlan, 1863), p. 31.

65. See E. Benveniste, *Problèmes de linguistique générale* (Paris: Gallimard, 1974), 2:91, 95.

66. This leads to the most absurd confusions of language and race. M. Müller, for example, in attempting to prove the common Arian descent of the languages of Northern India, claims that "the blood which circulates in their grammar is Arian blood" ("Last Results," p. 281); also, "It is said that blood is thicker than water, but it may be said with even greater truth that language is thicker than blood" (*Science of Language*, p. 35).

67. See for example P. Mass, *Textkritik* (Leipzig: Teubner, 1950).

68. This is not to ignore the existence of ancient Sanskrit grammars which, though prescriptive, do not offer the same abstract meditation upon the nature and function of verbal signs as found in the medieval Christian West.

Chapter One

1. Parts of this first chapter appeared under the title "Etymologies et généalogies: théories de langue, liens de parenté, et genre littéraire au XIIIᵉ siècle," *Les Annales* 5 (1981):946–962.

2. ["He pondered how he might make known to that last man of his line that Solomon, who lived so long before him, knew the truth of his coming"] *La Queste del Saint Graal*, ed. A. Pauphilet (Paris: Champion, 1949), p. 221.

3. See E. Auerbach, "Figura," in *Scenes from the Drama of European Literature* (New York: Meridan, 1959), pp. 11–78.

4. "Tot ausi come s'ele parlast a ses oirs qui aprés li estoient a venir" (*La Queste*, p. 212); ["And this was a sign that by the Virgin Mary the inheritance that had been lost in ancient days would be recovered"] ibid., p. 213. The medievals were aware of the homophony between the word for stick (stem) and for virgin.

5. ["For as soon as he (Adam) plucked a twig from it, he put it into the earth, and it took root by itself"] ibid., p. 214.

6. ["Nor from this one could another grow, thus died all the other plants made from this one"] Ibid., p. 219.

7. For the exact genealogical sequence, see ibid., pp. 134–135. What is striking is the extent to which the text emphasizes lineal continuity as against disruption, or the Incarnation as a new beginning.

8. For a particularly incisive discussion of this tradition, see G. Ladner, "Medieval and Modern Understanding of Symbolism: A Comparison," *Speculum* 54 (1979):223–256.

9. Augustine, *Les Confessions*, ed. A. Solignac (Paris: Desclée de Brouwer, 1962), 2:490.

10. Ibid., p. 494.

11. For an exhaustive discussion of the issue, see A. Borst, *Der Turmbau von Babel*, 6 vols. (Stuttgart: Anton Hiersemann, 1957).

12. ["Let us see now why all these animals of the field and all the birds of the sky were brought to Adam in order that he give them names and that thus there grew in some way the necessity of creating a woman for him from his rib"] *De Genesi ad litteram*, ed. P. Agnësse and A. Solignac (Paris: Desclée de Brouwer, 1972), 2:116.

13. Jerome, *Interpretatio Chronicae Eusebii Pamphili*, PL, 27: col. 66; and *Hebraicae Quaestiones in Libro Geneseos*, in *Corpus Christianorum* (Turnholt: Brepols, 1959), 72:5.

14. Jerome, *Hebraicae Quaestiones*, p. 21; see also B. Smalley, *The Study of the Bible in the Middle Ages* (Oxford: Blackwell, 1952), pp. 1–37, and especially B. Guenée, *Histoire et culture historique dans l'Occident médiéval* (Paris: Aubier, 1980), p. 19.

15. Jerome, *Hebraicae Quaestiones*, p. 41. Isidore, who cites Jerome, concurs: "Plerique primorum hominum ex propriis causis originem nominum habent. Quibus ita prophetice indita sunt vocabula, ut aut futuris aut praecedentibus eorum causis conveniant" ["Several of early mankind draw the origin of their names from proper causes. Their names were imposed in a prophetic manner so that they can apply either to their future or to their past causes"] (*Etym.*, 7:vi, i).

16. "Sicut autem Cain, quod interpretatur possessio, terrenae conditor ciuitatis, et filius eius, in cuius nomine condita est, Enoch, quod interpretatur dedicatio, indicat istam ciuitatem et initium et finem habere terrenum, ubi nihil speratur amplius, quam in hoc saeculo cerni potest: ita Seth quod interpretatur resurrectio, cum sit generationum seorsus commemoratarum pater, quid de filio eius sacra haec historia dicat, intuendum est" ["Now, as Cain signifying possession, the founder of the earthly city, and his son Enoch, meaning dedication, in whose name it was founded, indicate that this city is earthly both in its beginning and in its end—a city in which nothing more is hoped for than can be seen in this world—so Seth, meaning resurrection, and being the father of generations registered apart from the others, we must consider what this sacred history says of his son"] (Augustine, *De Civitate Dei*, ed. J. Welldon [London: Society for Promoting Christian Knowledge, 1924], 2:162.

17. ["From this same one, in fact, come the patriarchs, apostles, and the people of God. And from his lineage too comes Christ, whose name, from sunrise to sunset, is greatly on the lips of men"] *Etym.*, 7:vi, xvi.

18. Augustine, *De Genesi*, 2:122.

19. The Carolingian poet Milo, playing on the name of Andrew the Apostle, claims that the son fulfills the name of the parents: "Ac nomen patrium patrando viriliter implet" (cited in E. R. Curtius, *European Literature in the Latin Middle Ages*, ed. W. Trask [New York: Harper, 1953], p. 497).

20. Jerome, *Interpretatio*, col. 67.

21. See J. W. Thompson, *The History of Historical Writing* (New York: Macmillan, 1942), 1:130; J. Taylor, *The Universal Chronicle of Ranulf Higden* (Oxford: Clarendon Press, 1966), pp. 1–49.

22. ["And whatsoever Adam called every living creature, that was the name of the thing thereof"] Gen. 2:19.

23. [παρὰ Μωυσεῖ δὲ αἱ τῶν ὀνομάτων θέσεις ἐνάργειαι πραγμάτων εἰσὶν ἐμφαντικώταται, ὡς αὐτὸ τὸ πρᾶγμα ἐξ ἀνάγκης εὐθὺς εἶναι τοὔνομα καὶ <τοὔνομα καὶ> καθ᾽ οὗ τίθεται διαφέρειν μηδέν] Philo, *On the Cherubim*, ed. F. H. Colson (London: Heinemann, 1929), 2:43.

24. "Illa certe tunc loquebatur Adam et in ea lingua, si adhuc usque permanet, sunt istae uoces articulatae, quibus primus homo animalibus terrestribus et uolatilibus nomina inposuit" (*De Genesi*, 2:119).

25. "Litterae Latinae et Graecae ab Hebraeis videntur exortae. Apud illos enim prius dictum est aleph, deinde ex simili enuntiatione apud Graecos tractum est alpha, inde apud Latinos A. Translator enim ex simili sono alterius linguae litteram condidit, ut nosse possimus linguam Hebraicam omnium linguarum et litterarum esse matrem" ["Latin and Greek letters come from the Hebrew. For among the latter *aleph* was the first so named; then by the similarity of sound it was transmitted to the Greeks as *alpha*; likewise to the Latins as *A*. For the borrower fashioned the letter of the second language according to the similarity of sound so that we can know that the Hebrew language is the mother of all languages and letters"] (*Etym.*, 1:iii, iv).

26. *Metalogicon*, p. 23; Brunetto Latini, *Li Livres dou tresor*, ed. F. Carmody (Berkeley: University of California Press, 1948), p. 317.

27. "Impositores primi latini ydiomatis, mediante greco ydiomate, voces latinas imponebant. . . . Greci vero imposuerunt suas voces, mediante hebreo ydiomate. . . . Hebrei vero voces multas imposuerunt, mediantibus vocibus datis a Deo" ["The givers of the first Latin words imposed Latin sounds according to Greek words. . . . The Greeks truly imposed their sounds according to Hebrew words. . . . The Hebrews truly imposed many sounds according to those given by God"] (*Notices*, p. 131).

28. "Ergo utimur verbis aut eis quae propria sunt et certa quasi vocabula rerum paene una nata cum rebus ipsis . . ." (Cicero, *De Oratore*, ed. E. W. Sutton and H. Rackham [Cambridge: Harvard University Press, 1948], 2:118). "Propria sunt verba, cum id significant, in quod primo denominata sunt" (Quintilian, *Institutio Oratoria*, ed. H. E. Butler [Cambridge: Harvard University Press, 1969], 1:110). "Sunt autem signa vel propria, vel translata. Propria dicuntur, cum his rebus significandis adhibentur, propter quas sunt instituta . . ." (Augustine, *De Doctrina Christiana*, ed. G. Combès and J. Farges [Paris: Desclée de Brouwer, 1949], p. 258).

29. "Genera dicta a generando. Quicquid enim gignit aut gignitur, hoc potest genus dici et genus facere" (Varro, p. 602).

30. ["Genders, which are masculine and feminine, are properly named from generating' since they can generate"] Priscian, p. 141.

31. ["They are called the genera of verbs, since they generate. For if you add 'R' to the active it breeds the passive; likewise, if from the passive you take the 'R' away, it produces the active"] *Etym.*, 1:ix, vii; see also ibid., 9:ii, i.

32. "Patronymicum est, quod a propriis tantummodo derivatur patrum nominibus secundum formam Graecam" ["The Patronymic is applied to a word derived only from the proper names of fathers according to the Greek model"] (Priscian, p. 62).

33. "Et quod patronymica a masculino descendunt plerumque genere, rarissime autem a feminino nec proprie, quando a matribus fiunt, ut supra ostendimus, possessiva autem ab omnibus nascuntur generibus; et quod patronymica ad homines pertinet vel ad deos, possessiva vero ad omnes res" ["And while patronyms usually derive from the masculine class, but most rarely from the feminine, since as we previously showed, they are inappropriately derived from the maternal side, possessives, on the other hand, arise from all classes; and while patronyms pertain to men or to gods, possessives in fact pertain to all things"] (ibid., p. 68).

34. "La primiera maniera de derivatio so es de votz o de significat. es ayssi cum filhs leyals,. e naturals. lequals es. de leyal matrimoni. La segonda ques fay solamen en votz. es coma filhs naturals solamen lequals en autra maniera es appelatz bortz. La tersa ques fay solamen en significat. es coma filhs adoptius" (*Leys D'Amors*, ed. M. Gatien-Arnoult [Toulouse: Bon et Privat, 1841], 2:24).

35. "Filii Iauan Elisa et Tharsis, Cethim et Dodanim. Ad his diuisae sunt insulae nationum in terris suis, uir secundum linguam suam et cognationem suam et gentem suam. De Ionibus, id est de Graecis, nascuntur Elisei, qui uocantur Aeolides: unde et quinta lingua Graeciae aeolis appellatur, quam illi uocant πέμπτην διάλεκτον" ["The sons of Iaun were Elisa and Tharsis, Cethim and Dodanim. The islands in his lands were divided by them according to nation, and man was separated according both to his language and his nationality. From the Ionians, that is from the Greeks, come the Eliseans who are called Aeolides; the fifth language of Greece, which they call πέμπτην διάλεκτον is named Aeolic after them"] (Jerome, *Hebraicae Quaestiones*, p. 11).

36. Augustine, *De Civitate Dei*, 2:204.

37. "Nam priusquam superbia turris illius in diversos signorum sonos humanam divideret societatem, una omnium nationum lingua fuit, quae Hebraea vocatur; quam Patriarchae et Prophetae usi sunt non solum in sermonibus suis, verum etiam in litteris sacris" ["For before the proud undertaking of that tower divided human society among different languages there was one tongue for all peoples, which is called Hebrew. This the patriarchs and prophets used, not only in their conversations, but in the sacred writings as well"] (*Etym.*, 9:i, i).

38. ["Nations arise from speech and not speech from nations"] Ibid., 9:i, xiv.

39. Dante, *De Vulgari Eloquentia*, ed. P. Rajna (Florence: Le Monnier, 1896), p. 16.

40. Ibid., p. 99.

41. Even for the contemporary critic it is an extremely complex issue. The place of origins within the medieval *artes sermocinales* has, like almost all meditations upon beginnings, been misunderstood, displaced, distorted, and generally overdetermined by the meditating mediator. Those, for example, whose theological investment in the Middle Ages encourages a worshipful closeness to the *sacra pagina* have tended to be caught in the movement of that which they seek to describe and thus to transform Adam's founding act into something equivalent to a medieval cratylism of signs. On the other hand, those whose deep distrust of all forms of textual production encourages an equally theological unwillingness even to entertain the issues of beginnings, progression, or closure remain trapped in the "naturalized" intellectual assumptions of their own era, and hence are blind to one of the most consequential modes of thought of a profoundly "originary" age.

42. ἀκράτου γὰρ ἔτι τῆς λογικῆς φύσεως ὑπαρχούσης ἐν ψυχῇ, καὶ μηδενὸς ἀρρωστήματος ἢ νοσήματος ἢ πάθους παρεισεληλυθότος, τὰς φαντασίας τῶν

σωμάτων καὶ πραγμάτων ἀκραιφνεστάτας λαμβάνων, εὐθυβόλους ἐποιεῖτο τὰς κλήσεις, εὖ μάλα στοχαζόμενος τῶν δηλουμένων, ὡς ἅμα λεχθῆναί τε καὶ νοηθῆναι τὰς φύσεις αὐτῶν. ["For the native reasoning power in the soul being still unalloyed . . . , he received impressions made by bodies and objects in their sheer reality, and the titles he gave were fully apposite, for right well did he divine the creatures he was describing, with the result that their natures were apprehended as soon as their names were uttered"] (Philo, *On the Creation*, ed. F. H. Colson [London: Heinemann, 1929], 1:119).

43. Origen, *Contra Celsum*, ed. H. Chadwick (Cambridge: Cambridge University Press, 1953), p. 23; see also p. 299.

44. Cited in J. Jolivet, "Quelques cas de 'platonisme grammatical' au XIIe siècle," in *Mélanges René Crozet* (Poitiers: Société d'Etudes Médiévales, 1966), 1:99.

45. See W. S. Allen, "Ancient Ideas on the Origin and Development of Language," *Transactions of the Philological Society of London* (1948), pp. 35–60; R. H. Robins, *Ancient and Medieval Grammatical Theory in Europe* (London: G. Bell, 1951); and, for a study of cratylism as a modern as well as an ancient phenomenon, see G. Genette, *Mimologiques* (Paris: Seuil, 1976).

46. See A. Le Boulluec, "L'Allégorie chez les Stoïciens," *Poétique* 23 (1975): 291–300.

47. Aristotle, *On Interpretation* (London: Heinemann, 1938), p. 117.

48. ["Pythagoras Samius first formed the letter 'Y' according to the example of human life"] *Etym.*, 1:iii, vii; "Nam iudices eandem litteram 'Θ' adponebant ad eorum nomina, quos supplicio afficiebant" (ibid., 1:iii, viii).

49. This definition of letters will be adopted by twelfth-century grammarians; see R. W. Hunt, "Studies on Priscian in the Twelfth Century—II, The School of Ralph of Beauvais," *Medieval and Renaissance Studies* 2 (1950): 7.

50. ["Not all names were imposed by the ancients according to nature, but some also according to convention"] *Etym.*, 1:xxix, ii. Interestingly enough, the figure or shape of a letter can also exist either by the nature of the sound it represents or by convention (ibid., 1:iv, xvii).

51. "Et tamen si dicam vitam esse quamdam beatam, eamdemque sempiternam, quo nos Deo duce, id est ipsa veritate, gradibus quibusdam infirmo gressui nostro accommodatis perduci cupiam, vereor ne ridiculus videar, qui non rerum ipsarum quae significantur, sed consideratione signorum tantam viam ingredi coeperim" ["And yet, if I say that there is a blessed life, an eternal life to which I would like God, that is to say, truth itself, to lead us by steps proportionate to the weakness of our capacity, I fear appearing ridiculous, I who engage in such an undertaking by the study of signs instead of the study of the things signified"] (*De Magistro*, ed. F. J. Thonnard [Paris: Desclée de Brouwer, 1952], p. 66).

52. *De Ordine*, ed. R. Jolivet (Paris: Desclée de Brouwer, 1948), p. 434.

53. See *De Doctrina*, p. 240.

54. "Formata quippe cogitatio ab ea re quam scimus, verbum est quod in corde dicimus; quod nec graecum est, nec latinum nec linguae alicuius alterius; sed cum id opus est in eorum quibus loquimur perferre notitiam, aliquod signum quo significetur assumitur. Et plerumque sonus. . . ." ["For the thought formed from that thing which we know is the word which we speak in our heart, and this is neither Greek, nor Latin, nor any other language, but when we have to bring it to the knowledge of those to whom we are speaking, then some sign is assumed by which it may be known. And generally this is a sound. . . ."] (Augustine, *De Trinitate*, ed. G. Beschin [Rome: Città Nuova, 1973], p. 650).

55. *Glossulae super Porphyrium* in *Philosophische Schriften*, ed. B. Geyer (Munster: Aschendorff, 1923), 3:537; see also J. Jolivet, "Platonisme grammatical," p. 72.

56. Ibid., 3:567.

57. "Nam ille qui invenit gramaticam et dictiones imposuit ad significandum, debuit habere cognitionem rei significande et vocis que ei debuit imponi" (*Notices*, p. 123).

58. "Jam ergo intelligas volo, res quae significantur, pluris quam signa esse pendendas" (Augustine, *De Magistro*, ed. F. J. Thonnard [Paris: Desclée de Brouwer, 1941], p. 78).

59. ". . . vides profecto quanto verba minoris habenda sint, quam id propter quod utimur verbis. . . ." (ibid., p. 80).

60. "Verbis igitur nisi verba non discimus, imo sonitum strepitumque verborum. . . ." (ibid., p. 98).

61. *De Doctrina*, p. 350.

62. Ibid., pp. 312, 534.

63. ". . . nec linguam quippe eius nec membranas et atramentum nec significantes sonos lingua editos nec signa litterarum conscripta pelliculis corpus Christi et sanguinem dicimus, sed illud tantum quod ex fructibus terrae acceptum et prece mystica consecratum rite sumimus ad salutem spiritalem in memoriam pro nobis Dominicae passionis. . . ." ["for when we speak of the body and the blood of Christ, we certainly do not mean the tongue of the Apostle, or the parchment or the ink, or the vocalized sounds, or the alphabetical signs written on the skins. We refer only to that which, received from the fruits of the earth and consecrated by a mystical prayer, we take for our spiritual health in the memory of the Lord's passion. . . ."] (*De Trinitate*, p. 140).

64. Ibid., p. 158.

65. W. Kneale and M. Kneale, *The Development of Logic* (Oxford: Oxford University Press, 1975), p. 20.

66. Donatus, *Ars Minor*, ed. W. J. Wace, in *Wisconsin Studies in the Social Sciences* 11 (1926), p. 29; see also Priscian, p. 55.

67. In the traditional examples, a truly single entity is illustrated by a species (e.g., man) with only one member (e.g., the individual Plato or Socrates). The property of a class like man is to be found, according to some, in his capacity for philosophy, according to others, in his capacity for grammar, and, according to still others, in his capacity for laughter. Thus, not all men show an aptitude for philosophy, grammar, or laughter, but no other class of being is capable of one of the qualities unique to or proper to man. See Aristotle, *Topics* in *The Basic Works of Aristotle*, ed. R. McKeon (New York: Random House, 1941), p. 191; Porphyry, *The Introduction of Porphyry*, ed. O. F. Owen (London: George Bell, 1878), chap. 4 ("On Property"); Cassiodorus, *Introduction to Divine and Human Readings*, ed. A. P. Evans (New York: Columbia University Press, 1946), p. 161; Martianus Capella, *De Nuptiis Philologiae et Mercurii*, ed. A. Dick (Leipzig: Teubner, 1925), p. 160.

68. Aristotle, *Categoriae*, in *Basic Works*, p. 10.

69. Cassiodorus, *Divine Readings*, p. 168.

70. See J. Fontaine, *Isidore de Seville et la culture classique dans l'Espagne wisigothique* (Paris: Etudes Augustiniennes, 1959), p. 203.

71. "Modo per singulas partes diffiniendo currit: per *quot* numerum, per *quae* nomina, per *quid* substantiam requirit.—*Pars orationis*, .i. una species latinitatis: diffinitio est nominis. Sicut superius diximus, diffinitio a genere incipit et per species ad proprium tendit" ["The definition (of the noun) includes several parts. It asks of what number, name, and substance a thing is. It is a part of speech under

the surveillance of Latinity. Thus the noun is defined. As we said above, the definition starts with the genus and moves to the proper through the species"] (Remigius of Auxerre, *In Artem Donati Minorem Commentum*, ed. W. Fox [Leipzig: Teubner, 1902], p. 9).

72. Martianus Capella, *De Nuptiis*, p. 84.

73. "Ars itaque est quasi strata publica, qua ire, ambulare, et agere, sine calumnia et concussione omnibus ius est. Vitium est omnibus deuium, ut qui in eo iter actumue exercet, aut precipitium subeat, aut calumniam et concussionem interpellantium patiatur. Figura uero medium tenet locum" ["The art (of grammar) is, as it were, a public highway, on which all have the right to journey, walk, and act, immune from criticism or molestation. To use faulty grammar means that one is forsaking the proper thoroughfare. He who pursues such devious bypaths is likely either to end up at a precipice, or become an easy target for the darts and jousts of those who may challenge what he says. The figure (of speech), however, occupies an intermediate position"] (*Metalogicon*, p. 45). See also H. Lausberg, *Handbuch der literarischen Rhetorik* (Munich, Max Hueber, 1960), 1:35.

74. Donatus, *Ars Grammatica*, ed. H. Keil (Hildesheim: Georg Olms, 1961), p. 397.

75. Cited R. W. Hunt, "Studies on Priscian in the Eleventh and Twelfth Centuries," *Medieval and Renaissance Studies* 1 (1941): 212.

76. Cicero, *Topics*, ed. H. M. Hubbell (Cambridge: Harvard University Press, 1976), p. 408; see also p. 388. Quintilian's definition of etymology represents a succinct résumé of the semantic range of the term: "Etymologia, quae verborum originem inquirit, a Cicerone dicta est notatio, quia eius apud Aristotelem invenitur δύμβολον, quod est nota; nam verbum ex verbo ductum, id est veriloquium, ipse Cicero, qui finxit, reformidat. Sunt qui vim potius intuiti originationem vocent" ["Etymology inquires into the origin of words, and was called 'notation' by Cicero, on the grounds that the term used by Aristotle is δύμβολον, which may be translated by 'nota.' A literal rendering of ἐτυμολογία would be 'veriloquium,' a form which even Cicero, its inventor, shrinks from using. Some again, with an eye to the meaning of the word, call it 'origination'"] (*Institutio Oratio*, ed. H. E. Butler [Cambridge: Harvard University Press, 1969], 1:122).

77. For an extended discussion of the relation between rhetoric and space see F. Yates, *The Art of Memory* (Chicago: University of Chicago Press, 1966).

78. "Tiberis quod caput extra Latium, si inde nomen quoque exfluit in linguam nostram, nihil (ad) ἐτυμολόγον Latinum . . ." (Varro, p. 26).

79. "Locus est, ubi locatum qui esse potest, ut nunc dicunt, collocatum. . . . Ubi quidque consistit, locus" (ibid., p. 14); interestingly enough, Varro specifically links the notion of place to the act of generation: "Sic loci muliebres, ubi nascendi initia consistunt" ["So also *loci muliebres* 'woman's places,' where the beginnings of birth are situated"] (ibid.).

80. "Loqui ab loco dictum" (ibid., p. 222); ". . . is loquitur, qui suo loco quodque verbum sciens ponit. . . ." (ibid., p. 224).

81. The compilers and philosophers of the period after the fall of Rome seem to add little to the Classical notion of etymology. Varro had defined it as that part of speech "where the Greeks examine why and whence words are" (*De Lingua*, p. 5). Martianus Capella, in discussing various types of argument, mentions that "from *nota*, which the Greeks call etymology" (*De Nuptiis*, p. 237). Cassiodorus lists among the basic grammatical classifications the technique of etymology, "consisting of the true or probable demonstration of a word" (*Divine Letters*, p. 146).

Boethius too seems merely to repeat the Ciceronian definition of an argument "from the power of a name": "ex vi nominis argumentum elicitur, quam Graeci ἐτυμολογιαν appellant, id est verbum ex verbo veriloquium" (*In Topica Ciceronis, PL,* 64: col. 1110). For a general treatment of the subject, see G. de Poerck, "Etymologia et origo à travers la tradition latine," *Anamnhcic: Gedenkboek E. A. Leemans* (Brugges: De Temple, 1971), pp. 191–228; Lausberg, *Handbuch,* 1:77, 215, 255; E. Wofflin, "Die Etymologieen der lateinischen Grammatiker," *Archiv für Lateinische Lexicographie und Grammatik* 8 (1892): 421–440, 563–585.

82. P. Zumthor, "Etymologies," in *Langue, texte, énigme* (Paris: Seuil, 1975), p. 149.

83. Fontaine, *Isidore,* p. 203.

84. "Aliunde originem non trahunt" (*Etym.,* 1:viii, v).

85. ["The derivation of words, when the force of a verb or a noun is ascertained through interpretation"] Ibid., 1:xxix, i.

86. "Sunt autem etymologiae nominum aut ex causa datae, ut 'reges' a (regendo et) recte agendo, aut ex origine, ut 'homo,' quia sit ex humo, aut ex contrariis ut a lavando 'lutum,'. . . . Quaedam etiam facta sunt ex nominum derivatione, ut a prudentia 'prudens'; quaedam etiam ex vocibus, ut a garrulitate 'garrulus.' . . ." ["Thus some etymologies of names are drawn from the cause (of imposition), as 'kings' [*reges*] comes from ruling and acting fairly [*regendo et recte agende*]; some are drawn from the origin, for 'man' [*homo*] is so named because he is of the earth [*humus*]; some are drawn from contraries, as 'mud' [*lutum*] comes from 'washing' [*lavando*]. Also, some etymologies are formed from nominal derivation, as 'prudent' from 'prudence,' and some from sound, as 'garrulous' and 'garrulity'"] (*Etym.,* 1:xxix, iii).

87. J. Jolivet even maintains that words are, for Isidore, the equivalent of Platonic forms ("Platonisme grammatical," p. 94).

88. ["For Astronomy embraces the revolution of the heavens, the rise, setting, and motion of the heavenly bodies, and the origin of their names"] Ibid., 3:xxvii, i).

89. Zumthor, "Etymologies," p. 149.

90. E. R. Curtius writes of Isidore's *Etymologiae*: ". . . it may be called the basic book of the entire Middle Ages. It not only established the canonical stock of knowledge for eight centuries but also molded their thought categories" (*European Literature,* p. 496).

91. "Ut dicatur ethimologia quasi veriloquium, quoniam qui ethimologizat veram, id est primam, vocabuli originem assignat" (*Notices,* p. 147).

92. "Ethimologia . . . est expositio alicuius vocabuli per aliud vocabulum, sive unum sive plura magis nota, secundum rei proprietatem et litterarum similitudinem. . . ." ["Etymology is the exposition of one word by another whether by one sign or more, according to the property of the thing and the resemblance of letters. . . ."] (*Notices,* p. 147).

93. "Siquidem non est eloquens quisquis loquitur, aut qui quod uoluerit utcumque loquitur, sed ille dumtaxat qui animi sui arbitrium commode profert. Ipsa quoque commoditas exigit facultatem (que a facilitate dicitur) ut sequamur mores nostros, quibus gratum est in ea parte Stoicos imitari, qua ad faciliorem intelligentiam rerum et uerborum originem studiosius perscrutantur" ["Not everyone who speaks, nor even one who says what he wants to in some fashion, is eloquent. He alone is eloquent who fittingly and efficaciously expresses himself as he intends. This appropriate effectiveness postulates a faculty (so called from

the facility), to follow our wont of imitating the concern of the Stoics about the etymologies of words as a key to easier understanding of their meanings"] (*Metalogicon*, p. 22).

94. E. Faral, *Les Arts poétiques du XIIe et du XIIIe siècle* (Paris: Champion, 1971), p. 136.

95. Interestingly enough, Augustine finds the letter "V" to be consonant with harshness and violence, offering the examples *violenta, vomis, vincere* (*De Origine Verbi, PL*, 32: col. 1413). Though Migne attributes this text to Augustine, its authorship has been contested. The arbitrariness of conflicting certainties makes it clear that etymology as an intellectual strategy is more important than specific etymologies.

96. Hildebert, *PL*, 171: col. 1274; Marbod writes:

"Nomen commendat res nomine significata.
Ergo debemus naturam quaerere rerum,
Ex quo possimus de nomine cernere verum."

"The thing marked by the name prescribes the name.
Therefore we should seek out the nature of things,
For as a result we may discern the truth about the name."

[Ibid., col. 1671]

97. See Curtius, *European Literature*, p. 498.

98. *Leys D'Amors*, 2:29.

99. Origen, *Contra Celsum*, p. 23.

100. "Quid ultra provehar? Quidquid aliud annumerari potest, aut similitudine rerum et sonorum, aut similitudine rerum ipsarum, aut vicinitate, aut contrario, contineri videbis originem verbi, quam prosequi non quidem ultra soni similitudinem possumus. . . ." ["Of what use continuing? All that one can add would show in the principles of resemblance, proximity, or contrariety of things that origin of words which we cannot pursue beyond the resemblance of the sound to things. . . ."] (Augustine, *De Origine Verbi*, in *PL* 32: col. 1413).

101. Augustine, *De Doctrina*, p. 244.

102. Ibid., p. 258.

103. Jerome, *Hebraicae Quaestiones*, p. 1.

104. The most interesting contemporary treatment of the relationship between language and paternity is to be found in the work of J. Derrida; see especially *De la Grammatologie* (Paris: Éditions de Minuit, 1967) and "La Pharmacie de Platon," *Tel Quel* 32 (1968): 3–48; and 33 (1968): 18–59. See also J. Pépin, "L'herméneutique ancienne: Les mots et les idées," *Poétique* 23 (1975): 291–300.

105. Cited in Pépin, "L'herméneutique ancienne," p. 298.

106. Eusebius, *Ecclesiastical History*, ed. E. Capps and T. E. Page (London: Heinemann, 1926), 2:22.

107. *Allegoriae in Sacram Scripturam, PL*, 112: col. 1083.

108. "Quia ergo nihil creari posset siue ante tempora, quod quidem non est creatori coaeternum, siue ab exordio temporum siue in aliquo tempore, cuius creandi ratio, si tamen ratio recte dicitur, non in Dei uerbo patri coaeterno coaeterna uita uiueret, propterea scriptura, priusquam insinuet unamquamque creaturam, ex ordine, quo conditam dicit, respicit ad Dei uerbum. . . ." ["Nothing then could be created which, if before time is not coeternal with the Creator, or if at the beginning of time or at some time, does not base the reason for its creation—if the term 'reason' is not used improperly—in the partaking of a life coeternal in the Word of God coeternal to the Father. This is why Scripture, before enumerating each creature in the order of its creation, refers to the Word of God. . . ."] (Augustine, *De Genesi*, 1:164).

109. See Colish, *Mirror of Language*, p. 52.

110. Augustine, *De Trinitate*, p. 456.

111. "Appetunt tamen omnes quamdam similitudinem in significando, ut ipsa signa, in quantum possunt, rebus quae significantur similia sint" (Augustine, *De Doctrina*, p. 300).

Chapter Two

1. G. Duby, *La Société aux XIe et XIIe siècles dans la région mâconnaise* (Paris: Armand Colin, 1953), p. 137; and "Structures de parenté et noblesse dans la France du Nord aux XIe et XIIe siècles," in *Hommes et structures du moyen âge* (Paris: Mouton, 1973), p. 274. If, as the reader will note, I rely heavily upon Duby, it is because his studies of the medieval family are the most systematic and sustained to date.

2. Duby, *La Société*, p. 283.

3. G. Duby, "Lignage, noblesse et chevalerie au XIIe siècle dans la région mâconnaise: Une révision," in *Hommes et structures*, p. 416.

4. For Duby, see articles and books cited; P. Bonnassie, *La Catalogne du milieu du Xe à la fin du XIe siècle* (Toulouse: Publications de l'Université de Toulouse, 1975); R. Fossier, *La Terre et les hommes en Picardie jusqu'à la fin du XIIIe siècle* (Paris: Beatrice-Nauwelaerts, 1968); L. Génicot, *L'Economie namuroise au bas moyen âge* (Louvain: Bibliothèque de l'Université, 1960); R. Hajdu, "Family and Feudal Ties in Poitou, 1110–1300," *Journal of Interdisciplinary History* 8 (1977): 117–139; D. Herlihy, "The Agrarian Revolution in Southern France and Italy, 801–1150," *Speculum* 33 (1958): 23–41; and "Land, Family, and Women in Continental Europe, 701–1200," *Traditio* 18 (1962): 89–120; L. Musset, "L'Aristocratie normande au XIe siècle," in *La Noblesse au moyen âge, Xe–XIe siècles: Essais à la mémoire de Robert Boutruche*, ed. P. Contamine (Paris: Presses Universitaires de France, 1976), pp. 71–104.

5. I have developed elsewhere the thesis that the literary motif of the Wasteland is indeed related to such demographic dispersion. See "Wasteland and Round Table: The Historical Significance of Myths of Dearth and Plenty in Old French Romance," *New Literary History* 11 (1979–1980): 255–276.

6. See M. Bloch, *Feudal Society* (Chicago: University of Chicago Press, 1964): 2:194–197; Contamine, *La Noblesse*, p. 21; Duby, *Mâcon*, pp. 187, 243, 267, 436; Fossier, *Picardie*, pp. 518–551; P. Ourliac and J. de Malafosse, *Droit romain et ancien droit: les biens* (Paris: Presses Universitaires de France, 1961), p. 140.

7. The best discussion of such impediments is still that of A. Esmein, *Le Mariage en droit canonique* (Paris: Sirey, 1929), 1:236–348.

8. "Il souloit estre que l'en se venjoit par droit de guerre dusques ou setisme degré de lignage et ce n'estoit pas merveille ou tans de lors, car devant le setisme degré ne se pouoit fere mariages. Mes aussi comme il est raprochié que mariages se puet fere puis que li quars degré de lignage soit passés, aussi ne se doit on pas prendre pour guerre a persone qui soit plus loingtiene du lignage que ou quart degré. . . ." ["It used to be that one could resort rightfully to vengeance beyond the seventh degree of kinship, and this was not surprising in those days since one could not marry within the seventh degree. But since it now has been ruled that marriage can occur beyond the fourth degree, one should not take on the wars of those more distantly related than the fourth degree. . . ."] (*Coutumes de Beauvaisis*, ed. A. Salmon [Paris: J. Picard, 1970], 2: 1686: 362).

9. See Bonnassie, *Catalogne*, p. 281; Duby, "Structures de parenté," p. 278; Fossier, *Picardie*, p. 535; Hajdu, "Poitou," p. 127.

10. Duby, "Structures de parenté," p. 283.

11. See Duby, *Mâcon*, p. 418; *Medieval Marriage* (Baltimore: Johns Hopkins University Press, 1978), pp. 10–12; and "Les 'Jeunes' dans la société aristocratique dans la France du Nord-Ouest au XIIe siècle," in *Hommes et structures*, pp. 213–224.

12. Bonnassie, *Catalogne*, p. 281; Hajdu, "Poitou," p. 123.

13. *The Grand Coutumier de Normandie*, for example, stipulates: "Sorores autem in hereditate patris nullam portionem debent reclamare versus fratres vel eorum heredes, sed maritagium possunt requirere" ["Sisters, however, can claim no part of their father's inheritance against their brothers or their heirs; but they can claim the *maritagium*"] (ed. E.-J. Tardif [Rouen: Lestrignant, 1896], p. 83).

14. See Duby, *Medieval Marriage*, chap. 1; and *Mâcon*, p. 436; C. Donahue, "The Policy of Alexander the Third's Consent Theory of Marriage," *Proceedings from the Fourth International Congress of Medieval Canon Law* (Vatican: Biblioteca Apostolica Vaticana, 1976), pp. 256, 257; M. Sheehan, "Choice of Marriage Partner in the Middle Ages: Development and Application of a Theory of Marriage," *Studies in Medieval and Renaissance History* 1 (1978): 1–33; J. Turlan, "Recherches sur le mariage dans la pratique coutumière (XIIe-XIVe siècles)," *Revue Historique du Droit Français et Etranger* 35 (1957): 477–528. Where the right of wardship was concerned, the *Grand Coutumier* reads as follows: "Si autem femina in custodia fuerit, cum ad annos nubiles venerit, per consilium et licenciam domini sui ad consilium et consensum amicorum suorum et consanguineorum et propinquorum, prout generis nobilitas et feodorum valor requisierint, debet maritari, et in contractu matrimonii debet ejus feodum a custodia liberari" ["But if the woman were in the custody of a guardian when she arrived at a marriageable age, the counsel and freedom of power of her guardian should be wedded to the advice and consent of her friends, blood relatives, and kin, as the nobility of her race and the strength of alliances demanded, and in the marriage contract her alliance should be freed from the guardianship"] (*Grand Coutumier*, p. 105).

15. See Bonnassie, *Catalogne*, pp. 268 ff.; Duby, *Mâcon*, p. 481; Fossier, *Picardie*, pp. 263 ff.; P. Ourliac and J. Malafosse, *Histoire du droit privé*, vol. 3, *Le Droit familial* (Paris: Presses Universitaires de France, 1968).

16. ["Neither a fief of hauberk, nor fief of sergeanty which belongs to the seigneurie of the duke, nor barony shall be divided"] *Très Ancien Coutumier de Normandie*, ed. E.-J. Tardif (Rouen: Cagniard, 1881), p. 7.

17. *Les Etablissements de Saint Louis*, ed. P. Viollet (Paris: Renouard, 1881), 2: 36.

18. See Bonnassie, *Catalogne*, p. 281; Duby, *Mâcon*, pp. 268 ff.; and "Lignage, noblesse, et chevalerie," p. 408; Ourliac and Malfosse, *Le Droit familial*, pp. 9, 25.

19. Beaumanoir, *Coutumes de Beauvaisis*, 1: 494: 235.

20. See E. Le Roy Ladurie, "Family Structures and Inheritance Customs in Sixteenth Century France," in *Family and Inheritance, Rural Society in Western Europe 1200–1800*, ed. J. Goody, J. Thiesk, and E. P. Thompson (Cambridge: Cambridge University Press, 1976), p. 56; Ourliac and Malafosse, *Les Biens*, p. 26; *Le Droit familial*, pp. 37, 46.

21. See R. Aubenas, "La Famille dans l'ancienne Provence," *Les Annales* 8 (1936): 523–541; Duby, *Mâcon*, p. 280; "Structures de parenté," p. 270; and "Situation de la noblesse au début du XIIIe siècle," in *Hommes et Structures*, p. 344; Hajdu, *Poitou*, p. 127; Herlihy, "The Agrarian Revolution," p. 26.

22. ["The oldest knight shall have the fief of hauberk in its entirety"] *Très Ancien Coutumier*, 2:6; *Grand Coutumier*, p. 73.

23. Beaumanoir, *Coutumes de Beauvaisis*, 1:464, 465: 223; ["A noble can only give

to his children, other than the first, a third of his inheritance"] (*Etablissements,* 2:19).

24. Ladurie, "Family Structures," p. 56. Further evidence of this principle is contained in the fact that in the regions where lineage is strongest, Normandy in particular, property passes to the children whose father predeceases them before he inherits, a procedure known as "infinite representation."

25. "Immobile autem dicimus possessionem que de loco in locum transmoveri non potest, ut ager, pratum et omnes possessiones fundo terre inherentes" (*Grand Coutumier,* p. 209). See also Ourliac and Malafosse, *Les Biens,* p. 19.

26. Beaumanoir, *Coutumes de Beauvaisis,* 1: 672, 678: 311.

27. See Ourliac and Malafosse, *Les Biens,* pp. 16, 413.

28. Beaumanoir, for example, specifies that one succession is sufficient to create a *propre*: "Chascuns doit savoir que quiconques aquiert eritages, si tost comme l'aqueste vient a ses oirs, ce devient leur propres eritages puis que l'aqueste descent un seul degré" ["Everyone should know that whoever acquires an inheritance, as soon as the acquisition comes to his heirs, that it becomes a proper of inheritance since it descends a single degree"] (*Coutumes de Beauvaisis,* 1: 505: 243). Beaumanoir's prescription is also echoed in the adage "L'aquêt du père est le propre de l'enfant."

29. *Etablissements,* 2:173, 129.

30. This paragraph is based primarily on Guerevič's article "Représentations et attitudes à l'égard de la propriété pendant le haut moyen âge," *Annales* 27 (1972): 523–547.

31. Cited in Guerevič, "Représentations," p. 526.

32. For a discussion of the possible role of climate in demographic change, see G. Duby, *Guerriers et paysans. VII-XIIe siècle: Premier essor de l'économie européenne* (Paris: Gallimard, 1973), chap. 1.

33. See N. Denholm-Young, *History and Heraldry 1254 to 1310* (Oxford: Clarendon Press, 1965); W. H. St. John Hope, *A Grammar of English Heraldry* (Cambridge: Cambridge University Press, 1953); C. Kephart, *Origins of Heraldry in Europe* (Washington, D.C.: National Genealogical Society, 1953); R. Mathieu, *Le Système héraldique français* (Paris: J. B. Janin, 1946).

34. "Au XIIe siècle, la conception familiale était résolument dynastique: on remontait vers ses ancêtres par les mâles, et lorsque, à la fin du siècle, l'usage des armoiries commença de se répandre, la symbolique héraldique s'organisa de manière à conserver le souvenir de l'origine agnatique commune dans les branches latérales dès que celles-ci se constituèrent en lignages indépendants" (G. Duby, "La Noblesse dans la France médiévale: Une enquête à poursuivre," in *Hommes et structures,* p. 152).

35. G. Brault has written an excellent study of the blazon from a linguistic point of view: *Early Blazon: Heraldic Terminology in the Twelfth and Thirteenth Centuries with Special Reference to Arthurian Literature* (Oxford: Clarendon Press, 1972).

36. Carolingian onomastics indicate dynastic and tribal preferences for certain names according to thematic variables (e.g., *Sig*frid, son of *Sig*mund; Wald*bert* and Wolf*bert*, sons of Hrum*bert*; *Amala*fridus, son of Herman*afridus* and *Amala*-berga); alliterative resonance (e.g., the Burgundian Kings Gibica, Godomarus, Gislaharius, Gundaharius, Gundevechus, Gundobadus); or the integral transfer of the name of a grandparent, uncle, or father. See K. Michaëlsson, *Etudes sur les noms de personne français* (Uppsala: Almquist, 1927), p. 184.

37. D. Herlihy, for example, has demonstrated the relatively high percentage

of matronymics in use in southern France in the tenth through twelfth centuries (see "Land, Family and Women," pp. 93–95).

38. A. Giry, *Manuel de diplomatique* (Paris: Hachette, 1894), p. 360.

39. See Duby, "Structures de parenté," p. 273; A. Dauzat, *Les Noms de personne* (Paris: Delagrave, 1950), p. 37; Michaëlsson, *Etudes*, pp. 166, 174.

40. K. Schmid, "Heirat, Familienfolge, Geschlechterbewusstsein," in *Il Matrimonio nella società altomedievale* (Spoleto: Presso del Centro, 1977), pp. 103–137; and " 'De regia Stirpe Waiblingensium' Remarques sur la conscience de soi des Staufen," in *Famille et parenté dans l'occident médiéval* (Paris: Boccard, 1977), pp. 49–56; K. F. Werner, "Liens de parenté et noms de personne: un problème historique et méthodologique," in *Famille et parenté*, pp. 13–18, 25–34.

41. Musset, "L'Aristocratie normande," p. 95; Bonnassie, *Catalogne*, p. 285; Duby, *Mâcon*, p. 418; Fossier, *Picardie*, p. 545.

42. G. Duby, "Remarques sur la littérature généalogique en France aux XIe et XIIe siècles," in *Hommes et structures*, pp. 287–298; and "Structures de parenté," ibid., pp. 266–285. Recent findings point to the fact that such genealogies were not as restricted to the North and West as Duby's work implies. See L. Génicot, *Les Généalogies* (Turnhout: Brepols, 1975); B. Guenée, *Histoire et culture historique dans l'Occident médiéval* (Paris: Aubier, 1980), pp. 31–72.

43. Duby, "Structures de parenté," p. 283.

44. Ibid., p. 281.

45. Ibid., p. 280.

46. We will have occasion later to return to the close connection between genealogical and narrative sequence (see below, pp. 96–108).

47. See R. Hanning, *The Vision of History in Early Britain* (New York: Columbia University Press, 1966), pp. 92–120.

48. Geoffrey of Monmouth, *Historia regum Britanniae*, ed. San-Marte (Halle: Eduard Anton, 1854), p. 18.

49. Wace, *Le Roman de Rou*, ed. A. J. Holden (Paris: A. and J. Picard, 1970), v. 304.

50. Benoît de Sainte Maure, *Chroniques des ducs de Normandie*, ed. C. Fahlin (Uppsala: Almquist, 1967), v. 499.

51. Ibid., v. 531.

52. See G. Duby, *Les Trois Ordres ou l'imaginaire du féodalisme* (Paris: Gallimard, 1978).

53. See J. Corblet, "Etude iconographique sur l'arbre de Jesse," *Revue de l'Art Chrétien* 4 (1860): 49–61, 113–125; G. Ladner, "Medieval and Modern Understanding of Symbolism: A Comparison," *Speculum* 54 (1979): 223–256; E. Mâle, *L'Art Religieux en France* (Paris: Armand Colin, 1925), 4: 135–173; A. Watson, *The Early Iconography of the Tree of Jesse* (Oxford: Oxford University Press, 1934).

54. "Et egredietur uirga de radice Iesse, et flos de radice eius ascendet. Et requiescet super eum spiritus Domini. . . ." (Isa. 11:1–3).

55. Cited in Watson, *Early Iconography*, p. 69.

56. Ibid.

57. A. K. Porter, "Spain or Toulouse? and Other Questions," *Art Bulletin* 7 (1924): 15.

Chapter Three

1. *Girart de Vienne*, ed. W. Van Emden (Paris: A. and J. Picard, 1977), v. 8.

2. For a discussion of the term "geste," see K. Keuck, *Historia, Geschichte des Wortes und seiner Bedeutungen in der Antike und in den romanischen Sprachen* (Emsdetten: Heinrich and J. Lechte, 1934), pp. 47–55; W. Van Emden, "Contribution à

l'étude de l'évolution du mot 'geste' en ancien français," *Romania* 96 (1975): 105–122.

3. *Girart de Vienne*, v. 41.

4. See J. Frappier, *Les Chansons de geste du cycle de Guillaume d'Orange* (Paris: Société d'Edition d'Enseignement Supérieur, 1955), 1:67.

5. MS B2, for example, contains the following indication: "ci apres comence li sieges de barbastre"; MS 24370, "Ici comence la bataille des Sagytaires et la mort d'Aymeri" (cited in Frappier, ibid., p. 50). The only modern parallel to the *geste* of Monglane is the cycle of the Rougon-Macquart, but here the conceptual framework and mode of technical elaboration are so different as to render the comparison gratuitous.

6. See R. Bezzola, "De Roland à Raoul de Cambrai," in *Mélanges Hoepffner* (Paris: Les Belles Lettres, 1949), pp. 195–213; W. C. Calin, *The Old French Epic of Revolt* (Geneva: Droz, 1961); P. Matarasso, *Recherches historiques et littéraires sur "Raoul de Cambrai"* (Paris: Nizet, 1962); and my *Medieval French Literature and Law* (Berkeley: University of California Press, 1977), pp. 70–104.

7. No survey of the connection between families of heroes and of poems would be complete without mention of two mini*gestes* that function according to the same pattern as the larger cycles. The *Geste de Nanteuil*, e.g., includes the story of *Aye d'Avignon*, wife of Garnier de Nanteuil; *Gui de Nanteuil*, son of Aye and Garnier; *Parise la Duchesse*, Guy's sister. It also contained at one time the tale of the deeds of Doon de Nanteuil, another of the sons of Aye; but this work survives only in fragments. Finally, I mention in passing a group of epics known as the *Geste des Lorrains*, which chronicles the long series of wars between the families of Lorrain and Bordelais (*La Mort de Garin le Loherenc, Guibert de Mes, Hervis de Mes, Anséis de Mes, Yon*).

8. Cicero, *De Inventione*, ed. H. M. Hubbel (Cambridge: Harvard University Press, 1976), p. 54; see also the *Rhetorica ad Herennium*, ed. H. Caplan (Cambridge: Harvard University Press, 1977), p. 24; H. Lausberg, *Handbuch der literarischen Rhetorik* (Munich: Max Hueber, 1960), 1:165–167.

9. Quintilian, *Institutio Oratoria*, ed. H. E. Butler (Cambridge: Harvard University Press, 1969), 2:224.

10. Priscian, *De Praeexercitamentis Rhetoricis*, ed. H. Keil (Hildesheim: Georg Olms, 1961), p. 431.

11. Cited in E. Faral, *Les Arts poétiques du XIIe et du XIIIe siècle* (Paris: Champion, 1971), p. 56.

12. Ibid., p. 57.

13. Ibid.

14. Ibid., p. 200.

15. P. Zumthor, *Essai de poétique médiévale* (Paris: Seuil, 1972), p. 348.

16. Wace, *Le Roman de Rou*, ed. A. J. Holden (Paris: A. and J. Picard, 1970), vv. 43 ff.

17. Ibid., v. 1.

18. ["The lady said: I cannot believe that they are not of high lineage"] Cited in Godefroy, *Dictionnaire de l'Ancien Français*, 3: col. 618c; ["Ganor the Arab was of very high lineage"] *Aye d'Avignon*, ed. S. J. Borg (Geneva: Droz, 1967), v. 3279; ["Doz the venerable was of very great lineage"] cited in Godefroy, *Dictionnaire*, 3: col. 618c; ["In order to be victorious over those who are of the Devil's lineage"] cited in Tobler-Lommatsch, *Altfranzösisches Wörterbuch*, 3: col. 1404.

19. M. Parry, "Studies in the Epic Technique of Oral Verse-Making, I: Homer and Homeric Style," *Harvard Studies in Classical Philology* 41 (1930): 80. See also J. Rychner, *La Chanson de geste: essai sur l'art épique des jongleurs* (Geneva: Droz, 1955);

A. Lord, *The Singer of Tales* (New York: Atheneum, 1965); S. Nichols, *Formulaic Diction and Thematic Composition in the Chanson de Roland, University of North Carolina Studies in Romance Languages and Literatures* 36 (1961); J. Duggan, *The Song of Roland: Formulaic Style and Poetic Craft* (Berkeley: University of California Press, 1973).

20. E. Vance, *Reading the Song of Roland* (Englewood Cliffs, N.J.: Prentice-Hall, 1971), p. 32; A. Parry, "The Language of Achilles," *Transactions and Proceedings of the American Philological Association* 87 (1956): 3; E. Auerbach, "Roland against Ganelon," in *Mimesis*, trans. W. Trask (New York: Doubleday, 1957), pp. 83–107.

21. Auerbach, *Mimesis*, p. 92.

22. See J. Rychner, *L'Articulation des phrases narratives dans "La Mort Artu"* (Geneva: Droz, 1970); R. H. Bloch, "The Text as Inquest: Form and Function in the Pseudo-Map Cycle," *Mosaic* 8 (1975): 107–119.

23. See in particular Vance, *Reading Roland*, chap. 8; J. Halverson, "Ganelon's Trial," *Speculum* 42 (1967): 661–669.

24. This is not to imply that the family line remains free from deviation by marriage, the introduction of new members, or even illegitimacy, but that it stands, despite such obliquities, as a connected series.

25. K. Schmid, "Heirat, Familienfolge, Geschlechterbewusstsein," in *Il Matrimonio nella società altomedievale* (Spoleto: Presso del Centro, 1977), p. 128.

26. ["By my beard, if I ever see my noble sister Aude again, you will never lie in her arms"] *Roland*, v. 1719.

27. Trans. G. Brault.

28. ["At the baths at Aix the c . . . (?) are very large. There they baptized the Queen of Spain: They found for her the name Juliane"] *Roland*, v. 3984.

29. Trans. G. Brault; see n. 30 for interpretation of this last line.

30. Herein lies, I think, yet another meaning of the highly ambiguous last line of the poem ("Ci falt la geste que Turoldus declinet"): "Here ends the poem because Turoldus declines [is fatigued]"; "Here ends the cycle that Turoldus declines [narrates]"; "Here ends the chronicle that Turoldus portrays"; "Here breaks the narrative [*geste*] that Turoldus recounts"; but also, "Here ends the family [*geste*] that Turoldus delineates."

31. Two possible exceptions to this sweeping generalization are *Le Charroi de Nîmes* and *Le Pèlerinage de Charlemagne*.

32. ["I think that the world will not last long according to what Scripture says, since now the son fails the father and the father the son in turn."]

33.
> "Car qui l'autrui con capusa
> Lo sieu tramet al mazel,
> E qui l'estraing vol sentir,
> Lo sieu fai enleconir
> E·l met en la comunailla."
> [Marcabru, p. 205]

The following verses are also relevant:
> "Moillerat, per saint Ylaire,
> Son d'una foldat confraire,
> Qu'entre'els es guerra moguda
> Tals que cornutz fa cornuda,
> E cogotz copatz copada,
> Puois eis la coa de braire."
> [Ibid., p. 20]

"Husbands by Saint Hilary share a common folly, for among them there has irrupted a war such that the one who wears horns makes his wife wear them; the cuckold cuckolded cuckolds his wife, and then ends by braying."

> "Maritz qui l'autrui con grata
> Ben pot saber que·l sieus pescha
> E mostra com hom li mescha,
> Qu'ab eis lo sieu fust lo bata,
> Et aura·n tort si s'en clama,
> Car drech e raços deviza
> Que qui car compra car ven,
> Ar, segon la lei de Piza."
>
> [Ibid., p. 45; see also p. 32]

"The husband who scratches the cunt of another should know that his own sins on her side and prepares an evil brew and a beating with her own stick. He would be wrong to complain because right and reason judge this way: that he who buys dearly must sell dearly, according to the law of Pisa."

34.
> "Eyssamens son domnas trichans
> E sabon trichar e mentir
> Per que fan los autrus enfans
> Als maritz tener e noyrir";
>
> [Ibid., p. 166]

35.
> "Mos alos es
> En tal deves
> Res mas ieu non s'en pot jauzir . . . ,
> De pluzors sens
> Sui ples e prens
> De cent colors per mieills chauzir;
>   Fog porti sai
>   Et aigua lai,
> Ab que sai la flam' escantir."
>
> [Ibid., p. 67]

36. *The Life and Works of the Troubadour Raimbaut d'Orange,* ed. W. T. Pattison (Minneapolis: University of Minnesota Press, 1952), p. 75.

37. Ibid., p. 65.

38. Ibid., p. 191.

39. ["I mix words and I refine the melody, as the tongue is intertwined in a kiss"] *Les Poésies de Bernart Marti,* ed. E. Hoepffner (Paris: Champion, 1929), p. 11.

> "Maritz que marit fai sufren
> Deu tastar d'atretal sabor,
> Que car deu comprar qui car ven;
> E·l gelos met li guardador,
> Pueys li laissa sa molher prenh
> D'un girbaudo, filh de girbau."
>
> [Ibid., p. 34]

"A husband who tricks a husband must taste the same sauce, for he who buys dearly must sell dearly; and the jealous one provides a guardian who later leaves his wife pregnant with a rogue, son of a rogue."

40. Ibid., p. 5.

41. "Lo dreyt torna daus l'envers" (ibid., p. 4).

42. Zumthor, *Essai*, p. 218.

43. J. Boutière and A.-H. Schutz, *Biographies des troubadours* (Paris: Nizet, 1964), p. 264; cited in U. Mölk, *Trobar Clus Trobar Leu* (Munich: Fink, 1968), p. 104; *Jongleurs et troubadours gascons*, ed. A. Jeanroy (Paris: Champion, 1957), p. 13.

44. "Farai un vers de dreyt nien:
　　　Non er de mi ni d'autra gen,
　　　Non er d'amor ni de joven,
　　　　Ni de ren au,
　　　Qu'enans fo trobatz en durmen
　　　　Sobre chevau."

[William IX, p. 6]

"I will write a poem about nothing: It is not about me nor anyone else. It is not about love or youth, nor anything. It was composed while asleep upon my horse."

45. "He is held to be low-born who does not understand it [my verse] or who does not willingly learn it by heart; such a one who finds it to his taste will separate himself from love only with difficulty."

46. Peire d'Alvernha links such linguistic ambiguity directly to confusion or "puzzlement" in the household:

　　　"C'a un tenen, ses mot borrel,
　　　Deu de dir esser avinens;
　　　Quar qui trassail de Mauri en Miro
　　　Entre·l mieg faill—si no·s pren als ladriers!
　　　Com del treball quecs motz fa·s messatgiers,
　　　Qu'en devinaill met l'auzir, de maiso."

"For in a straightforward fashion, without fill-up phrases, one should be pleasant in one's speech, since he who wavers between Mauri and Miro slips down in-between—unless he hangs on to the sides! As each word acts as a herald of the labor [behind it], so he turns listening into a puzzle for the whole household." [*Anthology of Troubadour Lyric Poetry*, ed. and trans. A. R. Press (Austin: University of Texas Press, 1971), p. 90]

47. "Anc no li diz ni bat ni but,
　　　Ni fer ni fust no ai mentaugut,
　　　　Mas sol aitan:
　　　'Babariol, babariol,
　　　　Babarian.'"

[William IX, p. 10]

48. "Translatio est cum verbum in quandam rem transferetur ex alia re, quod propter similitudinem recte videbitur posse transferri" (*Ad Herennium*, p. 342); "Tropus est verbi vel sermonis a propria significatione in aliam cum virtute mutatio" (*Institutio Oratoria*, 3:300); Augustine, *De Doctrina Christiana*, ed. G. Combès and M. Farges (Paris: Desclée de Brouwer, 1949), p. 258. See Lausberg, *Handbuch*, 1:285–291; J. Murphy, *Rhetoric in the Middle Ages: A History of Rhetorical Theory from Saint Augustine to the Renaissance* (Berkeley: University of California Press, 1974), p. 33.

49. H. Keil, *Grammatici Latini* (Hildesheim: Georg Olds, 1961), 1:456.

50. Notker Labeo, *Ars Rhetorica*, ed. P. Piper (Freiburg, Tubingen: J. C. B. Mohr, 1882), p. 671.

51. Faral, *Arts poétiques*, p. 86.

52. D. M. Inguanez and H. M. Willard, *Alberici Casinensis Flores rhetorici*, in *Miscellanea Cassinese* 14 (1938): 38, 42; see also Mölk, *Trobar clus*, pp. 194–196.

53. See Mölk, *Trobar clus*, pp. 177–194; E. Köhler, *Trobadorlyrik und höfischer Roman* (Berlin: Rütter and Loening, 1962), pp. 133–150.

54. Faral, *Arts poétiques*, pp. 221–245.

55. ["Do not always allow a word to reside in its proper place: for such a residence is a source of shame for the word in question; it should avoid its proper places and after travelling establish elsewhere a pleasing site on another's property; there it should be a new guest"] Ibid., p. 220.

56. "Propria est quando voces in illo sensu proferuntur in quo prius sunt reperte, ut *homines rident*. Figurativa locutio est ubi voces de propria significatione ad aliam significationem transferuntur convenienter, ut *pratar rident*. Vitiosa est locutio ubi est translatio inconveniens, ut *Neptunias lacunas*" (*Notices*, p. 234; see also p. 83).

57. "Propria sunt verba, cum id significant, in quod primo denominata sunt; translata, cum alium natura intellectum alium loco praebent" (Quintilian, *Institutio Oratoria*, 1:110).

58. This is not to deny that metaphor stands as a powerful tool for the recuperation of a higher truth as it is used especially in Biblical exegesis.

59.   "Longius ut sit opus, ne ponas nomina rerum:
        Pone notas alias; nec plane detege, sed rem
        Innue per notulas; nec sermo perambulet in re,
        Sed rem circuiens longis ambagibus ambi
        Quod breviter dicturus eras, et tempora tardes, . . ."

[Faral, *Arts poétiques*, p. 204]

What Geoffrey suggests as a principle of poetic elaboration is what Raimbaut d'Aurenga intends by "caulking" with words (see above, p. 112), and Peire d'Alvernha by "filling up of phrases" (see n. 46, p. 54).

60. Albert of Monte Cassino, *Flores rhetorici*, p. 45.

61. *The Songs of Bernart de Ventadorn*, ed. S. G. Nichols (Chapel Hill: University of North Carolina Press, 1962), p. 87.

62. See P. Bec, "La Douleur et son univers poétique chez Bernard de Ventadour," *Cahiers de Civilisation Médiévale* 9 (1968): 545–571; 12 (1969): 25–33; G. Lavis, *L'Expression de l'affectivité dans la poésie lyrique française du moyen âge (XIIe–XIIIe s.): étude sémantique et stylistique du réseau lexical joie-douleur* (Paris: Les Belles Lettres, 1972).

63. Elsewhere Bernart affirms, ["a hundred times a day I die of sorrow, and I revive another hundred"] "cen vetz mor lo jorn de dolor/ e reviu de joi autras cen" (ibid., p. 132).

64. See Zumthor, *Essai*, p. 216.

65. Bernart de Ventadorn, *Songs*, p. 60.

66. "Mas totas res pot om en mal escrire" (ibid., p. 72).

67. Ibid., p. 68.

68. Ibid., p. 129.

69. The Chatelain de Coucy, for example, speaks of a "tresdous mals," of "loial folie ou sage traison," of walking "mort vivant." He is torn by paradoxes of joy and suffering that would have been familiar to Bernart:

        "Par mainte fois m'effroie
        Amors et foit pensant,

> Et sovent me rapaie
> Et done cuer ioiant:
> Ensi me fait vivre mesleement
> D'ire et de ioie."
>
> > > [*Die Lieder des Castellans von Coucy*, ed. F. Fath
> > > (Heidelberg: Theodor Groos, 1888), p. 53]

"Many times love scares me and makes me pensive, and often repays me and makes me joyful: Thus he makes me live ambiguously on pain and joy"

Again, like Bernart, the poet is suspended between conflicting emotions:

> "E ie sui, las, de che en tel balanche,
> K'a mains iointes aor
> Ma bele mort ou ma haute richor,
> Ne sai lekel, s'en ai ioie et paor,
> Si ke sovent cant la ou de cuer plor."
>
> > > [Ibid., p. 60]

"I am trapped in such a bind that, hands joined, I worship my sweet death or my good fortune. I do not know which, since I have such joy and fear that often I sing when my heart is full of tears."

The Chatelain de Coucy submits to a drama of uncertainty ("Ne ne sai, se vif ou non, / Ou se i'ai tort ou raison, / ou se i'aim ou ch'est noiens" [Ibid., p. 45]) that breeds paranoia and passivity: "Je ne m'en sai vengier fors au plorer"; "Tant com li plaist, me puet faire languir"; "Et quant mi mal li sont bel e plaisans, / Por ceu me hac et sui mes mal vueillans" ["I can only venge myself through tears"; "As long as it pleases her, she can make me languish"; "And to the degree that my hurt is sweet and pleasant to her, she hates me for it and I am more conscious of my wounds"] (ibid., pp. 55, 70, 59). The most thorough treatment of the "semiotics of interruption" in the verse of a northern poet is to be found in P. Haidu's "Text and History: The Semiosis of Twelfth-Century Lyric as Sociohistorical Phenomenon," *Semiotica* 33 (1981): 1–62.

70. Press, *Anthology*, p. 116 (editor's translation).

71. M. Shell, "Money and the Mind: The Economics of Translation in Goethe's *Faust*," *Modern Language Notes* 95 (1980): 515–562.

72. Albert of Monte Cassino, *Flores rhetorici*, p. 45.

Chapter Four

1. E. Köhler, "Zur Diskussion der Adelsfrage bei den Trobadors," in *Trobadorlyrik und höfischer Roman* (Berlin: Rütter and Loening, 1962), pp. 115–132.

2. Andreas Capellanus, *De Amore*, ed. S. Battaglia (Rome: Perrella, 1947), pp. 22, 42; see also Jean de Meun, *Rose*, vv. 18619, 18811, 18855.

3. Andreas, *De Amore*, pp. 24–176.

4. "Paubres e rics fai amdos d'un paratge"; "bel' e conhd', ab cors covinen, / m'a faih ric ome de nien" (*The Songs of Bernart de Ventadorn*, ed. S. Nichols [Chapel Hill: University of North Carolina Press, 1962], pp. 163, 81).

5. ["One doesn't love a lady for her lineage, but because she is beautiful and courtly and wise. In time you will learn this truth"] *Chansons de Conon de Béthune*, ed. A. Wallensköld (Helsingfors: Imprimerie Centrale de Helsingfors, 1891), p. 243.

6. "Lo plus fi, ab qu'aya meyns proder: / Qu'on meyns er ricx, mais vos o graziria" (cited in U. Mölk, *Trobar clus Trobar leu* [Munich: Fink, 1968], p. 22).

7. *Sämtliche Lieder des Trobadors Giraut de Bornelh*, ed. A. Kolsen (Halle: Niemeyer, 1910), 1:380.

8. "Virtute decet, non sanguine, niti: / Nobilitas animi sola est atque unica virtus" (Faral, *Arts poétiques du XIIe et du XIIIe siècle* [Paris: Champion, 1971], p. 116).

9. *Las Leys D'Amors*, ed. M. Gatien Arnoult (Toulouse: Bon et Privat, 1841), 3:20.

10. Ibid., p. 22.

11. Ibid., p. 24.

12. We spoke earlier of a distinction between a mode of possession appropriate to males (*l'immeuble, propre, real* estate) and to females (*les meubles*, personal property, chattel) (see above, pp. 71–73). Here it seems that we also affirm an affinity between the mobility of feminine property and the mobility of the discourse of the lyric. The quintessential form of mobile wealth is, of course, money, which we associated at the end of the preceding chapter with metaphor. The corresponding quintessential form of mobile literary language is the *canso* or *chanson*. It is, moreover, in this sense that we ought to conceive of the courtly lyric as feminine poetry and not because it is addressed to, speaks about, or idealizes women.

13. I am indebted to A. Leupin's "Ecriture naturelle et écriture hermaphrodite" for the initial introduction of Alain to the present discussion (*Digraphe* 9 [1976]: 119–141); see also E. Vance, "Désir, rhétorique et texte," *Poétique* 42 (1980): 137–155; M.-R. Jung, *Etudes sur le poème allégorique en France au moyen âge* (Berne: Francke, 1971), pp. 64–88; G. Raynaud de Lage, *Alain de Lille, poète du XIIe siècle* (Montreal: Institut d'Etudes Médiévales, 1951).

14. " . . . Venerem . . . collocavi, ut ipsa . . . humani generis seriem indefessa continuatione contexeret, ne Parcarum manibus intercisa discidii injurias sustineret" (*De Planctu*, 2:470).

15. "Praeterea Cypridi mea indixit praeceptio, ut ipsa in suis constructionibus, suppositiones appositionesque ordinarias observando, rem feminini sexus charactere praesignitam suppositionis destinaret officio; rem vero specificatem masculini generis intersignis sede collocaret appositi. . . ." ["Furthermore, my command enjoined Cypris that, in her constructions, she have regard to the ordinary rules for nouns and adjectives, and that she appoint that organ which is especially marked with the peculiarity of the feminine sex to the office of noun, and that she should put that organ characterized by the signs of the masculine sex in the seat of the adjective"] (ibid., p. 476).

16. "Dionae igitur duo dati sunt filii, descrepantia generis disparati, nascendi leges dissimiles. . . . Hymenaeus namque uterinae fraternitatis mihi affinis confinio, . . . ex Venere sibi Cupidinem propagavit in filium. Antigamus vero, scurrilis, ignobilitatis genere derivatus, adulterando cum Venere adulterinum filium jocum sibi joculatorie parentavit" ["To Dione, then, were given two sons, divided by difference in kind, unlike by law of their birth. . . . For Hymen, who is related to me by the bond of brotherhood from the same mother, . . . sired from Venus his son Cupid. But Antigamus, scurrilous and descended from a race of ignobility, by his adultery with Venus has lightly become the father of an illegitimate son Mirth"] (ibid., p. 481). It is to be noted that linguistic theory and ethics were implicated in each other throughout the period in question, grammar and rhetoric being organized in terms of *virtutes* and *vitia*.

17. " . . . sed potius se grammaticis constructionibus destruens, dialecticis conversionibus se invertens, rhetoricis coloribus decoloratis, suam artem in figuram, figuramque in vitium transferebat" (ibid., p. 480).

18. " . . . sibi legem generis deponentis assumere" (ibid., p. 477);
   "Predicat et subjicit, fit duplex terminus idem,
   Grammaticae leges ampliat ille nimis.
   Se negat esse virum, Naturae factus in arte,
   Barbarus; ars illi non placet, immo tropus.
   Non tamen ista tropus poterit translatio dici;
   In vitium melius ista figura cadit."

[Ibid., p. 429]

19. See Vance, "Désir, rhétorique et texte."

20. As is evident in even so brief a reading of Alain's text, nature and society are by no means conceived as antagonistic, but as allied, principles.

21. "Mes Nature, douce et piteuse,
   Quant el voit que Mors l'envieuse,
   Entre li et corruption,
   Vuelent metre a destrucion
   Quanque trovent, dedenz sa forge
   Touz jors martele, touz jorz forge,
   Touz jors ses pieces renovele
   Par generacion novele."

[*Rose*, v. 16005]

"But sweet and piteous Nature, who sees that envious Death along with corruption want to destroy all they can lay hold of, hammers and forges all the time to renew her pieces through new generation."

22. "Genius, dist elle, biau prestres,
   Qui des leus estes diex et mestres,
   Et selonc lor propriétés
   Toutes en ovre les metés,
   Et bien achevés le besoingne
   Si cum a chascun le besoingne. . . ."

[Ibid., v. 16285]

"'Genius,' she said, 'good priest who are god and master of places, and who, according to their properties, make them work together, and finish the task as each needs. . . .'"

23. "Nature, qui pensoit des choses
   Qui sont dessous le ciel encloses,
   Dedens sa forge entree estoit,
   Ou toute s'entente metoit
   A forgier singulieres pieces
   Por continuer les espieces. . . ."

[Ibid., v. 15893]

"Nature, who takes care of all earthly things, entered into her forge where she put all her effort into forging the individual pieces for the survival of the species. . . ."

24. "Jadiz au temps des premiers peres
   Et de nos premerainnes meres, . . .
   Furent amors loiaus et fines,
   Sanz convoitise et sanz rapines. . . ."

   . . . .
   "Encor n'i avoit roi ne prince
   Meffais, qui l'autrui tout et pince.

Tretuit pareil estre soloient,
Ne rienz propre avoir ne voloient."
[Ibid., vv. 8355, 8445]

"In the good old days of our first fathers and mothers, love was loyal and refined, without desire and without depredation. . . ."

"At that time there were not yet evil-doing kings or princes, who rob and squeeze others. Everyone was equal and no one desired to own anything for himself."

25.   "Biaus amis, je puis bien nommer,
Sanz moi faire mal renomer
Proprement, par le propre non
Chose qui n'est se bonne non.
Voire du mal seürement
Puis je bien parler proprement,
Car de nulle chose n'ai honte,
Se tele n'est qu'a pechié monte."
[Ibid., v. 6945]

"Sweet friend, I can, without incurring the risk of a bad reputation, name properly, by the proper name, any good thing. What's more, I can even speak properly of evil, for I am ashamed of nothing if it is not a sin."
26. ["How's that, by the body of Saint Homer, I wouldn't name properly my father's works?"; "But even if God made things, at least he did not make their names"] Ibid., vv. 7123, 7084; see D. Poirion, "De la signification selon Jean de Meun," forthcoming in *Archéologie du signe*, ed. L. Brind-Amour and E. Vance (Toronto: Pontifical Institute, 1982); and "Les Mots et les choses selon Jean de Meun," *Information Littéraire* 26 (1974): 7–11.

27.   "Se je, quant mis les nons as choses
Que si reprendre et blamer oses,
Coilles reliques appelasse
Et reliques coilles nomasse,
Tu, qui se m'en mort et depiques,
Me redeïsses de reliques
Que ce fust lais mos et vilains."
[*Rose*, v. 7109]

"If I had, when I imposed names on things (which you dare to reproach and blame), called balls 'relics,' you, who so bite and bother me, would have said that 'relics' is an ugly and evil word."
28. ["I know well how to change my clothes, put on one set and take the other off. . . . Now I am prince and now page, since I am master of all tongues"] Ibid., v. 11187.
29. " . . . cum jam me solum in mundo superesse philosophum estimarem nec ullam ulterius inquietationem formidarem, frena libidini cepi laxare, qui antea vixeram continentissime" (Abelard, *Historia*, p. 70).
30. "Apertis itaque libris, plura de amore quam de lectione verba se ingerebant, plura erant oscula quam sententie; sepius ad sinus quam ad libros reducebantur manus, crebrius oculos amor in se reflectebat quam lectio in scripturam dirigebat" (ibid., p. 72).
31. See R. Girard, "De 'La Divine Comédie' à la sociologie du roman," *Revue de l'Institut de Sociologie de Bruxelles* 36 (1963): 263–280.

32. ["It so happened that at the outset I devoted myself to analyzing the basis of our faith through illustrations based on human understanding, and I wrote for my students a certain tract on the unity and trinity of God"] *Historia*, p. 82.

33. "Non curamus, inquit ille, rationem humanam aut sensum vestrum in talibus, sed auctoritatis verba solummodo" (ibid., p. 84).

34. " . . . cum Deus Deum genuerit, nec nisi unus Deus sit, negarem tamen Deum se ipsum genuisse" (ibid., p. 84).

35. See M. Colish, *The Mirror of Language: A Study in the Medieval Theory of Knowledge* (New Haven: Yale University Press, 1968), chap. 2.

36. See J. Jolivet, *Arts du langage et théologie chez Abélard* (Paris: J. Vrin, 1969), pp. 306–307; M. de Gandillac, *Oeuvres choisies d'Abélard* (Paris: Aubier, 1945), pp. 51–58.

37. " . . . transmisi eam ad abbatiam quandam sanctimonialium . . . que Argenteolum appellatur, ubi ipsa olim puellula educata fuerat atque erudita, . . . Quo audito, avunculus et consanguinei seu affines ejus opinati sunt me nunc sibi plurimum illusisse, et ab ea moniali facta me sic facile velle expedire. Unde vehementer indignate et adversum me conjurati, . . . eis videlicet corporis mei partibus amputatis quibus id quod plangebant commiseram" [" . . . I sent her to a convent of nuns at Argenteuil . . . where she herself had been brought up and educated as a young girl. . . . When her uncle and his kinsmen heard of this, they were convinced that now I had completely played them false and had rid myself forever of Heloise by forcing her to become a nun. Violently insensed, they laid a plot against me . . . , for they cut off those parts of my body with which I had done that thing which was the cause of their sorrow"] (*Historia*, p. 79). It is interesting to note that Jean de Meun also focuses upon the kidnapping of Heloise rather than the sexual act as the cause of castration: "Car puisqu'el fu, si cum moi semble, / Par l'acort d'ambedeus ensemble, / D'Argentuel nonain revestue, / Fu la coille a Pierre tolue. . . ." ["Since it was by an agreement between them that she should take the veil at Argenteuil, Peter lost his balls. . . ."] (*Rose*, v. 8793).

38. I am indebted to E. Vance for bringing my attention to this point.

39. M. de Gandillac, for example, contrasts Abelard's sense of the strict intransmissibility of guilt with Saint Bernard's seemingly primogenital law of moral inheritance (see *Oeuvres choisies*, p. 59).

40. Petrus Abaelardus, *Dialectica*, ed. L. M. De Rijk (Assen: Van Gorcum, 1956), p. 128.

41. "Si vero interpretatio ethymologiam fecerit, ut videlicet magis secundum nominis compositionem quam secundum rei substantiam fiat. . . ." (ibid., p. 339).

42. ["Since an interpretation of this kind pursues the composition of the name only instead of revealing the property of the thing itself, it does not attain any credibility] Ibid.

43. Jolivet, *Abélard*, p. 74.

44. "Praeter rem et intellectum tertia exiit nominum significatio" (Abelard, *Philosophische Schriften*, ed. B. Geyer [Munster: Aschendorff, 1923], 1:24).

45. Ibid., p. 16. See also de Gandillac, *Oeuvres choisies*, p. 102; M. Carré, *Realists and Nominalists* (Oxford: Oxford University Press, 1946), p. 45; P. Vignaux, article on Nominalism in *Dictionnaire de théologie catholique* 11 (1931): cols. 718–784; M. Tweedale, *Abailard on Universals* (New York: North-Holland, 1976).

46. "Est autem universale vocabulum quod de pluribus singillatum habile est ex inventione sua praedicari, ut hoc nomen 'homo,' quod particularibus nominibus hominum coniungibile est secundum subjectarum rerum naturam quibus est impositum" (Abelard, *Philosophische Schriften*).

47. "Non itaque propositiones res aliquas designant simpliciter, quemadmodum nomina, immo qualiter sese ad invicem habent, utrum scilicet sibi conveniant annon, apponunt. . . ." (Abaelardus, *Dialectica*, p. 160).

48. Ibid.; Jolivet, *Abélard*, p. 82.

49. See G. Leff, *William of Ockham: The Metamorphosis of Scholastic Discourse* (Manchester: Manchester University Press, 1975), pp. 145 ff.; Vignaux, *Nominalism*, col. 7333; C. Panaccio, "Guillaume d'Occam: Signification et Supposition," in *Archéologie du signe*; Ockham, *Philosophical Writings*, ed. P. Boehner (New York: Nelson, 1962), pp. i–liv.

50. " . . . non est universale nisi per significationem, quia est signum plurium." ["Nothing is universal except by signification, by being a sign of several things"] (Ockham, *Philosophical Writings*, p. 33).

51. Occamist apocrypha notwithstanding, Ockham never mentions specifically the "razor" associated with his name. Boehner has culled a number of quotations upon which the concept of the razor can be built, and he resumes them as follows: "We are not allowed to affirm a statement to be true or to maintain that a certain thing exists, unless we are forced to do so either by its self-evidence or by revelation or by experience or by a logical deduction from either a revealed truth or a proposition verified by observation" (ibid., p. xx).

52. Actually, the *modistae* represent the second generation of speculative grammarians, refiners as they were of the works of William of Conches, Peter Helias, Robert Kilwardby. See R. Bursill-Hall, *Speculative Grammars of the Middle Ages* (Paris: Mouton, 1971), p. 35.

53. " . . . in duo diuiditur, scilicet in scienciam considerandi et obseruandi quid unaqueque dictio significet apud gentem illam cuius lingua est, et in scienciam obseruandi regulas illarum dictionum" (Dominicus Gundissalinus, *De Divisione Philosophiae*, ed. L. Baur [Munster: Aschendorff, 1903], p. 45).

54. " . . . illa uariatur apud omnes secundum diuersitatem linguarum, hec pene eadem est apud omnes secundum similitudinem regularum. . . ." (ibid., p. 46).

55. " . . . conditiones sunt impermutabiles et eedem apud omnes. . . ." (cited in J. Pinborg, *Sprachtheorie im Mittelalter* [Copenhagen: Arne Frost-Hansen, 1967], p. 27).

56. An anonymous Parisian grammarian expresses this relation as follows: "Grammatica est de sermone significante modos rerum generales . . . unde ipsa vox articulata non est eadem apud omnes ratione principiorum materialium, que sunt litere, sunt tamen heedem apud omnes ratione principiorum formalium, et voco principia formalia, quod litere sic ordinantur in sillaba, sillabe in dictione, et dictiones in oratione ab conformitate accidentium: et hee sunt eadem apud omnes" ["Grammar concerns speech that signifies the general modes for things; thus a particular sound is not articulated the same in all cases because of material principles, that is, letters; but it is articulated the same in all cases according to formal principles. By formal principles I mean how letters are arranged in a syllable, how syllables are arranged in a word, and how words are arranged in a phrase in keeping with accidents: these principles are constant in all cases"] (cited in Pinborg, *Sprachtheorie*, p. 28).

57. " . . . non erit subiectum grammaticae. . . ." (cited in Bursill-Hall, *Speculative Grammars*, p. 38). Robert states elsewhere: "Constructibilia et principia materialia constructionis et eorum principia essentialia eadem sunt apud omnes. . . . Diversificantur tamen apud diversos actualiter, ut per diversa accidentia et per diversas vocis appellationes" ["The compositional, material principles of construction and

their essential principles are the same in all cases . . . but in practice there is diversity among different elements, due, for instance, to different accidents and different names for a sound"] (*Notices*, p. 125). R. Bacon concurs: " . . . grammatica una et eadem est secundum substantiam in omnibus linguis, licet accidentaliter varietur" ["Grammar is one and the same according to substance in every language, though it is varied according to accidents"] (cited in Bursill-Hall, *Speculative Grammars*, p. 38).

58. An anonymous thirteenth-century commentator: "Utrum sit necessaria. Sic, et in se, quia procedit per principia, respectu quorum posteriora impossibile est aliter se habere. . . . Utrum modus sciendi demonstrativus possibilis sit in gramatica. Sic. Ut in aliis scientiis principia communia et principia propria sunt indemonstrabilia, cognitiones autem que ex hiis sequuntur per illa sunt demonstrabiles, sic est in gramatica" (*Notices*, p. 128).

59. See Bursill-Hall, *Speculative Grammars*, pp. 38, 83.

60. ["The properties of things are distinguished in turn by the parts of speech"] Cited in ibid., p. 93.

61. Ibid., p. 40.

62. ["Just as to the constitution of the species correspond genus and specific difference, so the general and specific modes of signification correspond to the constitution of the parts of speech"] Cited in ibid., p. 58.

63. "Inter istos autem terminos aliquae differentiae reperiuntur. Una est, quod conceptus sive passio animae naturaliter significat quidquid significat; terminus autem prolatus vel scriptus nihil significat nisi secundum voluntariam institutionem" (William of Ockham, *Summa logicae*, ed. P. Boehner [Saint Bonaventure, N.Y.: Franciscan Institute, 1951], 1:8).

64. Their grammatical model is, of course, still that of Latin.

65. Cited in R. W. Hunt, "Studies on Priscian in the Twelfth-Century—II: The School of Ralph of Beauvais," *Medieval and Renaissance Studies* 2 (1950): 26.

66. Bursill-Hall, *Speculative Grammars*, p. 59.

67. Here is where our use of the term metonymic breaks with that of R. Jakobson since he uses it to refer to syntax, and metaphor to refer to lexical substitution (*Essais de linguistique générale* [Paris: Editions de Minuit, 1963], pp. 43–67).

68. ["Grammar . . . is concerned with the expression of the concept of the mind through the congruent verbal term"] (cited in Bursill-Hall, *Speculative Grammars*, p. 67; see also pp. 60 ff.).

69. Ibid., p. 75; see also Pinborg, *Sprachtheorie*, pp. 29, 37.

70. ["Consequently, since tense belongs to verbs does it not also suit nouns?"] Abelard, *Dialectica*, p. 123; ["Not therefore in the signification of time is the noun seen to differ from the verb, but in its mode of signifying"] cited in ibid.

71. ["Hic in essentia cursus ostenditur, ibi in adjacentia"] Cited in J. Jolivet, "Comparaison des théories du langage chez Abélard et chez les nominalistes du XIVe siècle," in Peter Abelard, *Proceedings of the International Conference* (Hague: Nijhoff, 1974), p. 173.

72. ["A mode of signifying in speech to signify substance with quality"; "another mode of signifying to signify action or movement"] *Notices*, p. 154.

73. "Non distinguuntur partes orationis secundum distinctionem rerum, sed secundum distinctionem modorum significandi" (cited in Pinborg, *Sprachtheorie*, p. 48).

74. Thomas of Erfurt: ". . . in una et eadem re possunt reperiri diversae proprietates rei non repugnantes, a quibus sumi possunt diversi modi signifi-

candi activi licet una vox non imponatur ei, ut stat sub ombibus [*sic*] illis proprietatibus, sed quandoque imponatur una vox, ut stat sub una proprietate, quandoque
alia vox, ut sub alia proprietate" ["In one and the same thing different properties
can be found that do not contradict the things; from them different modes of
signifying the active element can be drawn, although one sign should not be
imposed upon it, since it is subsumed under all those properties; yet sometimes
one sign should be imposed when it is subsumed under one property, and
sometimes another sign, when it is subsumed under another property"] (Bursill-
Hall, *Speculative Grammars*, p. 76).

75. " . . . haec res, albedo, habet diversas proprietates, sub quibus possunt ei
imponi diversae voces. Nam si consideretur in ea modus entis, qui est modus
habitus et permanentis, sic significatur per vocem nominis absolute. Si autem
consideretur in ea modus entis, et cum hoc modus essentiae determinatae, sic
significatur voce nominis substantivi, ut albedo. Si autem consideretur in ea
modus entis et cum hoc modus inhaerentiae alteri secundum essentiam, sic
significatur in voce nominis adiectivi, ut albus" [" . . . this thing, *albedo* (whiteness), possesses different properties beneath which it can accept the imposition of
different signs. For if it is understood in the mode of being, which is the mode of
permanent condition, its meaning is then derived from the sign of the absolute
term. But if it is understood in the mode of being alone, with the mode of fixed
essence, then its meaning comes from the sign of the substantive, for instance
albedo. And if it is understood in the mode of being along with the mode of
adhering to something else in conformity with the essence, its meaning then is
expressed in the sign of the adjective, for instance *albus* (white)"] (ibid.).

Chapter Five

1. See J. Dauvillier, *Le Mariage dans le droit classique de l'Eglise* (Paris: Sirey, 1933),
pp. 13–52; G. Duby, *Medieval Marriage* (Baltimore: Johns Hopkins University
Press, 1978), pp. 1–24; A. Esmein, *Le Mariage en droit canonique* (Paris: Sirey, 1929),
1: 60–91; G. E. Howard, *A History of Matrimonial Institutions* (Chicago: University
of Chicago Press, 1904), 1:315, 351; J. Noonan, "Power to Choose," *Viator* 4 (1973):
419–434; E. Schillebeeckx, *Le Mariage* (Paris: Cerf, 1966), pp. 254–264; M. Sheehan,
"Choice of Marriage Partner in the Middle Ages: Development and Mode of
Application of a Theory of Marriage," *Studies in Medieval and Renaissance History*
1 (1978): 1–33.

2. *Petri Lombardi, Libri IV Sententiarum* (New York: Saint Bonaventure, 1916),
2: 917. See also Dauvillier, *Le Mariage*, pp. 12–17; Duby, *Medieval Marriage*, pp.
16–25; Esmein, *Le Mariage*, 1:131; Schillebeeckx, *Le Mariage*, p. 256.

3. Actually, there is some debate about the status of parental ratification in
Gratian's writing; see Dauvillier, *Le Mariage*, pp. 8, 23–29; Esmein, *Le Mariage*,
1:103; Howard, *Matrimonial Institutions*, p. 336; Schillebeeckx, *Le Mariage*, p. 258.

4. " . . . sufficiat secundum leges solus eorum consensus, de quorum conjunc-
tionibus agitur . . . " (*PL*, 187: col. 1392). Interestingly enough, the example used
in such a determination is that of Christ who, in dying, commended his mother to
his disciple and not to Joseph. Gratian reasons that, since Christ could not have
condoned divorce, the Virgin must not have been indissolubly married: "unde
apparet eos non fuisse conjuges" (cited in Esmein, *Le Mariage*, 1:122).

5. See C. Donahue, "The Policy of Alexander the Third's Consent Theory of
Marriage," *Proceedings from the Fourth International Congress of Medieval Canon Law*
(Vatican: Biblioteca Apostolica Vaticana, 1976), pp. 251–281.

6. For a discussion of Alexander's famous letter to the Bishop of Norwich concerning just such a case, see F. Pollock and F. Maitland, *The History of English Law* (Cambridge: Cambridge University Press, 1923), 2:372.

7. See H. A. Kelly, *Love and Marriage in the Age of Chaucer* (Ithaca: Cornell University Press, 1975).

8. For a particularly succinct correlation of the idea of consensualism and common property, see G. Vismara, "I Rapporti patrimoniali tra coniugi nell' alto medioevo," in *Il Matrimonio nella società altomedievale* (Spoleto: Presso del Centro, 1977), pp. 633–691.

9. Even the term "fief roturier" is often ambiguous, designating sometimes the nature of payment due on a particular holding and at other times the social status of the holder.

10. J. Yver, *Egalité entre Héritiers et exclusion des enfants dotés* (Paris: Sirey, 1966). See also E. Le Roy Ladurie, "Family Structure and Inheritance Customs in Sixteenth-Century France," in J. Goody, *Family and Inheritance, Rural Society in Western Europe 1200–1800* (Cambridge: Cambridge University Press, 1976), pp. 53–68; P. Ourliac and J. Malafosse, *Histoire du droit privé: le droit familial* (Paris: Presses Universitaires de France, 1968), pp. 403, 489, 490.

11. *Très Ancien Coutumier*, ed. E.-J. Tardif (Rouen: Cagniard, 1881), p. 9. See also the *Grand Coutumier de Normandie*, ed. E.-J. Tardif (Rouen: Lestrignant, 1896), p. 114; Yver, *Egalité*, pp. 90–107.

12. E. Le Roy Ladurie makes the curiously suggestive comment that "the customs of the West smiled on children, but not on love" ("Family Structure," p. 58).

13. See Yver, *Egalité*, pp. 195–221.

14. E. Vance, "Love's Concordance: The Poetics of Desire and the Joy of the Text," *Diacritics* 5 (1975): 45.

15. "Quibus duobus repertis, nata est illa librariorum et calculonom professio, velut quaedam grammaticae infantia. . . ." (*De Ordine*, ed. R. Jolivet [Paris: Desclée de Brouwer, 1948], p. 426).

16. " . . . not by nature, but by imposition; for this reason therefore it is called a piece of money" (cited in E. Bridrey, *La Théorie de la monnaie au XIVe siècle: Nicole Oresme* [Paris: V. Giard and E. Brière, 1906], p. 373).

17. "Populus una civitas est, cui est periculosa dissensio: quid est autem dissentire, nisi non unum sentire? Ex multis militibus fit unus exercitus: nonne quaevis multitudo eo minus vincitur, quo magis in unum coit? Unde ipsa coitio in unum 'cuneus' nominatus est, quasi 'co-uneus'" ["The people form a single city to which discord is dangerous: but what is discord if not diversity of sentiment? From many soldiers comes a single army: is not any multitude less subject to conquest to the degree that it maintains its cohesion? And whence does it come that that which holds separate things together is called 'cuneus' (coin), as if one said 'co-uneus'?"] (Augustine, *De Ordine*, p. 446).

18. Nicholas Oresme, *De Moneta*, ed. C. Johnson (London: Thomas Nelson, 1956), p. 22.

19. "Illud enim uocaretur libra, quod in ueritate non esset libra; quod est inconueniens, ut nunc dictum est" (ibid., p. 18).

20. Ibid., p. 9.

21. "Alia uero nomina monete sunt impropria, accidentalia seu denominatiua a loco, a figura, ab actore, uel aliquo tali modo." ["The other names of coins are not proper, but accidental or denominative from a place, a design or an authority, or in some other way"] (ibid.).

22. M. Bloch, *Esquisse d'une histoire monétaire de l'Europe* (Paris: Armand Colin, 1954), p. 25; "Economie nature ou économie argent," *Annales d'histoire sociale* 1 (1939): 7–16; P. Bonnassie, *La Catalogne du milieu du Xe à la fin du XIe siècle* (Toulouse: Université de Toulouse-le-Mirail, 1975), p. 369; C. Cippola, *Money, Prices, and Civilization in the Mediterranean World from the Fifth to the Seventeenth Century* (Princeton: Princeton University Press, 1956), pp 38–51; G. Duby, *The Early Growth of the European Economy* (Ithaca: Cornell University Press, 1974), p. 64.

23. See J. W. Baldwin, "Medieval Theories of Just Price," in *Transactions of the American Philosophical Society* (Philadelphia: American Philosophical Society, 1959); J. Ibanès, *La Doctrine de l'église et les réalités économiques au XIIIe siècle* (Paris: Presses Universitaires de France, 1967), pp. 34–55; J. F. McGovern, "The Rise of New Economic Attitudes—Economic Humanism, Economic Nationalism—during the Later Middle Ages and the Renaissance, A.D. 1200–1250," *Traditio* 26 (1970): 217–253; H. W. Spiegel, *The Growth of Economic Thought* (Englewood Cliffs, N.J.: Prentice-Hall, 1971), p. 61.

24. See T. Bisson, *Conservation of Coinage: Monetary Exploitation and Its Restraint in France, Catalonia and Aragon c. 1000–1200 A.D.* (Oxford: Oxford University Press, 1979).

25. "Economie nature," p. 13.

26. M. Bloch, *Esquisse*, pp. 41–75; Ibanès, *Doctrine*, pp. 52–55, 61–65.

27. Oresme, *De Moneta*, p. 14.

28. "Oportet igitur, si proporcio remaneat immutata, et unum nummisma mutet appellacionem, quod aliud eciam proporcionaliter immutetur; ut si primum uocetur duo denarii, secundum uocetur duo solidi, et tercium due libre" (ibid., p. 18).

29. Ibid., p. 21.

30. Thus profit is sanctioned, according to the criterion of cause, by risk, expense, or work, but not *ex cupiditate*. And it is sanctioned, according to the criterion of end or goal, if it is to be used in support of oneself, but not for the purpose of accumulation. Fraud too undergoes scholastic scrutiny according to whether the act gives rise to a contract (*dolus dans causam*), influences the terms of a sale (*dolus incidens*), or is unintentional (*dolus re ipsa*, e.g., a mistake in price). See especially R. de Roover, *La Pensée économique des scolastiques* (Paris: J. Vrin, 1971).

31. "A usurous will makes the usurer," says William of Auxerre, who also distinguishes between the absolute and the conditional volition of the debtor. Nonetheless, usury can be avoided by a host of legal exemptions or extrinsic titles of interest. A lender can, for example, legally be compensated for harm by the loan (*damnum emergens*), for delay or default (*mora*), for risk (*periculum sortis*), or for lost profit (*lucrum cessans*). Thus if the intention at the outset is profit, the transaction is usurious; but if profit is incurred through respect for the contract or by extraneous circumstances attached to it, the loan becomes licit. See J. Noonan, *The Scholastic Analysis of Usury* (Cambridge: Harvard University Press, 1957); Ibanès, *La Doctrine*, pp. 23–27.

32. See M. Shell, *The Economy of Literature* (Baltimore: Johns Hopkins University Press, 1978), especially chap. 1.

33. Aristotle, *Nicomachean Ethics*, ed. H. Rackham (New York: Barnes and Noble, 1952), p. 94.

34. See M. Bloch, *Feudal Society* (Chicago: University of Chicago Press, 1964), 2: 421; G. Duby, *European Economy*, pp. 221–224; *La Société aux XIe et XIIe siècles dans la région mâconnaise* (Paris: Armand Colin, 1953), pp. 516–527; E. Köhler, *Ideal und Wirklichkeit in der höfischen Epik* (Tubingen: Max Niemeyer, 1956), pp. 24–40.

35. Duby, *Mâcon*, p. 358. See also Ourliac and Malafosse, *Le droit familial*, p. 253; H. Pirenne, *Medieval Cities* (Princeton: Princeton University Press, 1970).

36. Ibid., p. 401.

37. Noonan, *Usury*, pp. 56–57.

38. Aristotle, *Politics* in *Basic Works*, ed. R. McKeon (New York: Random House, 1941), p. 1141.

39. ["... money, no matter how valuable, does not multiply by itself"] Cited in Ibanès, *La Doctrine*, p. 19; " . . . money does not breed money" (see Noonan, *Usury*, pp. 61–65); "Qui ergo utitur ea alio modo, ipse abutitur contra institutionem naturalem monete; facit enim, ut ait Aristotiles, quod denarius pariat denarium, quod est contra naturam. Adhuc autem, in istis mutacionibus ubi capitur lucrum, oportet uocare denarium illud quod in ueritate non est denarius et libram illud quod non est libra. . . ." ["Anyone therefore who uses it otherwise, misuses it against the natural institution of money, for he causes money to beget money, which, as Aristotle says, is against nature. And, besides. . . ." (*De Moneta*, p. 26).

40. There is surely a thesis to be written on the relationship in the Middle Ages between usury and poetry; see B. Fitz, "The Prologue to the *Lais* of Marie de France and the *Parable of the Talents*: Gloss and Monetary Metaphor," *Modern Language Notes* 90 (1975): 558–596.

41. Parts of the following discussion appeared under the title "Money, Metaphor, and the Mediation of Social Difference in Old French Romance," *Symposium* 35 (1981): 18–33.

42. ["The court Garin de Biaucaire was old and frail. . . . He had no heir, neither son nor daughter, except for a young man: this one was as I shall tell you"] *Aucassin*, p. 1.

43. ["May God never grant me anything I ask of him . . . if you do not give me Nicolette, my sweet friend whom I love so much"; "And if you want a wife, I will give you the daughter of a king or a count"] Ibid., p. 2.

44. See R. Bernheimer, *Wild Men in the Middle Ages* (Cambridge: Harvard University Press, 1952); P. Haidu, *Aesthetic Distance in Chrétien de Troyes* (Geneva: Droz, 1968), p. 119; M. Zink, *La Pastourelle: poésie et folklore au moyen âge* (Paris: Bordas, 1966).

45. I say "appears to favor," because the ultimate outcome of the meeting is more ambiguous than it looks: the shepherd—through a certain refusal to engage further in the war of words—wins the economic exchange despite Nicolette's effort to remain linguistically on top (cf. the shepherd Thibaut's similarly victorious refusal at the end of *Pathelin*). We will have occasion later to return to what seems like the added ambiguity of a "nominalizing noble" versus the appropriation by a nonnoble of a mode of speech more in keeping with the interests of aristocracy.

46. S. Monsonégo, *Etude stylo-statistique du vocabulaire des vers et de la prose dans la chantefable Aucassin et Nicolette* (Paris: Klincksieck, 1966), p. 43.

47. E. Vance, "The Word at Heart: *Aucassin et Nicolette* as a Medieval Comedy of Language," *Yale French Studies* 45 (1970), p. 41.

48. *La Vie de Saint Alexis*, ed. G. Paris (Paris: Champion, 1974), v. 36.

49. ["He took all his money with him and disbursed it all, which attracted people"; "Oh son, who will have my large inheritance, my vast lands of which I have many, and my palace in Rome?"] Ibid., vv. 91, 401.

50. "Plus aimet Deu que trestot son lignage" (ibid., v. 250).

51. ". . . quam assensu(m) parentum ipso tradente. vellet nollet Christina Burthredus illam sibi desponsandam accepit" (*The Life of Christina of Markyate*, ed. C. H. Talbot [Oxford: Clarendon Press, 1959], p. 44).

52. Ibid., p. 68.

53. "Ut quid degeneret? Ut quid parentes dishonoret? Mendicitas illius universe nobilitati erit notabile dedecus. Fiat modo quod nos volumus. omnia eius erunt" (ibid., p. 58).

54. See F. Barteau, *Les Romans de Tristan et Iseult: Introduction à une lecture plurielle* (Paris: Larousse, 1972), pp. 32–36.

55.   "En son cuer dit or croit sa feme

                Et mescroit les barons du reigne,

                Qui li faisoient chose acroire

                Que il set bien que n'est pas voire

                Et qu'il a prové a mençonge."

                              [*Le Roman de Tristan*, ed. E. Muret

                              (Paris: Champion, 1962), v. 287].

"In his heart he says that he believes his wife and does not believe the barons of the realm, who made him believe something that he knows is not true and that he has proven to be a lie."

56. Ibid., v. 1995.

57. See "Tristan, the Myth of the State and the Language of the Self," *Yale French Studies* 51 (1975): 61–81.

58. "Their lying so apart both pleased him and pained him. Pleased him, I mean, because of the fond idea that they were innocent; pained him, I mean, because he harboured suspicion. 'Merciful God,' he said to himself, 'what can be the meaning of this? If anything has passed between these two such as I have long suspected, why do they lie apart so? A woman should cleave to her man and lie close in his arms by his side. Why do these lovers lie thus?' And then he went on to himself: 'Is there anything behind it now? Is there guilt here, or is there not?' But with this Doubt was with him again. 'Guilt?' he asked. 'Most certainly, no!' Marc bandied these alternatives to and fro till, pathless man, he was in two minds about their passion" (Gottfried von Strassburg, *Tristan*, ed. A. T. Hatto [Middlesex: Penguin, 1972], p. 272).

59. Here I follow my earlier article cited above (n. 57). See also Barteau, *Romans de Tristan*, pp. 83–118.

60. "Il nos laissa por nos traïr:"; "Par cest change poon parçoivre, / Mestre, que il nos veut deçoivre" (Béroul, *Tristan*, vv. 2096, 2111).

61. *Les Fragments du Roman de Tristan*, ed. B. H. Wind (Geneva: Droz, 1960), v. 835 (Fragment Douce); see also vv. 826, 842, 879.

62. "Mialz voldroie estre desmanbree / Que de nos deus fust remanbree / L'amors d'Ysolt et de Tristan"(*Cligés*, ed. A Micha [Paris: Champion, 1957], v. 3105). J.-C. Payen suggests that much of subsequent courtly literature represents an attempt to come to grips with the Tristan story; see "Lancelot contre Tristan: la conjonction d'un mythe subversif (Réflexions sur l'idéologie romanesque au moyen âge)," in *Mélanges Le Gentil* (Paris: S.E.D.E.S., 1973) pp. 617–632.

63. See for example vv. 469–515, 618–864, 889–1038.

64. ["She opposes and responds to herself"] Ibid., v. 4364.

65. Ibid., v. 4415.

66. Ibid., v. 6161.

67. E. Vance, "Mervelous Signals: Poetics, Sign Theory, and Politics in Chaucer's *Troilus*," *New Literary History* 10 (1979): 307–311. See also his "Le Combat érotique chez Chrétien de Troyes," *Poétique* 12 (1972): 544–572.

68. ["She wanted to preserve her virginity in order to save him his inheritance"] *Cligés*, v. 3185.

69. Chrétien de Troyes, *Erec et Enide*, ed. M. Roques (Paris: Champion, 1963), vv. 2585, 2914, 2962, 3002, 3074, 3100.

70. Ibid., v. 6414.

71. *Equitan*, in *Les Lais de Marie de France*, ed. J. Lods (Paris: Champion, 1959), v. 197; Gurun's barons are similarly concerned in *Le Freisne*, v. 313. See also *Guigemar*, v. 645.

72. *Eliduc*, v. 91; ["Since he had a large inheritance, he took a wife in order to have children who, after him, would be his heirs"] *Yonec*, v. 18; ["He divided women and lands among all, except for one who had served him"] *Lanval*, v. 17.

73. *Guigemar*, v. 210.

74. Ibid., v. 229.

75. See D. Legge, *Anglo-Norman Literature and Its Background* (Oxford: Clarendon Press, 1963), pp. 137–175.

76. The editions referred to are Hue de Roteland, *Ipomedon*, ed. E. Kölbing and E. Koshwitz (Breslau: Wilhelm Koebner, 1889); Raoul de Houdenc, *Meraugis de Portlesguez*, ed. M. Friedwagner (Halle: Niemeyer, 1897); Renaut de Beaujeu, *Le Bel Inconnu*, ed. P. Williams (Paris: Champion, 1929); Gautier d'Arras, *Ille et Galeron*, ed. F. A. G. Cowper (Paris: Champion, 1926); *Partonopeu de Blois*, ed. J. Gildea (Pennsylvania: Villanova University Press, 1967); *Amadas et Ydoine*, ed. J. R. Reinhard (Paris: Champion, 1926).

77. *Partonopeu*, v. 313.

78. ["It is a great sin, it seems to me, to place a man and woman together if one knows they do not like each other"] *Ille et Galeron*, v. 5340.

79. See G. Duby, *Medieval Marriage*, pp. 105–107; and "Les 'Jeunes' dans la société aristocratique dans la France du Nord-Ouest au XIIe siècle," in *Hommes et structures du moyen âge* (Paris: Mouton, 1973), pp. 213–225; E. Köhler, "Sens et fonction du terme 'jeunesse' dans la poésie des troubadours," in *Mélanges R. Crozet*, ed. P. Gallais (Poitiers: Société d'Etudes Médiévales, 1966), pp. 569–583.

80. "Ja feme n'iert mais iretere / Ens el roiame d'Engletiere, / Por tant com j'aie a tenir tiere" (*Le Roman de Silence*, ed. L. Thorpe [Cambridge: W. Heffer, 1972], v. 314).

81. Ibid., v. 2067. See also v. 2539.

82. See vv. 2266, 2295, 2420, 2523, 5153.

Chapter Six

1. Parts of the following chapter appeared under the title "Wasteland and Round Table: The Historical Significance of Myths of Dearth and Plenty in Old French Romance," *New Literary History* 11 (1979–1980): 255–276.

2. For succinct resumés of some of the important explanations of sources, see J. Frappier, "Le Graal et ses feux divergents," *Romance Philology* 24 (1971): 373–440; R. S. Loomis, *The Grail: From Celtic Myth to Christian Symbol* (New York: Columbia University Press, 1963), p. 2; J. Marx, *La Légende arthurienne et le Graal* (Paris: Presses Universitaires de France, 1952), pp. 20–39.

3. As, for example, "Crient fu u plain et plus u gast"; "They shouted on the plain and then in the woodland" (Béroul, *Le Roman de Tristan*, ed. E. Muret [Paris: Champion, 1962], v. 1728).

4. "Il i soloit avoir .i. jaiant qui si estoit granz et cruex et orribles que nus n'osoit abiter en demi li roiaume; et destruoit si la terre et gastoit conme vos l'avez hui

trouvé" (*Le Haut livre du Graal Perlesvaus*, ed. W. Nitze and T. A. Jenkins [Chicago: University of Chicago Press, 1932], p. 216).

5. "Superveniet itaque ultio tonantis: quia omnis ager colonos decipiet. Arripiet mortalitas populum: cunctasque nationes evacuabit" (Geoffrey of Monmouth, *Historia regum Britanniae*, ed. San-Marte [Halle: E. Anton, 1854], p. 94); ["All emptied of people"] *Perlesvaus*, p. 225; ["After their death the lands remained wasted and exiled, and lacking in good knights"] *La Mort Artu*, ed. J. Frappier (Geneva: Droz, 1964), p. 232.

6. *Elucidation*, in *Der Percevalroman*, ed. A. Hilka (Halle: Max Niemeyer, 1932), v. 95.

7. ["The trees bore no fruit, and in the water there were no fish, except for small ones"] *La Queste del Saint Graal*, ed. A. Pauphilet (Paris: Champion, 1975), p. 204. See also *L'Estoire del Saint Graal*, ed. O. Sommer (Washington: Carnegie Institution, 1910), 1:290. Not only is gathering culture disrupted but pastoral life becomes impossible as well: "A tant s'en part Lanceloz de l'ermitage, et chevauche tant que il vient hors de la forest et trove une terre gaste et un païs grant et large, ou il n'abitoit ne bestes ne oisiax, car la terre estoit si seche et si povre qu'il n'i trovoient point de pouture" ["Then Lancelot left the hermitage and rode until he came out of the forest, and he found a Wasteland and a large land inhabited by neither beast nor bird, for the land was so dry and poor that they could find no pasture there"] (*Perlesvaus*, p. 136).

8. *Sone von Nansay*, ed. M. Goldschmidt (Tubingen: Literarischer Verein, 1899), v. 4843. Similarly, the Merlin of Geoffrey's *Historia* predicts that "every field shall fail the tiller of the soil" (see n. 5, above); and the author(s) of the *Estoire* specifies that "for a long time the fields were not cultivated by laborers, nor has grain grown nor anything else" ["de grant tans les terres as laboreurs ne furent gaaignies, ne ni croissoit bles ne autre chose"] (Sommer, 1:290).

9. See *Historia*, Book 1, chap. 14; Sommer, 2:135; see also pp. 98, 125, 164, 168, 176–77, 179, 190, 199, 289; *Huth*, 1:148; *Perlesvaus*, pp. 102, 216.

10. ["The father died of sorrow for the sons"] *Perceval*, v. 481.

11. ["It is the count Philip of Flanders, who is more worthy than Alexander"; "This is the tale of the Grail of which the count gave him the book; listen how he acquits himself of it"] Ibid., vv. 13, 66.

12. ["And he plants in such a worthy place that it can only turn to good"] Ibid., v. 9.

13. ["The count is such that he does not listen to vulgar jokes nor silly words"] Ibid., v. 21.

14. ["You would have been a knight, son, if it had pleased Lord God; and your father would have trained you along with your other relatives"] Ibid., v. 412.

15. The author of the *Perlesvaus* associates Perceval's name with disinheritance: "Damoisele, fet li rois, e qui est li chevaliers?—Sire, fet ele, il fu filz Julain le Gros des Vax de Kamaalot, e est apelez Pellesvax. —Por coi Pellesvax? fet li rois. —Sire, fet ele, quant il fu nez, on demanda son pere comment il avroit non en droit bautesme, et il dist qu'il voloit q'il eüst non Pellesvax, car li Sires des Mares le toloit la greigneur partie des Vax de Kamaalot, si voloit qu'il en sovenist son fil par cest non, se Dex le monteplioit tant qu'il fust chevaliers" ["My lady, said the king, who is this knight? —Lord, she said, he was the son of Julian the Great of the Valley of Camelot, and he is called Pellesvax. —Why Pellesvax? said the king. —Lord, she said, when he was born, they asked his father what should be his baptismal name, and he said that he wanted him to have the name Pellesvax, because the Lord des Mares had taken from him the greater part of the Valley of Camelot, and he wanted his son to remember this by this name, assuming that God would keep him until he became a knight"] *Perlesvaus*, p. 42.

16.   "Ce sont angle que je voi chi.
                        Et voir or ai je molt pechié,
                        Ore ai je molt mal esploitié
                        Que dis que c'estoient deable."
                                    [*Perceval*, v. 137]

"These are angels that I see here. For I have sinned and done badly to call them devils."
See P. Haidu's masterful reading of this passage (*Aesthetic Distance in Chrétien de Troyes* [Geneva: Droz, 1968], pp. 118–126).

17. ["Who are you?" —"I am a knight"; "What are you carrying?" . . . "I will tell you, it is my lance"; "What I am carrying is called a shield"; "Young man, this is my hauberk"] *Perceval*, vv. 175; 191, 197; 224; 263.

18. Mother to son: "Biax fix, un sens vos weil aprendre/ Ou il vos fait molt bon entendre. . . ." ["Dear son, I want to teach you a lesson to which you should listen well. . . ."] (ibid., v. 527).

19. Among these, Perceval mistakes Orgueilleux's tent for a Church. On the basis of his mother's instruction to revere God and her description of His house ("Une maison bele et saintisme / Ou il a cors sains et tresors" ["A beautiful and saintly house full of holy objects and treasure"] [v. 577]), Perceval misperceives Orgueilleux's encampment: "Diex, or voi je vostre maison" ["God, now I see your house"] (v. 655).

20. Orgueilleux's admonition seems, in fact, to be a direct response to Perceval's mother's injunction to "leave off the rest" ("Le sorplus je vos en desfent"):

                "Qui baise feme et plus n'i fait,
                Des qu'il sont sol a sol andui,
                Dont quit je qu'il remaint en lui.
                Feme qui se bouche abandone
                Le sorplus molt de legier done,
                S'est qui a certes i entende."
                                  [V. 3860]

"He who kisses a woman and does nothing more if they happen to be alone is, in my opinion, missing something. A woman who offers her mouth gives up the rest easily, if you want to know the truth."

21.   "Ne ne parlez trop volentiers:
                Nus ne puet estre trop parliers
                Qui sovent tel chose ne die
                Qui torné li est affolie,
                Car li sages dit et retrait:
                'Qui trop parole, il se mesfait.'
                Por che, biax amis, vos chastoi
                De trop parler. . . ."
                                  [V. 1648]

"Do not speak too willingly, for oftentimes one can be too talkative and say foolish things; this is why the wise man says and repeats: 'He who speaks too much does wrong.' For this reason, dear friend, I warn you not to speak too freely. . . ."

22. See also vv. 3244, 3290.

23. ["The young man understood very little of what his mother said"; "I would willingly find the king who makes knights"] Vv. 489, 493.

24. ["Lord, what does this Welshman say?"—"He is ignorant of the laws. . . . Welshmen are by nature more uncivilized than beasts at pasture"] Vv. 235, 243.

25. ["And the one who did not know his name guessed that his name was Perceval the Welsh"] v. 3573.

26. ["The one that is served from it is my brother. My sister and his was your mother; and the Rich Fisher-King is the son of this king"] Ibid., v. 6415. In the *Didot-Perceval*, Perceval is actually designated as heir to the Grail and Fisher-King: ". . . Li Rois Pesciere ne poroit morir dusqu'atant que vos ariés esté a se cort, et quant vous i ariés esté il seroit garis et vous bailleroit sa grasse et son vaissel, et seriés sire del sanc nostre Segnor Jhesucrist" ["The Fisher-King cannot die until you shall have been to his court; and when you shall have been there, he will be cured and will bestow upon you his grace and his vessel; and you will be lord of the blood of Our Lord Jesus Christ"] *Didot-Perceval*, ed. W. Roach [Philadelphia: University of Pennsylvania Press, 1941], p. 182. The actual succession takes place on p. 242.

27. Gauvain also stumbles upon his own lineage in the castle of Roche de Canguin, and he too fails to recognize his own mother, grandmother, and sister (*Perceval*, vv. 8739 ff.).

28. ["For I lost in one morning my father, who was a brave knight . . . and I was disinherited of all my land"] Sommer, 5:94; see also 5:17; ["Thus was Lancelot for three years in the keeping of the lady, and this without discomfort; for he believed her truly to be his mother"] Ibid., 3:22.

29. Ibid., 3:147.

30. ["And then he saw the letters that said 'here will lie Lancelot of the Lake, the son of King Ban of Benoyc; and he put the stone back and he knew well that it was his name that he saw"] Ibid., 3:152.

31. Bibliothèque nationale MS 768 reads: ". . . et l'autre fu fille au Roi mehaignié ce fu li rois Pellés qui fu peres Perlesvas." [". . . and the other was the daughter of the wounded king, that is King Pelles who was Perceval's father"] (cited in J. Roubaud, "Généalogie morale des Rois-Pêcheurs," *Change* 17 [1973], p. 238).

32. "Et saluez moi toz cels dou saint hostel et mon oncle li roi Pellés et mon aiol le Riche Roi Pescheor. . . ." ["And greet for me all those of the holy host and my uncle King Pellés, and my ancestor (grandfather?) the Rich Fisher-King"] (*La Queste*, p. 8).

33. ". . . les noveles de sa bele fille qui ert morte, cele en qui Galaad fu engendrez" (ibid., p. 259); ". . . del mellor cheualier du monde & de la fille au riche roy pescheor" (Sommer, 5:251).

34. Roubaud, "Généalogie morale," p. 245.

35. ["Then the brother knew his sister carnally; and the lady carried the one who one day would betray him (Arthur) and turn the land to destruction and suffering, as you shall be able to hear toward the end of the book"] *Huth*, 1:147.

36. *La Queste*, p. 95.

37. ["Thus began the battle on Salisbury Plain, by which the Realm of Logres was turned to destruction . . .; after their death the lands remained wasted and exiled and lacking in good knights. . . . Thus the father killed the son, and the son wounded the father fatally"] *La Mort Artu*, pp. 232, 245.

38. In the *Huth Merlin* it is a curious but telling confrontation between enemy brothers, whose names show a minimal phonetic difference (Balaan and Balaain), that brings on the Wasteland (*Huth*, 88:49–57).

39. ". . . ne le fist mie tant por la biaute de lui ne pour escauffement de char" (Sommer, 5:110).

40. "Pucelages est une vertuz que tuit cil et toutes celes ont qui n'ont en atouchement de charnel compaignie. Mais virginitez est trop plus haute chose et

plus vertuose: car nus ne la puet avoir, soit hom soit fame, por qu'il ait eu volenté de charnel assemblement" ["Chastity is a virtue that all men and women have who have never kept carnal company. But virginity is an even higher and more virtuous thing: for no one, either man or woman, can attain it who has had the will to carnal knowledge"] (*La Queste*, p. 213).

41. Ibid., p. 18. See also p. 278.

42. See J. Roubaud, "Enfances de la prose," *Change* 16 (1973): 361–364.

43. ["his surname was Lancelot, but his baptismal name was Galehos"] Sommer, 3:3.

44. Roubaud makes the link between such onomastic scrambling and the *trobar clus* project of "mixing words" (see "Enfances," p. 352, and infra pp. 111–116).

45. See in particular E. Vinaver, *The Rise of Romance* (Oxford: Oxford University Press, 1971), pp. 68–78.

46. ["But now the tale is silent about. . . . Now the tale says"; "But then the tale leaves off. . . . Now the tale says"; "But now the tale is silent about. . . . Now the tale says"] *La Queste*, pp. 26, 41, 51; see also pp. 56, 71, 115, 147, 162, 195, 210, 226, 244, 246, 262; J. Rychner, *L'Articulation des phrases narratives dans "La Mort Artu"* [Geneva: Droz, 1970]; T. Todorov, "La Quête du récit," *Critique* 262 [1969]: 195; R. H. Bloch, "The Text as Inquest: Form and Function in the Pseudo-Map Cycle," *Mosaic* 8 [1977]: 107–119.

47. ". . . si s'en esmiervilla moult, et puis mist la nuit et l'(u)eure en escrit" (*Huth*, 1:17).

48. Merlin to the judge: "Vous avés en escrit l'(u)eure toute et la nuit que je fui engenrés, si poés bien savoir quant je nasqui." ["You have in writing the hour and night that I was conceived; you know then when I was born"] (ibid., 1:24); ". . . Il meteroit en escrit toutes les fois que il girroit a vous, pour chou que il meismes avoit paour que vous ne couchissiés a autre homme" (ibid., 1:27).

49. ["And he had put into writing the hour and the night that you conceived him"] Ibid., 1:112.

50. "Par ceste raison sot cil les choses qui estoient dites et faites et alees de par l'anemi, et le seurplus que il sot des choses a venir vaut nostre sires que il seust contre les autres choses que il savoit pour endroit de la soie partie. Ore si se tourt a la quele que il vaurra; et se il veult il puet rendre au dyable son droit et a nostre signour le sien. Car plus n'i a dyables formé fors le cors, et nostre sires met ens l'esperit pour veoir et pour oir et pour entendre. . . ." ["In this way he knew from the Devil things that had been said and done; and the rest, that is, things to come, Our Lord wanted him to know in order to counterbalance the other things so that His side would also be represented. Thus Merlin could turn to whichever side he wanted; and if he wanted to, he could render to the Devil his own, or to God what was his. For the Devil formed only the body, and Our Lord endowed him with a spirit to see, hear, and listen. . . ."] (ibid., 1:19; see also 1:77, 94).

51. ["It will be about Joseph and the book of lineages that I recalled to you with your own and mine"] (Ibid., 1:32).

52. "Et Merlins s'en ala a Blaise en Norhomberlande, si li raconta tot et dist, et Blaises le mist en escrit et par son livre le resavons nous encore" ["And Merlin went off to Blaise in Northumberland, and recounted all; and Blaise put it into writing, and by his book we know it still"] (ibid., 1:90; see also 1:46, 61, 71, 85, 90, 98, 115, 133; 2:61, 139).

53. ["I will do the book willingly, but I beg of you in the name of the father and the son . . . that you neither deceive nor trick me"; "I know things said and done, and I know them through the satanic force"] Ibid., 1:31, 94.

54. "Lors dist li rois et tout cil qui l'oirent que nus n'est si sages conme Merlin

est. Et disent que il ne li orront jamais dire chose qui avenir doive que il ne metent en escrit. Ensi l'ont devisé (Ensi fu conmenciés uns livre que on apelle par nom le livre des prophecies Merlin. . . ." ["Then the king and all those that heard him (Merlin) said that no one is as wise as Merlin. And they said that they would never hear him say that a thing would come to pass that they would not put it into writing. Thus they decided. Thus was begun a book known by the name of the Prophecies of Merlin. . . ."] (ibid., 1:85).

55. ["I will never again speak publicly except in such an obscure way that they will not know what I say before seeing it"] Ibid.

56. ["This book does not tell who Merlin is or where he comes from"] Ibid. "Li rois n'entendi pas cele parole que Merlins li dist adont, car trop estoit obscure, si avint elle puis tout ensi que Merlins li devisa, si comme l'ystoire le conte qui de l'estoire dou saint graal en parole et est devisee" ["The king did not understand this word that Merlin spoke to him because it was too obscure; but things came to pass as Merlin said, and as the story of the Holy Grail tells"] (ibid., 2:61).

57. "Je ne di obscure parole dont vous n'en connissiés bien la verité ains que vous trespassés de cest siecle" (ibid., 1:275).

58. ["they put into writing nothing except that which he said"; "And Our Lord, who is powerful over everything, gave me the intelligence to know all things that will happen, in part"] Ibid., 1:85, 94.

59. *La Queste*, p. 164.

60. Ibid., p. 165.

61. "Des pechiez mortiex porte li peres son fes et li filz le suen; ne li filz ne partira ja as iniquitez au pere, ne li peres ne partira ja as iniquitez au filz; mes chascuns selonc ce qu'il avra deservi recevra loier" (ibid., p. 138).

62. *La Queste*, pp. 74–76.

63. "Scutella lata et aliquantum profunda, in qua preciosae dapes cum suo jure ditibus solent apponi graditim, unus morcellus post alium in diversis ordinibus" (cited in Marx, *Légende arthurienne*, p. 242; see also J. Frappier, "Le Graal et l'Hostie," in *Les Romans du Graal aux XIIe et XIIIe siècles* [Paris: Editions du Centre National de la Recherche Scientifique, 1956]: 63–81; Loomis, *The Grail*, pp. 58–60).

64. Wace, *Le Roman de Brut*, ed. I. Arnold (Paris: Champion, 1940), v. 9747. See also *Huth*, 1:97; Sommer, 2:54.

65. "Ne ja puis que il i averont sis ne vaurront en leur pais retourner ne de chi partir" (*Huth*, 1:96). See also Sommer, 2:55.

66. *La Queste*, p. 76.

67. See also Sommer, 2:55; *La Queste*, p. 77.

68. Robert de Boron, *Le Roman de l'Estoire dou Graal*, ed. W. Nitze (Paris: Champion, 1927), v. 2595.

69. ["They said: 'By this vessel are we separated from you'"] Ibid., v. 2627; ["By this vessel the good are separated from the bad"] Sommer, 2:54.

70. ["And when they had eaten the king had his clerks called before him, and they put into writing the adventures as Lancelot recounted them. And this is how we know them still"] Sommer, 4:296; see also 4:227; 5:190, 332, 333.

71. "Ia ne serrai al mangier deuant que aucune auenture i sera auenue de quel part ke che soit" (Sommer, 2: 320); the Queen elicits from her knights a similar pledge (ibid., p. 321).

72. See R. H. Bloch, "Merlin and the Modes of Medieval Legal Meaning"; *Medieval French Literature and Law* (Berkeley: University of California Press, 1977), p. 205.

73. See C. Berubé, *La Connaissance de l'individuel au moyen âge* (Paris: Presses Universitaires de France, 1964); R. Hanning, *The Individual in Twelfth-Century*

Romance (New Haven: Yale University Press, 1977); C. Morris, *The Discovery of the Individual 1050–1200* (New York: Harper, 1973); W. Ullmann, *The Individual and Society in the Middle Ages* (Baltimore: Johns Hopkins University Press, 1960).

74. For fuller discussion of this point, see my *Literature and Law*, pp. 227–239.

75. Abelard equated Christian morality with self-knowledge in a work entitled *Ethics: or Know Thyself* (1135). William of Saint Thierry adopted the Delphic dictum "Man, know thyself" in the prologue to his treatise on the nature of body and soul (*PL*, 180: col. 695). Ailred of Rievaulx asked rhetorically, "How much does a man know if he does not know himself?" (ibid., 195: col. 683). And John of Salisbury offered in the *Policraticus* what would have been an appropriate answer: "No one is more contemptible than he who scorns a knowledge of himself" (ed. C. C. J. Webb [Oxford: Oxford University Press, 1909], 1:19).

76. See *Literature and Law*, pp. 127–152.

77. ["It is sometimes necessary for me to hide myself from people"] *Huth*, 1:77.

78. See *Literature and Law*, pp. 231–236.

79. The "places" of the mind articulated in the lyric will gain theoretical expression in the allegory where the various components of an inner dynamic become coterminous with social reality.

Index

Abelard, Peter, 20, 48–49, 50, 141–49, 156, 159, 274n.75
Abraham, 35, 38
Acerbus Morena, 57
Adam, 32, 33, 38, 105; as namer, 35, 39, 40, 44, 45, 48, 51, 84
Adler, A., 15
Ado of Vienne, 38
Adultery: in *De Planctu Naturae*, 134; in *Lais* of Marie de France, 191; in love lyric, 110–11, 111–12, 114–15; in *Tristan*, 182–83, 186
Ailred of Rielvaux, 180
Alain de Lille, 20, 133–36, 137, 138, 140, 197
Albert the Great, St., 19, 165–66, 171, 173
Albert of Monte Cassino, 117, 119, 126

Alcuin, 97
Alexander III, pope, 162
Alexander of Lombard, 173
Alexander of Villedieu, 53, 118–19, 131
Alexandrian hermeneutics, 47
Alexandrian Judaism, exegetical tradition of, 35, 39, 45
Aliscans, 95
Allegorical poems, 17
Alod, 68, 74–75, 85, 163
Alphonse II, 130
Alterity of Middle Ages, 12
Amadas et Ydoine, 193, 194
Andreas Capellanus, 129–30
Anselm, St., 143, 149
Anthropologie structurale (Lévi-Strauss), 25–26
Appellation. *See* Names

275